500 best
Cookies, Bars
& Squares

500 best
Cookies, Bars
& Squares

Esther Brody

Robert
ROSE

500 Best Cookies, Bars & Squares
Text copyright © 2004 Esther Brody
Photographs copyright © 2004 Robert Rose Inc.

For complete cataloguing information, see page 381.

Disclaimer
The recipes in this book have been carefully tested by our kitchen and our tasters. To the best of our knowledge, they are safe and nutritious for ordinary use and users. For those people with food or other allergies, or who have special food requirements or health issues, please read the suggested contents of each recipe carefully and determine whether or not they may create a problem for you. All recipes are used at the risk of the consumer.

We cannot be responsible for any hazards, loss or damage that may occur as a result of any recipe use.

For those with special needs, allergies, requirements or health problems, in the event of any doubt, please contact your medical adviser prior to the use of any recipe.

Design & Production: PageWave Graphics Inc.
Editor: Sue Sumeraj
Index: Gillian Watts
Photography: Mark T. Shapiro
Food Styling: Kate Bush and Jill Snider
Props Styling: Charlene Erricson

Cover image: Dad's Favorite Chocolate Chip Cookies (see recipe, page 31), Almond Sugar Cookie Crisps (see recipe, page 48), Chewy Coconut Squares (see recipe, page 173), Traditional Peanut Butter Cookies (see recipe, page 46) and Classic Chocolate Nut Brownies (see recipe, page 129)

We acknowledge the financial support of the Government of Canada through the Book Publishing Industry Development Program (BPIDP) for our publishing activities.

Published by Robert Rose Inc.
120 Eglinton Avenue East, Suite 800, Toronto, Ontario, Canada M4P 1E2
Tel: (416) 322-6552 Fax: (416) 322-6936

Printed in Canada

6 7 8 9 FP 12 11 10 09 08 07

To my little granddaughter, Natty (Natalie), the love of my life, whose beautiful little face and smile, head full of curls, loving hugs and kisses and treasured moments that she and I, alone, share with special songs, stories and laughter, I wish you a lifetime of good health, happiness and success in everything you do and hope for. May your entire life be filled with the special love, smiles and laughter that you have brought into my life. I want you always to remember that Baba loves you with all her heart.

To my daughter, Lisa Michelle, and my son, Leonard. I am proud of the successes they have achieved in life.

To my twin sister, Cecille Shtabsky, and her family. I wish her a complete recovery.

In memory of my sister Betty Shapiro, who recently passed away, and who was also a best friend to me. You will never be forgotten by me, your children and grandsons.

And in memory of my parents, Mary and Louis Goldstein.

Contents

Introduction

Who doesn't remember the wonderful, warm aroma coming from the kitchen as Mom was baking cookies? I wanted to gobble them up as soon as they came out of the oven, but Mom always made us wait until they were cool enough to eat or she said we would get a stomachache.

The smells and flavors of spices such as cinnamon, nutmeg and ginger, as well as other wonderful ingredients, bring back memories of special times and holidays. Think of nuts — not just old standbys such as walnuts, but other varieties such as pecans, almonds, hazelnuts, cashews and macadamia nuts. Think of rich chocolate and fresh, dried and candied fruits. Put these together with some good-for-you, hearty, nutritious ingredients such as rolled oats, wheat germ, granola and whole wheat flour, and you have delicious, wholesome treats.

Everyone — young and old — loves baked goodies. There is no greater way of saying "Thanks," "Happy Holidays" or "Welcome to the Neighborhood!" Students at school away from home anxiously await parcels of homemade goodies. They are also perfect for fundraisers, bazaars, wedding or baby showers, and on and on.

Best of all, cookies, brownies, bars and squares are so easy to make. They are usually made from simple ingredients and are very versatile. They're great for coffee breaks, snacks or desserts, and most recipes are easy enough for even a novice cook to attempt as long as you follow the instructions. There is no limit to the way in which recipes can be varied according to your taste.

Even multi-layered bars or squares (my personal favorites), are much simpler to prepare than you might think. You just begin with a crumbly mixture for the base. Pour this mixture into your prepared baking pan, spread evenly all over the bottom of the pan, press down to form a solid crust and bake if required. Add the filling and spread evenly over top of the crust, then add whatever topping is required in your recipe. Then it's just a matter of following the instructions for baking, cooling and cutting.

Most baked goods can be stored at room temperature for several days, or even weeks, if they don't disappear first. Everyone I know has a cookie jar sitting on the counter within easy reach. I find that using a cookie tin, with an airtight lid, helps cookies and brownies keep that freshly baked flavor. Most baked goods will freeze well, but they should be cooled completely before being placed in tins or containers. I always place a sheet of waxed paper between each layer.

Baking can be fun. I remember years ago hearing about "cookie swaps," and later participated in a few. They have become popular events, especially near a holiday. Here's how they work. You bake a dozen cookies or brownies for each guest coming to the swap. If there will be 10 guests participating, you bake 10 dozen of, say, your peanut butter cookies. You'll come home with 10 dozen different goodies, one dozen of each kind brought by the other guests. It is a wise idea to bake your cookies a few days ahead so you won't be overwhelmed the day of the swap. Decide in advance what type of goodie you'll be bringing and let the hostess know so that there won't be duplication. The wrapping is part of the fun: place each dozen cookies into a decorated bag or some other unique wrapping such as a basket or decorative tin. A swap is a perfect excuse to have a party, but it's also a way to get together with old and new friends to share your favorite goodies and recipes. So have lots of recipe cards and pens ready.

Another way to enjoy your favorite cookies is to make them into a crust for pies, or any other desserts that call for a dough crust. You could use chocolate cookies, vanilla wafers, graham wafers or gingersnap cookies, just to name a few. Crush about 1½ cups (375 mL) of cookies into fine crumbs. Stir in about ¼ cup (50 mL) melted butter or margarine, and press into your pie plate. This type of crust can be chilled without baking, or baked at 350°F (180°C) for 10 minutes and then cooled.

In this book, you'll find many familiar recipes, as well as new recipes that are sure to create wonderful memories for your family and friends. Whether you're a novice or a long-time baker, once you start experimenting with these recipes and see the fantastic results, you will be inspired to make baking a part of your everyday life.

Happy baking!

— *Esther Brody*

Making Perfect Cookies, Brownies, Bars and Squares

One of the beauties of making cookies, brownies, bars and squares is that you don't need special equipment. Dough or batter can be mixed by hand in a large bowl with a wooden spoon or prepared in an electric mixer or a food processor. As long as you've followed a tried-and-true recipe, all these methods produce equally delicious results.

The right equipment

Although most cookies are easy to prepare, following certain rules of thumb will guarantee outstanding results. For instance, I recommend investing in heavy-duty cookie sheets. They will likely cost a bit more, but they are worth it because they won't rust and your cookies will bake more evenly. Cookie sheets differ from baking pans in that they don't have sides, which allows the heat to circulate around the cookies, helping to ensure more even baking. If you don't have heavy-duty cookie sheets, lower the temperature of your oven by 25°F (10°C).

For brownies, bars and squares, use heavy metal baking pans for best results. If all you have is a glass baking dish, reduce the oven temperature by 25°F (20°C) and decrease the baking time slightly.

Getting started

1. The secret to successful baking is paying close attention to the recipe. Before you begin, read the recipe carefully and assemble all the necessary equipment and ingredients. Adjust oven racks to the desired level and 15 minutes before you want to bake, preheat the oven to the required temperature.

2. Don't make ingredient substitutions and don't double or halve the recipe unless it states that you can do so.

3. Shortening, butter, margarine and occasionally vegetable oil all work equally well in cookie recipes. Use whichever the recipe specifies. I do not recommend the use of spreads sold in tubs for baking as these products contain a higher percentage of water than solid fats. Cookies made from spreads will expand too much and will not brown as well as those made from more solid fats. They will also be tough and more likely to stick to the cookie sheet. Don't substitute margarine or shortening when the recipe calls specifically for butter.

4. If a cookie recipe calls for shortening, be aware that substituting butter or margarine will produce different results. Because butter and margarine melt more quickly than shortening, cookies made from butter will lose their shape and spread out more. Cookies made from shortening hold their shape better.

5. Remove shortening, butter or margarine from the refrigerator to soften 1 hour before mixing unless the recipe specifies the use of cold butter.

6. Always use large eggs for baking.

7. Since eggs separate more easily when they are cold, separate the yolks from the whites as soon as you take eggs

out of the refrigerator. If you're not using them immediately, cover the yolks with cold water and return them to the refrigerator until you're ready to use them. (Drain the water off before using the yolks in a recipe.) If you're beating egg whites, allow them to come to room temperature for 5 to 10 minutes before beating. Do not leave eggs at room temperature for longer than 1 hour.

8. Make sure your ingredients are fresh:
   - Purchase ground spices in small amounts and store tightly sealed in a cool, dry place. Replace ground spices annually.
   - Ensure that leavening agents such as baking soda and baking powder are still functional. Baking soda will keep for up to $1\frac{1}{2}$ years in a glass jar with a tight lid or in its original container. To make sure it is still active, mix 1 tbsp (15 mL) baking soda in $\frac{1}{2}$ cup (125 mL) cold water. Add 1 tsp (5 mL) vinegar. If the mixture doesn't fizz, discard the baking soda. To test whether baking powder is still active, dissolve 1 tsp (5 mL) baking powder in $\frac{1}{3}$ cup (75 mL) hot tap water. The mixture should bubble up vigorously.
   - Buy seeds and nuts from a bulk food store with rapid turnover and store them in the refrigerator.
   - Keep marshmallows in the freezer.
   - Check the "best before" date on ingredients such as peanut butter, sour cream and yogurt.

9. Prepare pans as required. If the recipe indicates the sheet should be greased, I recommend the use of shortening. Place a dab of shortening on a piece of waxed paper and spread it in a thin, even layer over the pan. Grease pans only if the recipe specifies. For cookies, a general rule of thumb is that dough containing a high proportion of shortening is baked on ungreased sheets. Unnecessary or excessive greasing will cause cakes to be gummy and some cookies to spread too much.

In my opinion, butter, margarine or oil may cause baked goods to stick to the pan. Instead of greasing, you can line the pan with parchment or waxed paper, cut to fit. If a recipe calls for lightly greased, spraying with a vegetable spray is acceptable.

Mixing for best results

1. Measure ingredients carefully and accurately. Use measuring cups with a flat rim for dry ingredients so they can easily be leveled off. To measure less than $\frac{1}{4}$ cup (50 mL), use standard measuring spoons. Fill cups or spoons to overflowing, then level off using a straight-edged knife or spatula. Do not pack or bang on the table.

2. Unless a recipe calls for "sifted flour" — in which case it should be sifted first, then measured — flour is not sifted before it is measured. If a recipe calls for "sifting" the dry ingredients together, there is no need to sift the flour prior to measuring. Just sift all pre-measured ingredients together and proceed with the recipe.

3. If a recipe calls for "packed" or "firmly packed" brown sugar, spoon it into a measuring cup, pack it down with the back of a spoon, then level off.

4. Shortening, butter or margarine that is not sold in stick form should be measured in a cup that holds the exact amount when leveled off. Press firmly into the cup so that no air holes are left. Level off and scoop out.

5. Before mixing batter or dough, combine dry ingredients such as flour, baking powder, baking soda and salt in a bowl and mix thoroughly to ensure they are well blended.

6. If a recipe calls for a melted ingredient such as butter, shortening or chocolate, cool slightly before adding eggs. Otherwise, the eggs may curdle.

7. If a recipe calls for extracts or flavorings, mix them in after the butter and sugar have been creamed (and after eggs have been beaten in, if using) so they will be well incorporated into the dough.

8. Roll cookie dough out on a floured board unless otherwise specified.

9. When making cut cookies, dip the cookie cutter in flour so it won't stick to the dough. Cut the cookies as close together as possible to reduce the quantity of leftover scraps to re-roll; the more the dough is handled, the less tender your cookies will be.

10. Ensure that all cookies in a batch are the same size and shape to ensure even cooking.

11. Don't over-beat cake batter. When adding flour alternately with a liquid, keep the mixing to an absolute minimum, mixing only until the flour and liquid are incorporated into the batter. If using an electric mixer, beat on low speed. Over-mixing will make the cake tough.

12. When pouring batter into a baking pan, spread it evenly in the pan and take care to fill all corners so the baked cake will come out even. Use a spatula to spread the batter gently across the bottom of the pan and into the corners in a smooth, even layer without touching the sides of the pan.

13. Once the batter is in the baking pan, bang the pan on the counter two or three times. This will eliminate any large air pockets that will create holes in the finished product.

Helpful tips for baking cookies

1. Pay close attention to oven temperature as cookies bake in a very short time and quickly become overcooked. If your oven is hotter than mine, you may need to lower the temperature by 25°F (10°C) or shorten the suggested baking times. You will get a feel for how your oven bakes after making a couple of batches of cookies.

2. Adjusting the temperature of the dough can also help you get the cookie shape you want. If you want your cookies to maintain their shape during baking, chill them on the sheet for 15 minutes before placing them in the oven and increase the oven temperature a few degrees. If you want the cookies to flatten, place them in the oven when the dough is at room temperature and lower the oven temperature a few degrees.

3. When baking, place the cookie sheet on the middle rack of your oven. Ensure that the sheet is narrower than the oven rack and doesn't touch the sides of the oven so the heat can circulate properly. For best results, bake only one sheet of cookies at a time.

4. Begin checking to see if your cookies are done a few minutes before the time suggested in the recipe — oven temperatures vary, and every extra minute can make a big difference to the quality of cookies. Cookies are better if they are under- rather than overcooked. They should be a bit soft in the center when they are removed

from the oven. Drop cookies are done if they spring back into shape when you touch them lightly with your finger. Crisp cookies are done when lightly browned.

5. To prevent over-baking, remove cookies from the sheet within 3 minutes of taking them out of the oven unless the recipe specifies otherwise. Using a lifter, transfer warm cookies to a wire rack to cool.

Tips for baking, cooling and cutting brownies, bars and squares

1. For multi-layered bars and squares, with a crust topped by a fluid batter, the crust must be pre-baked before the batter is added to prevent it from becoming soggy. All the recipes in this book have taken this into account and are written accordingly. Follow the recipe instructions.

2. The position of the baking pan in the oven influences how the product turns out. Center the baking pan on the middle rack of the oven. For best results, bake only one cake at a time. If you are baking multiple cakes, make sure the pans don't touch each other or the sides of the oven. Also, don't place one pan directly underneath another.

3. Since temperatures (and therefore baking times) can vary dramatically between ovens, check for doneness a few minutes before the time indicated in the recipe. You will know your cake is done if you insert a tester into the center and it comes out clean and dry. You can also tell that cooking is complete if the cake shrinks slightly from the sides of the pan or the top springs back when touched lightly in the center with a fingertip.

4. Most brownies, bars and squares should be cooled completely in the baking pan before cutting. To prevent cakes from becoming soggy, cool them in the pan on a wire rack. This allows the bottom of the pan to be cooled by circulating air.

5. Sometimes it is appropriate to cut cakes before they are completely cooled. If the cake has a sticky filling, run a knife around the edge of the pan to loosen it as soon as it comes out of the oven. Crispy bars should be cut while still warm to prevent them from shattering. Then place the pan on a rack to cool.

6. When cutting brownies, bars and squares, use a sharp knife and a gentle, sawing motion to avoid squashing the cake. Brownies, bars and squares can be cut into a variety of sizes, depending upon the size of the pan. If you are trying to stretch the quantity of a recipe, cut smaller sizes. A general rule: the thicker and richer the cake, the smaller each portion should be.

7. Store brownies, bars and squares in a tightly covered container or in the baking pan, covered tightly with foil. Make sure they are completely cooled before storing.

Ingredient Methods

Toasting nuts

Spread nuts out in a single layer on a baking sheet and bake at 350°F (180°C) for about 7 minutes, stirring or shaking the pan once or twice, until lightly browned. After toasting hazelnuts, place them on a clean tea towel and rub together vigorously to remove the skin.

Making sugar-cinnamon mix

In a cup, mix together ¼ cup (50 mL) granulated sugar and 1 tsp (5 mL) ground cinnamon. Store in a jar.

Melting chocolate

The trick to melting chocolate is to ensure it doesn't "seize." Therefore, it is important that the chocolate does not come in contact with water, which will cause it to solidify into a grainy mass. If your chocolate seizes when melting, add 1 tsp (5 mL) shortening for every 2 squares (2 oz/60 g) of chocolate used and stir well until the mixture is smooth and creamy. Do not use butter, as it contains water.

To ensure that chocolate melts quickly and evenly on the stovetop, break it into small pieces (or use chocolate chips) and stir constantly. Chocolate should always be melted over low heat, in a double boiler, or in a bowl set on top of a saucepan of hot (not boiling) water. Grease your measuring cup or saucepan with shortening before melting chocolate for easy removal.

Chocolate also melts well in the microwave. Use chocolate chips, squares (each 1 oz /30 g) or small chunks. Place in a microwaveable bowl, cover tightly with plastic wrap and microwave on High for approximately 1 minute per ounce. (Times will vary depending upon the power of your microwave and the quantity of chocolate used.) Remove from oven and stir well.

Chocolate should be well wrapped and stored in an airtight container in a cool place. If the storage location is too warm, a gray/white color (called "bloom") will appear on the surface of chocolate. This does not affect the flavor of the chocolate, and the chocolate will return to its normal color when melted.

Using honey instead of sugar

You can replace sugar with honey in most recipes. (The reverse does not hold true, however; if a recipe specifically calls for honey, then that is what will work best.) When substituting honey for sugar, add ½ tsp (2 mL) baking soda for each 1 cup (250 mL) honey and reduce the amount of liquid by ¼ cup (50 mL). Also, reduce the oven temperature by 25°F (10°C), since recipes containing honey will brown faster.

Storing cookies

Most cookies can be stored at room temperature for up to three weeks in an airtight container with a tight-fitting lid. Crisp cookies should be stored in a container with a loose-fitting lid, unless you live in a humid climate, in which case they should be covered tightly. If crisp cookies do soften, heating them in a 300°F (150°C) oven for 5 minutes will crisp them up.

Freezing cookies and dough

Most cookie dough can be frozen for up to six months, and most cookies freeze well. To freeze cookies, cool completely and place in airtight freezer bags with a sheet of waxed paper between layers.

Baking Problems (and How To Solve Them)

If your cookies, brownies, bars and squares turn out less than perfect, chances are there's a simple solution to the problem. Here are some common examples.

Cookies stick to your cookie sheet

Check the recipe to see if the sheet should be greased. If not, there may be ingredients in the cookies, such as raisins, that are causing them to stick. In that case, transfer the cookies to a wire rack as soon as they come out of the oven so they won't have a chance to stick to the sheet.

Cookies crumble or break when you remove them from the cookie sheet

The sheet should be greased, or the cookies may have been left on the hot sheet too long after they were removed from the oven.

Cookies are too dry

Ingredients may not have been measured properly, the eggs may not have been large enough, or the cookies may have over-baked.

Cookies spread out too much

You may have used too much butter, shortening or liquid or too little flour. Always measure ingredients correctly in a standard measuring cup.

Cookies run into each other instead of baking separately

You may have made the cookies too large and/or placed them too close together on the cookie sheet. Cookies should be the size indicated in the recipe and be placed far enough apart (most recipes suggest 2 inches (5 cm) for medium-sized cookies) to allow for the appropriate amount of spreading. A dough that is too thin will also spread more than usual. Check to make sure you've measured the ingredients correctly.

Cookies bake unevenly

Use heavy-duty cookie sheets. Make sure all the cookies are the same size and that the cookie sheet is placed in the center of the oven on the middle rack. It should not touch the sides of the oven. Since the heat in the rear of the oven is usually more intense than in the front, turn the sheet around halfway through the baking process.

Cookies are too well done

Check to ensure that your oven temperature is not too hot. Begin checking for doneness a couple of minutes before the suggested baking time. Make cookies the size specified in the recipe and place them the recommended distance apart on the sheet.

Cookies are burned on the bottom only

The cookie sheet may be placed too low in the oven. It should be centered on the middle rack. Use a light- rather than a dark-colored sheet, as those with a dark surface absorb heat that may cause cookie bottoms to brown.

Cake expands over the top of the pan

The pan may be too small. Check the pan size in the recipe. Batter should fill the pan only one-half to three-quarters full, depending on the cake. If you follow this rule and your cake still expands too much, you might have added too much shortening, sugar or leavening agent to the batter. Check your measurements.

The texture of the cake is coarse and dense

There are a number of possible explanations for this problem. The oven temperature may be too low. Raise the temperature by 25°F (10°C) and note the results. Dense cakes also result from not having adequate fat in the batter or from not creaming the shortening or butter well enough. Shortening or butter should be well beaten with sugar until the mixture is smooth and creamy. Coarse, dense cakes can also result from over-beating the batter after the flour is added.

Cake is too dry

The most common reasons for this problem are over-baking and not having enough fat in the batter. If one of these isn't the cause, the batter may contain too much leavening agent (such as baking powder) or flour. Also, over-beating egg whites until they are too stiff can dry cakes out.

Cracks or bumps on top of cake

This problem results from too much flour in the batter or an oven that is too hot. Check these variables.

Cake has holes in it

Chances are the batter was not thoroughly mixed. Another possibility is too much egg in the batter — perhaps the eggs were too large, or you used too many. Always use large (never extra-large) eggs unless another size is called for in the recipe, and never add an extra egg just to use it up. Do not use 2 medium or small eggs as the equivalent of 1 large egg.

Cake crumbles when sliced

There may be too much fat or too much sugar in the batter. Always measure ingredients accurately.

Cake is soggy or has streaks at the bottom

There is too much baking powder or sugar in the batter, and it's likely that the ingredients were not mixed thoroughly enough. When mixing, ensure that ingredients are blended.

Crust on a multi-layered cake is too sticky and moist

This problem usually results from too much sugar. Check the recipe to make sure you measured the sugar correctly.

Cake rises higher on one side

Most likely, the batter was spread unevenly in the pan or the pan is slightly warped. Another possibility is that the pan was set too close to another pan or the side of the oven.

Cake burns on bottom

This is usually the result of uneven heat distribution in the oven. Because the back of the oven is often slightly hotter than the front, rotate the pan halfway through baking to achieve a more even heat distribution.

Drop Cookies

Drop cookies are the most popular type of cookie as they are so easy to make. Dropped from a spoon, onto a cookie sheet, they spread out as they bake. Many of the most common cookies, such as traditional chocolate chip, oatmeal, meringues and macaroons, are drop cookies. But the ingredients for drop cookies can be varied to produce a wide range of delectable treats, from fruit-filled and frosted cookies to chunky hermits.

continued on next page

Oat Bran Raisin Cookies

⅔ cup	uncooked oat bran cereal	150 mL
¼ cup	old-fashioned rolled oats	50 mL
3 tbsp	all-purpose flour	45 mL
½ tsp	baking powder	2 mL
3 tbsp	margarine, softened	45 mL
¼ cup	firmly packed brown sugar	50 mL
1	egg white, lightly beaten	1
2 tsp	water	10 mL
¼ tsp	vanilla	1 mL
2 tbsp	raisins	25 mL

This recipe makes a smaller batch of cookies than usual, but it can be doubled, if desired.

- *Preheat oven to 350°F (180°C)*
- *Cookie sheet, greased*

1. In a small bowl, mix together oat bran, rolled oats, flour and baking powder.
2. In a large bowl, beat together margarine and brown sugar until smooth and creamy. Stir in egg white, water and vanilla, mixing until thoroughly incorporated. Add flour mixture and mix well. Fold in raisins.
3. Drop by level tablespoonfuls (15 mL), about 2 inches (5 cm) apart, onto prepared cookie sheet. Using a fork or the bottom of a glass, flatten slightly. Bake in preheated oven for 12 to 15 minutes or until bottoms are slightly browned. Cool on sheet for 3 minutes, then transfer to wire racks to cool completely.

Makes about 1 dozen

Wholesome Banana Granola Drops

1½ cups	all-purpose flour	375 mL
½ tsp	baking soda	2 mL
½ tsp	salt	2 mL
1 tsp	ground cinnamon	5 mL
½ cup	butter or margarine, softened	125 mL
1 cup	firmly packed brown sugar	250 mL
1	egg	1
½ tsp	vanilla	2 mL
1 cup	mashed bananas	250 mL
1 cup	granola	250 mL

TIP: To keep bananas from turning brown, wrap individual bananas tightly in aluminum foil and refrigerate in the crisper drawer. This will slow down the ripening process.

- *Preheat oven to 375°F (190°C)*
- *Cookie sheet, greased*

1. In a small bowl, mix together flour, baking soda, salt and cinnamon.
2. In a large bowl, beat butter and brown sugar until smooth and creamy. Add egg, vanilla and bananas and beat until well blended. Add flour mixture and mix well. Stir in granola.
3. Drop by tablespoonfuls (15 mL), about 2 inches (5 cm) apart, onto prepared cookie sheet. Bake in preheated oven for 12 minutes or until golden brown. Immediately transfer to wire racks to cool.

Makes about 4 dozen

Banana Oatmeal Drops

1½ cups	all-purpose flour	375 mL
1¾ cups	quick-cooking oats	425 mL
1 tsp	salt	5 mL
1 tsp	ground cinnamon	5 mL
½ tsp	baking soda	2 mL
¼ tsp	ground nutmeg	1 mL
¾ cup	shortening, softened	175 mL
1 cup	firmly packed brown sugar	250 mL
1	egg	1
1 cup	mashed bananas	250 mL
½ cup	chopped pecans or walnuts	125 mL

> **TIP:** For a special treat, frost these cookies with Quick Banana Frosting or Creamy Lemon Frosting (see recipes, pages 358 and 364).

- *Preheat oven to 350°F (180°C)*
- *Cookie sheet, greased*

1. In a medium bowl, mix together flour, oats, salt, cinnamon, baking soda and nutmeg.
2. In a large bowl, beat shortening and brown sugar until smooth and creamy. Add egg and mashed bananas and mix well. Add flour mixture and mix well. Fold in nuts.
3. Drop by heaping teaspoonfuls (5 mL), about 2 inches (5 cm) apart, onto prepared cookie sheet. Bake in preheated oven for 12 to 15 minutes or until golden brown. Cool slightly on sheet, then transfer to wire racks to cool completely.

Makes about 5 dozen

Apple Oatmeal Cookies

1¾ cups	all-purpose flour	425 mL
½ tsp	baking powder	2 mL
½ tsp	baking soda	2 mL
½ tsp	salt	2 mL
½ cup	quick-cooking oats	125 mL
½ tsp	ground nutmeg	2 mL
½ tsp	ground cinnamon	2 mL
½ cup	shortening, softened	125 mL
1 cup	packed brown sugar	250 mL
2	eggs	2
1 cup	finely chopped peeled apples	250 mL
1 cup	raisins	250 mL
1 cup	chopped nuts	250 mL

- *Preheat oven to 400°F (200°C)*
- *Cookie sheet, greased*

1. In a medium bowl, mix together flour, baking powder, baking soda, salt, oats, nutmeg and cinnamon.
2. In a large bowl, beat shortening and brown sugar until smooth and creamy. Add eggs, one at a time, mixing until well incorporated. Mix in apples and raisins. Add flour mixture and mix well. Fold in nuts.
3. Drop by rounded teaspoonfuls (5 mL), about 2 inches (5 cm) apart, onto prepared cookie sheet. Bake in preheated oven for 10 to 12 minutes or until golden brown. Immediately transfer to wire racks to cool.

Makes about 6 dozen

TIP: To test if eggs are fresh, place them in a bowl of cold, salted water. They are fresh if they sink to the bottom and stay there.

Oatmeal Pudding Drops

1 cup	all-purpose flour	250 mL
1½ tsp	baking powder	7 mL
½ tsp	salt	2 mL
1	package (3 oz/85 g) Jello pudding, any flavor	1
¾ cup	shortening, softened	175 mL
2 tbsp	granulated sugar	25 mL
1	egg	1
1 tsp	vanilla	5 mL
1 cup	old-fashioned rolled oats	250 mL

- *Preheat oven to 350°F (180°C)*
- *Cookie sheet, ungreased*

1. In a small bowl, sift together flour, baking powder and salt.
2. In a large bowl, beat pudding powder, shortening, sugar, egg and vanilla until smooth and blended. Add flour mixture and mix well.
3. Drop by teaspoonfuls (5 mL), about 2 inches (5 cm) apart, onto cookie sheet. Bake in preheated oven for 15 minutes or until golden brown. Immediately transfer to wire racks to cool.

Makes about 3 dozen

Cranberry Orange Oatmeal Cookies

2 cups	all-purpose flour	500 mL
1 tsp	baking powder	5 mL
1/4 tsp	baking soda	1 mL
1/2 tsp	salt	2 mL
2 cups	quick-cooking oats	500 mL
1 cup	butter or margarine, softened	250 mL
1 1/2 cups	granulated sugar	375 mL
2	eggs	2
1 tsp	vanilla	5 mL
1 cup	raisins	250 mL
1 cup	coarsely chopped cranberries, fresh or frozen	250 mL
1 tbsp	grated orange zest	15 mL

- *Preheat oven to 375°F (190°C)*
- *Cookie sheet, greased*

1. In a large bowl, mix together flour, baking powder, baking soda, salt and oats.
2. In another large bowl, beat butter or margarine and sugar until smooth and creamy. Beat in eggs, one at a time, until well incorporated. Mix in vanilla. Add flour mixture and mix well. Fold in raisins, cranberries and orange zest.
3. Drop by rounded teaspoonfuls (5 mL), about 2 inches (5 cm) apart, onto prepared cookie sheet. Bake in preheated oven for 10 to 12 minutes or until edges are lightly browned. Immediately transfer to wire racks to cool.

Makes about 5 dozen

TIP: Freeze cranberries before chopping or grinding them to ease cleanup.

Peanut Butter 'n' Honey Oatmeal Drops

1 1/2 cups	all-purpose flour	375 mL
1 tsp	baking soda	5 mL
1 tsp	salt	5 mL
1 1/2 cups	quick-cooking rolled oats	375 mL
1 1/2 cups	crunchy peanut butter	375 mL
2 cups	liquid honey	500 mL
3	eggs	3
1 tbsp	water	15 mL
2 tsp	vanilla	10 mL
2 cups	raisins	500 mL

- *Preheat oven to 350°F (180°C)*
- *Cookie sheet, greased*

1. In a medium bowl, mix together flour, baking soda, salt and oats.
2. In a large bowl, mix together peanut butter, honey, eggs, water and vanilla until well blended. Add flour mixture and mix well. Fold in raisins. Refrigerate dough for 30 minutes until firm.
3. Drop by rounded teaspoonfuls (5 mL), about 2 inches (5 cm) apart, onto prepared cookie sheet. Bake in preheated oven for 12 to 15 minutes or until tops spring back when lightly touched. Immediately transfer to wire racks to cool.

Makes about 8 dozen

TIP: When you need to measure honey or syrup, grease the cup with cooking oil. If your recipe calls for oil, shortening or butter, measure that ingredient first, then use the cup to measure out honey or syrup.

Homemade Oatmeal Macaroons

2	egg whites	2
¾ cup	granulated sugar, divided	175 mL
½ cup	butter or margarine, melted	125 mL
2 cups	quick-cooking oats	500 mL
¼ cup	all-purpose flour	50 mL

TIP: Overbaked cookies can be crumbled and sprinkled over ice cream or fresh fruit or used as a topping for fruit crumbles.

- *Preheat oven to 350°F (180°C)*
- *Cookie sheet, lightly greased*

1. In a large bowl, beat egg whites until soft peaks form. Gradually add ¼ cup (50 mL) sugar, beating until stiff peaks form.
2. In another large bowl, mix together remaining sugar, butter or margarine, oats and flour. Fold into beaten egg whites until well blended.
3. Drop by level tablespoonfuls (15 mL), about 1 inch (2.5 cm) apart, onto prepared cookie sheet. Bake in preheated oven for 10 to 12 minutes or until lightly browned. Immediately transfer to wire racks to cool.

Makes about 3 dozen

Peaches 'n' Cream Oatmeal Cookies

1½ cups	whole wheat flour	375 mL
2½ cups	old-fashioned rolled oats	625 mL
2 tsp	baking powder	10 mL
1 tsp	salt	5 mL
⅔ cup	butter or margarine, softened	150 mL
¾ cup	granulated sugar	175 mL
¾ cup	packed brown sugar	175 mL
2	eggs	2
1½ tsp	vanilla	7 mL
3	diced peaches	3
¾ cup	raisins (optional)	175 mL

Although these cookies will taste better if made from freshly picked peaches, canned peaches make an acceptable substitute out of season.

TIP: To ripen fruits such as peaches, nectarines or plums, place the unripe fruit in a brown paper bag, close the bag and keep it on your kitchen counter or in an area away from direct sunlight or cold. It will be ripe in 1 to 3 days.

- *Preheat oven to 350°F (180°C)*
- *Cookie sheet, lightly greased*

1. In a large bowl, mix together flour, oats, baking powder and salt.
2. In another large bowl, beat butter or margarine and sugars until smooth and creamy. Beat in eggs, one at a time, until incorporated. Stir in vanilla. Add flour mixture and mix well. Fold in peaches and raisins. Refrigerate dough for 30 minutes, until firm.
3. Drop by rounded teaspoonfuls (5 mL), about 2 inches (5 cm) apart, onto prepared cookie sheet. Bake in preheated oven for 10 to 15 minutes or until golden brown. Immediately transfer to wire racks to cool.

Makes about 3 dozen

Chock-Full Oatmeal Cookies

2 cups	all-purpose flour	500 mL
1 tsp	baking soda	5 mL
½ tsp	salt	2 mL
1 cup	quick-cooking oats	250 mL
½ cup	butter, softened	125 mL
½ cup	granulated sugar	125 mL
¾ cup	packed brown sugar	175 mL
1	egg	1
2	egg whites	2
2 tsp	vanilla	10 mL
1 cup	semi-sweet chocolate chunks	250 mL
½ cup	dark raisins	125 mL

- *Preheat oven to 375°F (190°C)*
- *Cookie sheet, lightly greased*

1. In a medium bowl, mix together flour, baking soda, salt and oats.
2. In a large bowl, beat butter and sugars until smooth and creamy. Beat in egg, then egg whites, until incorporated. Stir in vanilla. Add flour mixture and mix well. Fold in chocolate and raisins until well combined.
3. Drop by level tablespoonfuls (15 mL), about 2 inches (5 cm) apart, onto prepared cookie sheet. Bake in preheated oven for 10 to 12 minutes or until golden brown. Immediately transfer to wire racks to cool.

Makes about 4 dozen

> **TIP:** Always use large-size eggs when baking cookies.

Golden Raisin Oat Cookies

2 cups	old-fashioned rolled oats	500 mL
1 cup	golden raisins	250 mL
2 cups	all-purpose flour	500 mL
1 tsp	baking soda	5 mL
½ tsp	salt	2 mL
1 cup	butter or margarine, softened	250 mL
1 cup	packed light brown sugar	250 mL
1 cup	granulated sugar	250 mL
2	eggs	2
2 tsp	vanilla	10 mL

- *Preheat oven to 350°F (180°C)*
- *Food processor*
- *Cookie sheet, ungreased*

1. Using a food processor, pulse oats and raisins until coarsely ground. Add flour, baking soda and salt and pulse once or twice to combine.
2. In a large bowl, beat butter or margarine and sugars until light and creamy. Beat in eggs, one at a time, until incorporated. Stir in vanilla. Add flour mixture and mix well.
3. Drop by tablespoonfuls (15 mL), about 2 inches (5 cm) apart, onto cookie sheet. Bake in preheated oven for 12 to 15 minutes or until golden brown. Immediately transfer to wire racks to cool.

Makes about 3 dozen

> **TIP:** To soften brown sugar that has hardened, add a slice of fresh bread. Close container tightly. The sugar will be soft in a few hours.

Peanut Butter Oat Cookies

1 cup	all-purpose flour	250 mL
1/2 tsp	baking powder	2 mL
1/2 tsp	baking soda	2 mL
1 1/2 cups	quick-cooking oats	375 mL
1/2 tsp	salt	2 mL
1/2 cup	butter, softened	125 mL
1/2 cup	granulated sugar	125 mL
1 cup	lightly packed brown sugar	250 mL
1	egg	1
6 tbsp	crunchy peanut butter	90 mL
2 tbsp	water	25 mL
1/2 tsp	vanilla	2 mL

- *Preheat oven to 350°F (180°C)*
- *Cookie sheet, greased*

1. In a medium bowl, mix together flour, baking powder, baking soda, oats and salt.
2. In a large bowl, beat butter and sugars until smooth and creamy. Beat in egg, until incorporated. Add peanut butter, water and vanilla and mix until smooth. Add flour mixture and mix well.
3. Drop by rounded tablespoonfuls (15 mL), 2 inches (5 cm) apart, onto prepared cookie sheet. Using your hand or the back of a spoon, press down slightly to flatten. Bake in preheated oven for 15 minutes or until golden brown. Immediately transfer to wire racks to cool.

Makes about 4 dozen

Maple Walnut Oatmeal Cookies

1 cup	all-purpose flour	250 mL
3 cups	quick-cooking oats	750 mL
1/2 tsp	baking soda	2 mL
1/2 tsp	salt	2 mL
1/4 tsp	ground cinnamon	1 mL
3/4 cup	butter or butter-flavored shortening, softened	175 mL
1 1/4 cups	firmly packed brown sugar	300 mL
1	egg	1
1 1/2 tsp	vanilla	7 mL
1 1/2 tsp	maple extract	7 mL
1/3 cup	milk	75 mL
1 cup	coarsely chopped walnuts	250 mL

- *Preheat oven to 375°F (190°C)*
- *Cookie sheet, greased*

1. In a large bowl, mix together flour, oats, baking soda, salt and cinnamon.
2. In another large bowl, beat butter or shortening and brown sugar until smooth and creamy. Beat in egg until incorporated. Stir in vanilla, maple extract and milk and mix well. Add flour mixture and mix well. Fold in nuts.
3. Drop by rounded tablespoonfuls (15 mL), about 2 inches (5 cm) apart, onto prepared cookie sheet. Using your hand or the back of a spoon, press down slightly to flatten. Bake in preheated oven for 10 to 12 minutes or until lightly browned. Cool on sheet for 2 minutes, then transfer to wire racks to cool completely.

Makes about 2 1/2 dozen

TIP: If you ever have a recipe that calls for half an egg, beat one egg lightly and use 2 tbsp (25 mL).

Oatmeal Lace Pennies

1 cup	old-fashioned rolled oats	250 mL
1 cup	granulated sugar	250 mL
3 tbsp	all-purpose flour	45 mL
¼ tsp	baking powder	1 mL
½ tsp	salt	2 mL
1	egg	1
½ cup	butter, melted	125 mL
½ tsp	vanilla	2 mL

- *Preheat oven to 350°F (180°C)*
- *Cookie sheet, lined with foil, bright side up*

1. In a medium bowl, mix together oats, sugar, flour, baking powder and salt.
2. In a large bowl, beat egg, butter and vanilla. Add flour mixture and mix well. (If dough seems too soft, chill for 15 to 20 minutes to firm.)
3. Drop by rounded teaspoonfuls (5 mL), about 2 inches (5 cm) apart, onto prepared cookie sheet. Bake in preheated oven for 8 to 10 minutes. Cool for 2 minutes on foil, then transfer to wire racks to cool completely.

Makes about 5½ dozen

Easy Oatmeal Drop Cookies

1 cup	all-purpose flour	250 mL
1 tsp	baking powder	5 mL
½ tsp	salt	2 mL
¾ cup	shortening, softened	175 mL
1 cup	lightly packed brown sugar	250 mL
2	eggs, beaten	2
1 tsp	vanilla	5 mL
⅓ cup	milk, divided	75 mL
3 cups	old-fashioned rolled oats	750 mL

- *Preheat oven to 375°F (190°C)*
- *Cookie sheet, greased*

1. In a large bowl, mix together flour, baking powder and salt.
2. Using two knives, a pastry blender or the tips of your fingers, cut in shortening until mixture resembles coarse crumbs. Stir in sugar, eggs, vanilla and half the milk. Beat until the mixture is smooth and blended. Mix together remaining milk and oats and fold into mixture.
3. Drop by rounded teaspoonfuls (5 mL), about 2 inches (5 cm) apart, onto prepared cookie sheet. Bake in preheated oven for 12 to 15 minutes or until golden brown. Immediately transfer to wire racks to cool.

Makes about 4 dozen

VARIATIONS

Date Nut Oatmeal Cookies
Add 1 cup (250 mL) chopped dates and 1 cup (250 mL) chopped nuts to the batter along with the oats.

Chocolate Chip Oatmeal Cookies
Add 1 cup (250 mL) chocolate chips to the batter along with the oats.

Raisin Oatmeal Cookies
Add ¾ cup (175 mL) raisins to the batter along with the oats.

Old-Fashioned Raisin Nut Oatmeal Cookies

1 cup	water	250 mL
1 cup	raisins	250 mL
2½ cups	all-purpose flour	625 mL
1 tsp	baking soda	5 mL
½ tsp	baking powder	2 mL
1 tsp	salt	5 mL
1 tsp	ground cinnamon	5 mL
½ tsp	ground cloves	2 mL
2 cups	quick-cooking rolled oats	500 mL
½ cup	chopped nuts	125 mL
¾ cup	shortening or butter, softened	175 mL
1½ cups	granulated sugar	325 mL
2	eggs	2
1 tsp	vanilla	5 mL

- *Preheat oven to 400°F (200°C)*
- *Cookie sheet, ungreased*

1. In a small saucepan, over medium heat, bring water and raisins to a boil. Simmer for 15 to 20 minutes or until raisins are plump. Drain, reserving liquid. If necessary, add water so liquid measures ½ cup (125 mL). Set raisins aside.
2. In a large bowl, mix together flour, baking soda, baking powder, salt, cinnamon, cloves, oats, nuts and reserved raisins.
3. In another large bowl, beat shortening or butter and sugar until smooth and creamy. Beat in eggs, one at a time. Stir in vanilla and reserved raisin liquid. Add flour mixture and mix well.
4. Drop by rounded teaspoonfuls (5 mL), 2 inches (5 cm) apart, onto cookie sheet. Bake in preheated oven for 8 to 10 minutes or until lightly browned. Cool for 3 minutes on sheet, then transfer to wire racks to cool completely.

Makes about 6 dozen

German Chocolate Cake Cookies

½ cup	butter or margarine, softened	125 mL
2	eggs	2
1	package (18¼ oz/515 g) chocolate cake mix	1
2 tbsp	all-purpose flour	25 mL
18	maraschino cherries, halved	18

TIP: For a treat, ice the cookies while they are still warm with Chocolate Icing (see Recipe, page 361).

- *Preheat oven to 350°F (180°C)*
- *Cookie sheet, greased*

1. In a large bowl, cream butter until smooth. Beat in eggs, one at a time, until incorporated. Mix in cake mix and flour. (Dough should be stiff.)
2. Drop by rounded teaspoonfuls (5 mL), about 2 inches (5 cm) apart, onto prepared cookie sheet. Press a cherry half into the top of each cookie. Bake in preheated oven for 10 to 12 minutes. Immediately transfer to wire racks to cool.

Makes 3 dozen

Chocolate Buttermilk Pyramids

2 cups	all-purpose flour	500 mL
½ cup	unsweetened cocoa powder	125 mL
2 tsp	baking powder	10 mL
½ tsp	baking soda	2 mL
1 tsp	salt	5 mL
½ cup	shortening, softened	125 mL
1 cup	granulated sugar	250 mL
2	eggs	2
½ tsp	vanilla	2 mL
1 cup	buttermilk	250 mL
	Confectioner's (icing) sugar, sifted (optional)	

> **TIP:** Keep a sugar shaker filled with confectioner's sugar available for dusting cookies.

- *Preheat oven to 350°F (180°C)*
- *Cookie sheet, ungreased*

1. In a medium bowl, mix together flour, cocoa, baking powder, baking soda and salt.
2. In a large bowl, beat shortening and sugar until smooth and creamy. Beat in eggs, one at a time, until well incorporated. Stir in vanilla. Add flour mixture alternately with buttermilk, mixing well after each addition.
3. Drop by rounded teaspoonfuls (5 mL), about 2 inches (5 cm) apart, onto cookie sheet. Bake in preheated oven for 12 to 15 minutes or until edges are lightly browned. Immediately transfer to wire racks to cool. Dust warm cookies with confectioner's sugar, if desired.

Makes about 4 dozen

Jam-Filled Chocolate Thumbprints

1¾ cups	all-purpose flour	425 mL
1 tsp	baking soda	5 mL
½ tsp	salt	2 mL
¾ cup	butter or margarine, softened	175 mL
¼ cup	granulated sugar	50 mL
½ cup	packed brown sugar	125 mL
2	eggs	2
1 tsp	vanilla	5 mL
1½ cups	mini chocolate chips	375 mL
	Raspberry jam	

> **TIP:** To decrystalize jam, jelly or syrup, place jar in a pan of cold water, over low heat. Heat gently and the crystals will disappear.

- *Preheat oven to 350°F (180°C)*
- *Cookie sheet, greased*

1. In a small bowl, mix together flour, baking soda and salt.
2. In a large bowl, cream butter or margarine and sugars until smooth and creamy. Add eggs, one at a time, beating until incorporated. Stir in vanilla. Add flour mixture and mix until just blended. Fold in chocolate chips and let stand for 10 minutes.
3. Drop by tablespoonfuls (15 mL), 2 inches (5 cm) apart, onto prepared cookie sheet. Using your thumb, a thimble or the back of a small spoon, make an indentation in each cookie. Bake in preheated oven for 10 to 12 minutes or until golden brown. Spoon raspberry jam into each indentation and transfer to wire racks to cool.

Makes about 4 dozen

Chocolate Meringue Kisses

¾ cup	granulated sugar	175 mL
¼ cup	unsweetened cocoa powder	50 mL
3	egg whites	3
¾ tsp	vanilla	4 mL
CHOCOLATE GLAZE		
3	squares (each 1 oz/28 g) semi-sweet chocolate	3
1 tbsp	shortening	15 mL

> **TIP:** If meringues have fallen, crumble them into pieces and use in parfait dishes with whipped cream, ice cream and fruit.

- *Preheat oven to 300°F (150°C)*
- *Cookie sheet, lined with parchment paper or foil and sprayed with nonstick spray*
- *Pastry bag with large star tip*

1. In a small bowl, mix together sugar and cocoa.
2. In a large bowl, beat egg whites and vanilla until soft peaks form. Gradually beat in sugar mixture until stiff peaks form.
3. Using a pastry bag, press stars onto prepared sheet, about 2 inches (5 cm) apart. Bake in preheated oven for 30 to 35 minutes or until lightly browned. Immediately transfer to wire racks to cool.
4. *Chocolate Glaze:* In a small saucepan, over low heat, melt chocolate and shortening, stirring constantly. Holding gently with your fingers, dip the top of each meringue into the glaze, then place on waxed paper to harden.

Makes about 4 dozen kisses

The Original Tollhouse Cookie

1 cup	all-purpose flour	250 mL
½ tsp	baking soda	2 mL
½ tsp	salt	2 mL
⅔ cup	butter, softened	150 mL
1 cup	lightly packed brown sugar	250 mL
1	egg	1
1½ tsp	vanilla	7 mL
½ cup	old-fashioned rolled oats	125 mL
½ cup	chopped nuts	125 mL
1 cup	chocolate chips or chunks	250 mL

> **TIP:** For a quick, delicious frosting, add maple syrup to confectioner's sugar and stir until thick and creamy. It's especially good on chocolate or mocha cookies.

- *Preheat oven to 375°F (190°C)*
- *Cookie sheet, greased*

1. In a small bowl, mix together flour, baking soda and salt.
2. In a large bowl, beat butter and brown sugar until smooth and creamy. Beat in egg until well incorporated. Stir in vanilla. Add flour mixture and mix well. Stir in rolled oats, nuts and chocolate chips or chunks.
3. Drop by rounded teaspoonfuls (5 mL), about 2 inches (5 cm) apart, onto prepared cookie sheet. Bake in preheated oven for 10 minutes or until golden brown. Immediately transfer to wire racks to cool.

Makes about 5 dozen

Chocolate Mint Chip Drops

2 cups	all-purpose flour	500 mL
¾ cup	unsweetened cocoa powder	175 mL
1 tsp	baking soda	5 mL
¼ tsp	salt	1 mL
1 cup	butter, softened	250 mL
¾ cup	granulated sugar	175 mL
1 cup	packed light brown sugar	250 mL
2	eggs	2
2 tsp	vanilla	10 mL
2 cups	mint chocolate chips	500 mL

TIP: You can also substitute chocolate chips for the mint chocolate chips and add ¼ tsp (1 mL) mint extract along with the vanilla.

- *Preheat oven to 375°F (190°C)*
- *Cookie sheet, ungreased*

1. In a medium bowl, combine flour, cocoa, baking soda and salt.
2. In a large bowl, beat butter and sugars until smooth and creamy. Add eggs, one at a time, mixing until well incorporated. Stir in vanilla. Add flour mixture and mix well. Fold in mint chocolate chips.
3. Drop by heaping teaspoonfuls (5 mL), about 2 inches (5 cm) apart, onto cookie sheet. Bake in preheated oven for 9 to 12 minutes or until cookies are crisp. Cool on sheet for 2 minutes, then transfer to wire racks to cool completely.

Makes about 5 dozen

Cream Cheese Chocolate Chip Cookies

1	package (10 oz/300 g) mini chocolate chips, divided	1
2¼ cups	all-purpose flour	550 mL
1½ tsp	baking soda	7 mL
½ cup	butter, softened	125 mL
8 oz	cream cheese, softened	250 g
1½ cups	granulated sugar	375 mL
1	egg	1
½ cup	chopped nuts	125 mL

TIP: Try making these cookies using raspberry or other flavored chips. For an added treat, drizzle melted chocolate chips over top of the cookies as soon as they come out of the oven.

- *Preheat oven to 350°F (180°C)*
- *Cookie sheet, ungreased*

1. In a small saucepan, over very low heat, melt 1 cup (250 mL) chocolate chips.
2. In a medium bowl, mix together flour and baking soda.
3. In a large bowl, beat butter, cream cheese and sugar until smooth and creamy. Beat in egg until well incorporated. Beat in melted chocolate until well combined. Add flour mixture and mix well. Fold in nuts and remaining chocolate chips.
4. Drop by tablespoonfuls (15 mL), about 2 inches (5 cm) apart, onto cookie sheet. Bake in preheated oven for 10 to 12 minutes or until cookies are firm around the edges. Immediately transfer to wire racks to cool.

Makes about 4 dozen

Dad's Favorite Chocolate Chip Cookies

3½ cups	all-purpose flour	875 mL
1 tsp	salt	5 mL
1 tsp	baking soda	5 mL
⅔ cup	shortening, softened	150 mL
⅔ cup	butter or margarine, softened	150 mL
1 cup	packed brown sugar	250 mL
1 cup	granulated sugar	250 mL
2	eggs	2
2 tsp	vanilla	10 mL
2	packages (12 oz/375 g) semi-sweet chocolate chips	2
1 cup	chopped nuts (optional)	250 mL

- *Preheat oven to 375°F (190°C)*
- *Cookie sheet, ungreased*

1. In a medium bowl, mix together flour, salt and baking soda.
2. In a large bowl, beat shortening, butter or margarine and sugars until smooth and creamy. Beat in eggs, one at a time, until incorporated. Stir in vanilla. Add flour mixture and mix well. Fold in chocolate chips and nuts, if using.
3. Drop by rounded teaspoonfuls (5 mL), about 2 inches (5 cm) apart, onto cookie sheet. Bake in preheated oven for 10 minutes or until lightly browned. Cool on sheet for 2 minutes, then transfer to wire racks to cool completely.

Makes about 7 dozen

Chocolate Chip Raspberry Cream Cheese Drops

2½ cups	all-purpose flour	625 mL
1 tsp	baking soda	5 mL
½ cup	butter or margarine, softened	125 mL
1½ cups	granulated sugar	375 mL
8 oz	cream cheese, softened	250 g)
1	egg	1
1 cup	semi-sweet chocolate chips, melted (see page 14)	250 mL
1 cup	mini raspberry chips	250 mL

- *Preheat oven to 350°F (180°C)*
- *Cookie sheet, ungreased*

1. In a medium bowl, mix together flour and baking soda.
2. In a large bowl, beat butter or margarine, sugar and cream cheese until smooth. Beat in egg and melted chocolate until well blended. Add flour mixture and mix well. Fold in raspberry chips.
3. Drop by rounded teaspoonfuls (5 mL), about 2 inches (5 cm) apart, onto cookie sheet. Bake in preheated oven for 12 to 15 minutes or until tops of cookies spring back when lightly touched. Immediately transfer to wire racks to cool.

Makes about 2 dozen

TIP: When baking cookie dough containing chocolate bits, flouring a greased baking sheet will prevent the chocolate from sticking and burning if it comes in direct contact with the baking sheet.

Orange Chocolate Chip Cookies

1 cup	all-purpose flour	250 mL
¼ tsp	salt	1 mL
½ cup	butter or margarine, softened	125 mL
½ cup	granulated sugar	125 mL
4 oz	cream cheese, softened	125 g
1	egg	1
1 tsp	vanilla	5 mL
1 tsp	orange zest	5 mL
1 cup	semi-sweet chocolate chips	250 mL

- *Preheat oven to 350°F (180°C)*
- *Cookie sheet, ungreased*

1. In a small bowl, mix together flour and salt.
2. In a large bowl, beat butter or margarine, sugar and cream cheese until smooth. Beat in egg until incorporated. Stir in vanilla and orange zest. Add flour mixture and mix well. Fold in chocolate chips.
3. Drop by teaspoonfuls (5 mL), about 1 inch (2.5 cm) apart, onto cookie sheet. Bake in preheated oven for 15 minutes or until edges are lightly browned. Immediately transfer to wire racks to cool.

Makes about 3 dozen

Golden Coconut Macaroons

2	egg whites	2
½ tsp	vanilla	2 mL
2 tbsp	cake flour	25 mL
½ cup	granulated sugar	125 mL
¼ tsp	salt	1 mL
2 cups	shredded coconut	500 mL

- *Preheat oven to 350°F (180°C)*
- *Cookie sheet, lined with waxed or parchment paper or foil*

1. In a large bowl, beat egg whites and vanilla until soft peaks form.
2. In another large bowl, sift together flour, sugar and salt. Fold in beaten egg whites, then fold in coconut, blending thoroughly.
3. Drop by rounded teaspoonfuls (5 mL), about 2 inches (5 cm) apart, onto prepared cookie sheet. Bake in preheated oven for 20 minutes or until golden brown. Immediately transfer to wire racks to cool.

Makes about 1½ dozen

VARIATIONS

Cherry Coconut Macaroons
Add ½ cup (125 mL) chopped candied cherries along with the coconut.

Chocolate Chip Macaroons
Substitute ½ cup (125 mL) chocolate chips for the coconut.

Cornflake Macaroons
Substitute 2 cups (500 mL) cornflakes for the coconut.

Hazelnut Macaroons
Substitute 2 cups (500 mL) finely ground hazelnuts for the coconut.

Ambrosia Coconut Drops

2 cups	all-purpose flour	500 mL
1 tsp	baking soda	5 mL
½ tsp	salt	2 mL
½ cup	butter, softened	125 mL
1¼ cups	granulated sugar	300 mL
2	eggs	2
1 cup	shredded coconut	250 mL
1 tbsp	orange zest	15 mL
½ cup	orange juice	125 mL

- *Preheat oven to 350°F (180°C)*
- *Cookie sheet, lightly greased*

1. In a medium bowl, sift together flour, baking soda and salt.
2. In a large bowl, beat butter and sugar until smooth and creamy. Beat in eggs, one at a time, until incorporated. Add flour mixture and mix well.
3. In a small bowl, combine coconut and orange zest and juice. Fold into batter.
4. Drop by teaspoonfuls (5 mL), about 2 inches (5 cm) apart, onto prepared cookie sheet. Bake in preheated oven for 10 to 12 minutes or until golden brown. Transfer to wire racks.

Makes about 4 dozen

Carrot Coconut Drops

2 cups	all-purpose flour	500 mL
2 tsp	baking powder	10 mL
½ tsp	salt	2 mL
½ cup	shortening, softened	125 mL
½ cup	butter, softened	125 mL
¾ cup	granulated sugar	175 mL
2	eggs	2
1 cup	mashed cooked carrots	250 mL
¾ cup	shredded coconut	175 mL

- *Preheat oven to 400°F (200°C)*
- *Cookie sheet, lightly greased*

1. In a medium bowl, mix together flour, baking powder and salt.
2. In a large bowl, beat shortening, butter and sugar until smooth and creamy. Beat in eggs, one at a time, until incorporated. Stir in carrots. Add flour mixture and mix well. Fold in coconut.
3. Drop by teaspoonfuls (5 mL), about 2 inches (5 cm) apart, onto prepared cookie sheet. Bake in preheated oven for 8 to 10 minutes or until golden brown. Transfer to wire racks.

Makes about 4 dozen

TIP: If desired, these cookies may be frosted with Orange Butter Icing (see recipe, page 365).

Sunny Lemon Yogurt Cookies

2½ cups + 2 tbsp	all-purpose flour	650 mL
1 tsp	baking powder	5 mL
½ tsp	baking soda	2 mL
1 tsp	salt	5 mL
2	eggs	2
1½ cups	granulated sugar	375 mL
⅓ cup	vegetable oil	75 mL
½ cup	low-fat lemon yogurt	125 mL
½ tsp	finely grated lemon zest	2 mL
1 tsp	freshly squeezed lemon juice	5 mL
	Confectioner's (icing) sugar, sifted (optional)	
	Lemon Butter Frosting (optional) (see recipe, page 364)	

- *Preheat oven to 375°F (190°C)*
- *Cookie sheet, lightly greased*

1. In a medium bowl, mix together flour, baking powder, baking soda and salt.
2. In a large bowl, beat eggs, sugar, oil, yogurt, lemon zest and juice until well blended. Add flour mixture and mix well.
3. Drop by rounded teaspoonfuls (5 mL), about 2 inches (5 cm) apart, onto prepared cookie sheet. Bake in preheated oven for 10 to 12 minutes or until lightly browned around the edges. Cool on sheet for 2 minutes, then transfer to wire racks to cool completely. Sprinkle with confectioner's sugar or frost, if desired.

Makes about 4 dozen

TIP: When a recipe calls for just a few drops of lemon juice, poke holes in an uncut lemon with a fork and squeeze out the required amount. The lemon can go back into the refrigerator and be used several more times.

Soft Raisin Cookies

1 cup	water	250 mL
2 cups	raisins	500 mL
3½ cups	all-purpose flour	875 mL
1 tsp	baking powder	5 mL
1 tsp	baking soda	5 mL
1 tsp	salt	5 mL
½ tsp	ground nutmeg	2 mL
½ tsp	ground cinnamon	2 mL
1 cup	shortening, softened	250 mL
1¾ cups	granulated sugar	425 mL
2	eggs	2
1 tsp	vanilla	5 mL

- *Preheat oven to 350°F (180°C)*
- *Cookie sheet, greased*

1. In a saucepan, over medium heat, bring water and raisins to a boil. Cook for 3 minutes, remove from heat and let cool. Do not drain.
2. In a medium bowl, mix together flour, baking powder, baking soda, salt, nutmeg and cinnamon.
3. In a large bowl, beat shortening and sugar until smooth and creamy. Beat in eggs, one at a time, until incorporated. Stir in vanilla. Gradually add flour mixture, blending thoroughly. Stir in raisins and liquid.
4. Drop by rounded teaspoonfuls (5 mL), about 2 inches (5 cm) apart, onto prepared cookie sheet. Bake in preheated oven for 12 to 15 minutes or until golden brown. Immediately transfer to wire racks to cool.

Makes about 6 dozen

Cinnamon Raisin Banana Cookies

2 cups	all-purpose flour	500 mL
¼ tsp	salt	1 mL
1 tsp	ground cinnamon	5 mL
1 cup	raisins	250 mL
½ cup	chopped nuts	125 mL
½ cup	butter or margarine, softened	125 mL
1 cup	granulated sugar	250 mL
2	eggs	2
1 cup	mashed bananas, about 2 to 3 medium	250 mL

- *Preheat oven to 375°F (190°C)*
- *Cookie sheet, lightly greased*

1. In a medium bowl, mix together flour, salt, cinnamon, raisins and nuts.
2. In a large bowl, beat butter or margarine and sugar until smooth and creamy. Beat in eggs, one at a time, until incorporated. Stir in banana. Add flour mixture and mix well.
3. Drop by rounded teaspoonfuls (5 mL), about 2 inches (5 cm) apart, onto prepared cookie sheet. Bake in preheated oven for 8 to 10 minutes or until golden brown. Immediately transfer to wire racks to cool.

Makes about 4 dozen

Zesty Prune Cookies

1¾ cups	all-purpose flour	425 mL
½ tsp	baking soda	2 mL
½ tsp	salt	2 mL
½ tsp	ground cinnamon	2 mL
½ tsp	ground nutmeg	2 mL
Pinch	ground cloves	Pinch
½ cup	butter or margarine, softened	125 mL
1 cup	packed brown sugar	250 mL
1	egg	1
¼ cup	milk	50 mL
1 cup	chopped prunes	250 mL
½ cup	chopped nuts	125 mL

- *Preheat oven to 400°F (200°C)*
- *Cookie sheet, ungreased*

1. In a small bowl, mix together flour, baking soda, salt, cinnamon, nutmeg and cloves.
2. In a large bowl, beat butter or margarine and sugar until smooth and creamy. Beat in egg until well incorporated. Stir in milk. Add flour mixture and mix well. Fold in prunes and nuts.
3. Drop by rounded teaspoonfuls (5 mL), 2 inches (5 cm) apart, onto cookie sheet. Bake in preheated oven for 8 to 10 minutes or until tops spring back when lightly touched. Immediately transfer to wire racks to cool.

Makes about 4½ dozen

Diced Rhubarb Cookies

2 cups	all-purpose flour or whole wheat flour or a combination of both	500 mL
2 tsp	baking powder	10 mL
Pinch	salt	Pinch
1 tsp	ground cinnamon	5 mL
½ tsp	ground nutmeg	2 mL
½ tsp	ground cloves	2 mL
½ cup	butter, softened	125 mL
1 cup	lightly packed brown sugar	250 mL
1	egg	1
¼ cup	milk	50 mL
1 cup	diced rhubarb	250 mL
1 cup	chopped walnuts	250 mL

- *Preheat oven to 350°F (180°C)*
- *Cookie sheet, greased*

1. In a medium bowl, combine flour, baking powder, salt, cinnamon, nutmeg and cloves.
2. In a large bowl, beat butter and sugar until smooth and creamy. Beat in egg until well incorporated. Mix in milk. Add flour mixture and beat until smooth. Fold in rhubarb and walnuts until well combined.
3. Drop by rounded teaspoonfuls (5 mL), 2 inches (5 cm) apart, onto prepared cookie sheet. Bake in preheated oven for 18 to 20 minutes or until crisp and lightly browned. Immediately transfer to wire racks to cool.

Makes about 3½ dozen

> **TIP:** If you are lactose intolerant, use lactose-reduced milk in baking. It can be substituted for regular milk and will not affect the results.

Hawaiian Pineapple Drops

2 cups	all-purpose flour	500 mL
1 tsp	baking powder	5 mL
½ tsp	baking soda	2 mL
¼ tsp	salt	1 mL
½ cup	butter or margarine, softened	125 mL
1 cup	lightly packed brown sugar	250 mL
1	egg	1
1 tsp	vanilla	5 mL
1 cup	crushed pineapple, well drained	250 mL

- *Preheat oven to 400°F (200°C)*
- *Cookie sheet, greased*

1. In a medium bowl, mix together flour, baking powder, baking soda and salt.
2. In a large bowl, beat butter or margarine and brown sugar until smooth and creamy. Beat in egg until well incorporated. Stir in vanilla. Add flour mixture and mix well. (Dough will look crumbly.) Add pineapple and mix until well blended.
3. Drop by tablespoonfuls (15 mL), 2 inches (5 cm) apart, onto prepared cookie sheet. Bake in preheated oven for 10 to 15 minutes or until golden brown. Immediately transfer to wire racks to cool.

Makes about 3 dozen

Orange Raisin Butter Cookies

1 cup	water	250 mL
2 cups	raisins	500 mL
4 cups	all-purpose flour	1 L
1 tsp	baking powder	5 mL
1 tsp	baking soda	5 mL
1 tsp	salt	5 mL
1½ tsp	ground cinnamon	7 mL
¼ tsp	ground nutmeg	1 mL
¼ tsp	ground allspice	1 mL
1 cup	shortening or butter, softened	250 mL
1¾ cups	granulated sugar	425 mL
3	eggs	3
2 tsp	vanilla	10 mL
2 tsp	grated orange zest	10 mL

TIP: To rehydrate raisins that have dried out, place in a sieve and steam over hot water for 3 to 5 minutes.

- *Preheat oven to 400°F (200°C)*
- *Cookie sheet, ungreased*

1. In a saucepan, over medium heat, bring raisins and water to a boil. Simmer for 5 minutes. Drain, reserving liquid. Set raisins aside.
2. In a large bowl, mix together flour, baking powder, baking soda, salt, cinnamon, nutmeg and allspice.
3. In another large bowl, beat shortening and sugar until smooth and creamy. Beat in eggs, one at a time, until incorporated. Stir in vanilla.
4. Add flour mixture to creamed mixture alternately with reserved raisin liquid, mixing until well blended. Fold in raisins and orange zest.
5. Drop by tablespoonfuls (15 mL), 2 inches (5 cm) apart, onto cookie sheet. Using the bottom of a glass dipped in flour, flatten slightly. Bake in preheated oven for 8 to 10 minutes or until golden brown. Cool on sheet for 3 minutes, then transfer to wire racks to cool completely.

Makes about 6 dozen

Hermits

3½ cups	all-purpose flour	875 mL
1 tsp	baking soda	5 mL
½ tsp	salt	2 mL
1 tsp	ground cinnamon	5 mL
1 tsp	ground nutmeg	5 mL
½ cup	butter or margarine, softened	125 mL
½ cup	shortening, softened	125 mL
2 cups	packed brown sugar	500 mL
2	eggs	2
½ cup	cold coffee	125 mL
1 cup	chopped nuts	250 mL
1½ cups	raisins	375 mL

- *Preheat oven to 375°F (190°C)*
- *Cookie sheet, ungreased*

1. In a medium bowl, sift together flour, baking soda, salt, cinnamon and nutmeg.
2. In a large bowl, beat butter or margarine, shortening and brown sugar until smooth and creamy. Add eggs, one at a time, beating until incorporated. Beat in coffee. Add flour mixture and blend well. Fold in nuts and raisins.
3. Drop by rounded teaspoonfuls (5 mL), about 2 inches (5 cm) apart, onto cookie sheet. Bake in preheated oven for 8 to 10 minutes. Cool for 2 minutes on sheet, then transfer to wire racks to cool completely.

Makes about 7 dozen

> *Hermits are a spicy and fruity drop cookie, originally from New England.*

Thrifty Hermit Cookies

3 cups	all-purpose flour	750 mL
2 tsp	baking powder	10 mL
¼ tsp	salt	1 mL
1 tsp	ground allspice	5 mL
1 tsp	ground cinnamon	5 mL
1 tsp	ground nutmeg	5 mL
1 cup	butter or margarine, softened	250 mL
1½ cups	granulated sugar	375 mL
1	egg	1
1 cup	chopped raisins	250 mL

- *Preheat oven to 375°F (190°C)*
- *Cookie sheet, greased*

1. In a medium bowl, mix together flour, baking powder, salt, allspice, cinnamon and nutmeg.
2. In a large bowl, beat butter or margarine and sugar until smooth and creamy. Beat in egg until well incorporated. Add flour mixture and mix well. Fold in raisins.
3. Drop by rounded teaspoonfuls (5 mL), about 2 inches (5 cm) apart, onto prepared cookie sheet. Bake in preheated oven for 10 to 15 minutes or until golden brown. Cool for 2 minutes, then transfer to wire racks to cool completely.

Makes about 4 dozen

...ies

500 mL	
5 mL	
500 g	
250 mL	
375 mL	
2	
10 mL	
6 mL	
1 mL	
250 mL	
175 mL	
125 mL	

- *Preheat oven to 375°F (190°C)*
- *Cookie sheet, greased*

1. In a medium bowl, mix together flour and baking soda. Add dates and toss to coat.
2. In a large bowl, beat shortening and brown sugar until smooth and creamy. Add eggs, one at a time, beating until well incorporated. Stir in vanilla, cinnamon and nutmeg until blended. Add oats and flour mixture, mixing until just incorporated. Fold in coconut and nuts.
3. Drop by tablespoonfuls (15 mL), about 2 inches (5 cm) apart, onto prepared cookie sheet. Bake in preheated oven for 8 to 10 minutes or until golden brown. Cool on sheet for 2 minutes, then transfer to wire racks to cool completely.

Makes about 5 dozen

...ps

		125 mL
		125 mL
		50 mL
		125 mL
		1
		5 mL
½ tsp	lemon extract	2 mL
3 cups less 2 tbsp	all-purpose flour	725 mL
1 tsp	baking soda	5 mL
½ tsp	ground cinnamon	2 mL
¼ tsp	ground nutmeg	1 mL
¼ tsp	ground ginger	1 mL
¼ tsp	salt	1 mL

- *Preheat oven to 375°F (190°C)*
- *Cookie sheet, greased*

1. In a saucepan, soak figs in boiling water for 10 minutes. Drain, cut off stems and discard. Cut figs into small pieces and set aside.
2. In a saucepan, combine shortening, sugar and molasses. Bring to a boil, remove from heat and cool to lukewarm. Beat in egg, vanilla and lemon extract.
3. In a large bowl, sift together flour, baking soda, cinnamon, nutmeg, ginger and salt. Stir flour mixture into molasses mixture until well blended. Fold in reserved figs.
4. Drop by rounded teaspoonfuls (5 mL), about 2 inches (5 cm) apart, onto prepared cookie sheet. Bake in preheated oven for 12 minutes or until golden brown. Immediately transfer to wire racks to cool.

Makes about 3 dozen

TIP: To cut sticky foods, such as figs, prunes, dates, marshmallows and candied fruits, use kitchen scissors. Rub the blades with oil or dip them occasionally in hot water.

Mixed Fruit 'n' Nut Drops

1¼ cups	all-purpose flour	300 mL
½ tsp	baking soda	2 mL
2 cups	quartered pitted dates	250 mL
1 cup	diced candied pineapple	250 mL
1 cup	halved candied cherries	250 mL
½ cup	butter, softened	125 mL
½ cup	packed brown sugar	125 mL
1	egg	1
1 tsp	vanilla	5 mL
½ tsp	ground cinnamon	2 mL
½ cup	chopped walnuts	125 mL
½ cup	chopped pecans	125 mL
½ cup	chopped hazelnuts	125 mL
	Corn syrup for glaze (optional)	

- *Preheat oven to 350°F (180°C)*
- *Mini baking cups or cookie sheet, lightly greased*

1. In a large bowl, combine flour, baking soda, dates, pineapple and cherries and toss until fruit is well coated.
2. In another large bowl, beat butter and brown sugar until smooth and creamy. Beat in egg until incorporated. Stir in vanilla and cinnamon. Add flour mixture and mix well. Fold in nuts.
3. Drop by rounded teaspoonfuls (5 mL) into mini baking cups placed on a cookie sheet or directly onto prepared sheet. Bake in preheated oven for 12 to 15 minutes or until tops look dry. Immediately transfer to wire racks to cool. If you prefer a glazed cookie, brush tops lightly with heated corn syrup.

Makes about 4 dozen

Orange Nut Cranberry Cookies

3 cups	all-purpose flour	750 mL
1 tsp	baking powder	5 mL
¼ tsp	baking soda	1 mL
½ tsp	salt	2 mL
½ cup	butter or margarine, softened	125 mL
1 cup	granulated sugar	250 mL
¾ cup	packed brown sugar	175 mL
1	egg	1
¼ cup	milk	50 mL
2 tbsp	orange juice	25 mL
2½ cups	coarsely chopped frozen cranberries	625 mL
¾ cup	chopped nuts	175 mL

- *Preheat oven to 375°F (190°C)*
- *Cookie sheet, greased*

1. In a medium bowl, mix together flour, baking powder, baking soda and salt.
2. In a large bowl, beat butter or margarine and sugars until smooth and creamy. Beat in egg until well incorporated. Add milk and orange juice and blend well. Add flour mixture to creamed mixture and mix well. Fold in cranberries and chopped nuts.
3. Drop by rounded teaspoonfuls (5 mL), about 2 inches (5 cm) apart, onto prepared cookie sheet. Bake in preheated oven for 10 to 15 minutes or until lightly browned. Immediately transfer to wire racks to cool

Makes about 6 dozen

Frosted Banana Split Drops

2 cups	all-purpose flour	500 mL
2 tsp	baking powder	10 mL
1/4 tsp	baking soda	1 mL
1/4 tsp	salt	1 mL
1/2 tsp	ground cinnamon	2 mL
1/4 tsp	ground cloves	1 mL
1 cup	packed brown sugar	250 mL
1/4 cup	butter or margarine, softened	50 mL
1/4 cup	shortening, softened	50 mL
2	eggs	2
1 cup	mashed bananas, about 2 to 3 medium	250 mL
1/2 cup	chopped nuts	125 mL
	Chocolate or Vanilla Icing or Fresh Strawberry Frosting	

- *Preheat oven to 375°F (190°C)*
- *Cookie sheet, lightly greased*

1. In a medium bowl, mix together flour, baking powder, baking soda, salt, cinnamon and ground cloves.

2. In a large bowl, beat sugar, butter or margarine and shortening until smooth and creamy. Beat in eggs, one at a time, until incorporated. Blend in bananas. Add flour mixture and mix well. Fold in nuts. Cover dough and refrigerate for about 1 hour, until chilled.

3. Drop by rounded teaspoonfuls (5 mL), about 2 inches (5 cm) apart, onto prepared cookie sheet. Bake in preheated oven for 8 to 10 minutes or until cookie springs back when lightly touched. Immediately transfer to wire racks to cool completely. Frost with Chocolate Icing (see recipe, page 361), Fresh Strawberry Frosting (see recipe, page 367) or Vanilla Icing (see recipe, page 367).

Makes about 4 dozen

Brandy Lace Roll-ups

¾ cup	all-purpose flour	175 mL
½ tsp	ground ginger	2 mL
½ cup	butter or margarine, softened	125 mL
½ cup	corn syrup	125 mL
⅓ cup	packed brown sugar	75 mL
2 tsp	brandy or freshly squeezed lemon juice	10 mL
1 cup	whipping (35%) cream	250 mL
1 tbsp	brandy (optional)	15 mL

TIP: For ease of rolling, bake roll-ups one cookie sheet at a time. The cookies are likely to harden before they can be rolled if you work with a larger quantity.

VARIATION

Brandy Lace Crisps
Leave cookies on cookie sheet to cool for 3 to 5 minutes, then transfer to a wire rack. Store in an airtight container away from other cookies.

- *Preheat oven to 375°F (190°C)*
- *Cookie sheet, lightly greased*
- *Cake or pastry decorating bag*

1. In a small bowl, mix together flour and ginger.
2. In a saucepan, over medium heat, melt butter or margarine, corn syrup and brown sugar, stirring frequently. Remove from element and stir in brandy or lemon juice. Add flour mixture, mixing until well blended.
3. Drop by rounded teaspoonfuls (5 mL), about 5 inches (12.5 cm) apart, onto prepared cookie sheet. Bake in preheated oven for 6 to 8 minutes or until cookies are a rich brown and have spread into 3- to 4-inch (7.5- to 10-cm) rounds.
4. Cool for 1 to 3 minutes on sheet. Then, while still warm and working quickly, wrap each cookie around a wooden spoon handle, allowing it to firm up before sliding off. Place roll on a wire rack to cool. If cookies become too crisp to roll, return to preheated oven for about 1 minute to soften. Fill roll-ups with fresh whipped cream, flavored with brandy, if desired. Use a decorating bag with a plain or fancy tip and pipe the whipped cream into each end of the roll-up.

Makes about 2½ dozen

Meringue Dainties

4	egg whites	4
2 tsp	vanilla	10 mL
½ tsp	cream of tartar	2 mL
1 cup	granulated sugar	250 mL

VARIATION

Meringue Shells
Shape batter into 3-inch (7.5-cm) mounds and bake for 1 to 1¼ hours. Remove from oven and, using a spoon, scoop out the soft centers. Return meringues to preheated oven 30 minutes, then transfer to wire racks. When cooled, fill centers with whipped cream or your favorite custard.

- *Preheat oven to 250°F (120°C)*
- *Cookie sheet, lined with greased foil*

1. Beat egg whites, vanilla and cream of tartar until soft peaks form. Beat in sugar, 2 tbsp (25 mL) at a time, until stiff peaks form.
2. Drop by rounded teaspoonfuls (5 mL), about 2 inches (5 cm) apart, onto prepared cookie sheet. Bake in preheated oven for 50 to 60 minutes or until lightly browned. Turn heat off and leave meringues to dry in oven for 30 minutes, then transfer to wire racks.

Makes about 3 dozen small meringues

Crisp Caramel Wafers

½ cup	all-purpose flour	125 mL
½ tsp	ground cardamom	2 mL
¼ cup	sliced almonds	50 mL
3 tbsp	butter	45 mL
¼ cup	corn syrup	50 mL
¼ cup	packed brown sugar	50 mL
½ tsp	vanilla	2 mL

TIP: To line a cookie sheet with parchment or waxed paper, simply cut the paper to fit the sheet and place on top.

- *Preheat oven to 350°F (180°C)*
- *Cookie sheet, lined with parchment or waxed paper*

1. In a small bowl, mix together flour, cardamom and almonds.
2. In a saucepan, over medium-low heat, bring butter, corn syrup and brown sugar to a boil, stirring constantly. Add vanilla and mix well. Set aside to cool slightly. Add flour mixture and stir until well blended.
3. Drop by rounded teaspoonfuls (5 mL), about 4 inches (10 cm) apart, onto prepared cookie sheet. Bake in preheated oven for 6 to 8 minutes or until golden brown. Cool on sheet for 5 minutes, then transfer to wire racks to cool completely.

Makes about 2½ dozen

Brown Sugar Cookies

3½ cups	all-purpose flour	875 mL
1 tsp	baking soda	5 mL
1 tsp	salt	5 mL
1 cup	shortening, softened	250 mL
2 cups	lightly packed brown sugar	500 mL
2	eggs	2
½ cup	buttermilk	125 mL

- Preheat oven to 400°F (200°C)
- Cookie sheet, lightly greased

1. In a medium bowl, mix together flour, baking soda and salt.
2. In a large bowl, beat shortening and brown sugar until smooth and creamy. Add eggs, one at a time, beating until incorporated. Beat in buttermilk. Add flour mixture and mix well. Cover dough and refrigerate for 1 hour.
3. Drop by teaspoonfuls (5 mL), about 2 inches (5 cm) apart, on prepared cookie sheet. Bake in preheated oven for 8 to 10 minutes or until cookie springs back when lightly touched. Immediately transfer to wire racks.

Makes about 6 dozen

VARIATIONS

Coconut Brown Sugar Cookies
Stir in 1 cup (250 mL) shredded coconut before chilling.

Fruit Nut Brown Sugar Cookies
Stir in 2 cups (500 mL) chopped candied fruit and 1 cup (250 mL) chopped nuts before chilling.

Cinnamon Mocha Cappuccino Cookies

2 cups	all-purpose flour	500 mL
1 tsp	baking powder	5 mL
½ tsp	ground cinnamon	2 mL
¾ cup less 1 tbsp	butter or margarine, softened	160 mL
1¼ cups	granulated sugar	300 mL
2	eggs	2
2 tsp	instant cappuccino or other strong coffee powder	10 mL
1 tbsp	boiling water	15 mL
⅓ cup	hot milk	75 mL
1 tsp	vanilla	5 mL
	Sugar-Cinnamon Mix (see recipe, page 14)	
1	square (1 oz/28 g) grated semi-sweet chocolate	1

- Preheat oven to 375°F (190°C)
- Cookie sheet, well-greased

1. In a medium bowl, mix together flour, baking powder and cinnamon.
2. In a large bowl, beat butter or margarine and sugar until smooth and creamy. Add eggs, one at a time, beating until incorporated.
3. In a small bowl, mix together coffee, water and hot milk, stirring until coffee dissolves. Stir in vanilla and add to creamed mixture. Add flour mixture and mix thoroughly.
4. Drop by teaspoonfuls (5 mL), about 2 inches (5 cm) apart, onto prepared cookie sheet. Sprinkle tops with sugar-cinnamon mix and grated chocolate. Bake in preheated oven for 10 minutes or until bottoms are golden brown. Immediately transfer to wire racks to cool.

Makes about 2½ dozen

Cornmeal Molasses Drops

1 cup	all-purpose flour	250 mL
1 cup	yellow cornmeal	250 mL
3 tsp	baking powder	15 mL
½ tsp	salt	2 mL
⅓ cup	cold butter, cut into small chunks	75 mL
2 tbsp	light molasses	25 mL
6 tbsp	milk	90 mL
¼ cup	golden raisins (optional)	50 mL

TIP: These cookies are also delicious if allowed to cool for 5 minutes, then served warm.

- *Preheat oven to 425°F (220°C)*
- *Cookie sheet, ungreased*

1. In a large bowl, mix together flour, cornmeal, baking powder and salt. Using two knives, a pastry blender or the tips of your fingers, cut in butter until mixture resembles coarse crumbs.

2. In a measuring cup, combine molasses and milk. Add to flour mixture and mix well. Fold in raisins, if using.

3. Drop by teaspoonfuls (5 mL), about 2 inches (5 cm) apart, onto cookie sheet. Bake in preheated oven for 13 to 15 minutes or until golden brown. Immediately transfer to wire racks to cool.

Makes about 2 dozen

Herb Drop Cookies

2¼ cups	all-purpose flour	550 mL
2 tsp	baking soda	10 mL
1 tsp	ground cinnamon	5 mL
½ tsp	ground cloves	2 mL
1 tbsp	ground ginger	15 mL
¼ tsp	salt	1 mL
½ cup	shortening, softened	125 mL
½ cup	granulated sugar	125 mL
1	egg	1
½ cup	molasses	125 mL
⅓ cup	strong, hot coffee	75 mL
2 tbsp	anise seeds	25 mL
2 tsp	crushed coriander seeds	10 mL
	Walnut or pecan halves (optional)	

VANILLA GLAZE: In a medium bowl, beat together 2 cups (500 mL) sifted confectioner's (icing) sugar, 1 tsp (5 mL) vanilla and enough milk to make the mixture spreadable.

- *Preheat oven to 350°F (180°C)*
- *Cookie sheet, greased*

1. In a medium bowl, mix together flour, baking soda, cinnamon, cloves, ginger and salt.

2. In a large bowl, cream shortening and sugar until smooth and creamy. Beat in egg until incorporated, then blend in molasses. Add flour mixture to creamed mixture, alternately with coffee, mixing well after each addition. Stir in anise and coriander seeds.

3. Drop by rounded teaspoonfuls (5 mL), about 2 inches (5 cm) apart, onto prepared cookie sheet. Top with nuts, if desired. Bake in preheated oven for 8 to 10 minutes or until golden brown. Immediately transfer to wire racks to cool. Top with Vanilla Glaze, if desired (see method, left).

Makes about 3½ dozen

Traditional Peanut Butter Cookies

1¼ cups	all-purpose flour	300 mL
¾ tsp	baking soda	4 mL
¾ tsp	salt	4 mL
½ cup	shortening, softened	125 mL
¾ cup	smooth peanut butter	175 mL
1¼ cups	firmly packed brown sugar	300 mL
1	egg	1
1 tbsp	vanilla	15 mL
3 tbsp	milk	45 mL

Although these cookies work well as drop cookies, you can also shape them into a 1-inch (2.5-cm) ball and flatten with tines of a fork dipped in flour.

- *Preheat oven to 375°F (190°C)*
- *Cookie sheet, ungreased*

1. In a small bowl, mix together flour, baking soda and salt.
2. In a large bowl, cream shortening, peanut butter and brown sugar until smooth. Beat in egg until incorporated. Mix in vanilla and milk until smooth. Add flour mixture and mix thoroughly.
3. Drop by rounded tablespoonfuls (15 mL), about 2 inches (5 cm) apart, onto cookie sheet. Bake in preheated oven for 6 to 8 minutes or until golden brown. Cool on sheet for 2 to 3 minutes, then transfer to wire racks to cool completely.

Makes about 3 dozen

Poppy Seed Drop Cookies

1 cup	poppy seeds	250 mL
½ cup	scalded milk	125 mL
1½ cups	all-purpose flour	375 mL
1 tsp	baking powder	5 mL
Pinch	salt	Pinch
½ tsp	ground cinnamon	2 mL
¼ tsp	ground cloves	1 mL
½ cup	butter, softened	125 mL
½ cup	granulated sugar	125 mL
2	squares (each 1 oz/28 g) unsweetened chocolate, melted (optional) (see page 14)	2

TIP: To keep spices fresh for as long as possible, grind your own and keep in jars, sealed tightly away from heat, light and moisture. Stored this way, spices will keep for about a year.

- *Preheat oven to 350°F (180°C)*
- *Cookie sheet, greased*

1. In a small bowl, soak poppy seeds in hot milk for 30 minutes. Set aside.
2. In another small bowl, mix together flour, baking powder, salt, cinnamon and cloves.
3. In a large bowl, beat butter and sugar until smooth and creamy. Stir in chocolate, mixing until well blended. Mix in poppy seed mixture. Add flour mixture and mix thoroughly.
4. Drop by rounded teaspoonfuls (5 mL), about 2 inches (5 cm) apart, onto prepared cookie sheet. Bake in preheated oven for 20 minutes or until browned. Immediately transfer to wire racks to cool.

Makes about 2½ dozen

Classic Sour Cream Drop Cookies

2¾ cups	all-purpose flour	675 mL
½ tsp	baking powder	2 mL
½ tsp	baking soda	2 mL
½ tsp	salt	2 mL
½ cup	shortening, softened	125 mL
1½ cups	granulated sugar	375 mL
2	eggs	2
1 tsp	vanilla	5 mL
1 cup	sour cream	250 mL

Preheat oven to 425°F (220°C)
Cookie sheet, lightly greased

1. In a medium bowl, mix together flour, baking powder, baking soda and salt.
2. In a large bowl, beat shortening and sugar until smooth and creamy. Add eggs, one at a time, beating until well incorporated. Stir in vanilla and sour cream and mix well. Gradually add flour mixture, mixing until well blended. Refrigerate dough for at least 1 hour.
3. Drop by rounded teaspoonfuls (5 mL), about 2 inches (5 cm) apart, onto prepared cookie sheet. Bake in preheated oven for 8 to 10 minutes or until lightly browned. Immediately transfer to wire racks to cool.

Makes about 5 dozen

VARIATIONS

Chocolate Sour Cream Drops
Mix in 2 squares (each 1 oz/28 g) melted unsweetened chocolate to the creamed mixture, before adding flour mixture. Fold in 1 cup (250 mL) chopped nuts before chilling dough.

Fruit Cream Drops
Fold in 1 cup (250 mL) chopped dates or other candied fruit before chilling dough.

Almond Sugar Cookie Crisps

2 cups	all-purpose flour	500 mL
1 tsp	baking soda	5 mL
1 tsp	cream of tartar	5 mL
1 cup	shortening, softened, (butter-flavored, if possible)	250 mL
1/2 cup	granulated sugar	125 mL
1/2 cup	packed brown sugar	125 mL
1	egg	1
1/2 tsp	vanilla	2 mL
1/2 tsp	almond extract	2 mL

TIP: Using a glass dipped in water and then sugar to press down and flatten the dough makes cookies thinner and crisper.

- *Preheat oven to 350°F (180°C)*
- *Cookie sheet, ungreased*

1. In a medium bowl, mix together flour, baking soda and cream of tartar.
2. In a large bowl, beat shortening and sugars until smooth and creamy. Beat in egg until well incorporated. Stir in vanilla and almond extract. Gradually add flour mixture and mix thoroughly.
3. Drop by tablespoonfuls (15 mL), about 2 inches (5 cm) apart, onto cookie sheet. Flatten with the bottom of a glass dipped in sugar. Bake in preheated oven for 10 to 12 minutes or until lightly browned. Immediately transfer to wire racks to cool. Recipe can be doubled, if desired.

Makes about 2 1/2 dozen

Whole Wheat Spice Cookies

1/4 cup	vegetable oil	50 mL
1/4 cup	molasses	50 mL
1/2 cup	granulated sugar	125 mL
1/4 cup	packed brown sugar	50 mL
2	eggs	2
1/2 cup	whole wheat flour	125 mL
1 1/2 cups	all-purpose flour	375 mL
2 tsp	baking soda	10 mL
1/4 tsp	salt	1 mL
1 tsp	ground ginger	5 mL
1 tsp	ground cinnamon	5 mL
1 tsp	ground cloves	5 mL

- *Preheat oven to 350°F (180°C)*
- *Cookie sheet, lightly greased*

1. In a medium bowl, whisk oil, molasses, sugars and eggs until blended.
2. In a large bowl, mix together flours, baking soda, salt, ginger, cinnamon and cloves. Make a well in the center and add the molasses mixture, mixing until thoroughly blended.
3. Drop by teaspoonfuls (5 mL), about 2 inches (5 cm) apart, onto prepared cookie sheets. Bake in preheated oven for 8 to 10 minutes or until cookies are firm to the touch. Cool on sheets for 5 minutes, then transfer to wire racks to cool completely.

Makes about 3 dozen

Wholesome Banana Granola Drops *(page 19)* ➤
Hermits *(page 38)*
Traditional Peanut Butter Cookies *(page 46)*
Baba Mary's Thimble Cookies *(page 341)*

Hand-Shaped Cookies

Hand-shaped cookies are, as their name suggests, molded into a shape by hand. The dough, which is firmer than drop cookie dough, is usually shaped into a small ball before baking. Often it is flattened slightly and imprinted with a simple pattern made by the tines of a fork or the bottom of a glass.

continued on next page

◄ Chinese Chews *(page 64)*
Esther's Famous Komish Bread Cookies *(page 335)*

Other Hand-Shaped Cookies

Nutmeg Pecan Butter Balls

½ cup	butter, softened	125 mL
⅓ cup	confectioner's (icing) sugar, sifted	75 mL
½ tsp	vanilla	2 mL
¼ tsp	ground nutmeg	1 mL
Pinch	salt	Pinch
1 cup	all-purpose flour	250 mL
½ cup	finely chopped pecans, toasted (see page 14)	125 mL
½ cup	coarsely chopped pecans, toasted	125 mL

- *Preheat oven to 350°F (180°C)*
- *Cookie sheet, ungreased*

1. In a large bowl, beat butter and confectioner's sugar until smooth and creamy. Beat in vanilla, nutmeg and salt until well blended. Gradually mix in flour and finely chopped pecans. Wrap dough tightly in plastic wrap and refrigerate for 2 to 3 hours, until firm.
2. Shape dough into 1-inch (2.5 cm) balls and roll in coarsely chopped pecans until coated. Place about 2 inches (5 cm) apart on cookie sheet. Bake in preheated oven for 12 to 15 minutes or until browned. Cool on cookie sheets for about 2 minutes, then, being careful to ensure cookies don't break, transfer to wire racks to cool completely.

Makes about 2 dozen

Surprise Potato Chip Crunchies

¾ cup	butter or margarine, softened	175 mL
¾ cup	granulated sugar	175 mL
1	egg yolk	1
1 tsp	vanilla	5 mL
1½ cups	all-purpose flour	375 mL
⅓ cup	finely crushed potato chips	75 mL
¼ cup	finely chopped nuts	50 mL
	Additional granulated sugar	

TIP: Freeze leftover raw egg whites individually in plastic ice-cube containers. Thaw for 15 to 30 minutes and use in recipes requiring egg whites only.

- *Preheat oven to 375°F (190°C)*
- *Cookie sheet, ungreased*

1. In a large bowl, beat butter and sugar until smooth and creamy. Beat in egg yolk and vanilla until well blended. Gradually add flour and mix well. Stir in potato chips and nuts.
2. Shape dough into 1-inch (2.5 cm) balls and place 2 inches (5 cm) apart on cookie sheet. For each ball, dip the bottom of a glass in sugar and flatten. Bake in preheated oven for 12 to 15 minutes or until golden brown. Leave on cookie sheet for 2 minutes to cool, then transfer to wire racks to cool completely.

Makes about 3 dozen

Cinnamon Pecan Snickerdoodles

3 cups	all-purpose flour	750 mL
1 tsp	baking powder	5 mL
1/4 tsp	salt	1 mL
1 cup	butter, softened (no substitutes)	250 mL
1 1/2 cups	granulated sugar	375 mL
2	eggs	2
1 tsp	vanilla	5 mL
1/3 cup	granulated sugar	75 mL
1 tbsp	ground cinnamon	15 mL
1 cup	almond, pecan or walnut halves	250 mL

• *Preheat oven to 350°F (180°C)*
• *Cookie sheet, lightly greased*

1. In a medium bowl, combine flour, baking powder and salt.
2. In a large bowl, beat butter and 1 1/2 cups (375 mL) sugar until smooth and creamy. Beat in eggs, one at a time. Stir in vanilla. Add flour mixture and mix well.
3. In a small bowl, mix together 1/3 cup (75 mL) sugar and cinnamon.
4. Shape dough into 1-inch (2.5 cm) balls, then roll in cinnamon mixture to coat. Place about 2 inches (5 cm) apart on prepared cookie sheet. Press half a nut into the top of each cookie. Bake in preheated oven for 12 to 15 minutes or until golden brown. Immediately transfer to wire racks to cool.

Makes about 5 dozen

Mexican Wedding Cakes

2 cups	all-purpose flour	500 mL
1/2 cup	confectioner's (icing) sugar, sifted	125 mL
1 cup	finely chopped pecans, toasted (see page 14)	250 mL
Pinch	salt	Pinch
1 tsp	vanilla	5 mL
1 cup	cold butter, cut into 1-inch (2.5 cm) chunks (no substitutes)	500 mL
	Additional confectioner's sugar	

• *Preheat oven to 325°F (160°C)*
• *Cookie sheet, ungreased*

1. In a large bowl, mix together flour, confectioner's sugar, pecans and salt until thoroughly combined. Add vanilla and mix well.
2. Using two knives, a pastry blender or your fingers, cut butter into flour mixture until mixture resembles crumbs. Knead dough gently until it begins to hold together.
3. Shape dough into 1-inch (2.5 cm) balls and place about 2 inches (5 cm) apart on cookie sheet. Bake in preheated oven for 25 minutes until lightly browned. Immediately transfer to wire racks and cool for 5 minutes. Dip both sides of cookies in confectioner's sugar and return to racks to cool completely.

Makes about 4 dozen

TIP: To easily make chopped nuts, place pieces in a plastic bag and crush with a rolling pin. Then pour directly into a measuring cup.

Sweet Cornflake Cookies

½ cup	butter or margarine, softened	125 mL
¼ cup	firmly packed light brown sugar	50 mL
2 tbsp	light corn syrup	25 mL
1	egg	1
1½ cups	all-purpose flour	375 mL
1 tsp	baking powder	5 mL
⅓ cup	raisins	75 mL
2 cups	honey-sweetened cornflakes, lightly crushed	500 mL

- *Preheat oven to 350°F (180°C)*
- *Cookie sheet, ungreased*

1. In a large bowl, beat butter or margarine, brown sugar and corn syrup until smooth. Add egg and beat until incorporated. Stir in flour and baking powder and mix until blended. Fold in raisins. Wrap dough tightly in plastic wrap and refrigerate about 30 minutes.

2. Shape dough into 1-inch (2.5 cm) balls, then roll in the crushed cornflakes. Place about 2 inches (5 cm) apart on cookie sheet. Flatten slightly with a fork dipped in flour. Bake in preheated oven for 15 to 18 minutes or until golden brown. Immediately transfer to wire racks to cool.

Makes about 2 to 3 dozen

Quick 'n' Easy Butter Nut Cookies

1 cup	butter, softened	250 mL
6 tbsp	confectioner's (icing) sugar, sifted	90 mL
2 tsp	vanilla	10 mL
2 cups	sifted cake flour (no substitutes)	500 mL
1 cup	finely chopped nuts	250 mL
	Confectioner's (icing) sugar, sifted	

- *Preheat oven to 350°F (180°C)*
- *Cookie sheet, ungreased*

1. In a large bowl, beat butter, sugar and vanilla until smooth and creamy. Gradually beat in flour until thoroughly blended. Fold in nuts. Cover and refrigerate for 30 minutes, until firm.

2. Shape dough into 1-inch (2.5 cm) balls. Place about 2 inches (5 cm) apart on cookie sheet and flatten slightly with a fork or the bottom of a glass dipped in flour. Bake in preheated oven for 25 minutes or until golden brown. Immediately transfer to wire racks and sprinkle with confectioner's sugar.

Makes 3 dozen

TIP: When you flatten dough with the bottom of a glass dipped in sugar, use a glass with cut designs on the bottom so the imprint will be left as a decoration on the cookie.

Chinese Almond Cookies

2½ cups	all-purpose flour	625 mL
1½ tsp	baking powder	7 mL
1 tsp	ground allspice	5 mL
½ tsp	ground cloves	2 mL
½ tsp	salt	2 mL
1 cup	butter or margarine, softened	250 mL
¾ cup	granulated sugar	175 mL
1	egg	1
1 tsp	almond extract	5 mL
½ cup	finely ground blanched almonds	125 mL
1	egg yolk	1
1 tbsp	water	15 mL
32	whole blanched almonds	32

TIP: To make these cookies even in size, shape the dough into a long roll. Divide the roll in half, quarters and eighths. Divide the smallest pieces into quarters for the correct size.

- *Preheat oven to 350°F (180°C)*
- *Cookie sheet, ungreased*

1. In a medium bowl, mix together flour, baking powder, allspice, cloves and salt.
2. In a large bowl, beat butter or margarine and sugar until light and creamy. Beat in egg until incorporated. Stir in almond extract. Add flour mixture and mix until blended.
3. Shape dough into 32 balls (see Tip, below) and place about 2 inches (5 cm) apart on cookie sheet. For each ball, dip the bottom of a glass in flour and flatten.
4. In a small bowl, whisk egg yolk with water. Lightly brush tops with mixture, then press an almond into the center of each cookie. Bake in preheated oven for 20 minutes or until lightly browned. Immediately transfer to wire racks to cool.

Makes 32 balls

Nutmeg Almond Balls

1 cup	butter, softened	250 mL
½ cup	granulated sugar	125 mL
1 tsp	vanilla	5 mL
2 cups	all-purpose flour	500 mL
¾ cup	ground almonds, toasted (see page 14)	175 mL
1 cup	confectioner's (icing) sugar, sifted	250 mL
1 tbsp	ground nutmeg	15 mL

Using the correct amount of flour is the secret to getting these balls to maintain their shape during baking.

- *Preheat oven to 300°F (150°C)*
- *Cookie sheet, ungreased*

1. In a large bowl, beat butter and sugar until light and creamy. Stir in vanilla. Gradually add flour, mixing until blended. Fold in almonds.
2. Shape dough into 1-inch (2.5 cm) balls. Place about 2 inches (5 cm) apart on cookie sheet. Bake in preheated oven for 18 to 20 minutes or until bottoms are lightly browned. Immediately transfer to wire racks to cool completely.
3. In a bowl, mix together confectioner's sugar and nutmeg. Gently roll balls in mixture until lightly coated.

Makes about 3½ dozen

Greek Almond Cookies

2 cups	all-purpose flour	500 mL
½ tsp	baking powder	2 mL
1 cup	butter, softened	250 mL
¼ cup + 2 tbsp	confectioner's (icing) sugar, sifted	50 mL + 25 mL
1	egg yolk	1
½ tsp	vanilla	2 mL
2 tbsp	brandy	25 mL
½ cup	finely chopped blanched almonds (see Tip on page 89)	125 mL

> **TIPS:** A Christmas tradition in Greece is to press a whole clove into the center of each cookie before baking.

- *Preheat oven to 325°F (160°C)*
- *Cookie sheet, ungreased*

1. In a medium bowl, mix together flour and baking powder.
2. In a large bowl, beat butter and ¼ cup (50 mL) confectioner's sugar until smooth and creamy. Add egg yolk, vanilla and brandy and beat until very light. Using a spoon, stir in almonds. Stir in flour mixture until a soft dough forms. Cover and refrigerate for 30 minutes, until firm.
3. Form level tablespoonfuls (15 mL) of dough into almond shapes and place about 1½ inches (4 cm) apart on cookie sheet. Bake in preheated oven for 25 to 30 minutes or until sandy in color. Immediately transfer to wire racks to cool.
4. Before serving or storing, sprinkle remaining 2 tbsp (25 mL) confectioner's sugar over tops of cookies.

Makes about 3 dozen

Dipped Biscuit Peanut Butter Balls

¾ cup	smooth peanut butter	175 mL
1	can (10 oz/300 mL) sweetened condensed milk	1
1	egg	1
1 tsp	vanilla	5 mL
2 cups	packaged biscuit mix	500 mL
6	squares (each 1 oz/28 g) semi-sweet chocolate, melted	6
4 tsp	vegetable oil	20 mL

> **TIP:** Keep vegetable oil in a squeeze bottle for when small amounts are needed.

- *Preheat oven to 350°F (180°C)*
- *Cookie sheet, ungreased*

1. In a large bowl, beat peanut butter, condensed milk, egg and vanilla until smooth and blended. Gradually add biscuit mix and mix well. Wrap dough tightly in plastic wrap and refrigerate for 30 minutes, until firm.
2. Shape dough into 1-inch (2.5 cm) balls and place about 2 inches (5 cm) apart on cookie sheet. Bake in preheated oven for 10 to 12 minutes or until lightly browned. Immediately transfer to wire racks to cool.
3. In a small bowl, mix melted chocolate with oil. Dip top half of each cookie in warm mixture and place on cookie sheet lined with waxed paper. Chill until chocolate has hardened.

Makes about 5 dozen

Crunchy Peanut Butter Cookies

1½ cups	all-purpose flour	375 mL
½ tsp	baking soda	2 mL
¼ tsp	salt	1 mL
½ cup	butter or margarine, softened	125 mL
½ cup	packed brown sugar	125 mL
½ cup	crunchy peanut butter	125 mL
1	egg	1
½ tsp	vanilla	2 mL
½ cup	chopped unsalted peanuts (optional)	125 mL

- *Preheat oven to 375°F (190°C)*
- *Cookie sheet, lightly greased*

1. In a small bowl, combine flour, baking soda and salt.
2. In a large bowl, beat butter or margarine, brown sugar and peanut butter until smooth and creamy. Beat in egg and vanilla. Stir in flour mixture and mix until a stiff dough forms.
3. Shape into 1-inch (2.5 cm) balls and place about 2 inches (5 cm) apart on prepared cookie sheet. Using a fork, flatten in a criss-cross pattern. If desired, sprinkle with chopped peanuts. Bake in preheated oven for 10 minutes or until lightly browned. Immediately transfer to wire racks to cool.

Makes about 2½ dozen

Mocha Cherry Crackles

1 cup	butter, softened	250 mL
½ cup	granulated sugar	125 mL
1 tsp	vanilla	5 mL
1 tsp	instant coffee granules	5 mL
¼ cup	unsweetened cocoa powder	50 mL
¼ tsp	salt	1 mL
2 cups	all-purpose flour	500 mL
½ cup	finely chopped maraschino cherries	125 mL
½ cup	finely chopped walnuts or pecans	125 mL
	Additional granulated sugar for coating cookies	

- *Preheat oven to 325°F (160°C)*
- *Cookie sheet, ungreased*

1. In a large bowl, beat butter and sugar until smooth and creamy. Beat in vanilla, then coffee, cocoa and salt until well combined. Add flour and mix well until blended. Fold in cherries and walnuts. Wrap dough tightly in plastic wrap and refrigerate for at least 1 hour.
2. Shape dough into 1-inch (2.5 cm) balls and roll in sugar until lightly coated. Place balls about 2 inches (5 cm) apart on cookie sheet. Bake in preheated oven for 20 minutes or until tops start to crack. Immediately transfer to wire racks to cool completely.

Makes about 3½ dozen

Rolled Orange Juice Balls

2½ cups	all-purpose flour	625 mL
1 tbsp	baking powder	15 mL
½ cup	shortening, softened	125 mL
½ cup	granulated sugar	125 mL
3	eggs	3
1 tsp	vanilla	5 mL
½ cup	orange juice	125 mL
	Confectioner's (icing) sugar, sifted	

TIP: If you don't need zest for a particular recipe before squeezing an orange or lemon for juice, grate the peel and freeze it for later use.

- *Preheat oven to 350°F (180°C)*
- *Cookie sheet, lightly greased*

1. In a medium bowl, mix together flour and baking powder.
2. In a large bowl, beat shortening and sugar until smooth and creamy. Add eggs, one at a time, beating well after each addition. Beat in vanilla. Add flour mixture, alternately with orange juice, beating constantly until a soft, sticky dough forms.
3. Scoop out dough 1 tablespoon (15 mL) at a time and roll in confectioner's sugar until it forms a ball. Place balls about 2 inches (5 cm) apart on prepared cookie sheet. Repeat with remaining dough. Bake in preheated oven for 15 minutes or until edges of cookies are lightly browned. Immediately transfer to wire racks to cool.

Makes about 3 dozen

Sugar-Cinnamon Lemon Cookies

1½ cups	all-purpose flour	375 mL
1 tsp	baking powder	5 mL
¼ tsp	salt	1 mL
1½ tsp	ground cinnamon	7 mL
½ tsp	grated lemon zest	2 mL
½ cup	butter or margarine, softened	125 mL
1 cup	granulated sugar	250 mL
1	egg	1
1 tsp	vanilla	5 mL
	Sugar-Cinnamon Mix (see recipe, page 14)	

- *Preheat oven to 350°F (180°C)*
- *Cookie sheet, lightly greased*

1. In a small bowl, mix together flour, baking powder, salt, cinnamon and lemon zest.
2. In a large bowl, beat butter or margarine and sugar until smooth and creamy. Beat in egg until well incorporated. Stir in vanilla. Add flour mixture and mix well. Wrap tightly in plastic wrap and refrigerate for 2 hours, until firm.
3. Shape dough into ¾-inch (2 cm) to 1-inch (2.5 cm) balls. Roll in sugar-cinnamon mix to coat. Place balls about 2 inches (5 cm) apart on prepared cookie sheet. Bake in preheated oven for 10 minutes or until lightly browned. Cool on sheet for 2 minutes, then transfer to wire racks to cool completely.

Makes about 3 dozen

Iced Lemon Butter Cookies

2 cups	all-purpose flour	500 mL
1 cup	confectioner's (icing) sugar, sifted	250 mL
1 tsp	baking powder	5 mL
¼ tsp	salt	1 mL
1 cup	butter, softened	250 mL
1 tsp	lemon extract	5 mL
1 tsp	grated lemon zest	5 mL
1	egg	1
LEMON BUTTER ICING		
1 cup	confectioner's (icing) sugar, sifted	250 mL
1 tbsp	butter, softened	15 mL
2½ tsp	freshly squeezed lemon juice	12 mL

TIP: A medium-sized lemon yields about 2 to 3 tbsp (25 to 45 mL) juice and 3 tsp (15 mL) grated zest. To always have freshly squeezed juice on hand, pour into ice-cube trays and freeze. When frozen, place in plastic bags until ready to use.

- *Preheat oven to 350°F (180°C)*
- *Cookie sheet, lightly greased*

1. In a medium bowl, mix together flour, confectioner's sugar, baking powder and salt.
2. In a large bowl, beat butter, lemon extract, lemon zest and egg until smooth and creamy. Add flour mixture and mix until a sticky batter forms. Wrap tightly in plastic wrap and refrigerate for at least 1 hour until firm.
3. Shape dough into 1-inch (2.5 cm) balls and place about 2 inches (5 cm) apart on prepared cookie sheet. Bake in preheated oven for 12 minutes or until cookie springs back when touched lightly. Cool for 2 minutes on cookie sheet, then transfer to a wire rack to cool completely.
4. *Lemon Butter Icing:* In a small bowl, beat together confectioner's sugar, butter and lemon juice until smooth and creamy. Spread icing on tops of cookies and let harden before storing.

Makes about 2½ dozen

Lemon Thumb Cookies

2 cups	butter, softened	500 mL
1½ cups	confectioner's (icing) sugar, sifted	375 mL
⅓ cup	freshly squeezed lemon juice	75 mL
4 cups	all-purpose flour	1 L
2 cups	finely chopped walnuts or pecans	500 mL
	Assorted jams, such as grape, raspberry, strawberry, apricot	

- *Preheat oven to 350°F (180°C)*
- *Cookie sheet, greased*

1. In a large bowl, cream together butter and confectioner's sugar until smooth. Beat in lemon juice until well blended. Gradually add flour and mix well. Wrap dough tightly in plastic wrap and refrigerate for 2 hours, until firm.

2. Shape dough into 1-inch (2.5 cm) balls and roll in chopped nuts. Place balls about 2 inches (5 cm) apart on prepared cookie sheet. Press your thumb in the center of each ball, leaving an indentation, and fill with multicolored jams. Bake in preheated oven for 12 to 15 minutes or until golden brown. Immediately transfer to wire racks to cool.

Makes about 6 dozen

Raspberry Chocolate Chip Crackles

¼ cup	butter (no substitutes)	50 mL
1	package (10 oz/300 g) raspberry chocolate chips	1
2 cups	all-purpose flour	500 mL
2 tsp	baking powder	10 mL
¼ tsp	salt	1 mL
1½ cups	granulated sugar	375 mL
4	eggs	4
½ cup	finely chopped walnuts	125 mL
	Confectioner's (icing) sugar, sifted	

- *Preheat oven to 300°F (150°C)*
- *Cookie sheet, greased*

1. In the top of a double boiler, over hot water, melt butter with 1 cup (250 mL) raspberry chocolate chips, stirring until smooth. Remove from hot water and set aside.

2. In a medium bowl, mix together flour, baking powder and salt.

3. In a large bowl, beat sugar with melted butter mixture. Add eggs, one at a time, beating until incorporated. Beat in flour mixture until well blended. Fold in walnuts and remaining raspberry chips. Wrap dough tightly in plastic wrap and refrigerate at least 1 hour.

4. Shape dough into 1-inch (2.5 cm) balls, then roll in confectioner's sugar. Place balls about 2 inches (5 cm) apart on prepared cookie sheets. Bake in preheated oven for 15 to 18 minutes or until cracked on the surface but set in the middle. Immediately transfer to wire racks to cool.

TIP: If you don't feel up to making a batch of cookies, try this easy treat. Stack four graham wafers on top of each other. Spread Chocolate Icing (see recipe, page 361) between the wafers, over the entire top and down all sides. Set aside to allow icing to harden, then cut into three rectangular cookies.

Makes about 4 dozen

The Original Dad's Cookie

1 cup	all-purpose flour	250 mL
¾ cup	oat bran	175 mL
1 cup	quick-cooking oats	250 mL
1 tsp	baking powder	5 mL
1 tsp	baking soda	5 mL
1½ tsp	ground cinnamon	7 mL
1 tsp	ground nutmeg	5 mL
1 tsp	ground allspice	5 mL
1 cup	butter or margarine, softened	250 mL
¼ cup	lightly packed brown sugar	50 mL
¾ cup	granulated sugar	175 mL
2 tbsp	molasses	25 mL
1	egg	1
1 tsp	vanilla	5 mL

- *Preheat oven to 300°F (150°C)*
- *Cookie sheet, ungreased*

1. In a medium bowl, mix together flour, oat bran, oats, baking powder, baking soda, cinnamon, nutmeg and allspice.
2. In a large bowl, beat butter or margarine and sugars until smooth. Beat in molasses, egg and vanilla until well blended. Add flour mixture and mix well.
3. Shape dough into 1-inch (2.5 cm) balls and place about 2 inches (5 cm) apart on cookie sheet. Using the tines of a fork dipped in flour, flatten. Bake in preheated oven for 15 minutes or until golden brown. Let cool on cookie sheet for 2 to 3 minutes, then transfer to wire racks to cool completely.

Makes about 5 dozen

Coconut Oatmeal Cookies

1½ cups	all-purpose flour	375 mL
1 tsp	baking powder	5 mL
1 tsp	baking soda	5 mL
1 cup	butter, softened	250 mL
1 cup	granulated sugar	250 mL
½ cup	packed brown sugar	125 mL
2	eggs	2
1 tsp	vanilla	5 mL
1½ cups	rolled oats (not instant)	375 mL
¾ cup	shredded coconut	175 mL

- *Preheat oven to 350°F (180°C)*
- *Cookie sheet, lightly greased*

1. In a small bowl, mix together flour, baking powder and baking soda.
2. In a large bowl, beat butter and sugars until smooth and creamy. Add eggs, one at a time, beating until well incorporated. Stir in vanilla. Add flour mixture and mix well. Stir in oats, then coconut, mixing until thoroughly combined.
3. Shape into 1-inch (2.5 cm) balls and place about 2 inches (5 cm) apart on prepared cookie sheet. Using the tines of a fork dipped in flour or your hand, flatten slightly. Bake in preheated oven for 8 to 10 minutes or until golden brown. Immediately transfer to wire racks to cool.

Makes about 3 dozen

Farm-Style Oatmeal Cookies

1½ cups	all-purpose flour	375 mL
1 tsp	baking soda	5 mL
1 tsp	ground cinnamon	5 mL
1 cup	shortening, softened	250 mL
1 cup	granulated sugar	250 mL
½ cup	lightly packed brown sugar	125 mL
1	egg, beaten	1
1 tsp	vanilla	5 mL
1½ cups	quick-cooking oats	375 mL
¾ cup	finely crushed walnuts or pecans	175 mL
	Additional granulated sugar	

- *Preheat oven to 350°F (180°C)*
- *Cookie sheet, greased*

1. In a small bowl, combine flour, baking soda and cinnamon.
2. In a large bowl, beat shortening and sugars until smooth and creamy. Beat in egg and vanilla. Add flour mixture and mix well. Mix in oats and walnuts or pecans. Wrap dough tightly in plastic wrap and refrigerate for 1 hour.
3. Shape dough into 1-inch (2.5 cm) balls and place about 2 inches (5 cm) apart on prepared cookie sheet. Flatten with a fork dipped in granulated sugar. Bake in preheated oven for 10 minutes or until golden brown. Immediately transfer to wire racks to cool.

Makes about 6 dozen

Chocolate Cherry Thumbprint Cookies

1½ cups	all-purpose flour	375 mL
½ cup	unsweetened cocoa powder	125 mL
¼ tsp	baking powder	1 mL
¼ tsp	baking soda	1 mL
½ cup	butter, softened	125 mL
1 cup	granulated sugar	250 mL
1	egg	1
1½ tsp	vanilla	7 mL
1	jar (10 oz/284 mL) maraschino cherries	1
4 tsp	reserved cherry juice	20 mL
¾ cup	mini chocolate chips	175 mL
½ cup	condensed milk	125 mL

- *Preheat oven to 350°F (180°C)*
- *Cookie sheet, ungreased*

1. In a medium bowl, sift together flour, cocoa, baking powder and baking soda.
2. In a large bowl, beat butter and sugar until smooth and creamy. Beat in egg, then vanilla until well incorporated. Mix in flour mixture until well blended.
3. Shape dough into 1-inch (2.5 cm) balls and place about 2 inches (5 cm) apart on cookie sheet. With your thumb, make an indentation in the center of each ball. Drain cherries and save the juice. Place a cherry in the center of each ball.
4. In a small saucepan, melt chocolate chips and condensed milk, stirring until mixture is smooth. Add cherry juice and mix well. Spoon 1 tsp (5 mL) of mixture over top of cookies, covering the cherry. Bake in preheated oven for 10 to 12 minutes or until golden brown. Transfer to wire racks to cool.

Makes about 4 dozen

Swedish Thimble Cookies

1½ cups	butter, softened	375 mL
¾ cup	packed light brown sugar	175 mL
3	eggs, separated	3
3 cups	sifted all-purpose flour	750 mL
¼ tsp	salt	1 mL
2 cups	finely chopped walnuts	500 mL
	Jam or jelly	

TIP: Always buy nuts in a store where the turnover is high, as they become rancid quickly. Wrap leftover nuts well and store in the refrigerator or freezer.

- *Preheat oven to 300°F (150°C)*
- *Cookie sheet, lined with waxed or parchment paper*

1. In a large bowl, beat butter and brown sugar until smooth and creamy. Beat in egg yolks, one at a time, until well incorporated. Gradually add flour and salt, mixing until all ingredients are well combined. (Dough will be very sticky.) Wrap dough tightly in plastic wrap and refrigerate for 1 hour.

2. Beat egg whites until peaks form. Place walnuts in a small bowl.

3. Shape dough into 1-inch (2.5 cm) balls. Dip each into beaten egg whites, then roll in walnuts to coat. Place balls about 2 inches (5 cm) apart on prepared cookie sheets. Using a thimble dipped in flour, make indentations in the center of each ball. Fill with your choice of jam or jelly, using about ¼ tsp (1 mL) each, just enough to fill the indentation.

4. Bake in preheated oven for 15 to 18 minutes or until lightly browned. Allow to cool on cookie sheet for 2 to 3 minutes, then transfer to wire racks to cool completely.

Makes about 5 dozen

A Honey of a Cookie

3½ cups	all-purpose flour	875 mL
2 tsp	baking soda	10 mL
1 cup	butter or margarine, softened	250 mL
1 cup	packed brown sugar	250 mL
2	eggs	2
6 tbsp	liquid honey	90 mL
1 tsp	vanilla	5 mL

TIP: When measuring spoonfuls of honey or molasses, coating the spoon lightly with oil helps the sticky ingredient to slide off and makes cleanup easier.

- *Preheat oven to 350°F (180°C)*
- *Cookie sheet, ungreased*

1. In a medium bowl, mix together flour and baking soda.
2. In a large bowl, beat butter and brown sugar until smooth and creamy. Add eggs, one at a time, beating until well incorporated. Beat in honey and vanilla until smooth. Add flour mixture and mix well. (Dough will be very thick.) Wrap dough tightly in plastic wrap and refrigerate until firm, at least 1 hour.
3. Shape dough into 1-inch (2.5 cm) balls and place about 2 inches (5 cm) apart on cookie sheet. Bake in preheated oven for 10 to 15 minutes or until golden brown. Immediately transfer to wire racks to cool.

Makes about 4 dozen

Sesame Seed Cookies

1½ cups	whole wheat flour	375 mL
1 tsp	baking powder	5 mL
¼ tsp	salt	1 mL
¼ cup	butter or margarine, softened	50 mL
¼ cup	liquid honey	50 mL
¼ cup	sesame paste (tahini)	50 mL
½ tsp	almond extract	2 mL
½ cup	sesame seeds, toasted (see page 14)	125 mL

TIP: When a recipe calls for room-temperature or softened butter, grate cold butter. It will soften very quickly.

- *Preheat oven to 350°F (180°C)*
- *Cookie sheet, lightly greased*

1. In a small bowl, mix together flour, baking powder and salt.
2. In a large bowl, beat butter or margarine, honey, sesame paste and almond extract until smooth. Add flour mixture and mix well. Stir in sesame seeds.
3. Shape dough into 1-inch (2.5 cm) balls and place about 2 inches (5 cm) apart on prepared cookie sheet. Using the tines of a fork dipped in flour, flatten, or using your hands, mold into crescent shapes. (Wet your hands first, if using to mold the dough.) Bake in preheated oven for 10 to 12 minutes or until lightly browned. Immediately transfer to wire racks to cool.

Makes about 2 dozen

Chinese Chews

¼ cup	butter or margarine, softened	50 mL
2	eggs	2
1 tsp	vanilla	5 mL
½ cup	liquid honey	125 mL
½ cup	lightly toasted sesame seeds, divided (see Tip, below)	125 mL
¼ cup	chopped raisins	50 mL
1 cup	chopped pitted dates	250 mL
½ cup	chopped walnuts	125 mL
¾ cup	whole wheat or all-purpose flour	175 mL
	Confectioner's (icing) sugar, sifted (optional)	

- *Preheat oven to 350°F (180°C)*
- *8-inch (2 L) square baking pan, greased*

1. In a bowl, beat butter or margarine, eggs, vanilla and honey until light and fluffy. Stir in ¼ cup (50 mL) sesame seeds, raisins, dates and walnuts and mix well. Gradually add flour, mixing until thoroughly blended.

2. Using your hands spread batter into prepared pan. Bake in preheated oven for 20 minutes, until set. Remove from oven and cut into fingers, about 2- by 1½ inches (5 by 4 cm). Using a lifter or a knife, lift out fingers. Cool very slightly, then shape into balls in the palm of your hands. On a plate, roll in remaining sesame seeds, then confectioner's sugar, if desired, until well coated. Cool on wire racks.

Makes about 2 dozen

TIP: If you prefer a sweeter cookie, use only ¼ cup (50 mL) sesame seeds and roll the cookies in ¼ cup (50 mL) confectioner's sugar.

Old-Fashioned Spice Balls

3 cups	all-purpose flour	750 mL
2 cups	granulated sugar	500 mL
4 tsp	baking soda	20 mL
1 tsp	salt	5 mL
1 tsp	ground cinnamon	5 mL
1 tsp	ground allspice	5 mL
1 tsp	ground ginger	5 mL
2½ cups	old-fashioned rolled oats	625 mL
⅔ cup	shortening, softened	150 mL
½ cup	butter or margarine	125 mL
2	eggs, lightly beaten	2
½ cup	warm corn syrup	125 mL

- *Preheat oven to 350°F (180°C)*
- *Cookie sheet, lined with parchment or waxed paper*

1. In a large bowl, mix together flour, sugar, baking soda, salt, cinnamon, allspice, ginger and rolled oats. Using two knives, a pastry blender or your fingers, cut in shortening and butter until mixture resembles coarse crumbs. Add eggs and warm syrup (be sure it is warm or dough will not be firm enough) and mix well.

2. Shape dough into 1-inch (2.5 cm) balls and place about 2 inches (5 cm) apart on prepared cookie sheet. Bake in preheated oven for 10 to 12 minutes or until golden brown. Immediately transfer to wire racks to cool.

Makes about 6 dozen

Ginger Snaps

2 cups	all-purpose flour	500 mL
3 tsp	baking soda	15 mL
¼ tsp	salt	1 mL
1 tsp	ground cinnamon	5 mL
1 tsp	ground ginger	5 mL
½ tsp	ground cloves	2 mL
¾ cup	shortening, softened	175 mL
1 cup	granulated sugar	250 mL
1	egg	1
¼ cup	molasses	50 mL
	Granulated sugar	

TIP: To measure solid shortening, line a measuring cup with plastic wrap and fill it with shortening. It lifts out easily and the cup stays clean.

- *Preheat oven to 350°F (180°C)*
- *Cookie sheet, greased*

1. In a medium bowl, mix together flour, baking soda, salt, cinnamon, ginger and cloves.
2. In a large bowl, beat shortening and sugar until smooth and creamy. Add egg and beat until well incorporated. Mix in molasses until well blended. Add flour mixture and stir well.
3. Shape dough into 1-inch (2.5 cm) to ¾-inch (2 cm) balls, then roll in granulated sugar. Place on prepared cookie sheet about 2 inches (5 cm) apart. Bake in preheated oven for 10 to 12 minutes, depending upon size of balls. Immediately transfer to wire racks to cool.

Makes 5 to 6 dozen

Crispy Cheddar Cookies

1 cup	all-purpose flour	250 mL
½ cup	butter	125 mL
1½ cups	shredded old Cheddar cheese	375 mL
1 cup	crisp rice cereal	250 mL
1	egg, beaten	1

- *Preheat oven to 350°F (180°C)*
- *Cookie sheet, ungreased*

1. In a large bowl, using two knives, a pastry blender or your fingers, combine flour and butter until mixture resembles coarse crumbs. Add cheese, cereal and egg and mix until well blended.
2. Shape dough into either 1-inch (2.5 cm) or ¾-inch (2 cm) balls and place 2 inches (5 cm) apart on cookie sheet. Flatten slightly with a fork. Bake in preheated oven for 15 to 17 minutes, depending upon size of balls, until golden brown. Immediately transfer to wire racks to cool.

Makes about 4 dozen smaller and 2½ dozen larger cookies

Wholesome Cheddar Bran Cookies

1¾ cups	all-purpose flour	425 mL
½ tsp	baking powder	2 mL
½ tsp	baking soda	2 mL
½ tsp	salt	2 mL
¾ cup	butter or margarine, softened	175 mL
1 cup	lightly packed brown sugar	250 mL
1	egg	1
1 tsp	vanilla	5 mL
3 cups	crushed bran flakes cereal	750 mL
½ cup	shredded Cheddar cheese	125 mL
½ cup	raisins	125 mL
½ cup	chopped pecans or other nuts	125 mL

- *Preheat oven to 350°F (180°C)*
- *Cookie sheet, ungreased*

1. In a small bowl, mix together flour, baking powder, baking soda and salt.
2. In a large bowl, beat butter or margarine and sugar until smooth and creamy. Beat in egg, then vanilla. Add flour mixture and mix well. Stir in bran flakes, cheese, raisins and nuts until mixture is crumbly.
3. Shape dough into 1-inch (2.5 cm) balls. Place about 2 inches (5 cm) apart on cookie sheet. Bake in preheated oven for 15 to 18 minutes or until lightly browned. Cool on cookie sheet for 3 to 5 minutes, then transfer to wire racks to cool completely.

Makes about 6 dozen

TIP: Before you grate cheese, spray the grater with non-stick cooking spray to ease cleanup.

Cut Cookies

Although cut cookies are the most fun to make, they are a bit trickier than drop or hand-shaped cookies because the dough must be the right consistency to roll. If it is too wet, it will stick to the rolling pin and if it is too dry it will crack. To make it easier to handle, the dough must be chilled, usually for at least an hour and often as long as overnight. If desired, you can wrap the dough tightly in plastic wrap and refrigerate for up to a week. When you're ready to bake, roll the dough out, thinly, and cut your cookies as close together as possible.

The Ultimate Sugar Cookie

2 cups	all-purpose flour	500 mL
1 1/2 tsp	baking powder	7 mL
1/2 tsp	salt	2 mL
1 cup	granulated sugar	250 mL
1/2 cup	butter, softened	125 mL
1	egg	1
1 tsp	vanilla	5 mL
1/4 tsp	each lemon and almond extract (optional)	1 mL
1 tbsp	milk or cream	15 mL
	Granulated or tinted sugar for sprinkling	

This is the classic cut cookie. For an extra-special version, add lemon and almond extract along with the vanilla.

VARIATIONS

Sour Cream Cookies
Sift 1/4 tsp (1 mL) ground nutmeg and 1/4 tsp (1 mL) baking soda with the flour. Reduce baking powder to 1/2 tsp (2 mL). Substitute 1/2 tsp (2 mL) lemon extract for the vanilla. Substitute 1/3 cup (75 mL) sour cream for the milk.

Lemon Sugar Cookies
Substitute 1 tsp (5 mL) lemon extract and 2 tsp (10 mL) grated lemon zest for the vanilla.

Chocolate Sugar Cookies
Add 2 squares (each 1 oz/28 g) melted unsweetened chocolate after the egg. If desired, add 1 cup (250 mL) finely chopped nuts to the flour mixture.

Shaped Sugar Cookies
Add 1/3 cup (75 mL) chopped almonds and the grated zest of 1/2 lemon to the flour mixture. Shape into 1-inch (2.5 cm) balls and flatten with a fork.

- *Preheat oven to 375°F (190°C)*
- *Cookie sheet, ungreased*
- *Cookie cutters*

1. In a medium bowl, sift together flour, baking powder and salt.

2. In a large bowl, cream sugar and butter until smooth. Beat in egg until well incorporated. Stir in vanilla, almond extract and lemon extract, if using, and milk or cream. Gradually add flour mixture and mix until dough is firm enough to handle. Wrap in plastic wrap and refrigerate for 1 hour.

3. On a lightly floured surface, roll dough out to 1/8-inch (0.25 cm) thickness. Using cookie cutters or a glass dipped in flour, cut out desired shapes. Place about 2 inches (5 cm) apart on cookie sheets and sprinkle with sugar. Bake in preheated oven for 8 to 10 minutes or until lightly browned. Immediately transfer to wire racks to cool.

Makes about 50 small cookies

Sugar, Spice 'n' Everything Nice Cookies

2 cups + 2 tbsp	all-purpose flour	525 mL
3/4 tsp	ground cinnamon	4 mL
1 tsp	ground cardamom	5 mL
1 tsp	ground ginger	5 mL
Pinch	freshly ground black pepper	Pinch
1 cup	butter, softened	250 mL
1/2 cup + 2 tbsp	packed brown sugar	125 mL + 25 mL
2 tsp	lemon zest	10 mL

- *Preheat oven to 325°F (160°C)*
- *Cookie sheet, lined with parchment or waxed paper*
- *Cookie cutters*

1. In a medium bowl, sift together flour, cinnamon, cardamom, ginger and black pepper.
2. In a large bowl, beat butter and sugar until smooth. Stir in lemon zest. Gradually add flour mixture until a soft dough forms. Shape dough into two flattened disks, wrap tightly in plastic wrap and refrigerate for 1 to 2 hours, until firm.
3. Place one at a time between two sheets of waxed paper and roll out to 1/4-inch (0.5 cm) thickness. Using cookie cutters or glass dipped in flour, cut out desired shapes. Place about 2 inches (5 cm) apart on prepared cookie sheet. Bake in preheated oven for 8 to 10 minutes or until golden brown. Transfer to wire racks.

Makes about 3 dozen

Ginger Spice Snaps

4 cups	all-purpose flour	1 L
1 tsp	baking soda	5 mL
1 1/2 tsp	salt	7 mL
1/2 tsp	ground nutmeg	2 mL
1/4 tsp	ground allspice	1 mL
1/2 tsp	ground cloves	2 mL
1 1/2 tsp	ground ginger	7 mL
1/2 cup	shortening, softened	125 mL
1 cup	granulated sugar	250 mL
1/2 cup	water	125 mL
1 cup	dark molasses	250 mL
	Granulated sugar for sprinkling	

- *Preheat oven to 375°F (190°C)*
- *Cookie sheet, well-greased*
- *Cookie cutters*

1. In a large bowl, mix together flour, baking soda, salt, nutmeg, allspice, cloves and ginger.
2. In another large bowl, cream shortening and sugar until smooth. Add water and molasses and mix well. Stir in flour mixture and mix until well blended and a soft dough forms. Wrap dough tightly in plastic wrap and refrigerate for at least 3 hours.
3. On a lightly floured surface, roll dough out to 1/4-inch (0.5 cm) thickness. Using cookie cutters or glass dipped in flour, cut into 3-inch (7.5 cm) circles. Sprinkle with sugar and place about 2 inches (5 cm) apart on prepared cookie sheet. Bake in preheated oven for 10 to 12 minutes or until browned. Cool on sheets for 5 minutes, then transfer to wire racks.

Makes about 4 dozen

Little Gingerbread People

2 cups	all-purpose flour	500 mL
1 tsp	baking powder	5 mL
1 tsp	baking soda	5 mL
1 tsp	ground cinnamon	5 mL
1 tsp	ground allspice	5 mL
1½ tsp	ground ginger	7 mL
½ cup	butter, softened	125 mL
½ cup	granulated sugar	125 mL
½ cup	molasses or dark corn syrup	125 mL
1	egg yolk	1
	Colored icings and candies for decoration	

- *Preheat oven to 350°F (180°C)*
- *Cookie sheet, ungreased*
- *Gingerbread children cookie cutters*

1. In a medium bowl, mix together flour, baking powder, baking soda, cinnamon, allspice and ginger.

2. In a large bowl, beat butter and sugar until smooth and creamy. Beat in molasses or corn syrup (mixture will look curdled) and then egg yolk until incorporated. Gradually add flour mixture, beating well. (Dough will be sticky.) Divide dough into four portions and shape into flattened disks. Wrap tightly in plastic wrap and refrigerate for 3 hours until firm.

3. On a floured surface, roll dough out to ¼-inch (0.5 cm) thickness and cut out figures. Place about 2 inch (5 cm) apart on cookie sheets. Bake in preheated oven for 6 to 8 minutes until slightly firm. Cool on sheets for 5 minutes, then transfer to wire racks. Decorate cookies with colored icings and candies, as desired.

Makes about 2½ dozen

Nurnbergers

2¾ cups	all-purpose flour	675 mL
½ tsp	baking soda	2 mL
1 tsp	ground cinnamon	5 mL
½ tsp	ground nutmeg	2 mL
½ tsp	ground allspice	2 mL
¼ tsp	ground cloves	1 mL
⅓ cup	cut-up citron (see Tip, below)	75 mL
½ cup	chopped nuts	125 mL
1 cup	liquid honey	250 mL
¾ cup	packed brown sugar	175 mL
1	egg	1
1 tsp	grated lemon zest	5 mL
1 tbsp	freshly squeezed lemon juice	15 mL
	Blanched almond halves	
	Candied cherries	
SUGAR GLAZE		
1 cup	granulated sugar	250 mL
½ cup	water	125 mL

> These delicious honey-spice cookies get their unusual name from the Bavarian city of Nurnberg, where they originated.

TIP: Citron is a semi-tropical fruit that looks like a huge lemon. It can be purchased as candied citron especially for baking in specialty stores and supermarkets.

- *Preheat oven to 400°F (200°C)*
- *Cookie sheet, lightly greased*
- *Cookie cutters*

1. In a medium bowl, mix together flour, baking soda, cinnamon, nutmeg, allspice, cloves, citron and nuts.
2. In a small saucepan, heat honey to boiling. Remove from heat and pour into a large bowl to cool thoroughly.
3. Add brown sugar, egg, lemon zest and juice to honey and mix well. Stir in flour mixture and mix until dough forms. Cover and refrigerate for at least 4 hours or preferably overnight.
4. Divide dough into four portions and return three to refrigerator. On a lightly floured surface, roll the first portion to ¼-inch (0.5 cm) thickness. Using cookie cutters or a glass dipped in flour, cut into 2-inch (5 cm) rounds and place on prepared cookie sheet. Press 5 almond halves, end to end, around the edge of the circle to form a rim and press a candied cherry in the center. Repeat with remaining dough.
5. Bake in preheated oven for 10 to 12 minutes or until cookie springs back when touched lightly with finger. Immediately transfer to wire racks to cool.
6. *Sugar Glaze:* In a small bowl, beat sugar and water. While cookies are still hot, brush tops lightly.

Makes about 5 dozen

Maple Syrup Cookies

3½ cups	all-purpose flour	875 mL
2 tsp	baking powder	10 mL
½ tsp	salt	2 mL
1 cup	butter, softened	250 mL
1 cup	firmly packed brown sugar	250 mL
2	eggs	2
1 tsp	vanilla	5 mL
⅓ cup	pure maple syrup	75 mL

TIP: For optimum results, bake cookies one sheet at a time. If you do bake two sheets at the same time, place one on the middle rack of your oven and the other on the next-lowest rung. Baking two sheets next to each other affects the heat flow and produces underbaked cookies.

- *Preheat oven to 350°F (180°C)*
- *Cookie sheet, greased*
- *Cookie cutters*

1. In a medium bowl, combine flour, baking powder and salt.
2. In a large bowl, beat butter and brown sugar until smooth and creamy. Beat in eggs, one at a time, until incorporated. Mix in vanilla and syrup. Add flour mixture in three batches, beating well after each addition. Wrap tightly in plastic wrap and refrigerate at least 4 hours.
3. Divide dough into four portions. Place between two sheets of waxed paper. Roll out, one portion at a time, to ⅛-inch (0.25 cm) thickness. Using cookie cutters or a glass dipped in flour, cut into desired shapes. Place about 2 inches (5 cm) apart on prepared sheet. Bake in preheated oven for 8 to 10 minutes or until edges are golden brown. Immediately transfer to wire racks.

Makes about 6 dozen

Danish Jam Squares

2 cups	all-purpose flour	500 mL
1 tbsp	granulated sugar	15 mL
3½ tsp	baking powder	17 mL
½ tsp	salt	2 mL
5 tbsp	shortening	75 mL
¾ cup	milk	175 mL
	Jam or jelly of your choice	

TIP: Whenever cookie dough is too sticky to work with, chilling it in the refrigerator for about 20 minutes will firm it up to the right consistency.

- *Preheat oven to 350°F (180°C)*
- *Cookie sheet, lightly greased*

1. In a large bowl, mix together flour, sugar, baking powder and salt.
2. Using two knives, a pastry blender or your fingers, work in shortening until mixture resembles coarse crumbs. Gradually stir in enough milk to make a soft dough.
3. On a lightly floured surface, knead dough lightly. Roll into a square about ⅛-inch (0.25 cm) thick and cut into 2½-inch (6 cm) squares. Place 1 tsp (5 mL) jam or jelly in the center of each. Bring the four corners to the center and pinch together, making a small, square envelope. Place about 2 inches (5 cm) apart on prepared cookie sheet. Bake in preheated oven for 15 to 20 minutes or until golden brown. Transfer to wire racks lined with waxed paper.

Makes about 2½ dozen

Cinnamon Sugar Diamonds

1⅔ cups	all-purpose flour	400 mL
½ tsp	baking powder	2 mL
¼ tsp	salt	1 mL
½ cup	butter or margarine, softened	125 mL
1 cup	granulated sugar	250 mL
2	egg yolks	2
1 tsp	vanilla	5 mL
1 tbsp	whipping (35%) cream, plus additional for glazing cookies	1 tbsp
1 tbsp	granulated sugar	15 mL
1 tsp	ground cinnamon	5 mL

TIP: To ease cleanup when making cut-out cookies, place a piece of plastic wrap loosely over the rolled dough. Using your cookie cutter, press down on the plastic wrap until your shape is cut. Your cookie cutter stays clean because the plastic wrap is between it and the dough.

- *Preheat oven to 375°F (190°C)*
- *Cookie sheet, greased*

1. In a small bowl, mix together flour, baking powder and salt.
2. In a large bowl, beat butter or margarine and sugar until smooth and creamy. Beat in egg yolks until well incorporated. Stir in vanilla and 1 tbsp (15 mL) whipping cream. Add flour mixture and mix well. Cover and refrigerate for several hours or overnight.
3. In a small bowl, mix together sugar and cinnamon. Set aside.
4. On a lightly floured surface, divide dough into three portions. Roll out one portion at a time to ⅛-inch (0.25 cm) thickness. Cut dough into diamond shapes, 3 inches (7.5 cm) long and 1½ inches (4 cm) at widest point. Place about 2 inches (5 cm) apart on prepared cookie sheet. Brush tops with additional whipping cream, then with sugar-cinnamon mixture. Bake in preheated oven for 5 to 6 minutes or until lightly browned. Cool slightly and then transfer to wire racks to cool completely.

Makes about 6 dozen

Apricot Cream Cheese Kolacky

2 cups	all-purpose flour	500 mL
2 tbsp	granulated sugar	25 mL
2 tsp	baking powder	10 mL
½ tsp	salt	2 mL
1 cup	butter or margarine, softened	250 mL
1 cup + 2 tbsp	softened cream cheese	275 mL
2	eggs	2
½ cup	apricot or cherry preserves	125 mL

> These sweet treats are part of both the Polish and Czech cultures. Often filled with poppy seeds or nuts, they're filled with fruit preserves and cream cheese here.

- *Preheat oven to 375°F (190°C)*
- *Cookie sheet, ungreased*
- *Cookie cutters*

1. In a medium bowl, mix together flour, sugar, baking powder and salt.

2. In a large bowl, beat butter and cream cheese until smooth. Beat in eggs, one at a time, until incorporated. Gradually add flour mixture, mixing until a stiff dough forms. Cover and refrigerate for 3 hours.

3. On a lightly floured surface, divide dough into four portions. Roll each portion to ¼-inch (5 cm) thickness. Using a cookie cutter or a glass dipped in flour, cut into circles. Dip your index finger in flour and make a deep indentation in the center of each round. Fill with a scant ¼ tsp (1 mL) preserves. (Do not use too much, as the fruit will spill over.) Place rounds about 2 inches (5 cm) apart on cookie sheet. Bake in preheated oven for about 15 minutes or until golden brown. Immediately transfer to wire racks.

Makes about 6 dozen

Apricot Bundles

1¼ cups	all-purpose flour	300 mL
½ tsp	baking powder	2 mL
¼ tsp	salt	1 mL
3 tbsp	butter, softened	45 mL
3 tbsp	margarine, softened	45 mL
½ cup	granulated sugar	125 mL
1	egg	1
2 tsp	grated orange zest	10 mL
½ tsp	vanilla	2 mL
APRICOT FILLING		
½ cup	chopped dried apricots	125 mL
⅓ cup	orange juice	75 mL
2 tbsp	light brown sugar	25 mL
	Confectioner's (icing) sugar, sifted	

- *Preheat oven to 350°F (180°C)*
- *Cookie sheet, lightly greased*

1. In a small bowl, mix together flour, baking powder and salt.
2. In a large bowl, beat butter, margarine and sugar until smooth and creamy. Beat in egg, orange zest and vanilla until well blended. Add flour mixture and mix until a soft dough forms. Wrap tightly in plastic wrap and refrigerate for at least 2 hours.
3. *Apricot Filling:* In a small saucepan, bring apricots, orange juice and brown sugar to a boil. Lower heat, cover and simmer for about 10 minutes, until apricots are soft. Allow to cool, then purée in food processor. If mixture is too thick, add a little orange juice.
4. On a lightly floured surface, divide dough into three portions. Roll each portion into a 6-inch (15 cm) square and cut into nine 2-inch (5 cm) squares. In a narrow diagonal line, spread a level teaspoonful (5 cm) of filling across each square diagonally, from one corner to the opposite corner. Fold the other two opposite corners together to make a triangle. Using your fingers or the tines of a fork, press to seal. Repeat with each piece of dough.
5. Place bundles about 2 inches (5 cm) apart on prepared cookie sheet. Bake in preheated oven for 10 to 12 minutes. Immediately transfer to wire racks to cool, then sprinkle with confectioner's sugar.

Makes about 2 dozen

Jam Crescents

3¼ cups	all-purpose flour	800 mL
½ tsp	baking powder	2 mL
½ tsp	salt	2 mL
1	envelope (⅓ oz/9 g) vanilla sugar	1
1 cup	butter, softened	250 mL
¼ cup	margarine or shortening, softened	50 mL
3	egg yolks	3
1 cup	sour cream	250 mL
	Plum or seedless raspberry jam	
	Granulated sugar	

- *Preheat oven to 350°F (180°C)*
- *Cookie sheet, ungreased*

1. In a medium bowl, combine flour, baking powder, salt and vanilla sugar.
2. In a large bowl, beat butter, margarine or shortening, egg yolks and sour cream until well blended. Add dry ingredients and beat until a soft dough forms. (If dough is sticky, transfer to a lightly floured board and knead in additional flour until right consistency is achieved.) Form dough into a large ball, then cut in half. Flatten each half into a disk and wrap tightly in plastic wrap. Refrigerate at least 2 hours, until dough is firm.
3. On a lightly floured surface, divide dough into 10 balls. Return nine to the refrigerator until ready to use and roll one ball into an 8-inch (20 cm) circle. Using a knife or a pastry cutter, fluted, if desired, cut into eight pie-shaped wedges.
4. Spread about ½ tsp (2 mL) jam on outer edge of each wedge. Beginning with the outer edge and finishing with the point in the center, roll up to form crescents. Sprinkle generously with sugar and shake off excess. Place, point-side down, about 2 inches (5 cm) apart on cookie sheet. Repeat with remaining dough.
5. Bake in preheated oven for 15 to 17 minutes or until bottom of crescents are golden brown. Immediately transfer to wire racks to cool.

Makes about 6½ dozen

Sliced Cookies

Often called refrigerator cookies, sliced cookies are among the easiest and most convenient cookies to make. You can mix the dough, shape it into a roll, wrap tightly in plastic wrap and refrigerate for as long as a week. When you're ready to bake, slice off pieces of dough — only as much as you want — and bake. You can always have warm cookies ready and waiting — even for unexpected guests.

Easy Elephant Ears

	Granulated sugar	
½ lb	frozen puff pastry, defrosted	250 g

- *Preheat oven to 425°F (220°C)*
- *Cookie sheet, ungreased*

1. Sprinkle a pastry board with a thick layer of sugar. Place puff pastry on top and roll into a neat oblong.
2. Fold one long side of puff pastry inward, like a jellyroll, but stopping at the center. Repeat on the other side, so the two rolls meet in the center. Cut into slices ¼ inch (0.5 cm) thick and press each slice in sugar.
3. Place slices on cookie sheet. Bake in preheated oven for 6 to 8 minutes. Turn over and bake for another 6 to 8 minutes or until golden brown.

Makes about 1 dozen

The Refrigerator Cookie

2 cups	all-purpose flour	500 mL
2 tsp	baking powder	10 mL
½ tsp	salt	2 mL
½ cup	shortening, softened	125 mL
¾ cup	granulated sugar	175 mL
½ cup	packed brown sugar	125 mL
1	egg	1
1 tsp	vanilla	5 mL
½ cup	chopped nuts	125 mL

- *Preheat oven to 425°F (220°C)*
- *Cookie sheet, lightly greased*

1. In a medium bowl, mix together flour, baking powder and salt.
2. In a large bowl, beat shortening and sugars until smooth and creamy. Beat in egg until well incorporated. Stir in vanilla and nuts. Add flour mixture and mix until a soft dough forms.
3. On a lightly floured surface, divide dough in half. Shape into two long rolls about 2 inches (5 cm) wide. Wrap each tightly in plastic wrap and refrigerate for at least 2 hours, until firm.
4. When ready to bake, remove from wrap and cut dough into slices ¼ inch (0.5 cm) thick. Place about 2 inches (5 cm) apart on prepared cookie sheet. Bake in preheated oven for 8 to 10 minutes or until golden brown. Immediately transfer to wire racks to cool.

Makes about 4 dozen

Easy Icebox Cookies

3 cups	all-purpose flour	750 mL
1 tsp	baking soda	5 mL
¼ tsp	salt	1 mL
1 cup	chopped walnuts (optional)	250 mL
1 cup	butter, softened	250 mL
2½ cups	firmly packed light brown sugar	625 mL
2	eggs	2
1 tbsp	vanilla	15 mL

VARIATIONS

Almond Icebox Cookies
Substitute 1 cup (250 mL) coarsely chopped slivered almonds for the walnuts.

Cranberry Icebox Cookies
Add ½ cup (125 mL) chopped, frozen or fresh cranberries along with the walnuts.

- *Preheat oven to 350°F (180°C)*
- *Cookie sheet, lined with parchment or waxed paper*

1. In a large bowl, mix together flour, baking soda, salt and nuts, if using.
2. In another large bowl, beat butter and brown sugar until smooth and creamy. Beat in eggs, one at a time, until incorporated. Stir in vanilla. Add flour mixture and mix well.
3. On a lightly floured surface, divide dough in half. Shape into two rolls about 2 inches (5 cm) wide. Wrap each roll tightly in plastic wrap. Refrigerate at least 3 hours or overnight.
4. When ready to bake, remove from wrap and cut dough into slices ¼ inch (0.5 cm) thick. Place about 2 inches (5 cm) apart on prepared cookie sheet. Bake in preheated oven for 12 to 15 minutes, until firm to the touch. Immediately transfer to wire racks to cool completely.

Makes about 6 dozen

Buttery Brown Sugar Slices

3½ cups	all-purpose flour	875 mL
1 tsp	baking soda	5 mL
½ tsp	salt	2 mL
1 cup	butter or margarine, softened	250 mL
2 cups	packed brown sugar	500 mL
2	eggs	2
1 tbsp	vanilla	15 mL
1 cup	finely chopped walnuts (optional)	250 mL

TIP: If brown sugar is caked and hard, place it in a jar with half an apple. Close lid tight and let stand for 1 day. Remove apple, fluff up sugar with a fork and put lid on tightly until ready to use.

- *Preheat oven to 350°F (180°C)*
- *Cookie sheet, ungreased*

1. In a medium bowl, combine flour, baking soda and salt.
2. In a large bowl, beat butter and brown sugar until smooth and creamy. Beat in eggs, one at a time, until incorporated. Stir in vanilla. Add flour mixture and mix well. Fold in nuts, if using.
3. On a lightly floured surface, divide dough in half. Shape into two rolls about 2 to 3 inches (5 to 7.5 cm) wide. Wrap each tightly in plastic wrap and refrigerate overnight.
4. When ready to bake, remove from wrap and cut dough into slices ¼ inch (0.5 cm) thick. Place about 2 inches (5 cm) apart on cookie sheet. Bake in preheated oven for 10 to 12 minutes or until golden brown. Immediately transfer to wire racks to cool.

Makes about 6 dozen

Butterscotch Pecan Cookies

1¼ cups	all-purpose flour	300 mL
½ tsp	baking powder	2 mL
¼ tsp	salt	1 mL
6 tbsp	butter or margarine, softened	90 mL
⅔ cup	packed brown sugar	150 mL
1	egg	1
½ tsp	vanilla	2 mL
½ cup	finely chopped pecans	125 mL

VARIATIONS

Butterscotch Date Cookies
Substitute 2 cups (500 mL) finely chopped pitted dates for the pecans.

Butterscotch Chews
For a soft, chewy cookie, add ¾ cup (175 mL) crushed cornflakes along with the pecans.

- *Preheat oven to 350°F (180°C)*
- *Cookie sheet, ungreased*

1. In a small bowl, combine flour, baking powder and salt.
2. In a large bowl, beat butter and brown sugar until smooth and creamy. Beat in egg until incorporated. Stir in vanilla. Gradually add flour mixture, mixing until well blended. Fold in pecans.
3. On a lightly floured surface, divide dough in half. Shape into two rolls about 2 inches (5 cm) wide. Wrap each log tightly in plastic wrap and refrigerate at least 2 hours.
4. When ready to bake, remove from wrap and cut dough into slices ¼ inch (0.5 cm) thick. Place about 2 inches (5 cm) apart on cookie sheet. Bake in preheated oven for 10 to 12 minutes until golden brown. Immediately transfer to wire racks to cool.

Makes about 4 dozen

Coffee Break Cinnamon Rolls

1	package (¼ oz/7 g) active dry yeast	1
⅔ cup	warm water	150 mL
2½ cups	biscuit mix	625 mL
¼ cup	packed brown sugar	50 mL
1 tsp	ground cinnamon	5 mL
½ cup	chopped pecans	125 mL
2 tbsp	melted butter	25 mL
TOPPING		
¼ cup	melted butter or margarine	50 mL
⅓ cup	packed brown sugar	75 mL
1 tsp	light corn syrup	5 mL

- *Preheat oven to 400°F (200°C)*
- *Jellyroll pan or large cookie sheet, lightly greased*

1. In a medium bowl, dissolve yeast in warm water. Add biscuit mix and beat to form a dough. On a floured surface, knead dough until smooth.
2. In a small bowl, mix together brown sugar, cinnamon and pecans.
3. Roll dough into a 12-inch (30 cm) square and brush with butter. Sprinkle with cinnamon mixture, then roll up like a jellyroll and cut into 12 slices. Place 2 inches (5 cm) apart on prepared pan or sheet and leave in a warm place to rise, about 1 hour. Bake in preheated oven 15 minutes.
4. *Topping:* In a small saucepan, over low heat, melt butter or margarine. Add brown sugar and corn syrup and, stirring constantly, bring to a boil. Five minutes before baking is completed, pour over rolls. Serve warm.

Makes 1 dozen

Mochaccino Cookies

2 cups	all-purpose flour	500 mL
¼ tsp	salt	1 mL
1 tsp	ground cinnamon	5 mL
½ cup	butter or margarine, softened	125 mL
½ cup	shortening, softened	125 mL
½ cup	lightly packed brown sugar	125 mL
½ cup	granulated sugar	125 mL
1	egg	1
1 tbsp	instant coffee granules dissolved in 1 tsp (5 mL) hot water	15 mL
2	squares (each 1 oz/28 g) unsweetened chocolate, melted (see page 14)	2

CHOCOLATE DIP

3 tbsp	shortening	45 mL
1½ cups	semi-sweet chocolate chips	375 mL

TIP: Pack any chilled cookie dough into juice cans. Seal the open end with foil secured by an elastic band. Keep in refrigerator. When ready to use, cut the end out of the can and push the dough out slowly, cutting slices as you push. Place on baking sheets and bake.

- *Preheat oven to 350°F (180°C)*
- *Cookie sheet, lightly greased*

1. In a medium bowl, mix together flour, salt and cinnamon.
2. In a large bowl, beat butter or margarine, shortening and sugars until smooth and creamy. Beat in egg. Add coffee mixture and melted chocolate and mix until thoroughly blended. Stir in flour mixture. Cover and refrigerate for at least 1 hour or until firm.
3. On a lightly floured surface, divide dough in half. Shape into two long logs about 2 to 2½ inches (5 to 6 cm) wide. Wrap each log tightly in plastic wrap and refrigerate at least 2 hours, until firm.
4. When ready to bake, remove from wrap and cut dough into slices ¼ inch (0.5 cm) thick. Place about 2 inches (5 cm) apart on prepared cookie sheet. Bake in preheated oven for 10 to 12 minutes or until edges are firm and bottoms are lightly browned. Immediately transfer to wire racks to cool. When cookies are slightly cooled, dip in chocolate, if desired.
5. *Chocolate Dip:* In a saucepan, over low heat, stir shortening and chocolate chips until melted and smooth. Using your fingers, dip top half of each cookie in mixture and place on cookie sheet lined with waxed paper. Refrigerate until chocolate hardens.

Makes about 3 dozen

Fruit and Nut Roly Poly

4 cups	all-purpose flour	1 L
2 tsp	baking powder	10 mL
¼ tsp	salt	1 mL
4	eggs	4
1 cup	granulated sugar	250 mL
1 cup	vegetable oil	250 mL
1 tsp	vanilla	5 mL
FILLING		
1 cup	finely chopped walnuts	250 mL
¼ cup	granulated sugar	50 mL
½ cup	peach preserves	125 mL
1¼ cups	diced dried fruits and raisins	300 mL
1 tbsp	grated orange zest	15 mL
¼ cup	fresh orange juice	50 mL
¼ cup	melted butter or margarine	50 mL
¼ cup	fine dry bread crumbs	50 mL

- *Preheat oven to 375°F (190°C)*
- *Cookie sheet, greased*

1. In a large bowl, sift together flour, baking powder and salt.
2. In another large bowl, beat eggs and sugar until light and fluffy. Beat in oil and vanilla until well blended. Stir in dry ingredients until a soft dough forms. (You may not use the entire flour mixture.)
3. *Filling:* In a large bowl, mix together walnuts, sugar, peach preserves, dried fruits and raisins, orange zest and juice.
4. On a lightly floured surface, divide dough into four equal portions. Roll one portion into a rectangle about ¼ inch (0.5 cm) thick. Brush with melted butter or margarine, leaving ½-inch (1 cm) border all around. Sprinkle bread crumbs lightly over top and spread one-quarter of the filling over this. Turn ends in and roll dough up like a jellyroll, making sure seam is sealed tight. Repeat with the remaining dough.
5. Place rolls, two at a time, on prepared cookie sheet. Bake in preheated oven for 30 to 35 minutes or until nicely browned. Cool on sheets, then cut into ½-inch (1 cm) slices.

Makes about 5 dozen

VARIATION

Jam and Nut Roly Poly
On each rolled out portion of dough, spread your favorite jam, leaving a ½-inch (1 cm) border. Sprinkle surface with chopped walnuts. Roll and bake as above. For variety, use different nuts and jam on each portion.

Apricot Cream Cheese Pinwheel Cookies

8 oz	cream cheese, softened	250 g
1 cup	butter, softened	250 mL
1/4 tsp	salt	1 mL
2 cups	all-purpose flour	500 mL
3/4 cup	apricot preserves	175 mL
1 cup	finely chopped walnuts	250 mL

TIP: Use an electric knife to cut rolled and chilled cookie dough. It makes perfect, even cookies quickly and easily.

- *Preheat oven to 350°F (180°C)*
- *Cookie sheet, lightly greased*

1. In a large bowl, beat cream cheese, butter and salt until smooth and creamy. Gradually add flour and mix until a soft dough forms. Cover and refrigerate overnight.
2. When ready to bake, combine apricot preserves and nuts in a small bowl.
3. On a lightly floured surface, roll dough into a 12- by 14-inch (30 by 35 cm) rectangle. Spread the apricot mixture all over, excluding edges. Beginning on one long side, roll up tightly, like a jellyroll. Ensure seam is sealed tight. Cut log in half, horizontally, and wrap each section tightly in plastic wrap. Refrigerate for at least 30 minutes, until firm.
4. Remove dough from wrap and cut each log into slices 1/2 inch (1 cm) thick. Place about 1 inch (2.5 cm) apart on prepared cookie sheet. Bake in preheated oven for 15 minutes or until golden. Immediately transfer to wire racks.

Makes about 4 1/2 to 5 dozen

Cinnamon Roll Slices

3/4 cup	butter or margarine, softened	175 mL
1 cup	granulated sugar	250 mL
1 tsp	baking soda	5 mL
3/4 cup	buttermilk (see Tip, page 103)	175 mL
3 cups	all-purpose flour	750 mL
	Softened butter to spread	
	Brown sugar	
	Ground cinnamon	

- *Preheat oven to 350°F (180°C)*
- *Cookie sheet, lightly greased*

1. In a large bowl, beat butter or margarine and sugar until smooth and creamy. Mix baking soda with buttermilk and stir into mixture. Gradually stir in flour until a dough forms.
2. On a floured surface, roll dough out to 1/4-inch (0.5 cm) thickness. Spread with butter, brown sugar and cinnamon. Roll up tightly like a jellyroll, making sure seam is sealed tight, and cut into 1-inch (2.5 cm) slices. Place about 2 inches (5 cm) apart on prepared cookie sheet. Bake in preheated oven for 20 to 25 minutes or until lightly browned. Immediately transfer to wire racks to cool.

Makes about 1 dozen

Chocolate 'n' Vanilla Spirals

1¼ cups	all-purpose flour	300 mL
¼ tsp	baking powder	1 mL
¼ tsp	salt	1 mL
½ cup	butter or margarine, softened	125 mL
¾ cup	granulated sugar	175 mL
1	egg	1
1 tsp	vanilla	5 mL
1	square (1 oz/28 g) unsweetened chocolate, melted and cooled (see page 14)	1

> **TIP:** For a fun and quick treat, dip the tips of salted pretzel sticks into melted chocolate and then into sprinkles. Place on a plate or a baking sheet covered in waxed paper until chocolate has set.

- *Preheat oven to 350°F (180°C)*
- *Cookie sheet, lightly greased*

1. In a small bowl, mix together flour, baking powder and salt.
2. In a large bowl, beat butter or margarine and sugar until smooth and creamy. Beat in egg until well incorporated. Stir in vanilla. Mix in flour mixture until a soft dough forms.
3. On a lightly floured surface, divide dough in half. Add melted chocolate to one of the halves and knead dough until it is uniformly chocolate-colored. Wrap both doughs tightly in plastic wrap and refrigerate for at least 1 hour, until dough is firm.
4. When ready to bake, remove from wrap, place plain dough between two sheets of waxed paper and roll out to a 16- by 16-inch (40 by 15 cm) rectangle. Remove waxed paper from top of plain dough, but leave waxed paper on bottom. Repeat with chocolate dough. Remove waxed paper from top of chocolate dough and invert chocolate onto the plain dough. Using a rolling pin, press together gently. Remove waxed paper from top and trim so both top and bottom are even. Using the waxed paper on the bottom to guide you, and starting from the long edge, roll dough up like a jellyroll, making sure seam is sealed tight. If necessary, roll back and forth on the work surface to make sure the roll is the same diameter from end to end. Wrap tightly in plastic wrap and refrigerate at least 2 hours or overnight.
5. Place roll, seam side down, on a cutting board and cut into slices ¼ inch (0.5 cm) thick. Place 2 inches (5 cm) apart on prepared cookie sheet. Bake in preheated oven for 10 to 12 minutes or until lightly browned. Immediately transfer to wire racks to cool.

Makes about 7 dozen

Tri-Color Neapolitan Cookies

2½ cups	all-purpose flour	625 mL
½ tsp	baking powder	2 mL
½ tsp	salt	2 mL
1 cup	butter, softened	250 mL
1½ cups	granulated sugar	375 mL
1	egg	1
1 tsp	vanilla	5 mL
½ tsp	almond extract	2 mL
6 drops	red food coloring	6 drops
½ cup	chopped walnuts	125 mL
¼ cup	unsweetened cocoa powder	1 mL

Because I have always loved Neapolitan ice cream, these cookies are one of my favorites.

TIP: In place of cocoa, add 1 square (1 oz/28 g) melted unsweetened chocolate to the dough.

- *Preheat oven to 350°F (180°C)*
- *9- by 5-inch (1.5 L) loaf pan, bottom and sides lined with waxed paper*
- *Cookie sheet, ungreased*

1. In a medium bowl, mix together flour, baking powder and salt.

2. In a large bowl, beat butter and sugar until smooth and creamy. Beat in egg until incorporated. Stir in vanilla. Gradually add flour mixture and mix until a soft dough forms.

3. Divide dough into three equal portions. Place one portion in a small bowl. Add almond extract and red food coloring and knead until fully integrated into the dough. Spread this portion evenly over the bottom of the prepared pan. Add nuts to another portion and knead well. Spread this portion evenly over the first layer. Add cocoa to the last portion and knead until it is evenly distributed throughout the dough. Spread this portion over the second layer. Cover with plastic wrap or waxed paper and refrigerate overnight.

4. When ready to bake, remove from pan and cut loaf in half lengthwise. Cut each half into slices ¼ inch (0.5 cm) thick. Place about 2 inches (5 cm) apart on cookie sheet. Bake in preheated oven for 10 to 12 minutes or until firm.

Makes about 6 dozen

Apple Fig Date Log

5 cups	all-purpose flour	1.25 L
2 tsp	baking powder	10 mL
1 tsp	baking soda	5 mL
½ tsp	salt	2 mL
1 cup	butter, softened	250 mL
1 cup	granulated sugar	250 mL
2	eggs	2
1 cup	sour cream	250 mL
2 tsp	vanilla	10 mL
	Confectioner's (icing) sugar, sifted	

FILLING

1¾ cups	finely chopped pitted dates	425 mL
1¾ cups	finely chopped figs	425 mL
6	peeled, finely chopped Granny Smith apples	6
½ cup	fresh orange juice	125 mL
⅓ cup	granulated sugar	75 mL
1 cup	chopped walnuts	250 mL

- *Preheat oven to 350°F (180°C)*
- *Cookie sheet, greased*

1. In a large bowl, combine flour, baking powder, baking soda and salt.
2. In another large bowl, beat butter and sugar until smooth and creamy. Beat in eggs, one at a time, until incorporated. Beat in sour cream and vanilla. Gradually add flour mixture, mixing until well blended. Wrap dough tightly in plastic wrap and refrigerate for at least 1 hour.
3. *Filling:* In a large pot, over medium heat, combine dates, figs, apples, orange juice and sugar. Cook, covered, stirring occasionally, for 25 minutes, until tender. Remove cover and cook, stirring, until mixture is dry, about 5 minutes. Remove from heat. When cool, mix in walnuts and refrigerate if not using immediately.
4. Divide dough into eight equal portions. On a lightly floured surface, shape one portion into a log, approximately 8 inches (20 cm) long. Roll log into a 10- by 5-inch (25 by 13 cm) rectangle. Spread ¾ cup (175 mL) filling down the middle of the rectangle. Fold each side over the filling and pinch together to seal. Place the log, seam side down, on prepared sheet. Repeat with remaining dough and filling.
5. Bake in preheated oven for 25 to 30 minutes or until golden brown. Immediately transfer to wire racks to cool. Sift the confectioner's sugar over the logs, then cut into slices ½ inch (1 cm) thick.

Makes about 6 dozen

Chocolate Chip Pecan Logs

2 cups	all-purpose flour	500 mL
½ tsp	baking powder	2 mL
½ tsp	salt	2 mL
½ cup	butter, softened	125 mL
4 oz	cream cheese, softened	125 g
½ cup	granulated sugar	125 mL
½ cup	lightly packed brown sugar	125 mL
1	egg	1
1 tsp	vanilla	5 mL
FILLING		
⅔ cup	semi-sweet chocolate chips	150 mL
⅔ cup	sweetened condensed milk	150 mL
½ cup	chopped pecans	125 mL
	Confectioner's (icing) sugar, sifted	

- *Preheat oven to 350°F (180°C)*
- *Cookie sheet, greased*

1. In a medium bowl, mix together flour, baking powder and salt.
2. In a large bowl, beat butter, cream cheese and sugars until smooth and creamy. Beat in egg and vanilla. Add flour mixture and mix until a soft dough forms.
3. On a lightly floured surface, divide dough into four portions. Shape each portion into a log, about 8 inches (20 cm) long. Repeat with remaining portions. Wrap tightly in plastic wrap and refrigerate for at least 2 hours.
4. *Filling:* In a small saucepan, over low heat, melt chocolate chips and milk, stirring until smooth. Fold in nuts and set aside.
5. On a well-floured surface, roll each log into a 10- by 5-inch (25 by 13 cm) rectangle. Spread one-quarter of the filling down the center of the rectangle, leaving about 1 inch (2.5 cm) at the sides so filling won't spill out. Fold into thirds, each side over the filling, to enclose the filling. Trim ends and pinch to seal.
6. Place logs about 2 inches (5 cm) apart, seam side down, on prepared cookie sheet. Bake in preheated oven for 20 to 25 minutes or until golden brown. Immediately dust with confectioner's sugar, then transfer to wire racks to cool. Once logs are cool, cut into slices ½ inch (1 cm) thick.

Makes about 4 dozen

Glazed Lemon Braids

½ cup	butter or margarine, softened	125 mL
1 cup	granulated sugar	250 mL
1	egg	1
	Zest of 1 lemon	
2 cups	all-purpose flour	500 mL
GLAZE		
	Juice of 1 lemon	
1½ cups	confectioner's (icing) sugar, sifted	375 mL

- *Preheat oven to 350°F (180°C)*
- *Cookie sheet, lightly greased*

1. In a large bowl, beat butter and sugar until crumbly. Beat in egg and lemon zest. Gradually add flour, mixing thoroughly after each addition until a soft dough forms.
2. Working with ¼ cup (50 mL) of dough at a time, divide in half. Shape each half into 7-inch (18 cm) long rope. Entwine the two ropes, as for braiding, then cut in half lengthwise. Place on prepared cookie sheet. Repeat with remaining dough.
3. Chill braids for 30 minutes, then bake in preheated oven until very lightly browned. Immediately transfer to wire racks to cool.
4. *Glaze:* In a small bowl, mix together confectioner's sugar and lemon juice. Brush over tops of warm cookies. Let set for 20 minutes.

Makes about 1½ dozen

Lemon Nutmeg Crisps

1 cup	all-purpose flour	250 mL
½ tsp	baking powder	2 mL
½ tsp	baking soda	2 mL
½ tsp	salt	2 mL
¼ tsp	ground nutmeg	1 mL
½ cup	butter, softened	125 mL
1½ cups	confectioner's (icing) sugar, sifted	375 mL
1 tbsp	grated lemon zest	15 mL
2	egg whites	2
½ tsp	vanilla	2 mL
¾ cup	ground walnuts	175 mL

- *Preheat oven to 300°F (150°C)*
- *Cookie sheet, lightly greased*

1. In a small bowl, mix together flour, baking powder, baking soda, salt and nutmeg.
2. In a large bowl, beat butter, confectioner's sugar and lemon zest until smooth. Beat in egg whites. Stir in vanilla and walnuts. Add flour mixture and mix until a soft dough forms. Refrigerate for 2 to 3 hours, until firm.
3. On a lightly floured surface, shape into two rolls about 2 inches (5 cm) wide. Wrap tightly in plastic wrap and refrigerate for 2 hours.
4. When ready to bake, remove from wrap and cut into slices ¼ inch (0.5 cm) wide. Place about 2 inches (5 cm) apart on prepared cookie sheet. Bake in preheated oven for 15 to 18 minutes or until lightly browned. Immediately transfer to wire racks to cool.

Makes about 5 dozen

Double Almond Sticks

½ cup	blanched almonds	125 mL
2 tbsp	granulated sugar	25 mL
1 cup	all-purpose flour	250 mL
⅓ cup	granulated sugar	75 mL
¼ tsp	salt	1 mL
½ cup	butter or margarine	125 mL
1	egg yolk	1
¼ tsp	almond extract	1 mL
1	egg white, lightly beaten	1

TIP: To blanch almonds, soak shelled nuts in boiling water for a few minutes. Rinse under cold water and skins will easily slip off.

- *Preheat oven to 350°F (180°C)*
- *Cookie sheet, ungreased*

1. In a food processor with a metal blade, process almonds until coarsely ground. In a small bowl, mix together 2 tbsp (25 mL) ground almonds with the 2 tbsp (25 mL) sugar and set aside. Set remaining almonds aside.

2. In a large bowl, mix together flour, ⅓ cup (75 mL) sugar, salt and remaining almonds. Using two knives, a pastry blender or your fingers, cut in butter until mixture resembles coarse crumbs. Stir in egg yolk and almond extract, mixing until a soft dough forms.

3. On a lightly floured surface, divide dough into six portions. Flour your hands and roll each portion into a long rope about 12 inches (30 cm) long. Brush tops generously with the beaten egg white and sprinkle with the reserved almond-sugar mixture.

4. Cut each rope into sticks 2 inches (5 cm) long. Place about 1 inch (2.5 cm) apart on cookie sheet. Bake in preheated oven for 15 minutes. Cool for 5 minutes, then transfer to wire racks to cool completely.

Makes about 3 dozen

Raspberry Nut Swirls

1¾ cups	all-purpose flour	425 mL
2 tsp	baking powder	10 mL
¼ tsp	salt	1 mL
½ cup	butter or margarine, softened	125 mL
1 cup	granulated sugar	250 mL
1	egg	1
1 tsp	vanilla	5 mL
½ cup	raspberry jam	125 mL
⅓ cup	finely chopped walnuts or pecans	75 mL

- *Preheat oven to 375°F (190°C)*
- *Cookie sheet, lightly greased*

1. In a small bowl, mix together flour, baking powder and salt.
2. In a large bowl, beat butter or margarine and sugar until smooth and creamy. Beat in egg until well incorporated. Stir in vanilla. Gradually add flour mixture, mixing until a dough forms. Turn out on a floured work surface and knead lightly.
3. Place dough between two sheets of waxed paper and roll out to a 12- by 10-inch (30 by 25 cm) rectangle.
4. In a small bowl, mix together jam and nuts. Spread mixture evenly over the dough, leaving a ½-inch (1 cm) border.
5. Starting at the long edge and using the waxed paper on the bottom as a guide, roll up like a jellyroll, making sure seam is sealed tight. Roll back and forth a couple of times to form an even roll. Wrap tightly in plastic wrap and refrigerate at least overnight.
6. When ready to bake, remove from wrap and cut dough into slices ¼ inch (0.5 cm) thick. Place about 2 inches (5 cm) apart on prepared cookie sheet. Bake in preheated oven for 10 to 15 minutes or until golden brown. Immediately transfer to wire racks to cool.

Makes 3½ dozen

Sandwich Cookies

The appeal of sandwich cookies is obvious. What could be better than a freshly baked cookie? Two freshly baked cookies spread with a mouth-watering filling and pressed together. I hope you'll try some of these delicious treats.

Chocolate Cream Delights

2½ cups	all-purpose flour	625 mL
1 tsp	baking powder	5 mL
1 tsp	salt	5 mL
¾ cup	shortening, softened	175 mL
1 cup	granulated sugar	250 mL
2	eggs	2
½ tsp	vanilla	2 mL
3	squares (each 1 oz/28 g) unsweetened chocolate, melted (see page 14)	3
	Granulated sugar	

FILLING

½ cup	butter, softened	125 mL
1½ cups	confectioner's (icing) sugar, sifted	375 mL
2	egg yolks	2
2 tsp	vanilla	10 mL

- *Preheat oven to 400°F (200°C)*
- *Cookie sheet, lightly greased*
- *Round cookie cutter*

1. In a medium bowl, sift together flour, baking powder and salt.
2. In a large bowl, beat shortening and sugar until smooth and creamy. Beat in eggs, one at a time, until incorporated. Stir in vanilla and chocolate. Gradually add flour mixture, mixing until a soft dough forms. Cover tightly and refrigerate for 1 to 2 hours or overnight.
3. On a lightly floured surface, roll out dough to ⅛-inch (0.25 cm) thickness. Using a round cookie cutter or a glass dipped in flour, about 2 inches (5 cm) in diameter, cut out cookies and place about 2 inches (5 cm) apart on prepared cookie sheet. Sprinkle generously with sugar and bake in preheated oven for 6 to 8 minutes until cookies are set. Immediately transfer to wire racks to cool.
4. *Filling:* In a medium bowl, beat butter and confectioner's sugar until smooth and creamy. Beat in egg yolks and vanilla until well blended.
5. On a work surface, spread filling on one cookie, then top with another to make a sandwich.

Makes 18 to 24 sandwiches

VARIATION

Chocolate Mint Cream Delights
Substitute store-bought or homemade vanilla icing for the filling and beat in ½ tsp (2 mL) peppermint extract and 2 to 3 drops green food coloring.

Chocolate Cream Puff Cookies

¼ cup	butter or margarine	50 mL
½ cup	water	125 mL
Pinch	salt	Pinch
½ cup	all-purpose flour	125 mL
2	eggs	2
2 tbsp	orange zest	25 mL
CHOCOLATE CREAM FILLING		
½ cup	semi-sweet chocolate chips	125 mL
2 tbsp	orange juice	25 mL
⅓ cup	finely chopped almonds	75 mL
½ cup	whipping (35 %) cream, whipped	125 mL
	Melted semi-sweet chocolate (optional)	

- *Preheat oven to 450°F (230°C)*
- *Cookie sheet, ungreased*

1. In a saucepan, over medium heat, bring butter, water and salt to a boil, stirring constantly. Quickly add flour and stir rapidly until mixture leaves the pan and forms a smooth ball. Remove from heat. Beat in eggs, one at a time, until incorporated. Stir in orange zest.

2. Drop batter by level teaspoonfuls (5 mL), about 2 inches (5 cm) apart, onto cookie sheet. Bake in preheated oven for 12 to 15 minutes. Immediately transfer to wire racks to cool.

3. *Filling:* In a saucepan, over low heat, melt chocolate chips. Stir in orange juice, remove from heat and allow to cool. Fold in almonds and whipped cream.

4. Using a sharp knife, cut puffs in half horizontally. Fill bottom with filling, then top. Drizzle melted chocolate over the tops, if desired. Refrigerate until ready to serve.

Makes about 4 dozen puffs

Chocolate-Filled Meringues

2	egg whites, room temperature	2
Pinch	salt	Pinch
½ tsp	vanilla	2 mL
½ cup	granulated sugar	125 mL
1	square (1 oz/28 g) bittersweet chocolate, melted (see page 14)	1

TIP: Don't beat egg whites in plastic bowls, as they retain oils. Use a very clean bowl with no traces of oil.

- *Preheat oven to 250°F (120°C)*
- *Cookie sheet, lined with parchment or foil*

1. In a large bowl, beat egg whites, salt and vanilla until frothy. Gradually add sugar, 2 tbsp (25 mL) at a time, beating until stiff, glossy peaks form.

2. Drop by level teaspoonfuls (5 mL), about 2 inches (5 cm) apart, onto prepared cookie sheet and, using a spatula, lightly flatten the tops. Bake in preheated oven for 40 to 45 minutes or until meringue is crisp. Immediately transfer cookies and liner to a wire rack. When completely cool, remove meringues from liner.

3. Spread chocolate over the bottom of one meringue and top with the bottom of another to form a sandwich.

Makes about 2 dozen sandwiches

Jam-Filled Cottage Cheese Squares

1 cup	margarine, softened	250 mL
1 cup	cottage cheese	250 mL
¼ tsp	baking powder	1 mL
2 cups	all-purpose flour	500 mL
	Strawberry jam or red jelly	

- *Preheat oven to 425°F (220°C)*
- *Cookie sheet, lightly greased*
- *Square cookie cutter*

1. In a large bowl, beat margarine and cottage cheese until well combined. Stir in baking powder and flour and mix well.
2. Shape dough into a ball, wrap tightly in plastic wrap and refrigerate for 1 hour.
3. On a floured surface, divide dough in half. Roll each half into a rectangle ⅛ inch (0.25 cm) thick. Cut into 2½-inch (6 cm) squares. Place a scant teaspoon (5 mL) jam in the center of each square. Fold corners up to center to make an envelope, pressing all edges together. Place about 2 inches (5 cm) apart on prepared baking sheet. Bake in preheated oven for 12 to 15 minutes or until golden brown. Immediately transfer to wire racks to cool.

Makes about 4 dozen

Jam-Filled Sandwiches

⅔ cup	all-purpose flour	150 mL
¾ tsp	baking soda	4 mL
½ tsp	ground cinnamon	2 mL
¾ cup	butter, softened	175 mL
½ cup	granulated sugar	125 mL
1 cup	lightly packed brown sugar	250 mL
1	egg	1
2 tsp	vanilla	10 mL
2 tbsp	water	25 mL
3 cups	rolled oats	750 mL
1½ cups	raspberry jam	375 mL

- *Preheat oven to 350°F (180°C)*
- *Cookie sheet, greased*

1. In a small bowl, mix together flour, baking soda and cinnamon.
2. In a large bowl, beat butter and sugars until smooth and creamy. Add egg and beat until incorporated. Stir in vanilla and water. Gradually add flour mixture, beating until well blended. Stir in oats.
3. Drop by level teaspoonfuls (5 mL), about 2 inches (5 cm) apart, onto prepared cookie sheet. Bake in preheated oven for 10 to 12 minutes until golden brown. Immediately transfer to wire racks to cool.
4. When cooled, spread with jam on the smooth side of one cookie and top with the smooth side of another cookie to form a sandwich.

Makes about 2½ dozen sandwiches

Date-Filled Cookies

1¾ cups	all-purpose flour	425 mL
1 tbsp	baking powder	15 mL
1 tsp	salt	5 mL
1 cup	shortening, softened	250 mL
1 cup	lightly packed brown sugar	250 mL
½ cup	milk	125 mL
2 cups	rolled oats	500 mL
DATE FILLING		
2 cups	chopped pitted dates	500 mL
1 tbsp	grated orange zest	15 mL
¾ cup	orange juice	175 mL
⅓ cup	water	75 mL

- *Preheat oven to 325°F (160°C)*
- *Cookie sheet, lightly greased*
- *Round cookie cutter*

1. In a small bowl, sift flour, baking powder and salt.
2. In a large bowl, beat shortening and brown sugar until smooth and creamy. Add milk and rolled oats and stir until well blended. Add flour mixture and mix until a soft dough forms. Wrap tightly in plastic wrap and refrigerate for 1 to 2 hours, until firm.
3. On a floured surface, roll out dough to ⅛-inch (0.25 cm) thickness. Using a cookie cutter or a glass dipped in flour, cut into rounds. Place about 2 inches (5 cm) apart on prepared cookie sheet. Bake in preheated oven for 12 to 15 minutes or until golden brown. Immediately transfer to wire racks to cool.
4. *Date Filling:* In a saucepan, over medium heat, bring dates, zest, juice and water to a boil, stirring constantly. Reduce heat to low, cover and simmer, stirring occasionally, for 40 to 50 minutes, until dates are very soft. Remove cover and cook, stirring for 5 minutes, until mixture becomes a thick paste. Cool completely.
5. Spread filling over the smooth side of a cooled cookie and top with the smooth side of another cookie to form a sandwich.

Makes about 2 dozen sandwiches, depending on size of rounds

Lemon-Filled Drops

2 cups	all-purpose flour	500 mL
1/4 tsp	salt	1 mL
1 cup	butter or margarine, softened	250 mL
1/2 cup	confectioner's (icing) sugar, sifted	125 mL
1 tsp	lemon extract	5 mL
	Confectioner's (icing) sugar for sprinkling	
FILLING		
1/4 cup	granulated sugar	50 mL
2 1/4 tsp	cornstarch	11 mL
1 tbsp	butter or margarine	15 mL
1 tsp	grated lemon zest	5 mL
4 tsp	freshly squeezed lemon juice	20 mL
1/4 cup	water	50 mL

- *Preheat oven to 400°F (200°C)*
- *Cookie sheet, ungreased*

1. In a medium bowl, mix together flour and salt.
2. In a large bowl, beat butter or margarine and confectioner's sugar until smooth and creamy. Stir in lemon extract. Add dry ingredients and mix until a soft dough forms. Cover tightly and refrigerate for 1 to 2 hours, until firm.
3. Shape dough into 1-inch (2.5 cm) balls and place about 2 inches (5 cm) apart on cookie sheet. Flatten slightly with the bottom of a glass dipped in granulated sugar. Bake in preheated oven for 8 to 10 minutes or until lightly browned. Immediately transfer to wire racks to cool.
4. *Filling:* In a saucepan, combine sugar and cornstarch. Add butter or margarine, lemon zest, lemon juice and water. Cook over medium heat, stirring constantly, until mixture comes to a boil. Boil until mixture thickens, about 1 minute. Set aside to cool.
5. Spread filling over the smooth side of a cooled cookie and top with the smooth side of another cookie to form a sandwich. Sprinkle with confectioner's sugar.

Makes about 2 dozen sandwiches

Jam Crescents (page 76) ➤
Easy Elephant Ears (page 78)

Lemon Raisin-Filled Squares

8 oz	cream cheese, softened	250 g
¼ cup	butter or margarine, softened	50 mL
1	egg	1
¼ tsp	vanilla	1 mL
1	package (18¼ oz/515 g) lemon cake mix	1

RAISIN FILLING

½ cup	raisins	125 mL
2 tbsp	water	25 mL
¼ cup	apricot preserves	50 mL

- *Preheat oven to 375°F (190°C)*
- *Cookie sheet, ungreased*
- *Square cookie cutter*

1. In a large bowl, beat cream cheese and butter or margarine until smooth. Beat in egg until incorporated. Stir in vanilla. Gradually add cake mix, mixing well after each addition, until a stiff dough forms. Wrap dough tightly in plastic wrap and refrigerate for 30 minutes, until chilled.

2. On a floured surface, roll out dough to ⅛-inch (0.25 cm) thickness. Using a square cookie cutter, cut out shapes.

3. *Raisin Filling:* In a saucepan, over medium heat, bring raisins, water and apricot preserves to a boil. Reduce heat to low and simmer until mixture combines, about 5 minutes. Set aside to cool.

4. Place half the squares about 2 inches (5 cm) apart on cookie sheet and spoon ½ tsp (2 mL) filling on the center of each. Using a sharp knife, cut a ½-inch (1 cm) "X" in the center of the remaining squares and place on top of the squares with filling. Press together to seal. Bake in preheated oven for 10 to 12 minutes or until lightly browned.

Makes about 2 dozen sandwiches

◄ Lacy Oatmeal Sandwiches *(page 106)*

Chocolate-Dipped Lemon Butter Cookies

1 cup	butter, softened	250 mL
½ cup	granulated sugar	125 mL
1	egg yolk	1
1 tsp	vanilla	5 mL
2 cups	all-purpose flour	500 mL
LEMON FILLING		
2 cups	confectioner's (icing) sugar, sifted	500 mL
½ cup	butter, softened	125 mL
2 tbsp	freshly squeezed lemon juice	25 mL
CHOCOLATE DIP		
4	squares (each 1 oz/28 g) semi-sweet chocolate	4
2 tbsp	butter	25 mL
	Finely chopped nuts (optional)	

- *Preheat oven to 350°F (180°C)*
- *Cookie sheet, ungreased*

1. In a large bowl, beat butter and sugar until smooth and creamy. Beat in egg yolk until incorporated. Stir in vanilla. Gradually add flour and mix until well blended.

2. Using your hands, shape into 1-inch (2.5 cm) balls. Flatten with the bottom of a glass dipped in sugar. Place about 2 inches (5 cm) apart on cookie sheet. Bake in preheated oven for 10 to 12 minutes or until firm. Immediately transfer to wire racks to cool.

3. *Lemon Filling:* Beat confectioner's sugar, butter and lemon juice until smooth and creamy. Spread filling on the flat surface of one cookie and top with the flat surface of another cookie to form a sandwich.

4. *Chocolate Dip:* In a small saucepan, melt chocolate with butter, stirring until smooth. Cool slightly, then dip half of each cookie into the chocolate. Dip chocolate-coated half in nuts, if desired. Set aside on waxed paper until chocolate hardens.

Makes about 2 dozen sandwiches

TIP: Use your slow cooker to melt chocolate in bulk and keep it warm as long as you need to. Break chocolate into chunks or 1-oz (28 g) pieces and turn to Low. Stir occasionally until melted.

Ice Cream Sandwiches

	Oatmeal, chocolate, chocolate chip or peanut butter cookies
	Ice cream, sherbet or frozen yogurt
	Chopped nuts, mini chocolate chips or sprinkles (optional)

1. Place desired number of cookies on work surface, smooth side up. Spread with a generous amount of ice cream or other filling. Top with another cookie, smooth side down, to form a sandwich.

2. For an added treat, roll the edges of the cookie sandwich in chopped nuts, mini chocolate chips or sprinkles or any other type of decorations.

3. Wrap sandwiches tightly in plastic wrap and freeze until ready to serve.

Use any of your favorite cookies to make these yummy ice cream sandwiches.

Linzer Cookies

2½ cups	all-purpose flour	625 mL
2 tsp	ground cinnamon	10 mL
½ tsp	ground cloves	2 mL
1 tbsp	grated lemon zest	15 mL
¼ tsp	salt	1 mL
1½ cups	finely ground walnuts	375 mL
1 cup	butter or margarine, softened	250 mL
1 cup	confectioner's (icing) sugar, sifted	250 mL
1	egg	1
1	egg yolk	1
1 tsp	vanilla	5 mL
	Seedless raspberry jam	
	Confectioner's (icing) sugar	

This variation on the classic Austrian Linzertorte is a particularly delectable cookie.

- *Preheat oven to 350°F (180°C)*
- *Cookie sheets, ungreased*
- *Round or star-shaped cookie cutter and smaller cookie cutter of the same shape*

1. In a large bowl, mix together flour, cinnamon, cloves, lemon zest, salt and walnuts.

2. In another large bowl, beat butter or margarine and confectioner's sugar until smooth and creamy. Beat in egg and egg yolk until well incorporated. Stir in vanilla. Gradually add flour mixture, mixing until a soft dough forms. Cover tightly and refrigerate for 2 to 3 hours, until firm.

3. On a floured surface, roll out dough to ⅛-inch (0.25 cm) thickness. Using a round or star-shaped cookie cutter, cut out dough. Place half the cookies on cookie sheet. Using a smaller cookie cutter of the same shape that you used above, cut out centers of the remaining cookies and place the cut cookies on cookie sheet. Bake in preheated oven for 10 to 12 minutes or until edges are lightly browned. Immediately transfer to wire racks to cool.

4. Spoon about 2 tsp (10 mL) jam onto each whole cookie. Dust confectioner's sugar onto cut cookie, then place on top of cookies with jam filling to form sandwiches.

Makes about 2 dozen sandwiches

Peanut Butter Mini Turnovers

2 cups	all-purpose flour	500 mL
1 tsp	baking powder	5 mL
¼ tsp	salt	1 mL
¾ cup	shortening, softened, (butter-flavored, if available)	175 mL
¾ cup	granulated sugar	175 mL
1	egg	1
1½ tsp	vanilla	7 mL
PEANUT BUTTER FILLING		
⅓ cup	smooth peanut butter	75 mL
3 tbsp	confectioner's (icing) sugar, sifted	45 mL
¼ cup	milk	50 mL
2	squares (each 1 oz/28 g) semi-sweet chocolate, melted (optional) (see page 14)	2

- *Preheat oven to 375°F (190°C)*
- *Cookie sheet, ungreased*
- *3-inch (7.5 cm) round cookie cutter*

1. In a medium bowl, mix together flour, baking powder and salt.

2. In a large bowl, beat shortening and sugar until smooth and creamy. Beat in egg until incorporated. Stir in vanilla. Gradually add flour mixture, mixing until a soft dough forms.

3. Divide dough in half and wrap each piece tightly in plastic wrap. Refrigerate for 1 to 2 hours, until firm.

4. *Peanut Butter Filling:* In a small bowl, mix together peanut butter, confectioner's sugar and milk until smooth.

5. On a lightly floured surface, roll one piece of dough out to ⅛-inch (0.25 cm) thickness. (Leave the other piece in the refrigerator while you work.) Using a 3-inch (7.5 cm) round cookie cutter dipped in flour, cut into rounds. Place half the rounds about 2 inches (5 cm) apart on cookie sheet. Spoon a rounded teaspoonful (5 mL) of filling onto the center of each and, using the back of a spoon, press filling slightly to flatten. Top with the remaining rounds. Using the tines of a fork, lightly press edges of cookies to seal. Repeat with remaining dough. Bake in preheated oven for 10 to 12 minutes, or until edges are lightly browned. Immediately transfer to wire racks to cool. When cookies are cool, drizzle melted chocolate over tops in a zigzag pattern, if desired.

Makes about 1½ dozen sandwiches

Peanut Butter Jelly Sandwiches

1¼ cups	all-purpose flour	300 mL
½ tsp	baking powder	2 mL
¾ tsp	baking soda	4 mL
¼ tsp	salt	1 mL
½ cup	shortening, softened	125 mL
½ cup	packed brown sugar	125 mL
½ cup	granulated sugar	125 mL
½ cup	smooth peanut butter	125 mL
1	egg	1
	Jam or jelly	

- *Preheat oven to 375°F (190°C)*
- *Cookie sheet, lightly greased*

1. In a small bowl, mix together flour, baking powder, baking soda and salt.
2. In a large bowl, beat shortening and sugars until smooth and creamy. Add peanut butter and egg and mix until well blended. Add dry ingredients and mix until a soft dough forms. Cover tightly and refrigerate for 1 hour, until firm.
3. Shape dough into 1-inch (2.5 cm) balls. Place about 2 inches (5 cm) apart on prepared cookie sheet. Bake in preheated oven for 10 to 12 minutes or until golden brown. Immediately transfer to wire racks.
4. When cool, place half the cookies on a pan, flat side up, and spread with jam. Top with remaining cookies, flat side down, to form a sandwich.

Makes about 2 dozen sandwiches

Cream Cheese Shortbread Sandwiches

8 oz	cream cheese, softened	250 g
3 tbsp	granulated sugar	45 mL
2 tbsp	coffee liqueur	25 mL
½ cup	chopped walnuts	125 mL
32	shortbread cookies, round or oblong, or chocolate wafers	32

1. In a medium bowl, beat cream cheese, sugar and liqueur until smooth and creamy. Fold in nuts.
2. Spread filling between two shortbread cookies or two chocolate wafers until all the cookies are used up. Refrigerate, covered, for 2 hours.

Makes about 16 sandwiches

Turn your favorite shortbread cookies or chocolate wafers into sandwich cookies with this great filling (see Shortbread recipes, page 117).

Mincemeat Refrigerator Rounds

2¾ cups	all-purpose flour	675 mL
½ tsp	baking soda	2 mL
1 tsp	salt	5 mL
1 cup	shortening, softened	250 mL
½ cup	granulated sugar	125 mL
½ cup	packed brown sugar	125 mL
2	eggs	2
½ cup	prepared mincemeat	125 mL
¼ cup	chopped nuts	50 mL
2 tbsp	chopped maraschino cherries (optional)	25 mL

- *Preheat oven to 400°F (200°C)*
- *Cookie sheet, ungreased*

1. In a medium bowl, mix together flour, baking soda and salt.
2. In a large bowl, beat shortening and sugars until smooth. Beat in eggs, one at a time, until incorporated. Gradually add dry ingredients, mixing until a soft dough forms.
3. Shape dough into two rolls about 2 inches (5 cm) wide. Wrap tightly in plastic wrap and refrigerate for 3 to 4 hours, until firm.
4. In a small bowl, mix together mincemeat, nuts and cherries, if using.
5. On floured surface, cut dough into slices ⅛ inch (0.25 cm) thick. Place half the slices about 2 inches (5 cm) apart on cookie sheet. Place a scant teaspoonful (5 mL) of the mincemeat mixture in the center of each and top with another slice. Bake in preheated oven for 8 to 10 minutes or until golden brown. Immediately transfer to wire racks to cool.

Makes about 2½ dozen sandwiches

Grandma's Whoopie Pies

½ cup	unsweetened cocoa powder	125 mL
½ cup	hot water (not boiling)	125 mL
2⅔ cups	all-purpose flour	650 mL
1 tsp	baking powder	5 mL
1 tsp	baking soda	5 mL
¼ tsp	salt	1 mL
½ cup	shortening, softened	125 mL
1½ cups	granulated sugar	375 mL
2	eggs	2
1 tsp	vanilla	5 mL
½ cup	buttermilk	125 mL
FILLING		
3 tbsp	all-purpose flour	45 mL
Pinch	salt	Pinch
1 cup	milk	250 mL
¾ cup	shortening, softened	175 mL
1½ cups	confectioner's (icing) sugar, sifted	375 mL
2 tsp	vanilla	10 mL

> **TIP:** If a recipe calls for buttermilk and you don't have any on hand, add 1 tbsp (15 mL) vinegar or lemon juice to each cup of regular milk for instant buttermilk.

- *Preheat oven to 350°F (180°C)*
- *Cookie sheet, lightly greased*

1. In a small bowl, combine cocoa and hot water and mix well. Set aside to cool for 5 minutes.

2. In a medium bowl, sift together flour, baking powder, baking soda and salt.

3. In a large bowl, beat shortening and sugar until smooth and creamy. Add eggs, one at a time, beating until well incorporated. Stir in vanilla. Add cocoa mixture and mix well. Add flour mixture alternately with buttermilk, mixing until thoroughly blended.

4. Drop dough by rounded teaspoonfuls (5 mL), about 2 inches (5 cm) apart, onto prepared baking sheet. Using a spoon or the palm of your hand, flatten slightly. Bake in preheated oven for 10 to 12 minutes until firm. Immediately transfer to wire racks to cool.

5. *Filling:* In a small saucepan, mix flour and salt. Slowly whisk in milk until smooth. Cook over medium heat, stirring constantly, for 5 to 8 minutes, until thick. Remove from heat, cover and place in refrigerator to cool completely.

6. In a medium bowl, beat shortening, confectioner's sugar and vanilla until smooth and creamy. Add chilled mixture and beat for 5 minutes, until light and fluffy.

7. On a work surface, spread filling over the flat surface of half the cookies. Top with remaining cookies, flat side down, to form sandwiches. Store in the refrigerator.

Makes about 2 dozen sandwiches

Apricot Almond Sandwiches

2½ cups	all-purpose flour	625 mL
¼ tsp	baking soda	1 mL
¼ tsp	salt	1 mL
½ cup	shortening, softened	125 mL
1 cup	granulated sugar	250 mL
2	eggs	2
1 tsp	vanilla	5 mL
FILLING		
⅔ cup	granulated sugar	150 mL
⅔ cup	water	150 mL
1 tsp	freshly squeezed lemon juice	5 mL
2 cups	canned apricots, mashed	500 mL
½ cup	finely chopped almonds	125 mL

- *Preheat oven to 375°F (190°C)*
- *Cookie sheet, ungreased*
- *Round cookie cutter*

1. In a medium bowl, mix together flour, baking soda and salt.

2. In a large bowl, beat shortening and sugar until smooth and creamy. Beat in eggs, one at a time, until well incorporated. Stir in vanilla. Gradually add flour mixture, mixing until a soft dough forms. Cover and refrigerate for 1 to 2 hours, until firm.

3. *Filling:* In a saucepan, over low heat, mix together sugar, water, lemon juice, apricots and almonds. Cook, stirring, until thickened, about 15 minutes. Set aside to cool.

4. On a floured work surface, divide dough in half. One at a time, roll out each half to ⅛-inch (0.25 cm) thickness. Using a round cookie cutter, cut circles in one portion and place 1 inch (2.5 cm) apart on cookie sheet. Using the same cutter, cut out the other portion then, using the open side of a thimble, or a pastry cutter make a small hole in the center 1 inch (2.5 cm) apart and place on sheet. Bake in preheated oven or until edges are lightly browned. Immediately transfer to wire racks to cool.

5. When cool, spread filling on the solid cookie and top with the cut out cookie.

Makes about 15 sandwiches

Just Peachy Sandwich Cookies

⅔ cup	butter or margarine, softened	150 mL
½ cup	confectioner's (icing) sugar, sifted	125 mL
2 tsp	grated lemon zest	10 mL
½ tsp	ground nutmeg	2 mL
1¾ cups	all-purpose flour	425 mL
PEACH FILLING		
½ cup	peach preserves	125 mL
1 tbsp	granulated sugar	15 mL

TIP: Drop a bay leaf into your sugar and flour canisters to keep unwanted pests away. It does not change the taste.

- *Preheat oven to 325°F (160°C)*
- *Cookie sheet, ungreased*

1. In a large bowl, beat butter or margarine, confectioner's sugar, lemon zest and nutmeg until smooth and creamy. Gradually stir in flour, until thoroughly blended.

2. Shape dough into 1-inch (2.5 cm) balls and place 2 inches (5 cm) apart on cookie sheet. Using the bottom of a glass or the tines of a fork dipped in sugar, flatten slightly. Bake in preheated oven for 12 to 15 minutes or until golden brown. Immediately transfer to wire racks to cool.

3. *Peach Filling:* In a small saucepan, over low heat, bring preserves and sugar to a boil, stirring constantly. Cook, stirring, for 2 minutes, until sugar dissolves and mixture is syrupy. Remove from heat and set aside to cool completely.

4. On a work surface, place half the cookies, flat side up. Spread each with about ½ tsp (2 mL) of the filling. Top with remaining cookies, flat side down, to form a sandwich. Press together gently. Dab any leftover filling on top of each sandwich as a garnish.

Makes 2 dozen sandwiches

Lacy Oatmeal Sandwiches

⅔ cup	all-purpose flour	150 mL
2 cups	quick-cooking rolled oats	500 mL
⅔ cup	butter or margarine, melted	150 mL
1 cup	granulated sugar	250 mL
¼ cup	corn syrup	50 mL
¼ cup	milk	50 mL
FILLING		
1 cup	semi-sweet chocolate chips, melted	250 mL
1 cup	white chocolate chips, melted	250 mL

> **TIP:** Drizzle any leftover chocolate over the tops of the cookies for added decoration.

- *Preheat oven to 375°F (190°C)*
- *Cookie sheet, lined with buttered foil*

1. In a medium bowl, mix together flour and oats.
2. In a large bowl, mix together butter or margarine, sugar and corn syrup. Add milk and mix well. Stir in flour mixture and mix thoroughly.
3. Drop batter by level teaspoonfuls (5 mL), about 3 inches (7.5 cm) apart, onto prepared cookie sheet and, using the back of a spoon or the tines of a fork, press down slightly on each. Bake in preheated oven for 8 to 10 minutes or until cookies have spread and are browned around the edges. Immediately transfer foil and cookies to wire racks. When cool, peel cookies off the foil.
4. On a work surface, spread a thin layer of semi-sweet chocolate on the bottom of some cookies and white chocolate on others. Top each with the bottom side of remaining cookies.

Makes about 2 dozen sandwiches

Biscotti

Crisp and delicious, biscotti are a traditional Italian biscuit, perfect for dunking in a glass of milk or your morning coffee. Most of my biscotti recipes contain butter, which makes them richer and less crunchy than the traditional Italian versions. But because they are baked twice, they are drier than most other cookies.

Apricot Almond Biscotti

3 cups	all-purpose flour	750 mL
2 tsp	baking powder	10 mL
¼ tsp	salt	1 mL
¾ cup	butter, softened	175 mL
¾ cup	granulated sugar	175 mL
2	eggs	2
1 tsp	almond extract	5 mL
1 tsp	orange zest	5 mL
½ cup	blanched chopped almonds, toasted (see page 14)	125 mL
1 cup	finely chopped dried apricots	250 mL

> **TIP:** When cutting the partially cooked dough, always use a sharp knife with a serrated edge and cut in a light sawing motion — otherwise, the cookies will crumble.

- *Preheat oven to 325°F (160°C)*
- *Cookie sheet, ungreased*

1. In a medium bowl, mix together flour, baking powder and salt.
2. In a large bowl, beat butter and sugar until smooth and creamy. Add eggs, one at a time, beating until well incorporated. Stir in almond extract and orange zest. Add almonds and apricots and mix well. Gradually add flour mixture, mixing until a dough forms.
3. On a lightly floured surface, divide dough in half. Shape into two rolls about 8 inches (20 cm) long. Place at least 2 inches (5 cm) apart on cookie sheet. Bake in preheated oven for 30 to 35 minutes or until golden brown.
4. Cool for 5 minutes on cookie sheet, then cut into slices ½ inch (1 cm) thick. Place on cookie sheet and return to oven to dry for 15 minutes. Turn slices over and bake for 5 minutes more. Immediately transfer to wire racks to cool.

Makes about 2½ dozen

Chocolate Almond Biscotti

2¾ cups	all-purpose flour	675 mL
2½ tsp	baking powder	12 mL
1 tsp	salt	5 mL
½ cup	butter, softened	125 mL
1½ cups	granulated sugar	375 mL
2	eggs	2
3	squares (each 1 oz/28 g) semi-sweet chocolate, melted (see page 14)	3
1 tbsp	grated orange zest	15 mL
¼ cup	orange juice	50 mL
3	squares (each 1 oz/28 g) semi-sweet chocolate, coarsely chopped	3
¾ cup	walnut pieces, toasted	175 mL
¾ cup	whole blanched almonds, toasted	175 mL

TIP: For an added treat, dip one end of the biscotti in additional melted chocolate.

- *Preheat oven to 350°F (180°C)*
- *Cookie sheet, greased and floured*

1. In a medium bowl, combine flour, baking powder and salt.
2. In a large bowl, beat butter and sugar until smooth and creamy. Add eggs, one at a time, beating until incorporated. Stir in melted chocolate. Add orange zest and juice and mix well. Gradually add flour mixture, mixing until a dough forms. Fold in chocolate and nuts.
3. Divide dough in half. Form two rolls about 2 inches (5 cm) wide. Place at least 2 inches (5 cm) apart on prepared sheet. Bake in preheated oven for 30 minutes.
4. Cool on cookie sheet for 10 minutes, then transfer to a cutting board and cut into slices ½ to ¾ inch (1 to 2 cm) thick. Return to oven and bake for 10 minutes. Turn slices over and bake for 10 minutes more. Immediately transfer to wire racks to cool.

Makes about 4 dozen

Chocolate Nut Coffee Biscotti

2 cups	all-purpose flour	500 mL
2 cups	unsweetened cocoa powder	500 mL
2 cups	granulated sugar	500 mL
1 tsp	baking powder	5 mL
1 tsp	baking soda	5 mL
6	eggs	6
Pinch	salt	Pinch
¾ cup	coffee or brandy	50 mL
2 tsp	vanilla	10 mL
2 cups	coarsely chopped walnuts, toasted (see page 14)	500 mL

- *Preheat oven to 300°F (150°C)*
- *Cookie sheet, lightly greased and floured*

1. In a large bowl, combine flour, cocoa, sugar, baking powder and baking soda. Make a well in center.
2. In another large bowl, beat eggs and salt. Add coffee or brandy and vanilla. Pour into well and mix until a soft dough forms. Fold in walnuts.
3. Divide dough in half. Form into two rolls about 10 inches (25 cm) long. Place about 2 inches (5 cm) apart on prepared cookie sheet. Bake in preheated oven for 50 minutes until loaf looks dry. Transfer to a cutting board and cut into slices ½ inch (1 cm) thick. Return to sheet and bake for 20 minutes. Turn slices over and bake 20 minutes more. Immediately transfer to wire racks.

Makes about 3½ dozen

Chocolate Chip Biscotti

1¾ cups	all-purpose flour	425 mL
2 tsp	baking powder	10 mL
½ cup	chocolate chips	125 mL
¾ cup	whole unblanched almonds	175 mL
2	eggs	2
⅓ cup	melted butter	75 mL
¾ cup	granulated sugar	175 mL
2 tsp	vanilla	10 mL
1½ tsp	grated orange zest	7 mL
½ tsp	almond extract	2 mL
1	egg white, lightly beaten	1

TIP: Chill your rolling pin in the freezer before using so dough will not stick to it.

- *Preheat oven to 350°F (180°C)*
- *Cookie sheet, ungreased*

1. In a large bowl, combine flour, baking powder, chocolate chips and almonds. Make a well in the center.
2. In another bowl, beat eggs, butter, sugar, vanilla, zest and almond extract. Spoon into well and mix until a sticky dough forms.
3. Divide dough in half, then shape into 2 rolls, 10 to 12 inches (25 to 30 cm) long. Place about 2 inches (5 cm) apart on cookie sheet. Brush tops with egg white. Bake in preheated oven for 20 minutes. Cool on cookie sheet for 5 minutes, then cut into slices ½ to ¾ inch (1 to 2 cm) thick. Stand cookies upright on sheet and bake for another 20 to 25 minutes or until golden. Immediately transfer to wire racks to cool.

Makes about 3½ dozen

Italian-Style Biscotti

3 cups	all-purpose flour	750 mL
2 tsp	baking powder	10 mL
½ tsp	salt	2 mL
4	eggs, slightly beaten	4
1 cup	granulated sugar	250 mL
½ cup	melted butter	125 mL
2 tsp	vanilla	10 mL
1 tsp	almond extract	5 mL
2 tsp	anise extract	10 mL
¾ cup	finely chopped blanched almonds	175 mL

TIP: Anise extract is available in many supermarkets. If you can't find it there, try a specialty store.

- *Preheat oven to 350°F (180°C)*
- *Cookie sheet, lightly greased*

1. In a medium bowl, mix together flour, baking powder and salt.
2. In a large bowl, beat eggs, sugar and melted butter until well blended. Add extracts and almonds and mix well. Add dry ingredients and mix until a soft dough forms.
3. On a lightly floured surface, divide dough in half. Shape into two rolls, about 12 inches (30 cm) long. Place about 2 inches (5 cm) apart on prepared cookie sheet. Bake in preheated oven for 20 minutes or until just beginning to brown around the edges.
4. Cool on sheet for 10 minutes, then transfer to a cutting board and cut into slices ½ inch (1 cm) thick. Place on sheet and bake for 12 minutes. Turn slices over and bake for 5 to 10 minutes more, until golden brown.

Makes about 4 dozen

Cherry Nut Biscotti

2 cups	all-purpose flour	500 mL
1 cup	granulated sugar	250 mL
1 tsp	baking powder	5 mL
2 tsp	lime zest	10 mL
¼ cup	cold butter, cut into small pieces	50 mL
¾ cup	dried tart cherries	175 mL
3	eggs	3
1¼ cups	shelled pistachios or nuts of your choice	300 mL

- *Preheat oven to 350°F (180°C)*
- *Cookie sheet, greased*
- *Food processor*

1. In a food processor, combine flour, sugar, baking powder and zest. Pulse until zest is very fine. Add butter and cherries and pulse until cherries are coarsely chopped.

2. In a small bowl, beat eggs lightly. Spoon out 1 tbsp (15 mL) beaten egg and set aside. Add remainder to flour mixture, along with the nuts, and pulse until dough is evenly moistened. (The dough will be sticky.)

3. On a well-floured surface, divide dough into four portions. Shape each into rolls 9 inches (23 cm) long. Place on prepared sheet at least 2 inches (5 cm) apart. Press lightly to flatten and brush with reserved egg. Bake in preheated oven for 25 minutes or until golden brown.

4. Cool on sheets for about 15 minutes, then transfer to a cutting board. Cut into slices ½ inch (1 cm) thick and place upright on sheet. Bake 15 minutes more or until crisp. Immediately transfer to wire racks to cool.

Makes about 6 dozen

Cinnamon Oatmeal Biscotti

2½ cups	all-purpose flour	625 mL
1 cup	quick-cooking rolled oats	250 mL
1 tsp	baking powder	5 mL
¼ tsp	baking soda	1 mL
2 tsp	ground cinnamon	10 mL
¼ tsp	salt	1 mL
1 cup	chopped pecans, toasted (see page 14)	250 mL
½ cup	butter, softened	125 mL
⅔ cup	packed brown sugar	150 mL
2	eggs	2
½ cup	liquid honey	125 mL
2 tsp	vanilla	10 mL

TIP: If you run out of brown sugar, make your own by mixing 2 tbsp (25 mL) molasses into 1 cup (250 mL) granulated sugar.

- *Preheat oven to 350°F (180°C)*
- *Cookie sheet, greased*

1. In a large bowl, mix together flour, oats, baking powder, baking soda, cinnamon, salt and pecans.

2. In another large bowl, beat butter and brown sugar until smooth and creamy. Beat in eggs, one at a time, until well incorporated. Mix in honey, then vanilla. Add flour mixture and mix until well combined.

3. Divide dough in half. Shape into two rolls about 10 inches (25 cm) long. Place about 2 inches (5 cm) apart on prepared cookie sheet. Bake in preheated oven for 30 minutes or until lightly brown.

4. Cool on sheet for 5 minutes, then transfer to a cutting board and cut into slices ½ inch (1 cm) thick. Stand slices up on sheet and reduce oven heat to 325°F (160°C). Bake for 25 to 30 minutes longer or until golden brown. Immediately transfer to wire racks to cool.

Makes about 3 dozen

Coffee House Biscotti

2 cups + 2 tbsp	all-purpose flour	525 mL
1 tsp	baking powder	5 mL
1/4 tsp	salt	1 mL
1/2 cup	butter, softened	125 mL
1 cup	granulated sugar	250 mL
2	eggs	2
1 tsp	vanilla	5 mL
	Grated zest of 1 large lemon	
1 cup	coarsely chopped hazelnuts, toasted (see page 14)	250 mL

- *Preheat oven to 350°F (180°C)*
- *Cookie sheet, ungreased*

1. In a medium bowl, combine flour, baking powder and salt.
2. In a large bowl, beat butter and sugar until smooth and creamy. Beat in eggs, one at a time, until incorporated. Mix in vanilla and lemon zest. Gradually add flour mixture, mixing until a soft dough forms. Fold in nuts.
3. Divide dough in half. Shape into two rolls about 10 inches (25 cm) long. Place about 2 inches (5 cm) apart on cookie sheet. Bake in preheated oven for 30 minutes until golden.
4. Cool on sheet for 10 minutes, then transfer to a cutting board and cut into slices 1/2 inch (1 cm) thick. Return to sheet and bake for 10 minutes until lightly browned. Turn slices over and bake 10 minutes more. Immediately transfer to wire racks.

Makes about 3 dozen

Cranberry Pistachio Biscotti

3 cups	all-purpose flour	750 mL
1 tbsp	baking powder	15 mL
1/4 tsp	salt	1 mL
3	eggs	3
3/4 cup	granulated sugar	175 mL
1/2 cup	melted butter	125 mL
2 tsp	vanilla	10 mL
1/3 cup	chopped dried cranberries	75 mL
1/2 cup	unsalted pistachios or almonds	125 mL

- *Preheat oven to 350°F (180°C)*
- *Cookie sheet, greased*

1. In a medium bowl, combine flour, baking powder and salt.

2. In a large bowl, beat eggs, sugar, butter and vanilla until blended. Gradually add dry ingredients until a sticky dough forms. Using floured hands, work in cranberries and nuts until evenly distributed and dough is smooth.

3. Divide dough in half. Shape into two rolls about 10 inches (25 cm) long. Place about 2 inches (5 cm) apart on prepared cookie sheet. Bake in preheated oven for 20 minutes or until browned.

4. Cool on sheet for 10 minutes, then cut into slices 1/2 to 3/4 inch (1 to 2 cm) thick. Arrange slices upright on cookie sheet. Lower oven heat to 300°F (150°C) and bake for 20 to 25 minutes or until firm and dry. Immediately transfer to wire racks.

Makes about 3 dozen

Lemon Orange Cocoa Biscotti

3 cups	all-purpose flour	750 mL
1 cup	granulated sugar	250 mL
5½ tsp	baking powder	27 mL
½ tsp	salt	2 mL
¾ cup	unsweetened cocoa powder	175 mL
½ cup	coarsely chopped slivered almonds, toasted (see page 14)	125 mL
½ cup	melted butter	125 mL
½ cup	water	125 mL
4	eggs	4
1 tsp	vanilla	5 mL
	Grated zest of 3 lemons	
	Grated zest of 2 oranges	

- *Preheat oven to 375°F (190°C)*
- *Cookie sheet, lightly greased*

1. In a large bowl, combine flour, sugar, baking powder, salt, cocoa and almonds. Make a well in the center.
2. In another bowl, whisk butter, water, eggs, vanilla, lemon and orange zests. Pour into well and mix until a stiff dough forms.
3. Divide dough in half. Shape into two rolls about 12 by 3 inches (30 by 7.5 cm). Place about 2 inches (5 cm) apart on prepared cookie sheet. Bake in preheated oven for 25 to 30 minutes. Immediately cut into slices ½ to ¾ inch (1 to 2 cm) thick.
4. Lower oven heat to 350°F (180°C). Place slices on cookie sheet and bake for 10 minutes. Turn slices over and bake for 10 minutes more. Immediately transfer to wire racks.

Makes about 4 dozen

Lemon Almond Biscotti

1¾ cups	all-purpose flour	425 mL
¾ cup	granulated sugar	175 mL
1 tbsp	baking powder	15 mL
2 tbsp	finely grated lemon zest	25 mL
¾ cup	coarsely chopped almonds	175 mL
2	eggs	2
⅓ cup	olive oil	75 mL
1 tsp	vanilla	5 mL
½ tsp	almond extract	2 mL

- *Preheat oven to 325°F (160°C)*
- *Cookie sheet, greased*

1. In a large bowl, mix together flour, sugar, baking powder, lemon zest and almonds. Make a well in the center.
2. In another bowl, whisk eggs, oil, vanilla and almond extract. Pour into well and mix until a soft, sticky dough forms.
3. Divide dough in half. Shape into two rolls about 10 inches (25 cm) long. Place about 2 inches (5 cm) apart on prepared cookie sheet. Bake in preheated oven for 20 minutes.
4. Cool on sheet for 5 minutes, then cut into slices ½ inch (1 cm) thick. Return to sheet and bake for 10 minutes. Turn slices over and bake for 10 minutes more. Immediately transfer to wire racks.

Makes about 3 dozen

Shortbread

Traditional Scottish shortbread is one of the best-known and best-loved cookies in the world. Served with tea, there are few more satisfying afternoon treats.

Basically, shortbread is some combination of butter and flour, worked together and flavored. Many excellent cooks believe that the best way to "work" the butter into the flour mixture is with your fingers, as it allows you to "feel" the dough as it combines. A food processor, fitted with a metal disk, also does a good job of combining the butter with the flour mixture. If using this method, cut the butter into 1-inch (2.5 cm) cubes. Don't process the dough too much, as it will destroy the "crumb."

Many cooks have shortbread tricks. When making sweet shortbread, some use extra-fine sugar (see Tip, page 124). Others swear by rice flour (see Tip, page 126). As you bake these shortbreads, you will soon get a feel for what techniques work best for you.

Ginger Shortbread

1 cup	butter, softened	250 mL
½ cup	confectioner's (icing) sugar, sifted	125 mL
¼ tsp	salt	1 mL
3 tbsp	finely chopped candied ginger	45 mL
2 cups	all-purpose flour	500 mL

- *Preheat oven to 300°F (150°C)*
- *8-inch (2 L) square baking pan, ungreased*

1. In a large bowl, beat butter, sugar and salt until smooth and creamy. Mix in ginger until well incorporated. Gradually sift in flour, mixing well after each addition.

2. Press dough into pan and, using a fork, prick deeply all over. Bake in preheated oven for 50 to 60 minutes or until golden brown. Cool in pan for 5 minutes, then invert onto a cutting board. Using a knife, score 32 bars, 2 by 1 inch (5 by 2.5 cm). When cool enough to handle, using a lifter, transfer to wire racks to cool.

Makes 32 bars

Cheddar Shortbread

2 cups	all-purpose flour	500 mL
1 tsp	salt	5 mL
Pinch	cayenne (optional)	Pinch
1 cup	butter or margarine, softened	250 mL
1½ cups	shredded Cheddar cheese	375 mL

- *Preheat oven to 425°F (220°C)*
- *Cookie sheet, greased*

1. In a medium bowl, combine flour, salt and cayenne, if using.

2. In a large bowl, cream butter. Beat in cheese, using a spoon, until well blended. Gradually add flour mixture, mixing thoroughly after each addition. Turn out on a floured surface and knead lightly.

3. Shape dough into an 8-inch (20 cm) square and cut into 4- by 1-inch (10 by 2.5 cm) bars. Place on prepared sheet and bake in preheated oven for 25 minutes or until golden brown. Immediately transfer to wire racks to cool.

Makes 32 bars

VARIATION

Food Processor Method
This method also works well and has the advantage of fully integrating the Cheddar into the dough. Cut butter into 1-inch (2.5 cm) cubes and place in freezer. In a food processor, using the metal blade, add flour, salt and cayenne. Pulse until blended. Add cheese and pulse until well combined. Add chilled butter and pulse just until a dough forms. Turn out on a floured board and knead lightly. Follow Step 3, right.

Refrigerator Nut Shortbread

3 cups	cake and pastry flour	750 mL
½ cup	rice flour	125 mL
¾ cup	granulated sugar	175 mL
1½ cups	butter, softened	375 mL
	Finely chopped almonds or pecans	

TIP: Refrigerator dough cookies are very convenient because you can make the dough ahead of time. When you're ready to bake, you can slice and bake as many cookies as you like.

- *Preheat oven to 300°F (150°C)*
- *Cookie sheet, ungreased*

1. In a large bowl, combine flours and sugar.
2. In another large bowl, beat butter until smooth. Gradually add flour mixture, mixing thoroughly after each addition. Knead lightly.
3. Divide dough in half and shape into two logs, each about 1½ inches (4 cm) in diameter. Roll logs in nuts until evenly coated. Wrap tightly in plastic wrap and twist ends to seal. Chill in refrigerator for 1 to 2 hours, until firm.
4. Cut dough into ¼-inch (0.5 cm) rounds and place on cookie sheet. Bake in preheated oven for 20 to 25 minutes or until golden brown. Cool on cookie sheet for 5 minutes, then transfer to wire racks to cool completely.

Makes about 6 dozen

Cherry Nut Refrigerator Shortbread

1 cup	all-purpose flour	250 mL
½ cup	confectioner's (icing) sugar, sifted	125 mL
½ cup	cornstarch	125 mL
¾ cup	chopped candied cherries	175 mL
½ cup	chopped pecans	125 mL
¾ cup	butter, softened	175 mL

- *Preheat oven to 375°F (190°C)*
- *Cookie sheet, ungreased*

1. In a medium bowl, mix together flour, confectioner's sugar and cornstarch. Add cherries and pecans and mix thoroughly.
2. In a large bowl, cream butter. Gradually add flour mixture, mixing thoroughly after each addition. Knead lightly. Shape dough into a roll about 1½ inches (4 cm) wide. Wrap tightly in plastic wrap and refrigerate for at least 4 hours.
3. When ready to bake, cut roll into slices ¼ inch (0.5 cm) thick and place on cookie sheet. Bake in preheated oven for 8 to 12 minutes or until golden brown. Immediately transfer to wire racks to cool.

Makes about 3 dozen

Orange Shortbread

1 cup	butter, softened	250 mL
1/3 cup	berry sugar	75 mL
1/4 tsp	salt	1 mL
1 tbsp	grated lemon zest	15 mL
2 tbsp	grated orange zest	25 mL
2 cups	all-purpose flour	500 mL

TIP: Berry or fruit sugar is extra-fine granulated sugar, which you can buy at most supermarkets. Many people believe it improves the quality of shortbread.

- *Preheat oven to 300°F (150°C)*
- *Cookie sheet, ungreased*

1. In a bowl, beat butter and sugar until smooth and creamy. Add salt and zests and blend in well.
2. Gradually add flour, mixing thoroughly after each addition. Knead lightly. Shape into a roll, wrap tightly in plastic wrap and refrigerate for at least 2 hours or overnight, if desired.
3. When ready to bake, cut dough into 1/4-inch (0.5 cm) slices and place on cookie sheet. Bake in preheated oven 10 minutes or until lightly browned. Immediately transfer to wire racks to cool.

Makes about 2 dozen

Chocolate Shortbread

3/4 cup	all-purpose flour	175 mL
1 tbsp	cornstarch	15 mL
Pinch	salt	Pinch
3 tbsp	unsweetened cocoa powder	45 mL
1/2 cup	butter, softened	125 mL
1/2 cup	confectioner's (icing) sugar, sifted	125 mL
1/2 tsp	vanilla	2 mL

- *Preheat oven to 325°F (160°C)*
- *Cookie sheet, ungreased*

1. In a small bowl, sift together flour, cornstarch, salt and cocoa.
2. In a large bowl, beat butter, confectioner's sugar and vanilla until smooth and creamy. Gradually add flour mixture, mixing thoroughly after each addition. Knead briefly.
3. Shape dough into 1-inch (2.5 cm) balls and place about 2 inches (5 cm) apart on cookie sheet. Using the bottom of a glass or the tines of a fork to make a criss-cross pattern, flatten slightly. Bake in preheated oven for 20 minutes or until firm. Cool slightly, then transfer to wire racks or waxed paper–lined platter to cool completely.

Makes about 2 1/2 to 3 dozen

Lemon Poppy Seed Shortbread

1 cup	all-purpose flour	250 mL
½ cup	confectioner's (icing) sugar, sifted	125 mL
½ cup	cornstarch	125 mL
2 tbsp	grated lemon zest	25 mL
1 tbsp	poppy seeds	15 mL
¾ cup	butter, softened	175 mL

TIP: Put lemon and orange zest in water, in a saucepan, and let simmer. You'll have a refreshing, wonderful aroma all through the house.

- *Preheat oven to 300°F (150°C)*
- *Cookie sheet, ungreased*
- *Cookie cutters*

1. In a medium bowl, mix together flour, sugar, cornstarch, lemon zest and poppy seeds.
2. In a large bowl, cream butter. Gradually add flour mixture, mixing well after each addition. Knead lightly.
3. On a lightly floured surface, roll out dough to ¼-inch (0.5 cm) thickness. Using cookie cutters, cut into desired shapes. Alternately, shape dough into 1-inch (2.5 cm) balls and flatten slightly with a fork and place on cookie sheets. Bake in preheated oven for 15 to 20 minutes or until lightly browned. Immediately transfer to wire racks to cool.

Makes about 2 dozen

Old-Time Oatmeal Shortbread

1 cup	all-purpose flour	250 mL
½ tsp	baking soda	2 mL
2 cups	quick-cooking rolled oats	500 mL
1 cup	butter, softened	250 mL
½ cup	firmly packed brown sugar	125 mL
1 tsp	vanilla	5 mL

- *Preheat oven to 350°F (180°C)*
- *Cookie sheet, ungreased*
- *Cookie cutters*

1. In a medium bowl, mix together flour, baking soda and oats.
2. In a large bowl, beat butter, brown sugar and vanilla until smooth and creamy. Gradually add flour mixture, mixing thoroughly after each addition. Knead lightly. Wrap tightly in plastic wrap and refrigerate for at least 2 hours.
3. On a lightly floured surface, roll out dough to ¼-inch (0.5 cm) thickness. Using cookie cutters or a glass dipped in flour, cut into desired shapes and place on cookie sheet. Bake in preheated oven for 10 to 12 minutes or until golden brown. Immediately transfer to wire racks to cool.

Makes about 4 dozen

Original Scottish Shortbread

1 cup	butter, softened	250 mL
¾ cup	granulated or fruit extra-fine sugar	175 mL
2½ cups	sifted all-purpose flour	625 mL

- *Preheat oven to 300°F (150°C)*
- *Cookie sheet, ungreased*
- *Cookie cutter*

1. In a large bowl, beat butter and sugar until smooth. Gradually add flour, mixing thoroughly after each addition. Knead lightly. Wrap tightly in plastic wrap and refrigerate for 1 to 2 hours.
2. On a lightly floured surface, roll out dough to about ½-inch (1 cm) thickness. Using a cookie cutter or a glass dipped in flour, cut into desired shapes and place on cookie sheet. Bake in preheated oven for 20 to 25 minutes or until golden brown. Immediately transfer to wire racks to cool.

Makes about 3 dozen

VARIATIONS

Honey Shortbread Cookies
Reduce sugar to ½ cup (125 mL). After beating butter and sugar, add ¼ cup (50 mL) liquid honey.

Butterscotch Shortbread Cookies
Use 1 cup (250 mL) firmly packed brown sugar in place of granulated sugar.

Cream Cheese Shortbread

4 oz	cream cheese, softened	125 g
1 cup	butter, softened	250 mL
½ cup	granulated sugar	125 mL
1 tsp	vanilla	5 mL
2 cups	sifted all-purpose flour	500 mL

- *Preheat oven to 375°F (190°C)*
- *Cookie sheet, ungreased*
- *Cookie cutters*

1. In a large bowl, beat cream cheese and butter until smooth. Add sugar and mix until creamy. Stir in vanilla. Gradually add flour, mixing well after each addition. Knead lightly.
2. On a lightly floured surface, roll out dough to ¼-inch (0.5 cm) thickness. Using a cookie cutter or a glass dipped in flour, cut into desired shapes and place on cookie sheet. Bake in preheated oven for 8 to 10 minutes. Immediately transfer to wire racks to cool.

Makes about 3 dozen

Grandma's Traditional Shortbread

½ cup	confectioner's (icing) sugar	125 mL
½ cup	cornstarch	125 mL
1 cup	all-purpose flour	250 mL
¾ cup	butter, softened	175 mL

TIP: Give your shortbread a professional look by dipping the shapes into melted white or dark chocolate and then sprinkling the chocolate with finely chopped nuts.

- *Preheat oven to 300°F (150°C)*
- *Cookie sheet, ungreased*
- *Cookie cutters*

1. In a medium bowl, sift together sugar, cornstarch and flour.
2. In a large bowl, cream butter. Using two knives, a pastry blender or your fingers, work flour in until a smooth dough forms. Knead lightly. Wrap dough in plastic wrap and refrigerate for about 30 minutes.
3. On a lightly floured surface, roll out dough to ¼-inch (0.5 cm) thickness. Using cookie cutters or the top of a glass dipped in flour, cut into desired shapes and place on cookie sheet. Bake in preheated oven for 15 to 20 minutes or until lightly browned. Immediately transfer to wire racks to cool.

Makes about 2 dozen

Classic Xmas Shortbread

1 cup	butter, softened	250 mL
⅔ cup	packed brown sugar	150 mL
2 cups	sifted all-purpose flour	500 mL

TIP: Dip the ends of plain shortbread cookies into melted chocolate. Let excess drip into saucepan, then place on a cookie sheet until chocolate hardens.

- *Preheat oven to 350°F (180°C)*
- *Cookie sheet, lightly greased*
- *Cookie cutters*

1. In a large bowl, cream butter and brown sugar until smooth. Gradually add flour, mixing thoroughly after each addition. Knead lightly.
2. Shape dough into a ball. Roll out on floured working surface to about ¼-inch (0.5 cm) thickness. Using cookie cutters or a glass dipped in flour, cut into desired shapes and place on prepared sheet. Bake in preheated oven for 12 to 15 minutes or until golden brown. Immediately transfer to wire racks to cool.

Makes about 3 dozen

Spicy Shortbread Wedges

1 cup	butter, softened	250 mL
1 cup	packed brown sugar	250 mL
2 tbsp	grated orange zest	25 mL
1 tbsp	ground cinnamon	15 mL
¾ tsp	ground cloves	4 mL
2 tbsp	ground ginger	25 mL
1 tsp	baking soda	5 mL
2 cups	all-purpose flour	500 mL
	Granulated sugar	

TIP: If a recipe calls for superfine sugar, whirl regular granulated sugar in a blender until fine.

- *Preheat oven to 325°F (160°C)*
- *Two 8-inch (20 cm) round cake pans, ungreased*

1. In a large bowl, beat butter, brown sugar, orange zest, cinnamon, cloves, ginger and baking soda until smooth and creamy. Gradually add flour, mixing thoroughly after each addition. Knead lightly.
2. Divide dough in half. Place half in one pan and press evenly over bottom. Repeat with remaining dough in second pan. Sprinkle tops with granulated sugar and bake in preheated oven for 25 to 30 minutes or until tops look dry and slightly crackled and edges are higher than the centers. Cool in pans for 5 minutes, then invert onto a cutting board. Cut each cake into 16 wedges.

Makes 32 wedges

Whipped Shortbread

2 cups	butter, softened	500 mL
1 tsp	vanilla	5 mL
½ cup	cornstarch	125 mL
3 cups	all-purpose flour	750 mL
1 cup	confectioner's (icing) sugar, sifted	250 mL
	Maraschino cherries (optional)	

- *Preheat oven to 300°F (150°C)*
- *Cookie sheet, ungreased*

1. In a large bowl, beat butter until smooth. Stir in vanilla. Add cornstarch, flour and confectioner's sugar and beat until dough is a smooth consistency resembling whipped cream.
2. Drop by teaspoonfuls (5 mL), about 2 inches (5 cm) apart, onto cookie sheet. Bake in preheated oven for 15 minutes or until golden brown. Top with a maraschino cherry, if desired. Immediately transfer to wire racks to cool.

Makes about 9 dozen

Shortbread Wedges with Peanut Butter and Jam

1¼ cups	all-purpose flour	300 mL
½ tsp	baking powder	2 mL
¼ tsp	salt	1 mL
3 tbsp	butter, softened	45 mL
½ cup	smooth peanut butter	125 mL
½ cup	granulated sugar	125 mL
1	egg	1
½ tsp	vanilla	2 mL
	Grape jam or jelly	

- *Preheat oven to 350°F (180°C)*
- *9-inch (23 cm) round pie plate or quiche pan, sprayed with vegetable spray*

1. In a small bowl, mix together flour, baking powder and salt.
2. In a large bowl, beat butter, peanut butter and sugar until smooth and creamy. Add egg and vanilla and beat until well blended. Gradually add flour mixture, mixing thoroughly after each addition. Knead lightly. Wrap dough tightly in plastic wrap and chill in refrigerator for several hours or overnight.
3. Press dough into bottom of prepared pan. Using a knife, score 18 pie-shaped wedges. (Do not cut all the way to the bottom.) Bake in preheated oven for 10 minutes. Using the tip of a wooden spoon, press random grooves into the dough. Fill with grape jam or jelly and return to the oven for 8 more minutes. Place plate on a wire rack to cool. Cut into 18 wedges.

Makes 18 wedges

Raisin Shortbread Wedges

1/3 cup	orange juice	75 mL
3/4 cup	seedless raisins	175 mL
1 1/2 cups	sifted all-purpose flour	375 mL
1/4 cup	granulated sugar	50 mL
1/2 cup	butter, softened	125 mL

> **TIP:** Some cooks believe the use of rice flour improves shortbread. Try substituting rice flour for one-fifth of the all-purpose flour in this or any other shortbread recipe.

- *Preheat oven to 350°F (180°C)*
- *Cookie sheet, greased*

1. In a small saucepan, bring orange juice and raisins to a slow boil. Cover and cool, if possible, overnight.
2. In a medium bowl, mix together flour and sugar.
3. In a large bowl, cream butter. Gradually add flour mixture, mixing thoroughly after each addition. Knead dough thoroughly.
4. Divide dough in quarters and shape into rounds, about 1/4 inch (0.5 cm) thick. Place one round on prepared cookie sheet and spread cooled raisin mixture over the entire surface. Top with another round, pressing down firmly. Using your fingers dipped in flour, pinch edges together. Prick entire top with a fork. Bake in preheated oven about 20 minutes or until golden. Mark into 8 segments as you would a pie, and when cool, remove from cookie sheet.

Makes 32 wedges

Brownies

The Basic Brownie

¾ cup	all-purpose flour	175 mL
½ tsp	salt	2 mL
½ tsp	baking powder	2 mL
2	squares (each 1 oz/28 g) unsweetened chocolate	2
⅓ cup	shortening or butter, softened	75 mL
1 cup	granulated sugar	250 mL
2	eggs	2
½ cup	chopped walnuts or pecans	125 mL
	Cocoa Frosting, optional (see page 362)	
	Confectioner's (icing) sugar, for dusting (optional)	

TIP: For a light-textured brownie, beat eggs more thoroughly. For a firmer brownie, beat eggs less.

- *Preheat oven to 350°F (180°C)*
- *8-inch (2 L) square cake pan, greased*

1. In a small bowl, mix together flour, salt and baking powder.
2. In a large saucepan, over low heat, melt chocolate with shortening, stirring until smooth. Remove from heat and set aside to cool slightly.
3. When chocolate mixture has cooled, stir in sugar. Add eggs and beat just until blended. Blend in flour mixture. Stir in nuts.
4. Spread batter evenly in prepared pan. Bake in preheated oven for 30 to 35 minutes or until a tester inserted in the center comes out clean. Place pan on a wire rack to cool completely, then cut into squares. If desired, frost with Cocoa Frosting or your favorite chocolate frosting. Or sift confectioner's sugar over top.

Makes 16 brownies

Old-Time Brownies

1¾ cups	cake flour, sifted	425 mL
¾ tsp	baking soda	4 mL
1 tsp	salt	5 mL
1⅓ cups	granulated sugar	325 mL
5	egg yolks	5
2½	squares (each 1 oz/28 g) unsweetened chocolate, melted	2½
1 tsp	vanilla	5 mL
1 cup	sour cream	250 mL
1 cup	chopped walnuts	250 mL

TIP: If you run out of unsweetened chocolate, substitute 3 level tbsp (45 mL) unsweetened cocoa powder and 1 tbsp (15 mL) butter for every 1 oz (28 g) unsweetened chocolate.

- *Preheat oven to 400°F (200°C)*
- *Three 12-cup muffin tins, greased or paper-lined*

1. In a small bowl, mix together flour, baking soda and salt.
2. In a large bowl, beat sugar and egg yolks until thickened. Blend in melted chocolate. Stir in vanilla. Gradually add flour mixture, alternately with sour cream, stirring until just combined. Stir in nuts.
3. Spoon into prepared tin, filling cups about three-quarters full. Bake in preheated oven for about 15 minutes or until a tester inserted in center of a brownie comes out clean. Place pan on a wire rack to cool slightly, then remove from cups and cool completely on rack.

Makes 36 brownies

Caramel Candy Brownies

FILLING

1	bag (14 oz/397 g) caramels, unwrapped (about 45 caramels)	1
2 tbsp	milk	25 mL

BASE AND TOPPING

4	squares (each 1 oz/28 g) unsweetened chocolate	4
¾ cup	butter or margarine	175 mL
2 cups	granulated sugar	500 mL
3	eggs	3
1 tbsp	milk	15 mL
1 cup	all-purpose flour	250 mL
1 cup	chopped pecans, divided	250 mL

- *Preheat oven to 350°F (180°C)*
- *9-inch (2.5 L) square cake pan, greased*

1. *Filling:* In a microwave-safe bowl, on medium power, heat caramels and milk for 3 minutes. Remove from oven and stir until melted and smooth. (Alternatively, heat caramels and milk in a saucepan over low heat, stirring until smooth and melted.) Keep warm while preparing brownie batter.

2. *Base and Topping:* In a large saucepan, over low heat, melt chocolate and butter, stirring constantly, until smooth. Remove from heat and set aside to cool slightly. When mixture has cooled, stir in sugar. Add eggs and beat until just blended. Stir in milk. Blend in flour. Stir in nuts.

3. Spread half the batter evenly in prepared pan. Spoon filling over batter. Sprinkle ¾ cup (175 mL) of the nuts over top. Drop remaining batter by spoonfuls over nuts, then sprinkle with remaining nuts. Bake in preheated oven for 30 to 35 minutes or until a tester inserted in the centre comes out clean. Place pan on a wire rack to cool completely, then cut into squares.

Makes 24 brownies

Classic Chocolate Nut Brownies

4	squares (each 1 oz/28 g) unsweetened chocolate	4
¾ cup	butter or margarine	175 mL
2 cups	granulated sugar	500 mL
3	eggs	3
1 tsp	vanilla	5 mL
1 cup	all-purpose flour	250 mL
1¼ cups	chopped nuts	300 mL
	Frosting (optional)	

- *Preheat oven to 350°F (180°C)*
- *13- by 9- inch (3.5 L) cake pan, greased*

1. In a large saucepan, over low heat, melt chocolate and butter, stirring until smooth. Set aside to cool slightly.

2. When chocolate mixture has cooled, stir in sugar. Add eggs and vanilla and beat until just combined. Blend in flour. Stir in nuts.

3. Spread batter evenly in prepared pan. Bake in preheated oven for 30 to 35 minutes or until a tester inserted in the center comes out clean. Place pan on a wire rack to cool completely. If desired, frost, then cut into squares.

TIP: Plain brownies freeze well wrapped tightly in a double layer of plastic wrap or foil. To avoid condensation, thaw completely before unwrapping.

Makes 36 brownies

Cheesecake Swirl Brownies

FILLING

4 oz	cream cheese, softened	125 g
2 tbsp	granulated sugar	25 mL
1	egg	1

BASE AND TOPPING

1 cup	all-purpose flour	250 mL
1/2 cup	unsweetened cocoa powder, sifted	125 mL
3/4 cup	granulated sugar	175 mL
1/2 tsp	baking powder	2 mL
1/2 cup	mini chocolate chips	125 mL
1/4 cup	chopped walnuts	50 mL
1/4 cup	vegetable oil	50 mL
1/4 cup	unsweetened applesauce	50 mL
1/4 cup	milk	50 mL
1 tsp	vanilla	5 mL
1	egg	1

- *Preheat oven to 350°F (180°C)*
- *8-inch (2 L) square cake pan, greased*

1. *Filling:* In a small bowl, beat cream cheese and sugar until smooth. Beat in egg until incorporated. Set aside.
2. *Base and Topping:* In a large bowl, mix together flour, cocoa, sugar and baking powder. Stir in chocolate chips and walnuts.
3. In another small bowl, whisk together oil, applesauce, milk, vanilla and egg until well blended. Add to flour mixture and mix until combined. Reserve 1 cup (250 mL) of mixture for topping and spread remainder evenly in prepared pan. Spread cream cheese filling evenly over batter. Drop reserved batter, by spoonfuls, over filling.
4. Run a knife through the batter at 1-inch (2.5 cm) intervals across the width of the pan, to create a marbling effect. Bake in preheated oven for 25 minutes or until a tester inserted in the center comes out clean. Place pan on a wire rack to cool completely, then cut into squares.

Makes 16 brownies

Coffee Mocha Brownies

3	squares (each 1 oz/28 g) unsweetened chocolate	3
1/2 cup	butter	125 mL
2 tsp	instant espresso or coffee powder	10 mL
1 1/4 cups	granulated sugar	300 mL
2	eggs	2
1 tsp	vanilla	5 mL
2/3 cup	all-purpose flour	150 mL
1/2 tsp	salt	2 mL
1/2 cup	coarsely chopped bittersweet chocolate	125 mL
1/2 cup	chopped pecans, toasted (see page 14)	125 mL

- *Preheat oven to 350°F (180°C)*
- *9-inch (2.5 L) square cake pan, lightly greased*

1. In a large saucepan, over low heat, melt chocolate, butter and coffee, stirring constantly, until mixture is smooth and coffee is dissolved. Set aside to cool slightly.
2. When chocolate has cooled, stir in sugar. Add eggs and vanilla and mix until blended. Blend in flour and salt. Stir in bittersweet chocolate and pecans.
3. Spread evenly in prepared pan. Bake in preheated oven for 25 to 30 minutes or until a tester inserted in the center comes out almost clean but with some moist crumbs. Place pan on a wire rack to cool completely, then cut into squares.

Makes 24 brownies

Cherry Cream Brownies

FILLING

3 oz	cream cheese, softened	90 g
¼ cup	granulated sugar	50 mL
½ tsp	vanilla	2 mL
¼ tsp	almond extract	1 mL
1	egg	1
⅓ cup	maraschino cherries, drained and chopped	75 mL

BASE AND TOPPING

½ cup	all-purpose flour	125 mL
½ tsp	baking powder	2 mL
¼ tsp	salt	1 mL
⅓ cup	unsweetened cocoa powder	75 mL
½ cup	butter or margarine, melted	125 mL
1 cup	granulated sugar	250 mL
2	eggs, beaten	2
1 tsp	vanilla	5 mL

- *Preheat oven to 350°F (180°C)*
- *9-inch (2.5 L) square cake pan, greased*

1. *Filling:* In a small bowl, beat cream cheese and sugar until smooth. Beat in egg until incorporated. Stir in almond extract, vanilla and cherries and mix until blended.
2. *Base and Topping:* In a small bowl mix together flour, baking powder and salt.
3. In a large bowl, sift cocoa into melted butter and mix until smooth. Stir in sugar. Add eggs and vanilla, beating until just combined. Blend in flour mixture.
4. Spread half the batter evenly in prepared pan. Spread filling over top. Drop remaining batter, by spoonfuls, over filling. Run a knife through the batter and filling to create a marbling effect. Bake in preheated oven for 35 to 40 minutes or until a tester inserted in the centre comes out clean. Place pan on a wire rack to cool completely, then cut into squares.

Makes 24 brownies

Original Fudge Brownies

½ cup	butter or margarine	125 mL
2	squares (each 1 oz/28 g) unsweetened chocolate	2
1 cup	granulated sugar	250 mL
2	eggs	2
½ tsp	vanilla	2 mL
½ cup	all-purpose flour	125 mL
Pinch	salt	Pinch
1 cup	chopped walnuts	250 mL

- *Preheat oven to 350°F (180°C)*
- *8-inch (2 L) square cake pan, greased*

1. In a saucepan, over low heat, melt butter and chocolate, stirring until smooth. Set aside to cool slightly.
2. When chocolate mixture has cooled, stir in sugar. Add eggs and vanilla and mix just until blended. Blend in flour and salt. Stir in nuts.
3. Spread batter evenly in prepared pan. Bake in preheated oven for 30 minutes or until a tester inserted in the center comes out clean. Place pan on a wire rack to cool completely, then cut into squares.

Makes 16 brownies

TIP: To line a pan with foil, turn the pan upside down, then smooth the foil around the pan to shape it. Turn the pan over and grease the bottom and sides before placing foil inside the pan. This prevents the foil from shifting.

Chocolate Butter Pecan Brownies

1½ cups	all-purpose flour	375 mL
1 tsp	baking powder	5 mL
1 tsp	salt	5 mL
1 cup	chopped pecans	250 mL
⅔ cup	butter	150 mL
4	squares (each 1 oz/28 g) unsweetened chocolate	4
2 cups	granulated sugar	500 mL
4	eggs	4
FROSTING		
¼ cup	butter	50 mL
2 cups	confectioner's (icing) sugar, sifted	500 mL
3 tbsp	whipping (35%) cream	45 mL
2 tsp	vanilla	10 mL
GLAZE		
1 tbsp	butter	15 mL
1	square (1 oz/28 g) unsweetened chocolate	1

- *Preheat oven to 350°F (180°C)*
- *13- by 9-inch (3.5 L) cake pan, greased*

1. In a medium bowl, mix together flour, baking powder, salt and pecans.
2. In a saucepan, over low heat, melt butter and chocolate, stirring until smooth. Remove from heat and set aside to cool slightly.
3. When butter mixture has cooled, stir in sugar. Add eggs and beat just until blended. Blend in flour mixture.
4. Spread batter evenly in prepared pan. Bake in preheated oven for 30 to 35 minutes or until tester inserted in the center comes out clean. Place pan on a wire rack to cool completely.
5. *Frosting:* In a saucepan, over low heat, melt butter. Remove from heat. Gradually add confectioner's sugar, alternately with cream, beating until smooth. Stir in vanilla. Spread evenly over brownies.
6. *Glaze:* In another saucepan, or in a microwave oven (see Tip, page 129), melt butter and chocolate until smooth. Cool slightly, then drizzle over top of frosting. When cooled, cut into squares.

Makes 36 brownies

Low-Fat Brownies

½ cup	cake flour	125 mL
½ cup	unsweetened cocoa powder	125 mL
¼ tsp	salt	1 mL
¾ cup	granulated sugar	175 mL
6 tbsp	unsweetened applesauce	90 mL
1	egg	1
2	egg whites	2
2 tbsp	vegetable oil	25 mL
1½ tsp	vanilla	7 mL
1 tbsp	chopped walnuts or pecans	15 mL

- *Preheat oven to 350°F (180°C)*
- *8-inch (2 L) square cake pan, greased*

1. In a small bowl, sift together flour, cocoa and salt.
2. In a large bowl, beat sugar, applesauce, egg, egg whites, oil and vanilla until blended. Blend in flour mixture. Spread batter evenly in prepared pan. Sprinkle walnuts over top. Bake in preheated oven for 25 minutes or until a tester inserted in the center comes out clean. Place pan on a wire rack to cool completely, then cut into squares.

Makes 16 brownies

Chocolate Mint Dream Brownies

¾ cup	butter or margarine	175 mL
1⅔ cups	semi-sweet chocolate chips	400 mL
1½ cups	all-purpose flour	375 mL
¼ tsp	salt	1 mL
1¾ cups	granulated sugar	425 mL
6	eggs	6
2 tsp	vanilla	10 mL
12	small chocolate-covered mints	12
½ cup	white chocolate chips	125 mL
2 tbsp	whipping (35%) cream	25 mL

- *Preheat oven to 350°F (180°C)*
- *13- by 9-inch (3.5 L) cake pan, greased*

1. In a saucepan, over low heat, melt butter and chocolate chips, stirring until smooth. Set aside to cool slightly.
2. In a small bowl, mix together flour and salt.
3. When chocolate mixture has cooled, stir in sugar. Add eggs and vanilla and beat until just blended. Blend in flour mixture.
4. Spread half the batter evenly in prepared pan. Arrange mints evenly over batter, pressing down lightly. Spoon remaining batter over top. Bake in preheated oven for 30 to 35 minutes or until tester inserted in the center comes out clean. Place pan on a wire rack to cool completely, then chill for 2 hours.
5. Meanwhile, in a saucepan, over low heat, melt white chocolate chips and cream, stirring constantly, until smooth. Drizzle mixture over top of chilled brownies and cut into squares.

Makes 36 brownies

Ice Cream Chocolate Brownies

1	package (15½ oz/440 g) brownie mix or brownie mix with chocolate chunks	1
1 cup	crushed peanut brittle	250 mL
6 cups	softened vanilla ice cream	1.5 L
½ cup	ready-to-serve whipped chocolate frosting	125 mL

TIP: To prevent ice crystals from forming on ice cream after the carton has been opened, fit a piece of plastic wrap snugly on top of the ice cream before resealing the carton.

- *Preheat oven to 350°F (180°C)*
- *13- by 9-inch (3.5 L) cake pan, greased on bottom only*

1. Prepare brownie mix as directed on package. Spread evenly in prepared pan. Bake in preheated oven for 25 to 30 minutes or until tester inserted in the center comes out clean. Place pan on a wire rack to cool completely.
2. In a clean bowl, fold nut brittle into softened ice cream. Spread evenly over cooled base. Cut into squares.
3. In a saucepan, over low heat, heat frosting until melted, stirring constantly. Drizzle over top of squares in zig-zag lines. Serve immediately. Any leftover brownies can be frozen until firm, then wrapped in plastic and stored in the freezer up to 1 month.

Makes 20 brownies

Frypan Brownies

1½ cups	all-purpose flour	375 mL
½ tsp	baking soda	2 mL
Pinch	salt	Pinch
½ cup	butter, margarine or shortening, softened	125 mL
1 cup	packed brown sugar	250 mL
1	egg	1
1½ tsp	vanilla	7 mL
2	squares (each 1 oz/28 g) unsweetened chocolate, melted and cooled	2
½ cup	milk	125 mL
1 tsp	shortening	5 mL
	Chocolate Butter Frosting (optional, see page 360), shredded or flaked coconut or confectioner's (icing) sugar (optional)	

* *Preheat a medium-size electric frypan to 300°F (150°C) with vent closed*

1. In a small bowl, mix together flour, baking soda and salt.
2. In a large bowl, beat butter and brown sugar until smooth and creamy. Beat in egg until incorporated. Stir in vanilla and melted chocolate. Gradually blend in flour mixture alternately with milk until just incorporated.
3. Brush frypan with shortening. Spread batter evenly over pan. Cover and cook in preheated pan for 25 minutes or until top is no longer sticky. Open vent for the last 5 minutes.
4. Using a spatula, loosen cake around the edges, then invert onto a wire rack. Cool completely, then cut into squares. If desired, frost with Chocolate Butter Frosting, sprinkle with coconut or dust with confectioner's sugar.

Makes 36 brownies

TIP: To melt chocolate in a microwave, use chocolate chips, chocolate squares (each 1 oz/28 g) or small chunks of chocolate. Place in a microwave-safe bowl, cover tightly with plastic wrap and microwave on High approximately 1 minute per ounce (28 g). (Times will vary depending upon the power of your microwave and the quantity of chocolate used.) Remove from microwave and stir until melted and smooth.

Coconut Macaroon Brownies

BROWNIE BATTER

4	squares (each 1 oz/28 g) unsweetened chocolate	4
¾ cup	butter or margarine	175 mL
2 cups	granulated sugar	500 mL
3	eggs	3
1 tsp	vanilla	5 mL
1 cup	all-purpose flour	250 mL
1 cup	chopped almonds, toasted	250 mL

COCONUT MACAROON BATTER

8 oz	cream cheese, softened	250 g
⅔ cup	granulated sugar	150 mL
2	eggs	2
2 tbsp	all-purpose flour	25 mL
2 cups	flaked coconut	500 mL
1 cup	chopped almonds, toasted (see page 14)	250 mL

CHOCOLATE GLAZE

2	squares (each 1 oz/28 g) semi-sweet chocolate, melted	2
	Whole almonds (optional)	

- *Preheat oven to 350°F (180°C)*
- *13- by 9-inch (3.5 L) cake pan, greased*

1. *Brownie Batter:* In a saucepan over low heat, melt chocolate and butter, stirring constantly, until smooth. Set aside to cool slightly.

2. When chocolate mixture has cooled, stir in sugar. Add eggs and vanilla and mix until blended. Blend in flour. Stir in almonds. Spread batter evenly in prepared pan.

3. *Coconut macaroon batter:* In a large bowl, beat cream cheese and sugar until smooth. Add eggs, one at a time, beating until incorporated. Blend in flour. Stir in coconut and almonds.

4. Spread coconut macaroon batter evenly over brownie batter and bake for 35 to 40 minutes or until a tester inserted in the center comes out clean. Place pan on a wire rack to cool completely, then drizzle with melted chocolate. Cut into squares and, if desired, place 1 whole almond on top of each.

Makes 36 brownies

Malted Milk Brownies

1½ cups	all-purpose flour	375 mL
½ tsp	baking powder	2 mL
½ tsp	salt	2 mL
4	squares (each 1 oz/28 g) semi-sweet chocolate	4
2	squares (each 1 oz/28 g) unsweetened chocolate	2
¾ cup	butter or margarine	175 mL
4	eggs, beaten	4
1½ cups	granulated sugar	375 mL
1 tbsp	vanilla	15 mL
TOPPING		
3 tbsp	milk	45 mL
1 tsp	vanilla	5 mL
¾ cup	unsweetened malted milk powder	175 mL
3 tbsp	butter or margarine, softened	45 mL
1 cup	confectioner's (icing) sugar, sifted	250 mL

TIP: For an added treat, chop malted milk balls or a malted milk chocolate bar into pieces and sprinkle over top.

- *Preheat oven to 350°F (180°C)*
- *13- by 9-inch (3.5 L) cake pan, greased*

1. In a small bowl, mix together flour, baking powder and salt.
2. In a saucepan, over low heat, melt chocolates and butter, stirring constantly, until smooth. Remove from heat and set aside to cool slightly.
3. When mixture has cooled, stir in sugar. Add eggs and vanilla and beat until blended. Blend in flour mixture.
4. Spread batter evenly in prepared pan. Bake in preheated oven for 25 to 30 minutes, until tester inserted in the center comes out clean. Place pan on a wire rack to cool completely.
5. *Topping:* In a small bowl, combine milk, vanilla and malted milk powder until blended. In another bowl, cream butter. Gradually add confectioner's sugar, alternately with milk mixture, beating well after each addition until mixture is smooth and spreadable. Spread evenly over cooled brownies. When topping is firm, cut into squares.

Makes 36 brownies

Orange Cream Walnut Brownies

BASE

½ cup	butter or margarine, softened	125 mL
2 tbsp	confectioner's (icing) sugar, sifted	25 mL
1 cup	all-purpose flour	250 mL

TOPPING

2 tbsp	all-purpose flour	25 mL
½ tsp	baking powder	2 mL
Pinch	salt	Pinch
2	eggs, beaten	2
1 cup	packed brown sugar	250 mL
½ cup	flaked coconut	125 mL
1 cup	chopped walnuts	250 mL

ORANGE CREAM FROSTING

1¼ cups	confectioner's (icing) sugar, sifted	300 mL
2 tbsp	butter or margarine, melted	25 mL
1½ tsp	grated orange zest	7 mL
1½ tsp	orange juice	7 mL

TIP: To get every drop of juice from citrus fruits, bring them to room temperature and roll them on the counter before squeezing.

- *Preheat oven to 350°F (180°C)*
- *9-inch (2.5 L) square cake pan, ungreased*

1. *Base:* In a medium bowl, beat butter and confectioner's sugar until smooth and creamy. Gradually add flour, mixing until a soft dough forms. Press evenly into bottom of pan. Bake in preheated oven for 10 minutes or until golden brown. Place pan on a wire rack to cool for 5 minutes.

2. *Topping:* In a medium bowl mix together flour, baking powder and salt. Add eggs and brown sugar and beat until just combined. Stir in coconut and nuts. Spoon evenly over baked crust. Bake 25 minutes longer or until top is firm. Place pan on a wire rack to cool completely, then frost with Orange Cream Frosting.

3. *Frosting:* In a small bowl, beat icing sugar, butter and orange juice until blended and smooth. Add zest and mix well. Spread evenly over cooled cake, then cut into squares.

Makes 24 brownies

Peanut Butter Brownies

¾ cup	smooth peanut butter	175 mL
¼ cup	milk	50 mL
2 cups	packed brown sugar	500 mL
2	eggs	2
1 cup	all-purpose flour	250 mL
FROSTING AND GLAZE		
¾ cup	smooth peanut butter, divided	175 mL
4	squares (each 1 oz/28 g) semi-sweet chocolate	4

- *Preheat oven to 350°F (180°C)*
- *9-inch (2.5 L) square cake pan, greased*

1. In a saucepan, over low heat, melt peanut butter in milk, stirring constantly. Remove from heat and set aside to cool slightly.
2. When mixture has cooled, stir in sugar. Add eggs and beat until just combined. Blend in flour.
3. Spread evenly in prepared pan. Bake in preheated oven for 35 to 40 minutes or until a tester inserted in the center comes out clean. Place pan on a wire rack to cool completely.
4. *Frosting:* In a saucepan, over low heat, melt ½ cup (125 mL) peanut butter with chocolate, stirring constantly, until smooth. Spread evenly over cooled brownies.
5. In another saucepan, over low heat, melt remaining peanut butter, stirring, until smooth. (Alternatively, in a microwaveable bowl, heat peanut butter on High for about 1 minute, until melted.) Spoon over frosting, then swirl with a knife to create a marble effect. Chill until firm, then cut into squares.

Makes 24 brownies

Rocky Road Brownies

BASE

2 cups	all-purpose flour	500 mL
1 tsp	baking soda	5 mL
½ cup	shortening	125 mL
½ cup	butter or margarine	125 mL
1 cup	strong, brewed coffee	250 mL
¼ cup	unsweetened cocoa powder, sifted	50 mL
2 cups	granulated sugar	500 mL
2	eggs	2
1 tsp	vanilla	5 mL
½ cup	buttermilk	125 mL

FROSTING

¼ cup	milk	50 mL
½ cup	butter or margarine	125 mL
2 tbsp	unsweetened cocoa powder, sifted	25 mL
1 tsp	vanilla	5 mL
3½ cups	confectioner's (icing) sugar, sifted	875 mL

TOPPING

1 cup	white mini marshmallows	250 mL
½ cup	unsalted peanuts	125 mL
3	squares (each 1 oz/28 g) semi-sweet chocolate, melted	3

TIP: For fast, easy cleanup when food is stuck to pans, boil a little vinegar and water in the pan before washing. You won't need to do any scrubbing.

- *Preheat oven to 400°F (200°C)*
- *13- by 9-inch (3.5 L) cake pan, greased*

1. *Base:* In a medium bowl, mix together flour and baking soda.
2. In a large saucepan, over medium heat, bring shortening, butter, coffee and cocoa to a boil, stirring constantly. Remove from heat and set aside to cool slightly.
3. When mixture has cooled, stir in sugar. Beat in eggs and vanilla. Gradually blend in flour mixture, alternately with buttermilk, until just incorporated. Spread evenly in prepared pan. Bake in preheated oven for 35 minutes or until a tester inserted in the center comes out clean.
4. *Frosting:* In a saucepan, over low heat, heat milk, butter and cocoa, stirring constantly, until steaming (not boiling). Remove from heat. Gradually add confectioner's sugar, beating until mixture is smooth and spreadable. Beat in vanilla. Spread frosting over warm cake.
5. *Topping:* Sprinkle marshmallows and peanuts evenly over cake. Bake 2 to 3 minutes longer, until marshmallows are slightly melted. Drizzle melted chocolate over top. Place pan on a wire rack to cool completely, then cut into squares.

Makes 36 brownies

Sour Cream Coffee Brownies

BASE

¾ cup	all-purpose flour	175 mL
½ tsp	baking powder	2 mL
¼ tsp	salt	1 mL
¾ cup	butter or margarine, softened	175 mL
6	squares (each 1 oz/28 g) semi-sweet chocolate	6
1 tbsp	instant coffee powder	15 mL
¾ cup	packed brown sugar	175 mL
2	eggs	2
1 tsp	vanilla	5 mL

CHEESECAKE TOPPING

8 oz	cream cheese, softened	250 g
½ cup	granulated sugar	125 mL
2	eggs	2
1 tsp	vanilla	5 mL
3 tbsp	coffee liqueur or strong coffee	45 mL
½ tsp	ground cinnamon	2 mL
2 tbsp	all-purpose flour	25 mL

SOUR CREAM TOPPING

1½ cups	sour cream	375 mL
⅓ cup	granulated sugar	75 mL

- *Preheat oven to 350°F (180°C)*
- *13- by 9-inch (3.5 L) cake pan, greased*

1. *Base:* In a small bowl, mix together flour, baking powder and salt.
2. In a large saucepan, over low heat, heat butter, chocolate and coffee, stirring until mixture is smooth and melted and coffee has dissolved. Set aside to cool slightly.
3. When mixture has cooled, stir in brown sugar. Add eggs and vanilla and beat until combined. Blend in flour mixture. Spread batter evenly in prepared pan.
4. *Cheesecake Topping:* In a medium bowl, beat cream cheese and sugar until smooth. Beat in eggs, one at a time, until incorporated. Stir in vanilla, liqueur and cinnamon until blended. Blend in flour. Spread evenly over base. Bake 20 minutes longer or until top is almost set.
5. *Sour Cream Topping:* In a small bowl, mix together sour cream and sugar. Spread carefully over top of brownies. Bake for 10 minutes longer. Place pan on a wire rack to cool completely, then cut into squares.

Makes 36 brownies

Chocolate Fudge Cake Brownies

2 cups	cake flour, sifted	500 mL
2 tsp	baking powder	10 mL
½ tsp	salt	2 mL
½ cup	butter, margarine or shortening, softened	125 mL
1 cup	granulated sugar	250 mL
1	egg	1
2	squares (each 1 oz/28 g) unsweetened chocolate, melted	2
1 tsp	vanilla	5 mL
¾ cup	milk	175 mL
	No-Cook Fudge Frosting (see recipe, page 363) (optional)	

- *Preheat oven to 325°F (160°C)*
- *8-inch (2 L) square cake pan, greased*

1. In a medium bowl, mix together flour, baking powder and salt.
2. In a large bowl, beat butter and sugar until smooth and creamy. Beat in egg until incorporated. Stir in melted chocolate and vanilla. Gradually blend in flour mixture alternately with milk until just incorporated.
3. Spread batter evenly in prepared pan. Bake in preheated oven for 55 to 60 minutes, or until tester inserted in the center comes out clean. Place pan on a wire rack to cool completely. If desired, frost, then cut into squares.

Makes 16 brownies

Chocolate Pecan Brownies

1 cup	all-purpose flour	250 mL
Pinch	salt	Pinch
⅔ cup	chopped pecans	150 mL
½ cup	butter or margarine, softened	125 mL
1 cup	granulated sugar	250 mL
3	eggs	3
2 tsp	vanilla	10 mL
¾ cup	chocolate-flavored syrup	175 mL
	Whole pecans for garnish (optional)	
	Confectioner's (icing) sugar (optional)	

- *Preheat oven to 350°F (180°C)*
- *9-inch (2.5 L) square cake pan, greased*

1. In a small bowl, mix together flour, salt and pecans.
2. In a large bowl, beat butter and sugar until smooth and creamy. Add eggs, one at a time, beating until incorporated. Stir in vanilla and chocolate syrup. Blend in flour mixture.
3. Spread batter evenly in prepared pan. Bake in preheated oven for 35 to 40 minutes or until a tester inserted in the center comes out clean. Place pan on a wire rack to cool completely, then cut into squares. Garnish each brownie with a pecan or dust with confectioner's sugar, if desired.

Makes 24 brownies

> **VARIATION**
> **Chocolate Walnut Brownies**
> Substitute walnuts for the pecans.

Raspberry Cream Cheese Brownies

FILLING

8 oz	cream cheese, softened	250 g
3 tbsp	granulated sugar	45 mL
1	egg	1
1 tsp	vanilla	5 mL

BASE AND TOPPING

½ cup	butter or margarine, softened	125 mL
¾ cup + 1 tbsp	granulated sugar	190 mL
1	egg	1
3	squares (each 1 oz/28 g) semi-sweet chocolate, melted and cooled	3
2	squares (each 1 oz/28 g) unsweetened chocolate, melted and cooled	2
1 cup	all-purpose flour	250 mL
Pinch	salt	Pinch
¼ cup	raspberry jam	50 mL

- *Preheat oven to 350°F (180°C)*
- *8-inch (2 L) square cake pan, greased*

1. *Filling:* In a small bowl, beat cream cheese and sugar until smooth. Add egg and beat until incorporated. Stir in vanilla. Set aside.
2. *Base and Topping:* In a large bowl, beat butter and sugar until smooth and creamy. Beat in egg until incorporated. Stir in melted chocolates. Blend in flour and salt. Set aside 1 cup (250 mL) of mixture and spread remainder evenly in prepared pan. Spread filling evenly over batter. Drop reserved batter, by spoonfuls, over filling. Using a teaspoon (5 mL), drop jam on top of batter. Run a knife through the jam and batter to make a zigzag design.
3. Bake in preheated oven for 35 to 40 minutes or until a tester inserted in the center comes out almost clean, but with just a few moist crumbs. Place pan on a wire rack to cool completely, then cut into squares.

Makes 16 brownies

1-2-3 Brownies

1	package (14 oz/425 g) fudge brownie mix	1
⅓ cup	water	75 mL
¼ cup	plain yogurt	50 mL

TIP: For a quick and easy chocolate frosting, melt a large bittersweet or milk chocolate bar and spread over cake.

- *Preheat oven to 350°F (180°C)*
- *8-inch (2 L) square cake pan, greased*

1. In a large bowl, mix together brownie mix, water and yogurt until well combined. Spread batter evenly in prepared pan. Bake in preheated oven for 25 minutes or until a tester inserted in the center comes out clean. Place pan on a wire rack to cool completely, then cut into squares.

Makes 16 brownies

Brownies from a Mix

2¼ cups	packed Cake Brownie Mix (see recipe, below)	550 mL
2	eggs, beaten	2
1 tsp	vanilla	5 mL
½ cup	chopped walnuts	125 mL

TIP: If you accidentally break an egg on the floor, sprinkle heavily with salt and leave for 5 to 10 minutes. The dried egg will sweep easily into your dustpan.

- *Preheat oven to 350°F (180°C)*
- *8-inch (2 L) square cake pan, greased*

1. In a large bowl, mix together Cake Brownie Mix, eggs and vanilla until blended. Stir in walnuts.
2. Spread batter evenly in prepared pan. Bake in preheated oven for 30 to 35 minutes or until a tester inserted in the center comes out clean. Place pan on a wire rack to cool completely, then cut into squares.

Makes 16 brownies

Cake Brownie Mix

2 cups	granulated sugar	500 mL
1 cup	all-purpose flour	250 mL
¾ cup	unsweetened cocoa powder, sifted	175 mL
1 tsp	baking powder	5 mL
¾ tsp	salt	4 mL
1 cup	shortening, softened	250 mL

1. In a large bowl, mix together sugar, flour, cocoa, baking powder and salt. Using two knives, a pastry blender or your fingers, cut in shortening until mixture resembles coarse crumbs. Store in an airtight container in a cool, dry place.

Makes 4½ packed cups (1.125 L)

Chocolate Banana Brownies

1	package (15.5 oz/440 g) chocolate chip brownie mix		1
⅔ cup	finely chopped walnuts	150 mL	
1 cup	mashed ripe bananas (2 or 3 medium)	250 mL	
	Chocolate Butter Frosting (see page 360)		

> **TIP:** If desired, sprinkle top of brownies with some chopped nuts, or when serving, place 2 or 3 thin slices of fresh banana on top.

- *Preheat oven to 350°F (180°C)*
- *13- by 9-inch (3.5 L) cake pan, greased*

1. Prepare mix according to package directions. Add walnuts and bananas and mix until blended. Spread batter evenly in prepared pan. Bake in preheated oven for 25 to 30 minutes or until tester inserted in the center comes out clean. Place pan on a wire rack to cool completely. Frost with Chocolate Butter Frosting. Cut into squares.

Makes 36 brownies

Black Forest Brownies

1	package (14 oz/425 g) fudge brownie mix		1
4 oz	cream cheese, softened	125 g	
¼ cup	granulated sugar	50 mL	
2	eggs		2
1 tsp	vanilla	5 mL	
2 tbsp	all-purpose flour	25 mL	
1	can (19 oz/540 mL) cherry pie filling		1
¼ cup	semi-sweet chocolate chips	50 mL	

- *Preheat oven to 350°F (180°C)*
- *13- by 9-inch (3.5 L) cake pan, greased*

1. Prepare brownie mix according to package directions. Spread half the batter evenly in prepared pan. Set remainder aside.
2. In a medium bowl, beat cream cheese and sugar until smooth. Beat in eggs, one at a time, until incorporated. Stir in vanilla. Blend in flour. Set aside.
3. Spread pie filling evenly over top of batter in pan. Sprinkle chocolate chips evenly across top. Spoon cream cheese mixture over chocolate chips. Drop remaining batter by spoonfuls over cream cheese mixture. Using a knife, lightly draw circles in cream cheese and top layer of fudge batters to create marbling effect. Bake in preheated oven for 45 to 50 minutes or until a tester inserted in the centre comes out clean. Place pan on a wire rack to cool completely, then cut into squares.

Makes 36 brownies

Apricot Almond Biscotti *(page 108)* ➢

Unbelievable Orange Brownies

1	package (14 oz/425 g) fudge brownie mix	1
1	whole orange	1

- *Preheat oven to 350°F (180°C)*
- *8-inch (2 L) square cake pan, greased*

1. Wash orange, cut into quarters and remove the seeds. In a food processor, process until almost smooth.
2. Prepare brownies as directed on package, but substitute the processed orange for the quantity of water in the package instructions.
3. Bake as directed. Place pan on a wire rack to cool completely, then cut into squares.

Makes 16 brownies

Broadway Blondies

1½ cups	all-purpose flour	375 mL
1½ tsp	baking powder	7 mL
½ tsp	salt	2 mL
½ cup	butter	125 mL
1½ cups	packed brown sugar	375 mL
2	eggs	2
1½ tsp	vanilla	7 mL
¾ cup	coarsely chopped pecans	175 mL

> *Blondies are brownies with a butterscotch rather than a chocolate flavor.*

- *Preheat oven to 325°F (160°C)*
- *9-inch (2.5 L) square cake pan, greased*

1. In a small bowl, mix together flour, baking powder and salt.
2. In a large saucepan, over low heat, melt butter. Gradually add sugar, stirring until smooth. Set aside to cool slightly.
3. When butter mixture has cooled, add eggs and vanilla and beat until just blended. Blend in flour mixture. Stir in pecans.
4. Spread batter evenly in prepared pan. Bake in preheated oven for 50 to 60 minutes or until a tester inserted in the center comes out clean. Place pan on a wire rack to cool completely, then cut into squares.

Makes 24 blondies

◄ Original Scottish Shortbread *(page 122)*

Chocolate Chip Blondies

2 cups	all-purpose flour	500 mL
1 tsp	baking powder	5 mL
¼ tsp	salt	1 mL
⅔ cup	butter, softened	150 mL
2 cups	packed brown sugar	500 mL
2	eggs	2
1 cup	semi-sweet chocolate chips	250 mL
1 cup	peanut butter chips	250 mL
½ cup	coarsely chopped walnuts	125 mL
½ cup	coarsely chopped pecans	125 mL

- *Preheat oven to 350°F (180°C)*
- *13- by 9-inch (3.5 L) cake pan, greased*

1. In a medium bowl, mix together flour, baking powder and salt.
2. In a large bowl, beat butter and brown sugar until smooth and creamy. Add eggs, one at a time, beating until incorporated. Stir in vanilla. Blend in flour mixture. Stir in chocolate and peanut butter chips, walnuts and pecans.
3. Spread batter evenly in prepared pan. Bake in preheated oven for 30 to 35 minutes or until golden brown. Place pan on a wire rack to cool completely, then cut into squares.

Makes 30 blondies

> **TIP:** If you can't live without chocolate, add chocolate chips to a blondie batter.

Toffee-Spice-Raisin Blondies

2 cups	all-purpose flour	500 mL
½ tsp	baking soda	2 mL
½ tsp	ground cinnamon	2 mL
½ tsp	ground nutmeg	2 mL
¼ tsp	ground cloves	1 mL
1¼ cups	packed brown sugar	300 mL
1 cup	butter or margarine, softened	250 mL
2	eggs	2
2 tbsp	milk	25 mL
1½ cups	raisins	375 mL

- *Preheat oven to 375°F (190°C)*
- *13- by 9-inch (3.5 L) cake pan, greased*

1. In a medium bowl, mix together flour, baking soda, cinnamon, nutmeg and cloves.
2. In a large bowl, beat brown sugar and butter until smooth and creamy. Beat in eggs until incorporated. Stir in milk. Gradually blend in flour mixture. Stir in raisins.
3. Spread batter evenly in prepared pan. Bake in preheated oven for 20 minutes or until a tester inserted in the center comes out clean. Place pan on a wire rack to cool completely, then cut into squares.

Makes 36 blondies

Chocolate Bars and Squares

Chocolate Chip Nut Bars

BASE		
1 cup	all-purpose flour	250 mL
¼ cup	granulated sugar	50 mL
⅓ cup	butter or margarine	75 mL

TOPPING		
2 tbsp	butter or margarine	25 mL
1 cup	semi-sweet chocolate chips	250 mL
½ cup	light corn syrup	125 mL
½ cup	granulated sugar	125 mL
2	eggs	2
⅔ cup	chopped pecans or walnuts	150 mL

- *Preheat oven to 350°F (180°C)*
- *9-inch (2.5 L) square cake pan, greased*

1. *Base:* In a small bowl, mix together flour and sugar. Using two knives, a pastry blender or your fingers, work butter in until mixture resembles coarse crumbs. Press evenly into prepared pan. Bake in preheated oven for 12 to 15 minutes or until golden brown. Place pan on a rack to cool slightly.

2. *Topping:* In a large saucepan, over low heat, melt butter and chocolate chips, stirring until smooth. Remove from heat and set aside to cool slightly. When mixture has cooled, beat in sugar and corn syrup. Beat in eggs. Stir in nuts. Spread evenly over base and bake 25 to 35 minutes longer or until topping is set. Place pan on a wire rack to cool completely, then cut into bars.

Makes 24 bars

Chocodamias

¼ cup	butter or margarine	50 mL
6	squares (each 1 oz/28 g) semi-sweet chocolate, divided	6
¾ cup	granulated sugar	175 mL
2	eggs	2
1 tsp	vanilla	5 mL
1¼ cups	all-purpose flour	300 mL
½ tsp	baking powder	2 mL
¾ cup	chopped macadamia nuts	175 mL

TIP: Dry ingredients — such as baking powder, baking soda and cocoa — sometimes have a tendency to pack down in their containers, so stir to loosen before measuring.

- *Preheat oven to 350° F (180° C)*
- *9-inch (2.5 L) square cake pan, greased*

1. In a large saucepan, over low heat, melt butter and 3 squares of chocolate, stirring until smooth. Set aside to cool slightly. Chop remaining chocolate into chunks. Set aside.

2. When chocolate mixture has cooled, stir in sugar. Add eggs and vanilla, mixing just until incorporated. Blend in flour and baking powder. Stir in chopped chocolate and nuts. Spread evenly in prepared pan. Bake in preheated oven for 20 to 25 minutes or until a tester inserted in center comes out clean. Place pan on a wire rack to cool completely, then cut into bars.

Makes 24 bars

Gooey Caramel-Pecan Chocolate Bars

BASE

1 cup	all-purpose flour	250 mL
¼ cup	granulated sugar	50 mL
Pinch	salt	Pinch
6 tbsp	cold butter	90 mL
3 tbsp	ice water	45 mL

FILLING

3 tbsp	butter	45 mL
⅓ cup	light corn syrup	75 mL
1⅓ cups	packed brown sugar	325 mL
½ cup	whipping (35%) cream	125 mL
1 tsp	white vinegar	5 mL
Pinch	salt	Pinch
1 tsp	vanilla	5 mL

TOPPING

¾ cup	chopped pecans, toasted (on page 14)	175 mL
3	squares (each 1 oz/28 g) semi-sweet chocolate	3

> **TIP:** To keep salt easy to pour, add a few grains of rice to the salt shaker.

- Preheat oven to 425°F (220°C)
- 8-inch (2 L) square cake pan, lined with greased foil

1. *Base:* In a medium bowl, mix together flour, sugar and salt. Using two knives, a pastry blender or your fingers, cut butter in until mixture resembles coarse crumbs. Sprinkle water, 1 tbsp (15 mL) at a time, over mixture, mixing lightly after each addition. (Dough should just be moist enough to hold together.) Press evenly into prepared pan. Bake in preheated oven for 15 to 20 minutes or until golden brown. Place pan on a rack to cool completely.

2. *Filling:* In a saucepan, over high heat, combine butter, syrup, brown sugar, cream, vinegar and salt. Bring to a boil, reduce heat to low and simmer, stirring constantly, for 5 minutes. Remove from heat and stir in vanilla until bubbling stops (about 20 seconds). Pour filling over cooled base.

3. *Topping:* Sprinkle top with pecans and set aside to cool. In a small saucepan, over low heat, melt chocolate, stirring until smooth. Cool slightly, then drizzle over pecans. Chill until chocolate sets. Using foil to lift, transfer to a cutting board and cut into bars.

Makes 18 bars

Easy Chocolate Delight Bars

BASE

1¼ cups	all-purpose flour	300 mL
1 tsp	baking powder	5 mL
½ cup	butter or margarine, melted	125 mL
1 tsp	granulated sugar	5 mL
1	egg yolk	1
2 tbsp	water	25 mL
2 cups	semi-sweet chocolate chips or chunks	500 mL

TOPPING

2	eggs	2
¾ cup	granulated sugar	175 mL
6 tbsp	butter, melted	90 mL
2 tsp	vanilla	10 mL
2 cups	finely chopped nuts	500 mL

- *Preheat oven to 350°F (180°C)*
- *13- by 9-inch (3.5 L) cake pan, greased*

1. *Base:* In a small bowl, mix together flour and baking powder.
2. In a large bowl, beat butter, sugar, egg yolk and water until blended. Blend in flour mixture. Press mixture evenly into prepared pan. Bake in preheated oven for 10 minutes. Sprinkle chocolate chips over top and bake 1 minute longer or until chocolate begins to melt. Remove from oven and spread chocolate evenly over top of base. Place pan on a wire rack to cool slightly.
3. *Topping:* Beat eggs, sugar, melted butter and vanilla until smooth and blended. Stir in nuts. Spread over top of chocolate. Bake 30 to 35 minutes longer or until a tester inserted in the center comes out clean.

Makes 36 bars

Fudgey Toffee Bars

½ cup	butter or margarine, melted	125 mL
1½ cups	graham wafer crumbs (about 22 wafers)	375 mL
1	can (10 oz/300 mL) sweetened condensed milk	1
1 cup	toffee bits	250 mL
1 cup	semi-sweet chocolate chips	250 mL
1 cup	chopped nuts	250 mL

- *Preheat oven to 350°F (180°C)*
- *13- by 9-inch (3.5 L) cake pan, lightly greased*

1. In a small bowl, mix together melted butter and graham wafer crumbs. Press evenly into prepared pan.
2. Pour condensed milk evenly over base. Sprinkle an even layer of toffee bits over milk, then a layer of chocolate chips, then a layer of nuts. Using a spatula, firmly press top layer into base.
3. Bake in preheated oven for 20 to 25 minutes or until lightly browned. Place pan on a wire rack to cool completely, then cut into bars.

Makes 36 bars

Fudgey Chocolate Oatmeal Bars

BASE

3 cups	quick-cooking oats	750 mL
2½ cups	all-purpose flour	625 mL
1 tsp	baking soda	5 mL
1 tsp	salt	5 mL
1 cup	butter or margarine, softened	250 mL
2 cups	packed brown sugar	500 mL
2	eggs	2
2 tsp	vanilla	10 mL

TOPPING

1	can (14 oz/398 mL) sweetened condensed milk	1
2 cups	semi-sweet chocolate chips	500 mL
2 tbsp	butter or margarine	25 mL
½ tsp	salt	2 mL
2 tsp	vanilla	10 mL
1 cup	chopped walnuts	250 mL

TIP: To freshen stale nuts, spread them on a baking sheet and heat in a 250°F (120°C) oven for 5 to 10 minutes.

- *Preheat oven to 350°F (180°C)*
- *13- by 9-inch (3.5 L) cake pan, greased*

1. *Base:* In a large bowl, mix together oats, flour, baking soda and salt.
2. In another large bowl, beat butter and brown sugar until smooth and creamy. Beat in eggs until incorporated. Stir in vanilla. Blend in flour mixture. Press two-thirds of mixture evenly into prepared pan. Set remainder aside.
3. *Topping:* In a saucepan over low heat, combine condensed milk, chocolate chips, butter and salt, stirring until chocolate is melted and mixture is smooth. Remove from heat and stir in vanilla and walnuts. Spread evenly over base, then sprinkle top with reserved base mixture. Bake in preheated oven for 25 to 30 minutes or until top is golden brown. Place pan on a wire rack to cool completely, then cut into bars.

Buttermilk Chocolate Squares

2	squares (each 1 oz/28 g) unsweetened chocolate, coarsely chopped	2
½ cup	boiling water	125 mL
2 cups	cake flour, sifted	500 mL
2 tsp	baking powder	10 mL
½ tsp	baking soda	2 mL
½ tsp	salt	2 mL
½ cup	shortening, softened	125 mL
2 cups	packed brown sugar	500 mL
2	eggs, separated	2
1 tsp	vanilla	5 mL
½ cup	buttermilk	125 mL
½ cup	water	125 mL
½ cup	chopped nuts	125 mL

COCOA FROSTING

6 tbsp	butter, softened	90 mL
½ cup	unsweetened cocoa powder, sifted	125 mL
3½ cups	confectioner's (icing) sugar, sifted	875 mL
¼ cup	milk (approximate)	50 mL
1½ tsp	vanilla	7 mL

TIP: When melting chocolate for any recipe, mix a little flour into the remains of melted chocolate. It gets the last bit of chocolate out of the pan and into the batter.

- Preheat oven to 350°F (180°C)
- 13- by 9-inch (3.5 L) cake pan, greased

1. In a saucepan, over low heat, stir chocolate with boiling water until chocolate is melted and smooth. Set aside to cool for 10 minutes.
2. In a medium bowl, mix together flour, baking powder, baking soda and salt.
3. In a large bowl, beat shortening and brown sugar until smooth and creamy. Beat in egg yolks until incorporated. Stir in vanilla and chocolate mixture. Gradually blend in flour mixture alternately with buttermilk, then water, until just incorporated. Stir in nuts.
4. In a clean bowl, beat egg whites until soft peaks form. Fold into batter, then spread mixture evenly in prepared pan. Bake in preheated oven for 35 to 40 minutes or until a tester inserted in the center comes out clean. Place pan on a wire rack to cool completely.
5. *Frosting:* In a large bowl, beat butter and cocoa until smooth. Gradually add confectioner's sugar alternately with milk, beating until smooth. (Add just enough milk to make the right consistency for spreading.) Beat in vanilla. Spread evenly over cake. Cut into squares.

Makes 36 squares

Chocolate Carrot Nut Squares

2 cups	all-purpose flour	500 mL
1/3 cup	unsweetened cocoa powder, sifted	75 mL
2 tsp	baking powder	10 mL
2 tsp	ground cinnamon	10 mL
1 1/4 tsp	baking soda	6 mL
1 tsp	salt	5 mL
1 1/2 cups	granulated sugar	375 mL
4	eggs, beaten	4
1 1/2 cups	vegetable oil	375 mL
1 tsp	vanilla	5 mL
2 cups	grated carrots	500 mL
1/2 cup	flaked coconut	125 mL
1/2 cup	chopped pecans	125 mL
2 cups	crushed pineapple, drained	500 mL
	Chocolate Butter Frosting (see page 360) or Chocolate Velvet Frosting (see page 362) (optional)	
	Crushed pineapple (optional)	

- *Preheat oven to 350°F (180°C)*
- *13- by 9-inch (3.5 L) cake pan, greased*

1. In a large bowl mix together flour, cocoa, baking powder, cinnamon, baking soda and salt. Make a well in the center. Add sugar, eggs, oil and vanilla; mix until blended. Stir in carrots, coconut, pecans and pineapple.

2. Spread evenly in prepared pan. Bake in preheated oven for 50 to 55 minutes or until a tester inserted in the center comes out clean. Place pan on a wire rack to cool completely. Frost, then spread crushed pineapple over top, if desired. Cut into squares.

Makes 36 squares

Viennese Chocolate Bars

BASE

1 cup	butter, softened	250 mL
½ cup	granulated sugar	125 mL
2	egg yolks	2
2½ cups	all-purpose flour	625 mL

FILLING

1	jar (10 oz/284 mL) raspberry jam or jelly	1
1 cup	semi-sweet chocolate chips	250 mL

TOPPING

4	egg whites	4
¼ tsp	salt	1 mL
1 cup	granulated sugar	250 mL
2 cups	finely chopped pecans	500 mL

TIP: If you have jam, jelly or syrup that has crystallized, place the bottle in a pan of cold water and heat gently. The crystals will disappear.

- *Preheat oven to 350°F (180°C)*
- *13- by 9-inch (3.5 L) cake pan, greased*

1. *Base:* In a large bowl, beat butter and sugar until smooth and creamy. Beat in egg yolks until incorporated. Blend in flour. Shape dough into a ball and knead lightly. Press evenly into prepared pan. Bake in preheated oven for 15 to 20 minutes or until lightly browned. Place pan on rack to cool slightly.

2. *Filling:* Stir jam or jelly until smooth, then spread evenly over base. Sprinkle chocolate chips evenly over top. Set aside.

3. *Topping:* In a bowl, beat egg whites with salt until frothy. Gradually beat in sugar until stiff peaks form. Fold in pecans. Spread gently over chocolate chips and bake 25 minutes longer or until lightly browned. Place pan on a wire rack to cool completely, then cut into bars.

Makes 36 bars

Mashed Potato Chocolate Squares

2 cups	all-purpose flour	500 mL
3½ tsp	baking powder	17 mL
1 tsp	ground cinnamon	5 mL
½ tsp	ground nutmeg	2 mL
½ tsp	ground mace	2 mL
½ tsp	ground cloves	2 mL
½ cup	milk	125 mL
2 cups	granulated sugar	500 mL
⅔ cup	butter or margarine, softened	150 mL
4	eggs	4
1 cup	hot mashed potatoes	250 mL
2	squares (each 1 oz/28 g) unsweetened chocolate, melted	2
1 cup	chopped nuts	250 mL
	Chocolate Butter Frosting (see recipe, page 360) or Chocolate Velvet Frosting (see recipe, page 362)	

- *Preheat oven to 350° F (180° C)*
- *13- by 9-inch (3.5 L) cake pan, greased*

1. In a medium bowl, mix together flour, baking powder, cinnamon, nutmeg, mace and cloves.

2. In a large bowl, beat sugar and butter until smooth and creamy. Beat in eggs, one at a time, until incorporated. Add potatoes and chocolate and mix well. Gradually blend in flour mixture alternately with milk until just incorporated. Stir in nuts.

3. Spread evenly in prepared pan. Bake in preheated oven for 30 to 35 minutes or until a tester inserted in the center comes out clean. Place pan on a wire rack to cool completely, then frost with a chocolate frosting of your choice. Cut into squares.

Makes 36 squares

Cherry Pie Cocoa Bars

1¾ cup	all-purpose flour	425 mL
¼ cup	unsweetened cocoa powder, sifted	50 mL
1 cup	granulated sugar	250 mL
1 cup	butter	250 mL
1	egg, lightly beaten	1
1 tsp	almond extract	5 mL
1	can (19 oz/540 mL) cherry pie filling	1
2 cups	semi-sweet chocolate chips	500 mL
1 cup	chopped almonds	250 mL

- *Preheat oven to 350°F (180°C)*
- *13- by 9-inch (3.5 L) cake pan, greased*

1. In a large bowl, mix together flour, cocoa and sugar. Using two knives, a pastry blender or your fingers, work butter in until mixture resembles coarse crumbs. Add egg and almond extract and mix until blended. Set aside 1 cup (250 mL) of mixture for topping and press remainder evenly into prepared pan. Spoon pie filling evenly over base.

2. In a large bowl, combine chocolate chips, almonds and reserved base mixture. Sprinkle over top of filling. Bake in preheated oven for 35 to 40 minutes, until top is golden. Chill for 2 to 3 hours, then cut into bars.

Makes 36 bars

Raspberry Chocolate Crumb Squares

BASE

1½ cups	quick-cooking rolled oats	375 mL
1½ cups	all-purpose flour	375 mL
½ cup	granulated sugar	125 mL
½ cup	packed brown sugar	125 mL
1 tsp	baking powder	5 mL
Pinch	salt	Pinch
1 cup	butter or margarine	250 mL

TOPPING

1 cup	raspberry jam or preserves	250 mL
1 cup	semi-sweet chocolate chips	250 mL
¼ cup	chopped almonds	50 mL
3	squares (each 1 oz/28 g) semi-sweet chocolate, chopped into small pieces	3

- *Preheat oven to 375°F (190°C)*
- *9-inch (2.5 L) square cake pan, ungreased*

1. *Base:* In a large bowl, mix together oats, flour, sugars, baking powder and salt. Using two knives, a pastry blender or your fingers, cut butter in until mixture resembles coarse crumbs. Set aside 1 cup (250 mL) of mixture and press remainder evenly into prepared pan. Bake in preheated oven for 10 minutes. Place pan on rack to cool slightly.

2. *Topping:* Stir jam until smooth and spread evenly over warm base. Sprinkle chocolate chips evenly over jam.

3. Combine reserved oat mixture with almonds. Sprinkle evenly over chocolate and gently pat down. Bake 30 to 35 minutes longer or until golden brown. Place pan on a wire rack to cool completely.

4. In a saucepan, over low heat, melt chocolate, stirring until smooth. Set aside to cool slightly. When cake has cooled, drizzle melted chocolate over top. Set aside until chocolate sets, then cut into squares.

Makes 24 squares

Chocolate Macaroon Bars

BASE

⅓ cup	butter or margarine, melted	75 mL
⅓ cup	granulated sugar	75 mL
1¼ cups	graham wafer crumbs (about 17 or 18 wafers)	300 mL
¼ cup	unsweetened cocoa powder, sifted	50 mL

TOPPING

2 cups	fresh white bread crumbs (about 4 slices)	500 mL
2⅔ cups	flaked coconut	650 mL
1	can (14 oz/398 mL) sweetened condensed milk	1
2	eggs, lightly beaten	2
2 tsp	vanilla	10 mL
1 cup	semi-sweet mini chocolate chips	250 mL

- *Preheat oven to 350°F (180°C)*
- *13- by 9-inch (3.5 L) cake pan, lightly greased*

1. *Base:* In a medium bowl, mix together butter, sugar, graham crumbs and cocoa until blended. Press evenly into prepared pan. Bake in preheated oven for 10 minutes.

2. *Topping:* In a large bowl, mix together bread crumbs, coconut, milk, eggs and vanilla. Stir in chocolate chips. Spread evenly over baked base. Bake 30 minutes longer or until lightly browned. Place pan on a wire rack to cool completely, then cut into bars. Store, covered, in refrigerator.

Makes 36 bars

Chocolate Chip Dream Bars

½ cup	butter or margarine, melted	125 mL
1½ cups	graham wafer crumbs (about 22 wafers)	375 mL
1	can (14 oz/398 mL) sweetened condensed milk	1
1 cup	semi-sweet chocolate chips	250 mL
1 cup	flaked coconut	250 mL
1 cup	chopped nuts	250 mL

- *Preheat oven to 350°F (180° C)*
- *13- by 9-inch (3.5 L) cake pan, lightly greased*

1. In a small bowl, mix together butter and graham wafer crumbs. Press evenly into prepared pan. Pour condensed milk over base.

2. Working in layers, sprinkle evenly with chocolate chips, then coconut, then nuts. Using a spatula, press down firmly. Bake in preheated oven for 25 to 30 minutes or until top is golden. Place pan on a wire rack to cool completely, then cut into bars.

Makes 36 bars

TIP: For a healthy snack, combine raisins and nuts left over from baking and chop coarsely.

Chocolate Mallow Sensations

FILLING

1	square (1 oz/28 g) unsweetened chocolate	1
2 tbsp	butter or margarine	25 mL
1/3 cup	chopped walnuts	75 mL

BASE

3/4 cup	all-purpose flour	175 mL
1 tsp	baking powder	5 mL
1/2 tsp	salt	2 mL
1 1/4 cups	packed brown sugar	300 mL
2	eggs	2
1/2 cup	flaked coconut	125 mL

TOPPING

20	large marshmallows, cut in half	20
2 tbsp	butter or margarine	25 mL
2	squares (each 1 oz/28 g) unsweetened chocolate	2
1 cup	confectioner's (icing) sugar, sifted	250 mL
1	egg, lightly beaten	1
1 tsp	vanilla	5 mL

TIP: To cut sticky foods (like marshmallows, dates or prunes) easily, use kitchen scissors, dipping them frequently in hot water.

- *Preheat oven to 375°F (190°C)*
- *8-inch (2 L) square cake pan, greased*

1. *Filling:* In a saucepan, over low heat, melt chocolate with butter, stirring until smooth. Stir in walnuts. Set aside.

2. *Base:* In a small bowl, mix together flour, baking powder and salt.

3. In a medium bowl, beat brown sugar and eggs until smooth and creamy. Blend in flour mixture. Spoon half this batter into another medium bowl and stir in coconut. Stir filling into remaining batter.

4. Spread coconut batter evenly in prepared pan. Spread chocolate-walnut batter evenly over top. Bake in preheated oven for 25 to 30 minutes or until a tester inserted in the center comes out clean.

5. *Topping:* Remove from oven and arrange marshmallow halves on top. Bake 2 minutes longer, until marshmallows are softened. Place pan on wire rack to cool.

6. In a saucepan, over low heat, melt butter and chocolate, stirring until smooth. Cool slightly, then beat in egg and vanilla. Gradually add confectioner's sugar, beating until mixture is smooth. Working quickly, spread topping over marshmallow layer. Place pan on a wire rack to cool completely, then cut into bars.

Makes 20 bars

Chocolate Marshmallow Squares

BASE

2	squares (each 1 oz/28 g) unsweetened chocolate	2
½ cup	butter	125 mL
1 cup	all-purpose flour	250 mL
½ tsp	baking powder	2 mL
¼ tsp	baking soda	1 mL
¼ tsp	salt	1 mL
1 cup	granulated sugar	250 mL
2	eggs	2
1 tsp	vanilla	5 mL
½ cup	unsweetened applesauce	125 mL

TOPPING

2½ cups	miniature marshmallows, divided	625 mL

GLAZE

2 tbsp	butter	25 mL
½ cup	granulated sugar	125 mL
2 tbsp	milk	25 mL
¼ cup	semi-sweet chocolate chips	50 mL

- *Preheat oven to 350°F (180°C)*
- *13- by 9-inch (3.5 L) cake pan, greased*

1. *Base:* In a saucepan, over low heat, melt chocolate and butter, stirring until smooth. Set aside to cool slightly.
2. In a small bowl, mix together flour, baking powder, baking soda and salt.
3. When chocolate mixture has cooled, stir in sugar. Add eggs and vanilla; beat until blended. Stir in applesauce. Blend in flour mixture. Spread evenly in prepared pan. Bake in preheated oven for 20 to 30 minutes or until a tester inserted in the center comes out clean.
4. *Topping:* Set aside ½ cup (125 mL) of the marshmallows and sprinkle remainder evenly over cake. Bake for 2 minutes longer or until marshmallows soften.
5. *Glaze:* In a saucepan, over medium heat, combine butter, sugar and milk. Stir constantly until mixture comes to a boil, then boil for 1 minute. Remove from heat. Stir in chocolate chips and reserved marshmallows until melted and smooth. Immediately drizzle over top of warm cake. Place pan on a wire rack to cool completely, then cut into squares.

Makes 36 squares

Grasshopper Cream Cheese Bars

BASE

¾ cup	all-purpose flour	175 mL
⅓ cup	unsweetened cocoa powder, sifted	75 mL
⅓ cup	granulated sugar	75 mL
6 tbsp	butter or margarine	90 mL

TOPPING

8 oz	cream cheese, softened	250 g
¼ cup	granulated sugar	50 mL
1	egg	1
½ tsp	peppermint extract	2 mL
4 or 5	drops green food coloring	4 or 5
¼ cup	milk	50 mL

- *Preheat oven to 350°F (180°C)*
- *8-inch (2 L) square cake pan, ungreased*

1. *Base:* In a medium bowl, mix together flour, cocoa and sugar. Using two knives, a pastry blender or your fingers, cut butter in until mixture resembles coarse crumbs. Set aside 1 cup (250 mL) of mixture and press remainder evenly into pan. Bake in preheated oven for 15 minutes or until lightly browned. Place medium pan on a wire rack to cool slightly.

2. *Topping:* In a medium bowl, beat cream cheese and sugar until smooth. Beat in egg, peppermint extract and food coloring until blended. Blend in milk. Spread topping evenly over baked base. Sprinkle remaining base mixture over top and bake 20 to 25 minutes longer or until crumbs are golden. Place pan on a wire rack to cool completely, then cut into bars. Store, covered, in refrigerator.

Makes 16 bars

Mocha Cream Cheese Bars

BASE		
¼ cup	butter or margarine, melted	50 mL
1½ cups	finely crushed chocolate wafers (about 30 wafers)	375 mL

TOPPING		
8 oz	cream cheese, softened	250 g
⅔ cup	granulated sugar	150 mL
3	eggs	3
3 tbsp	unsweetened cocoa powder, sifted	45 mL
¼ cup	milk	50 mL
3 tbsp	strong coffee	45 mL

> **TIP:** If you prefer frostings that are not-too-sweet, combine an 8-oz (250 g) package of softened cream cheese with a 16 oz (500 g) can of prepared frosting and mix until well blended.

- *Preheat oven to 350°F (180°C)*
- *9-inch (2.5 L) square cake pan, greased*

1. *Base:* In a small bowl, mix together butter and wafers. Press evenly into prepared pan. Set aside.

2. *Topping:* In a large bowl, beat cream cheese and sugar until smooth. Beat in eggs, one at a time, until incorporated. Add cocoa, milk and coffee, beating until well blended. Spread mixture evenly over base. Bake in preheated oven for 30 to 35 minutes or until set. Place pan on a wire rack to cool completely, then cut into bars. Store, covered, in the refrigerator.

Makes 24 bars

Coffee Mocha Cheesecake Diamonds

BASE

6	squares (each 1 oz/28 g) semi-sweet chocolate	6
¾ cup	butter or margarine	175 mL
1 tbsp	instant coffee powder	15 mL
2	eggs	2
¾ cup	packed brown sugar	175 mL
¾ cup	all-purpose flour	175 mL
½ tsp	baking powder	2 mL

CHEESECAKE LAYER

8 oz	cream cheese, softened	250 g
½ cup	granulated sugar	125 mL
2	eggs	2
2 tbsp	strong coffee or coffee liqueur	25 mL
2 tbsp	all-purpose flour	25 mL

SOUR CREAM TOPPING

1½ cups	sour cream	375 mL
3 tbsp	granulated sugar	45 mL
	Chocolate-covered almonds or espresso beans (optional)	

- *Preheat oven to 350°F (180°C)*
- *13- by 9-inch (3.5 L) cake pan, greased*

1. *Base:* In a saucepan, over low heat, melt chocolate and butter, stirring until smooth. Add coffee powder and mix well. Set aside to cool slightly.

2. In a large bowl, beat eggs and brown sugar. Add cooled chocolate mixture and mix well. Blend in flour and baking powder. Spread evenly in prepared pan. Chill for 10 minutes.

3. *Cheesecake layer:* In a medium bowl, beat cream cheese and sugar until smooth. Add eggs, one at a time, beating until incorporated. Stir in coffee until blended. Blend in flour. Spread evenly over base. Bake in preheated oven for 20 minutes or until set.

4. *Sour Cream Topping:* In a small bowl, mix together sour cream and sugar. Spread over warm cheesecake. Bake 10 minutes longer. Place pan on a wire rack to cool completely. When cool, cut cake into 6 long strips, then cut strips across on diagonal into diamond shapes. If desired, top each with a chocolate-covered almond or espresso bean.

Makes 36 diamonds

Marbled Cream Cheese Squares

FILLING

8 oz	cream cheese, softened	250 g
¼ cup	granulated sugar	50 mL
1	egg	1
2 tbsp	all-purpose flour	25 mL

BASE

¾ cup	butter or margarine	175 mL
4	squares (each 1 oz/28 g) unsweetened chocolate	4
1½ cups	granulated sugar	375 mL
3	eggs	3
1 tbsp	milk	15 mL
1 cup	all-purpose flour	250 mL
1 cup	chopped nuts	250 mL

TIP: When baking cakes, never open the oven door until the minimum time is up or cakes will collapse.

- *Preheat oven to 350°F (180°C)*
- *9-inch (2.5 L) square cake pan, greased*

1. *Filling:* In a medium bowl, beat cream cheese and sugar until smooth. Beat in egg until incorporated. Blend in flour. Set aside.

2. *Base:* In a saucepan, over low heat, melt butter and chocolate, stirring until smooth. Set aside to cool slightly.

3. When mixture has cooled, stir in sugar. Beat in eggs until blended. Stir in milk. Blend in flour. Stir in nuts.

4. Spread half the batter evenly in prepared pan. Spread filling evenly over base. Spread remaining batter evenly over filling. Run a knife through the layers to create a marbling effect. Bake in preheated oven for 35 to 40 minutes or until a tester inserted in the center comes out clean. Cool completely in pan, then cut into squares.

Makes 24 squares

Vanilla Fudge Cream Bars

1	package (18¼ oz/515 g) dark chocolate or devil's food cake mix	1
½ cup	butter or margarine, melted	125 mL
2	eggs	2
½ cup	chocolate fudge sundae sauce	125 mL
1	container (15 oz/420 g) ready-to-serve vanilla frosting	1
8 oz	cream cheese, softened	250 g

- *Preheat oven to 350°F (180°C)*
- *13- by 9-inch (3.5 L) cake pan, ungreased*

1. In a medium bowl, mix together cake mix, butter, 1 of the eggs and chocolate fudge sauce until blended. (Mixture will be crumbly.) Press evenly into pan.
2. In another medium bowl, beat frosting mix with cream cheese until smooth. Set 1 cup (250 mL) of mixture aside and add 1 egg to remainder in bowl. Beat until blended and smooth. Spread evenly over base.
3. Bake in preheated oven for 30 to 35 minutes or until set. Place pan on a wire rack to cool completely, then frost with reserved cream cheese mixture. Cut into bars. Store, covered, in refrigerator.

Makes 36 bars

Chocolate Cookie and Cream Squares

BASE

2⅔ cups	chocolate cookie crumbs	650 mL
⅔ cup	butter or margarine, melted	150 mL
½ cup	granulated sugar	125 mL

TOPPING

16 oz	cream cheese, softened	500 g
1 cup	granulated sugar	250 mL
4	eggs	4
2 cups	broken chunks chocolate cookies with white cream filling, divided	500 mL
6	squares (each 1 oz/28 g) semi-sweet chocolate	6
½ cup	whipping (35%) cream	125 mL

- *Preheat oven to 350°F (180°C)*
- *13- by 9-inch (3.5 L) cake pan, ungreased*

1. *Base:* In a medium bowl mix together cookie crumbs, butter and sugar. Press evenly into pan. Bake in preheated oven for 8 to 10 minutes. Place pan on a wire rack to cool slightly.
2. *Topping:* In a large bowl, beat cream cheese and sugar until smooth. Beat in eggs, one at a time, until incorporated. Spread half the mixture evenly over warm base and sprinkle with 1¾ cups (425 mL) of cookie chunks. Spread remaining batter over top. Bake 35 to 40 minutes longer or until center is almost set. Place pan on a wire rack to cool, then chill for at least 3 hours.
3. In a saucepan, over low heat, stir chocolate and whipping cream until melted and smooth. Pour over chilled cake. Sprinkle remaining cookie pieces over top. Cut into squares.

Makes 36 squares

Rocky Road Bars

½ cup	butter or margarine, melted	125 mL
1½ cups	graham wafer crumbs (about 22 wafers)	375 mL
1½ cups	flaked coconut	375 mL
1½ cups	chopped nuts	375 mL
1½ cups	semi-sweet chocolate chips	375 mL
1½ cups	miniature marshmallows	375 mL
1	can (10 oz/300 mL) sweetened condensed milk	1
3	squares (each 1 oz/28 g) semi-sweet chocolate, melted	3

- *Preheat oven to 350°F (180°C)*
- *13- by 9-inch (3.5 L) cake pan, greased*

1. In a small bowl, mix together melted butter and graham wafer crumbs. Press evenly into prepared pan. Working in layers, sprinkle coconut, then nuts, then chocolate chips and, finally, marshmallows evenly over base. Drizzle condensed milk evenly over top.
2. Bake in preheated oven for 25 to 30 minutes or until top is golden brown. Remove from oven. Drizzle with melted chocolate. Place pan on a wire rack to cool completely, then cut into bars.

Makes 36 bars

Chocolate Swirl Squares

BASE		
2 cups	packaged biscuit mix	500 mL
¼ cup	granulated sugar	50 mL
1	egg	1
⅔ cup	milk or water	150 mL
3 tbsp	melted butter or margarine, divided	45 mL
⅓ cup	semi-sweet chocolate chips or pieces, melted	75 mL
TOPPING		
¼ cup	granulated sugar	50 mL
⅓ cup	flaked coconut	75 mL
¼ cup	chopped nuts	50 mL

TIP: Don't overbeat cake batter. Overbeating will remove too much air and make finished cakes flat and heavy.

- *Preheat oven to 400°F (200°C)*
- *8-inch (2 L) square cake pan, greased*

1. *Base:* In a medium bowl, mix together biscuit mix, sugar, egg, milk and 2 tbsp (25 mL) of the melted butter until blended. Spread evenly in prepared pan. Pour melted chocolate evenly over batter. Run a knife through batter to create a marbling effect.
2. *Topping:* In a small bowl, mix together sugar, coconut, nuts and remaining melted butter.
3. Spread mixture evenly over base. Bake in preheated oven for 20 to 25 minutes or until a tester inserted in center comes out clean. Place pan on a wire rack to cool slightly and serve warm or cool completely then cut into squares.

Makes 16 squares

Chocolate Chip Meringue Squares

2 cups	all-purpose flour	500 mL
1 tsp	baking soda	5 mL
½ cup	butter or margarine, softened	125 mL
½ cup	granulated sugar	125 mL
1½ cups	packed brown sugar, divided	375 mL
2	eggs, separated	2
1 tsp	vanilla	5 mL
1 tbsp	water	15 mL
1 cup	semi-sweet chocolate chips or pieces	250 mL

- *Preheat oven to 325°F (160°C)*
- *13- by 9-inch (3.5 L) cake pan, lightly greased*

1. In a medium bowl, mix together flour and baking soda.
2. In a large bowl, beat butter and granulated sugar and ½ cup (125 mL) of the brown sugar until smooth and creamy. Beat in egg yolks until incorporated. Stir in vanilla and water. Blend in flour mixture. Spread mixture evenly in prepared pan. Sprinkle chocolate chips evenly over top, pressing lightly into the dough.
3. In a clean bowl, beat egg whites until soft peaks form. Gradually beat in remaining brown sugar until stiff peaks form.
4. Spread evenly over dough. Bake in preheated oven for 30 minutes or until meringue is golden brown. Place pan on a wire rack to cool completely, then cut into squares.

Makes 36 squares

Creole Cake Squares

3 tbsp	butter or margarine, melted	45 mL
2	squares (each 1 oz/28 g) unsweetened chocolate, melted	2
1⅓ cups	cake flour, sifted	325 mL
1¾ tsp	baking powder	9 mL
¼ tsp	salt	1 mL
1 cup	granulated sugar	250 mL
2	eggs	2
½ cup	milk	125 mL
	Butter Frosting (see recipe, page 360)	

- *Preheat oven to 325°F (160°C)*
- *8-inch (2 L) square cake pan, greased*

1. In a saucepan, over low heat, melt butter and chocolate, stirring until smooth. Set aside to cool slightly.
2. In a small bowl, mix together flour, baking powder and salt.
3. When chocolate mixture has cooled, stir in sugar. Add eggs and beat until just blended. Gradually blend in flour mixture alternately with milk until just incorporated.
4. Spread evenly in prepared pan. Bake in preheated oven for 45 to 50 minutes or until a tester inserted in the center comes out clean. Place pan on a rack to cool completely, then frost with any flavor of Butter Frosting. Cut into squares.

Makes 16 squares

Polish Chocolate Squares (Mazurek)

1/3 cup	shortening, softened	75 mL
1 1/2 cups	granulated sugar	375 mL
6	eggs, separated	6
1 1/2 tsp	vanilla	7 mL
6	squares (each 1 oz/28 g) unsweetened chocolate, melted	6
1 2/3 cups	dry bread crumbs, divided	400 mL
	Whipped (35%) cream (optional)	

- *Preheat oven to 350°F (180°C)*
- *13- by 9-inch (3.5 L) cake pan, greased*

1. In a large bowl, beat shortening and sugar until smooth and creamy. Add egg yolks, one at a time, and beat until incorporated. Stir in vanilla and melted chocolate. Add 1 1/2 cups (375 mL) of the bread crumbs and mix well.

2. In a clean bowl, beat egg whites until soft peaks form. Carefully fold into batter until blended.

3. Dust prepared baking pan with remaining bread crumbs. Spread batter evenly in pan. Bake in preheated oven for 35 minutes. Place pan on a wire rack to cool completely, then cut into squares. Serve plain or with whipped cream, if desired.

Makes 36 squares

Sour Cream Chocolate Squares

1 cup	all-purpose flour	250 mL
3/4 tsp	baking soda	4 mL
1/2 cup	milk	125 mL
1/2 cup	sour cream	125 mL
1/4 cup	butter or margarine	50 mL
2	squares (each 1 oz/28 g) unsweetened chocolate, chopped	2
1 cup	granulated sugar	250 mL
1	egg	1
1/2 tsp	vanilla	2 mL
FROSTING		
2	squares (each 1 oz/28 g) unsweetened chocolate, melted	2
1/2 cup	sour cream	125 mL
2 1/4 cups	confectioner's (icing) sugar, sifted	550 mL

- *Preheat oven to 350°F (180°C)*
- *8-inch (2 L) square cake pan, greased*

1. In a small bowl, mix together flour and baking soda. In a cup, combine milk and sour cream.

2. In a saucepan, melt butter and chocolate, stirring until smooth. Remove from heat and set aside to cool slightly.

3. When mixture has cooled, stir in sugar. Add egg and vanilla and beat until blended. Gradually blend in flour mixture alternately with milk mixture until just incorporated. Spread evenly in prepared pan. Bake in preheated oven for 25 to 30 minutes or until a tester inserted in center comes out clean. Cool in pan for about 10 minutes, then transfer to a wire rack to cool completely.

4. *Frosting:* Beat melted chocolate and sour cream until smooth and blended. Gradually beat in confectioner's sugar until smooth and spreadable. Spread frosting over cake and cut into squares.

Makes 16 squares

Chocolate-Lover's Banana Squares

BASE

2 tbsp	butter or margarine	25 mL
½ cup	mashed ripe banana (1 large)	125 mL
1	egg, beaten	1
1 tsp	vanilla	5 mL
¼ cup	water	50 mL
1 cup	all-purpose flour	250 mL
1 tsp	baking powder	5 mL
½ cup	granulated sugar	125 mL
¾ cup	unsweetened cocoa powder, sifted	175 mL
½ tsp	salt	2 mL
¼ tsp	ground cinnamon	1 mL

TOPPING

½ cup	packed brown sugar	125 mL
¼ cup	unsweetened cocoa powder, sifted	50 mL
1¼ cups	boiling water	300 mL

> **TIP:** Score bars or squares that are topped with chocolate as soon as the topping is applied. This prevents the chocolate from cracking later.

- *Preheat oven to 350°F (180°C)*
- *8-inch (2 L) square cake pan, ungreased*

1. *Base:* In a saucepan, over low heat, melt butter. Remove from heat and stir in banana, egg, vanilla and water until blended. Set aside.

2. In a large bowl, mix together flour, baking powder, sugar, cocoa, salt and cinnamon. Add banana mixture and mix well (batter will be thick). Spread evenly in pan.

3. *Topping:* In a small bowl, beat brown sugar, cocoa and boiling water until smooth and blended. Pour evenly over base. Bake in preheated oven for 35 to 40 minutes or until a tester inserted in the centre of the cake comes out clean (the fudgey sauce on top will be wet). Place pan on a wire rack to cool for 5 minutes, then cut into squares.

Makes 16 squares

Black and White Chocolate Bars

1¼ cups	all-purpose flour, divided	300 mL
⅓ cup	raisins	75 mL
½ cup	chopped walnuts	125 mL
½ cup	butter or margarine	125 mL
6	squares (each 1 oz/ 28 g) white chocolate, chopped into small chunks, divided	6
⅔ cup	granulated sugar	150 mL
3	eggs	3
2 tsp	vanilla	10 mL
4	squares (each 1 oz/ 28 g) bittersweet chocolate, chopped into small chunks	4

- *Preheat oven to 350°F (180°C)*
- *9-inch (2.5 L) square cake pan, lightly greased*

1. In a small bowl, mix together 2 tbsp (25 mL) of flour, raisins and walnuts. Set aside.
2. In a large saucepan, over low heat, melt butter and half the white chocolate chunks, stirring until smooth. Remove from heat and set aside to cool slightly.
3. When mixture has cooled, stir in sugar. Beat in eggs and vanilla just until blended. Blend in remaining flour. Stir in raisin-walnut mixture and remaining white and bittersweet chocolate.
4. Spread evenly in prepared pan. Bake in preheated oven for 30 minutes or until a tester inserted in center comes out clean. Place pan on a wire rack to cool completely, then cut into bars.

Makes 24 bars

White Chocolate Dream Bars

BASE

2⅓ cups	all-purpose flour	575 mL
2 cups	old-fashioned rolled oats	500 mL
1 cup	packed brown sugar	250 mL
1 tsp	baking soda	5 mL
1 cup	butter or margarine, melted	500 mL

TOPPING

1½ cups	white chocolate chips	375 mL
1 cup	slivered almonds	250 mL
1 cup	toffee bits	250 mL
1⅓ cups	caramel sundae sauce	325 mL
⅓ cup	all-purpose flour	75 mL

- *Preheat oven to 350°F (180°C)*
- *13- by 9-inch (3.5 L) cake pan, greased*

1. *Base:* In a large bowl, mix together flour, oats, brown sugar and baking soda. Add butter and mix thoroughly. Set aside 1 cup (250 mL) of mixture and press remainder evenly into prepared pan. Bake in preheated oven for 12 to15 minutes or until lightly browned. Place pan on a wire rack to cool slightly.
2. *Topping:* In a medium bowl, combine white chocolate chips, almonds and toffee bits. Sprinkle evenly over base.
3. In a separate bowl, blend caramel sauce with flour. Drizzle over chocolate layer, then sprinkle remaining base mixture over top. Bake 20 to 25 minutes longer or until golden brown. Place pan on a wire rack to cool completely, then cut into bars.

Makes 36 bars

Raspberry Almond White Triangles

½ cup	butter or margarine	125 mL
6	squares (each 1 oz/28 g) white chocolate, chopped	6
½ cup	granulated sugar	125 mL
2	eggs	2
1½ tsp	vanilla	7 mL
¼ tsp	salt	1 mL
1 cup	all-purpose flour	250 mL
	Raspberry jam, to taste	
1½ cups	white chocolate chips	375 mL
⅓ cup	sliced almonds	75 mL

TIP: Use only the size of pan called for in your recipe. The difference between an 8-inch (2 L) square cake pan and a 9-inch (2.5 L) square cake pan can mean the difference between a moist, chewy bar or square and an underbaked, heavy failure.

- *Preheat oven to 325°F (160°C)*
- *9-inch (2.5 L) square cake pan, greased*

1. In a large saucepan, over low heat, melt butter and chocolate, stirring until smooth. Set aside to cool slightly.
2. When mixture has cooled, stir in sugar. Add eggs and vanilla and beat until just combined. Blend in salt, then flour.
3. Spread half the batter evenly in prepared pan. Bake in preheated oven for 25 minutes or until golden brown. Place pan on a wire rack to cool for 10 minutes.
4. Stir jam until smooth and spread evenly over top of warm cake.
5. Stir chocolate chips into remaining batter and drop, by spoonfuls, over jam layer. Sprinkle almonds on top. Bake 35 to 40 minutes longer or until lightly browned. Place pan on a wire rack to cool completely. Cut into 16 squares, then cut each square into 2 triangles.

Makes 32 triangles

Coconut Bars and Squares

Southern Coconut Squares

2 cups	all-purpose flour	500 mL
2½ tsp	baking powder	12 mL
½ tsp	salt	2 mL
⅔ cup	shortening, softened	150 mL
1 cup	granulated sugar	250 mL
3	eggs	3
1 tsp	almond extract	5 mL
⅔ cup	milk	150 mL
1 cup	flaked coconut	250 mL

TIP: To prevent coconut from becoming moldy, toast in a skillet until golden, then store in an airtight container.

- *Preheat oven to 375°F (190°C)*
- *8-inch (2 L) square cake pan, greased*

1. In a medium bowl, mix together flour, baking powder and salt.
2. In a large bowl, beat shortening and sugar until smooth and creamy. Beat in eggs, one at a time, until incorporated. Stir in almond extract. Gradually blend in flour mixture alternately with milk until just incorporated. Stir in coconut.
3. Spread evenly in prepared pan. Bake in preheated oven for 25 minutes or until golden brown. Place pan on a wire rack to cool completely, then cut into squares.

Makes 16 squares

Double Nut Coconut Bars

BASE

½ cup	butter or margarine, melted	125 mL
1½ cups	finely crushed graham wafer crumbs (about 22 wafers)	375 mL

TOPPING

1	can (14 oz/398 mL) sweetened condensed milk	1
1 cup	semi-sweet chocolate chips	250 mL
1½ cups	shredded coconut	375 mL
¾ cup	chopped Brazil nuts	175 mL
¾ cup	chopped cashews	175 mL

- *Preheat oven to 350°F (180°C)*
- *13- by 9-inch (3.5 L) cake pan, lined with foil extending over ends*

1. *Base:* In a small bowl, mix together butter and wafer crumbs. Press evenly into prepared pan.
2. *Topping:* Pour condensed milk evenly over crumbs. Working in layers, spread chocolate chips, coconut, Brazil nuts and cashews over crumbs. Using a spatula, press down gently.
3. Bake in preheated oven for 25 to 30 minutes or until coconut is lightly browned. Place pan on a wire rack to cool completely. Transfer cake with foil to a cutting board and cut into bars.

Makes 36 bars

Coconut Bars Supreme

BASE

1¼ cups	all-purpose flour	300 mL
¼ cup	packed brown sugar	50 mL
½ cup	butter, margarine or shortening	125 mL

TOPPING

2 tbsp	butter, margarine or shortening, melted	25 mL
½ cup	granulated sugar	125 mL
½ cup	corn syrup	125 mL
2	eggs	2
1 tsp	vanilla	5 mL
¼ tsp	ground cinnamon	1 mL
¼ tsp	ground nutmeg	1 mL
⅔ cup	coarsely chopped almonds	150 mL
½ cup	flaked coconut	125 mL

> **TIP:** To soften brown sugar, place a slice of soft bread in the package or container and close tightly. In a couple of hours, the sugar will be soft again.

- *Preheat oven to 375°F (190°C)*
- *9-inch (2.5 L) square cake pan, greased*

1. *Base:* In a medium bowl, mix together flour and brown sugar. Using two knives, a pastry blender or your fingers, cut butter in until mixture resembles coarse crumbs. Press evenly into prepared pan. Bake in preheated oven for 15 minutes.

2. *Topping:* In another medium bowl, beat butter, sugar, syrup, eggs, vanilla, cinnamon and nutmeg until blended. Stir in almonds and coconut.

3. Spread evenly over base. Bake 20 to 25 minutes longer or until top is set. Place pan on a wire rack to cool completely, then cut into bars.

Makes 24 bars

Chewy Coconut Squares

¼ cup	butter or margarine	50 mL
1 cup	packed brown sugar	250 mL
½ cup	all-purpose flour	125 mL
1 tsp	baking powder	5 mL
½ tsp	salt	2 mL
1	egg, beaten	1
1 tsp	vanilla	5 mL
¾ cup	sweetened shredded coconut	175 mL

> **TIP:** If your coconut has dried out, sprinkle it with milk and let stand until it softens.

- *Preheat oven to 350°F (180°C)*
- *8-inch (2 L) square cake pan, greased*

1. In a saucepan, over low heat, melt butter with brown sugar, stirring until sugar dissolves. Remove from heat and cool slightly.

2. In a large bowl, mix together flour, baking powder and salt. Add egg, vanilla and butter mixture and mix until blended. Stir in coconut. Spread evenly in prepared pan. Bake in preheated oven for 20 to 25 minutes or until golden brown. Place pan on a wire rack to cool and cut into squares while slightly warm.

Makes 16 squares

Golden Butterscotch Triangles

3/4 cup	all-purpose flour	175 mL
1 tsp	baking powder	5 mL
1/4 tsp	salt	1 mL
1/4 cup	butter or margarine	50 mL
1 cup	packed brown sugar	250 mL
1	egg	1
1 tsp	vanilla	5 mL
1/3 cup	flaked coconut	75 mL
1/3 cup	chopped nuts	75 mL

TIP: Whenever I make anything flavored with butterscotch, I replace vanilla with almond extract. It seems to enhance the flavor.

- *Preheat oven to 350°F (180°C)*
- *8-inch (2 L) square cake pan, lightly greased*

1. In a small bowl, mix together flour, baking powder and salt.
2. In a medium bowl, beat butter and brown sugar until smooth and creamy. Beat in egg until incorporated. Stir in vanilla. Blend in flour mixture. Stir in coconut and chopped nuts.
3. Spread mixture evenly in prepared pan. Bake in preheated oven for 20 to 25 minutes or until lightly browned. Place pan on a wire rack to cool completely, then cut into squares.

Makes 16 squares

Coconut Dream Squares

BASE

1/2 cup	butter or margarine, softened	125 mL
1 tbsp	packed brown sugar	15 mL
1 cup	all-purpose flour	250 mL
Pinch	salt	Pinch

TOPPING

2 tbsp	all-purpose flour	25 mL
1 1/2 tsp	baking powder	7 mL
Pinch	salt	Pinch
1 1/4 cups	packed brown sugar	300 mL
2	eggs, beaten	2
3/4 cup	chopped walnuts	175 mL
1/2 cup	shredded coconut	125 mL
	Butter Frosting (optional, see Tip, below)	

TIP: If desired, frost with Butter Frosting (see page 360), flavored with 1 1/2 tsp (7 mL) almond extract instead of vanilla, before cutting into squares.

- *Preheat oven to 350°F (180°C)*
- *8-inch (2 L) square cake pan, lightly greased*

1. *Base:* In a medium bowl, beat butter and brown sugar until smooth and creamy. Blend in flour and salt. Press evenly into prepared pan. Bake in preheated oven for 15 minutes or until lightly browned. Place pan on a wire rack to cool.
2. *Topping:* In a medium bowl, mix together flour, baking powder and salt. Add brown sugar and eggs and mix until blended. Stir in walnuts and coconut.
3. Spread evenly over cooled base. Bake 20 to 25 minutes longer or until golden brown. Place pan on a rack to cool completely, then cut into squares.

Makes 16 squares

Coconut Chews

BASE

¾ cup	butter or shortening, softened	175 mL
¾ cup	confectioner's (icing) sugar, sifted	175 mL
1½ cups	all-purpose flour	375 mL

TOPPING

2 tbsp	all-purpose flour	25 mL
½ tsp	baking powder	2 mL
½ tsp	salt	2 mL
1 cup	packed brown sugar	250 mL
2	eggs	2
½ tsp	vanilla	2 mL
½ cup	chopped walnuts	125 mL
½ cup	flaked coconut	125 mL

ORANGE LEMON FROSTING (OPTIONAL)

2 tbsp	butter or margarine, melted	25 mL
1½ cups	confectioner's (icing) sugar, sifted	375 mL
3 tbsp	orange juice	45 mL
1 tsp	freshly squeezed lemon juice	5 mL

> **TIP:** To keep freshly baked cakes from sticking to wire cooling racks, spray racks with non-stick cooking spray.

- *Preheat oven to 350°F (180°C)*
- *13- by 9-inch (3.5 L) cake pan, ungreased*

1. *Base:* In a medium bowl, beat butter and confectioner's sugar until smooth and creamy. Gradually blend in flour until a soft dough forms. Press evenly into pan. Bake in preheated oven for 12 to 15 minutes or until lightly browned.

2. *Topping:* In a small bowl, mix together flour, baking powder and salt.

3. In another medium bowl, beat brown sugar, eggs and vanilla until smooth and blended. Blend in flour mixture. Stir in walnuts and coconut. Spread evenly over hot base and bake 20 minutes longer, until top is set. Place pan on a wire rack to cool slightly.

4. *Frosting (optional):* Beat butter, confectioner's sugar, orange juice and lemon juice until smooth and spreadable. Spread frosting over warm cake. When completely cooled, cut into bars.

Makes 36 bars

Coconut Fudge Bars

BASE

1 cup	all-purpose flour	250 mL
½ cup	chopped walnuts	125 mL
¼ cup	unsweetened cocoa powder, sifted	50 mL
1 cup	butter or margarine, softened	250 mL
1½ cups	granulated sugar	375 mL
3	eggs	3
1 tsp	vanilla	5 mL

TOPPING

1	can (14 oz/398 mL) sweetened condensed milk	1
1 cup	shredded coconut	250 mL

FROSTING

¼ cup	unsweetened cocoa powder	50 mL
2 cups	confectioner's (icing) sugar	500 mL
2 tbsp	butter or margarine, melted	25 mL
⅓ cup	evaporated milk	75 mL
½ tsp	vanilla	2 mL

> **TIP:** Fresh milk cannot be used when evaporated milk is called for in a recipe. But evaporated milk, mixed with an equal amount of water, can be substituted for fresh milk.

- *Preheat oven to 350°F (180°C)*
- *13- by 9-inch (3.5 L) cake pan, greased*

1. *Base:* In a small bowl, mix together flour, walnuts and cocoa.
2. In a large bowl, beat butter and sugar until smooth and creamy. Beat in eggs until incorporated. Stir in vanilla. Blend in flour mixture.
3. Spread evenly in prepared pan. Bake in preheated oven for 30 minutes or until tester inserted in the center comes out clean.
4. *Topping:* In a small bowl, mix together condensed milk and coconut.
5. Spread evenly over hot base. Bake for 20 minutes longer or until coconut is lightly browned. Place pan on a wire rack to cool slightly.
6. *Frosting:* Sift together cocoa and confectioner's sugar. Beat in butter, evaporated milk and vanilla until smooth. Spread over warm cake. Chill until cooled completely, then cut into bars.

Makes 36 bars

Coco-Nut Crumb Bars

BASE		
2 cups	chocolate chip cookie crumbs	500 mL
¼ cup	butter or margarine, melted	50 mL

TOPPINGS		
2 cups	flaked coconut	500 mL
1	can (14 oz/398 mL) sweetened condensed milk	1
2 cups	semi-sweet chocolate chips	500 mL

- *Preheat oven to 350°F (180°C)*
- *13- by 9-inch (3.5 L) cake pan, ungreased*

1. *Base:* In a medium bowl, mix together cookie crumbs and melted butter. Press evenly into pan. Bake in preheated oven for 10 minutes.
2. *Toppings:* Remove pan from oven and sprinkle coconut over base. Pour condensed milk over coconut.
3. Bake 18 to 20 minutes longer or until coconut begins to brown around the edges of the cake. Place pan on a wire rack to cool.
4. In a saucepan, over low heat, melt chocolate chips, stirring until smooth. Spread melted chocolate evenly over top of coconut. Chill until completely cooled, then cut into bars.

Makes 36 bars

Pineapple Coconut Bars

BASE		
1	package (18¼ oz/515 g) yellow cake mix	1

FILLING		
1	package (4-serving size) vanilla instant pudding mix	1
1¼ cups	milk	300 mL
2 cups	drained crushed pineapple	500 mL

TOPPING		
1	envelope (1⅓ oz/42.5 g) whipped topping mix	1
3 oz	cream cheese, softened	90 g
¼ cup	granulated sugar	50 mL
½ tsp	vanilla	2 mL
½ cup	flaked coconut, toasted	125 mL

- *Preheat oven to 350°F (180°C)*
- *13- by 9-inch (3.5 L) cake pan, greased*

1. *Base:* Prepare and bake cake mix according to package directions. Place pan on a wire rack to cool.
2. *Filling:* In a bowl, beat pudding mix and milk. Set aside. When mixture has thickened, fold in pineapple. Spread mixture evenly over cake.
3. *Topping:* In a medium bowl, prepare whipped topping according to package directions. Set aside.
4. In a medium bowl, beat cream cheese and sugar until smooth. Stir in vanilla. Add 1 cup (250 mL) of whipped topping and beat until blended. Fold in remaining topping and spread mixture evenly over pudding layer. Sprinkle coconut over top. Cover pan and chill thoroughly (3 to 4 hours), then cut into bars.

Makes 36 bars

Apple Pie Coconut Squares

BASE

1½ cups	all-purpose flour	375 mL
¼ tsp	salt	1 mL
½ cup	butter or margarine, softened	125 mL
½ cup	packed brown sugar	125 mL
1 tsp	vanilla	5 mL
1⅓ cups	flaked coconut	325 mL

TOPPING

1	can (19 oz/540 mL) apple pie filling	1
1 tbsp	freshly squeezed lemon juice	15 mL
½ tsp	ground cinnamon	2 mL
¼ tsp	ground mace	1 mL

- *Preheat oven to 375°F (190°C)*
- *8-inch (2 L) square cake pan, greased*

1. Base: In a small bowl, mix together flour and salt.
2. In a large bowl, beat butter and brown sugar until smooth and creamy. Stir in vanilla. Blend in flour mixture. Stir in coconut. Spread half the mixture evenly in prepared pan.
3. Topping: In a clean bowl, mix apple pie filling, lemon juice, cinnamon and mace until blended. Spoon evenly over base. Top with remaining coconut mixture.
4. Bake in preheated oven for 20 to 25 minutes. Place pan on a rack to cool completely, then cut into squares.

Makes 16 squares

> **TIP:** These squares are also delicious served hot with ice cream.

Maraschino Coconut Squares

BASE

½ cup	butter, softened	125 mL
3 tbsp	confectioner's (icing) sugar, sifted	45 mL
1 cup	all-purpose flour	250 mL

TOPPING

¼ cup	all-purpose flour	50 mL
½ tsp	baking powder	2 mL
¼ tsp	salt	1 mL
½ cup	granulated sugar	125 mL
2	eggs, lightly beaten	2
1 tsp	vanilla	5 mL
¾ cup	chopped walnuts	175 mL
½ cup	flaked coconut	125 mL
½ cup	maraschino cherries, diced and drained	125 mL

- *Preheat oven to 350°F (180°C)*
- *8-inch (2 L) square cake pan, lightly greased*

1. *Base:* In a small bowl, cream butter and confectioner's sugar. Blend in flour just until dough forms. Press evenly into prepared pan. Bake in preheated oven for 20 minutes or until edges are lightly browned.
2. *Topping:* In a medium bowl, mix together flour, baking powder and salt. Add sugar, eggs and vanilla and mix well. Stir in walnuts, coconut and cherries until blended.
3. Spread evenly over baked base. Bake 25 minutes longer. Place pan on a wire rack to cool completely, then cut into squares.

Makes 16 squares

Lemon Coconut Squares

BASE

½ cup	packed brown sugar	125 mL
½ cup	butter, softened	125 mL
1½ cups	all-purpose flour	375 mL

TOPPING

2 tbsp	all-purpose flour	25 mL
½ tsp	baking powder	2 mL
¼ tsp	salt	1 mL
1 cup	granulated sugar, divided	250 mL
3	eggs, separated	3
2 tbsp	grated lemon zest	25 mL
⅓ cup	freshly squeezed lemon juice	75 mL
2 cups	shredded coconut	500 mL

TIP: To squeeze a few drops of lemon juice without wasting the rest of the lemon, prick the peel at one end of the lemon with a fork, squeeze out the required quantity, then refrigerate the lemon. It will be fresh enough to use several more times.

- Preheat oven to 325°F (160°C)
- 13- by 9-inch (3.5 L) cake pan, ungreased

1. *Base:* In a large bowl, beat brown sugar and butter until smooth and creamy. Gradually add flour, mixing until mixture resembles coarse crumbs. Press evenly into pan. Bake in preheated oven for 10 to 15 minutes or until edges are lightly browned.

2. *Topping:* In a medium bowl, mix together flour, baking powder, salt and ½ cup (125 mL) of the sugar. In another bowl, lightly beat egg yolks, lemon zest and juice. Add to flour mixture and mix until blended. Stir in coconut.

3. In a clean bowl, beat egg whites until frothy. Gradually add remaining sugar and beat until stiff peaks form. Fold into flour mixture until blended.

4. Spread evenly over base. Bake 20 to 25 minutes longer or until nearly set. Place pan on a rack to cool completely, then cut into squares.

Makes 36 squares

Coconut Nests

BASE

1 cup	packed brown sugar	250 mL
1 cup	butter or margarine, softened	250 mL
1	egg	1
1 tsp	vanilla	5 mL
2 cups	all-purpose flour	500 mL
1 tsp	salt	5 mL

TOPPING

¼ to ½ cup	raspberry jam	50 to 125 mL
½ cup	shredded coconut (approximate)	125 mL

- Preheat oven to 350°F (180°C)
- 9-inch (2.5 L) square cake pan, lightly greased

1. *Base:* In a large bowl, beat brown sugar and butter until smooth and creamy. Beat in egg until incorporated. Stir in vanilla. Gradually blend in flour and salt. Press evenly into prepared pan. Bake in preheated oven for 20 to 25 minutes or golden brown. Place pan on rack to cool slightly.

2. *Topping:* Stir jam until smooth and spread over warm base. Sprinkle liberally with coconut until top has a nest-like appearance (you may wish to use more than ½ cup/125 mL of coconut). Place pan on a wire rack to cool completely, then cut into squares.

Makes 24 squares

Raspberry Coconut Bars

BASE		
1½ cups	all-purpose flour	375 mL
¼ tsp	salt	1 mL
¾ cup	granulated sugar, divided	175 mL
¾ cup	shortening	175 mL
2	eggs, separated	2
¼ tsp	almond extract	1 mL
TOPPING		
1 cup	raspberry jam or preserves	250 mL
½ cup	flaked coconut	125 mL

- *Preheat oven to 350°F (180°C)*
- *13- by 9-inch (3.5 L) cake pan, ungreased*

1. *Base:* In a small bowl, mix together flour and salt.
2. In a large bowl, beat ¼ cup (50 mL) of the sugar and shortening until smooth and creamy. Beat in egg yolks until incorporated. Stir in almond extract. Blend in flour mixture. Spread evenly in pan. Bake in preheated oven for 15 minutes.
3. *Topping:* Stir jam or preserves until smooth, then spread evenly over hot base. Sprinkle coconut evenly over top. Set aside.
4. In a clean bowl, beat egg whites until foamy. Gradually beat in remaining sugar until stiff peaks form. Spread evenly over top of coconut. Bake for 25 minutes longer, until top is lightly browned. Place pan on a wire rack to cool completely, then cut into bars.

Makes 36 bars

Coconut Jam Squares

BASE		
1¼ cups	all-purpose flour	300 mL
¼ cup	granulated sugar	50 mL
½ cup	shortening	125 mL
TOPPING		
1 cup	raspberry jam	250 mL
2	eggs, beaten	2
2 tsp	vanilla	10 mL
1 cup	granulated sugar	250 mL
½ tsp	baking powder	2 mL
2 cups	flaked coconut	500 mL

- *Preheat oven to 350°F (180°C)*
- *9-inch (2.5 L) square cake pan, greased*

1. *Base:* In a medium bowl, combine flour and sugar. Using two knives, a pastry blender or your fingers, cut shortening in until mixture resembles coarse crumbs. Press evenly into prepared pan.
2. *Topping:* Stir jam until smooth and spread evenly over base.
3. In a large bowl, beat eggs, vanilla, sugar and baking powder until blended. Stir in coconut. Spread evenly over jam. Bake in preheated oven for 25 to 30 minutes or until golden brown. Place pan on a wire rack to cool completely, then cut into squares. Or serve warm, topped with whipped cream, if desired.

TIP: Other flavors of jam, such as cherry, strawberry, apricot or peach, also work well in this recipe.

Makes 24 squares

Chocolate Coconut Raspberry Squares

BASE

1/3 cup	granulated sugar	75 mL
1 1/4 cups	all-purpose flour	300 mL
1/2 cup	butter or margarine	125 mL
1	egg yolk	1

TOPPING

1 1/3 cups	raspberry jam or preserves	325 mL
2 cups	flaked coconut	500 mL
1	can (10 oz/300 mL) sweetened condensed milk	1
5	squares (each 1 oz/28 g) semi-sweet chocolate	5
1 tbsp	butter or margarine	15 mL

TIP: When beating ingredients, 150 strokes by hand are equal to 1 minute of beating with an electric mixer.

- *Preheat oven to 350°F (180°C)*
- *9-inch (2.5 L) square cake pan, lightly greased*

1. *Base:* In a medium bowl mix together sugar and flour. Using two knives, a pastry blender or your fingers, cut in butter until mixture resembles coarse crumbs. Add egg yolk and mix well. Press evenly into prepared pan. Bake in preheated oven for 18 to 20 minutes or until lightly browned.

2. *Topping:* Stir jam until smooth and spread over hot base. In a medium bowl, mix together coconut and condensed milk and spread evenly over jam. Bake 25 minutes longer or until set. Place pan on a wire rack to cool completely.

3. In a small saucepan, over low heat, melt chocolate and butter, stirring until smooth. Spread evenly over coconut and smooth with a spatula. Chill until set, then cut into squares.

Makes 24 squares

Bridge Mix Coconut Bars

3 tbsp	butter or margarine, melted	45 mL
1/2	package (18 1/2 oz/515 g) white cake mix	1/2
3/4 cup	semi-sweet chocolate chips	175 mL
1 1/2 cups	miniature marshmallows	375 mL
1 cup	flaked coconut	250 mL
1 cup	chopped nuts	250 mL
1 1/4 cups	milk	300 mL

TIP: For a richer version of this recipe, substitute 1 can (10 oz/300 mL) sweetened condensed milk for the regular milk.

- *Preheat oven to 350°F (180°C)*
- *13- by 9-inch (3.5 L) cake pan, ungreased*

1. Spread melted butter evenly over the bottom of pan. Sprinkle evenly with cake mix, then top with chocolate chips, marshmallows, coconut and nuts. Pour milk evenly over top.

2. Bake in preheated oven for 25 to 30 minutes or until golden brown. Place pan on a wire rack to cool completely, then cut into bars.

Makes 36 bars

Creamy Apricot Coconut Bars

BASE

1	package (18¼ oz/515 g) lemon cake mix	1
¼ cup	packed brown sugar	50 mL
¼ cup	butter or margarine, softened	50 mL
2	eggs	2
¼ cup	water	50 mL
1 cup	flaked coconut	250 mL
1 cup	chopped dried apricots	250 mL

FROSTING

3 oz	cream cheese, softened	90 g
1 tbsp	milk (approximate)	15 mL
Pinch	salt	Pinch
1 tsp	vanilla	5 mL
2½ cups	confectioner's (icing) sugar, sifted	625 mL
⅛ tsp	each red and yellow food coloring, mixed to make apricot-orange color	0.5 mL

- *Preheat oven to 375°F (190°C)*
- *13- by 9-inch (3.5 L) cake pan, greased*

1. *Base:* In a large bowl, mix together half the cake mix, brown sugar, butter, eggs and water until blended and smooth. Stir in remaining cake mix, coconut and apricots. Spread evenly in prepared pan. Bake in preheated oven for 25 to 30 minutes or until a tester inserted in the center comes out clean. Place pan on a wire rack to cool completely.

2. *Frosting:* In a medium bowl, beat cream cheese, 1 tbsp (15 mL) of milk, salt and vanilla until smooth and creamy. Gradually beat in confectioner's sugar, adding additional milk, 1 tsp (5 mL) at a time, if necessary, until mixture is smooth and spreadable. Beat in coloring, a bit at a time, until desired shade is achieved. Spread evenly over cake. Cut into bars.

Makes 36 bars

TIP: Here's how to protect your frosted cake without having the plastic wrap stick to the frosting. Stick miniature marshmallows on the ends of toothpicks, then stick the toothpicks around the top and sides of the cake, then cover with plastic wrap. After the cake has been unwrapped, the marshmallows make a nice snack.

Fruit Bars and Squares

continued on next page

Apple Cake Bars

⅔ cup	packed brown sugar	150 mL
1 tsp	ground cinnamon	5 mL

BASE

1⅓ cups	all-purpose flour	325 mL
¾ cup	granulated sugar	175 mL
1 tbsp	baking powder	15 mL
¼ cup	butter or margarine	50 mL
1	egg, beaten	1
¾ cup	milk	175 mL
1 tsp	vanilla	5 mL
2 to 4	apples, peeled, cored and sliced	2 to 4

- *Preheat oven to 350°F (180°C)*
- *8-inch (2 L) square cake pan, greased*

1. *Topping:* In a small bowl, mix together brown sugar and cinnamon. Set aside.
2. *Base:* In large bowl, mix together flour, sugar and baking powder. Using two knives, a pastry blender or your fingers, cut butter in until mixture resembles coarse crumbs. Add egg, milk and vanilla and mix well. Spread half evenly in prepared pan. Sprinkle evenly with half the topping mixture. Sprinkle with remaining base mixture.
3. Arrange apple slices over top of cake, pushing them into the batter. Sprinkle with remaining topping. Bake in preheated oven for 50 to 60 minutes or until a tester inserted in the center comes out clean. Place pan on a wire rack to cool completely, then cut into bars.

Makes 24 bars

Sliced Apple Bars

BASE

4 cups	all-purpose flour	1 L
2 cups	granulated sugar	500 mL
½ tsp	salt	2 mL
1 cup	butter or margarine	250 mL

TOPPING

5 cups	peeled sliced tart apples	1.25 L
1 tsp	ground cinnamon	5 mL

TIP: To prevent sliced apples from turning brown, soak them for 10 minutes in moderately salted water after slicing.

- *Preheat oven to 375°F (190°C)*
- *13- by 9-inch (3.5 L) cake pan, greased*

1. *Base:* In a large bowl, mix together flour, sugar and salt. Using two knives, a pastry blender, or your fingers, cut butter in until mixture resembles coarse crumbs. Scoop out ½ cup (125 mL) of mixture and set aside. Spread half of remainder evenly in prepared pan. Bake in preheated oven for 10 minutes. Place pan on a wire rack to cool slightly.
2. *Topping:* In a large bowl, mix together, apples, cinnamon and reserved base mixture. Spread evenly over warm base. Top with the remaining base mixture. Bake in preheated oven for 30 to 35 minutes or until lightly browned. Place pan on a rack to cool completely, then cut into bars.

Makes 36 bars

Apple Kuchen Bars

* *Preheat oven to 375°F (190°C)*
* *9-inch (2.5 L) square cake pan, ungreased*

BASE

2 cups	all-purpose flour	500 mL
2 tbsp	granulated sugar	25 mL
Pinch	salt	Pinch
¾ cup	butter	175 mL
1	egg, lightly beaten	1

FILLING

⅓ cup	all-purpose flour	75 mL
⅓ cup	packed brown sugar	75 mL
1 tbsp	butter or margarine, softened	15 mL
	Zest of 1 orange	
½ tsp	ground cinnamon	2 mL
5	apples, preferably Granny Smith, peeled, cored and thinly sliced	5

TOPPING

2 tbsp	granulated sugar	25 mL
½ tsp	ground cinnamon	2 mL

TIP: To make an inexpensive room freshener, cover orange peels with water in a small saucepan and simmer over low heat, adding more water as needed. Your house will smell like a citrus grove.

1. *Base:* In a medium bowl, mix together, flour, sugar and salt. Using two knives, a pastry blender or your fingers, cut butter in until mixture resembles coarse crumbs. Add egg and mix until a dough forms. Shape into two equal balls; wrap dough tightly in plastic wrap and chill for about 1 hour.

2. On a floured work surface, roll out one portion of the dough to fit the bottom of pan. If necessary, cut dough to fit.

3. *Filling:* In another bowl, mix together flour, sugar, butter, zest, cinnamon and apples. Spread evenly over dough. Roll remaining dough out as for first portion and place on top of apple mixture, cutting to fit the pan.

4. *Topping:* In a small bowl, mix together sugar and cinnamon; sprinkle over top of base.

5. Bake in preheated oven for 40 to 50 minutes or until golden brown. Place pan on a wire rack to cool completely, then cut into bars.

Makes 24 bars

Cinnamon Applesauce Squares

BASE AND TOPPING

3 cups	all-purpose flour	750 mL
¼ cup	granulated sugar	50 mL
1 tbsp	baking powder	15 mL
1½ tsp	salt	7 mL
⅓ cup	butter or margarine	75 mL
2	eggs, beaten	2
6 to 8 tbsp	milk	90 to 125 mL

FILLING

2 cups	applesauce	500 mL
	Ground cinnamon	

GLAZE

1	egg yolk	1
1 tbsp	cold water	15 mL
	Granulated sugar	

- *Preheat oven to 350°F (180°C)*
- *13- by 9-inch (3.5 L) cake pan, greased*

1. *Base and Topping:* In a large bowl mix together flour, baking powder, sugar and salt. Using two knives, a pastry blender or your fingers, cut butter in until mixture resembles coarse crumbs. Add eggs and enough milk to make a dough, mixing lightly with a fork. Form dough into a ball and divide into two equal portions.

2. On a floured work surface, roll one portion into a rectangle, just a bit larger than the pan. Ease pastry into the bottom of prepared pan, bringing the dough a bit up the sides.

3. *Filling:* Spread applesauce evenly over dough and sprinkle lightly with cinnamon. Roll out remaining dough as for first portion and place on top of applesauce mixture. Seal the edges.

4. *Glaze:* Beat egg yolk and water and brush base with the mixture, then sprinkle generously with sugar. Bake in preheated oven for 40 to 45 minutes or until well browned. Place pan on a wire rack and cool completely, then cut into squares. Serve warm or cooled.

Makes 36 squares

Apricot Crumble Squares

BASE

2 cups	all-purpose flour	500 mL
1/2 tsp	baking powder	2 mL
1/4 tsp	salt	1 mL
1/2 cup	butter, softened	125 mL
1/3 cup	granulated sugar	75 mL
1	egg	1
1 tsp	vanilla	5 mL

TOPPING

2 cups	sliced apricots (drained if canned)	500 mL
1 tsp	granulated sugar	5 mL
1/2 tsp	ground cinnamon	2 mL

- *Preheat oven to 400°F (200°C)*
- *8-inch (2 L) square cake pan, ungreased*

1. *Base:* In a medium bowl, mix together flour, baking powder and salt.
2. In a large bowl, beat butter and sugar until smooth and creamy. Beat in egg and vanilla until incorporated. Blend in flour mixture, just until a dough forms. Spread dough evenly in pan. Bake in preheated oven for 6 to 7 minutes, until lightly browned.
3. *Topping:* Arrange apricots evenly over top of base. Sprinkle with sugar and cinnamon.
4. Bake 10 to 12 minutes longer or until golden brown. Place pan on a wire rack to cool completely, then cut into squares.

Makes 16 squares

Cream Cheese–Frosted Banana Bars

BASE

2 cups	all-purpose flour	500 mL
1 tsp	baking soda	5 mL
Pinch	salt	Pinch
2 cups	granulated sugar	500 mL
1/2 cup	butter or margarine, softened	125 mL
3	eggs	3
1 tsp	vanilla	5 mL
1 1/2 cups	mashed ripe bananas (3 or 4 large)	375 mL

FROSTING

8 oz	cream cheese, softened	250 g
1/2 cup	butter or margarine, softened	125 mL
2 tsp	vanilla	10 mL
3 1/2 to 4 cups	confectioner's (icing) sugar, sifted	825 mL to 1 L

- *Preheat oven to 350°F (180°C)*
- *13- by 9-inch (3.5 L) cake pan, greased*

1. *Base:* In a medium bowl, mix together flour, baking soda and salt.
2. In a large bowl, beat sugar and butter until smooth and creamy. Beat in eggs, one at a time, until incorporated. Stir in vanilla, then bananas. Blend in flour mixture. Spread evenly in prepared pan. Bake in preheated oven for 30 to 35 minutes or until a tester inserted in the center comes out clean. Place pan on a wire rack to cool completely.
3. *Frosting:* Beat cream cheese and butter until smooth and creamy. Stir in vanilla. Gradually beat in confectioner's sugar until smooth and spreadable. Spread over top of cooled cake and cut into bars.

Makes 36 bars

Banana Oatmeal Crunch Squares

BASE

2 cups	all-purpose flour	500 mL
1 cup	old-fashioned rolled oats	250 mL
2 tsp	baking powder	10 mL
1 tsp	baking soda	5 mL
½ tsp	salt	2 mL
¼ tsp	ground nutmeg	1 mL
½ cup	shortening, softened	125 mL
1¼ cups	granulated sugar	300 mL
2	eggs	2
1 tsp	vanilla	5 mL
¾ cup	buttermilk	175 mL
1½ cups	mashed ripe bananas (4 or 5 medium)	375 mL

TOPPING

¼ cup	shortening	50 mL
¾ cup	packed brown sugar	175 mL
⅓ cup	evaporated milk	75 mL
1½ cups	flaked coconut	375 mL
¾ cup	chopped walnuts	175 mL

- *Preheat oven to 350°F (180°C)*
- *13- by 9-inch (3.5 L) cake pan, greased*

1. *Base:* In a medium bowl, mix together flour, oats, baking powder, baking soda, salt and nutmeg.

2. In a large bowl, beat shortening and sugar until smooth and creamy. Beat in eggs until incorporated. Stir in vanilla. Blend in flour mixture alternately with buttermilk, then bananas, until just incorporated. Spread evenly in prepared pan. Bake in preheated oven for 35 to 40 minutes or until a tester inserted in the center comes out clean. Place pan on a wire rack to cool slightly.

3. *Topping:* Preheat broiler. In a saucepan, over low heat, melt shortening. Remove from heat and stir in brown sugar, milk, coconut and walnuts. Spread evenly over top of warm cake. Place pan under broiler and broil until top is golden brown. Place pan on a rack to cool completely, then cut into squares.

Makes 36 squares

Blueberry Pie Squares

1 cup	butter or margarine, softened	250 mL
1½ cups	granulated sugar	375 mL
4	eggs	4
1 tsp	almond extract	5 mL
2 tsp	baking powder	10 mL
2 cups	all-purpose flour	500 mL
1	can (19 oz/540mL) blueberry pie filling	1

TIP: Protect the finish on non-stick baking pans by using a plastic knife to cut bars or squares.

- *Preheat oven to 350°F (180°C)*
- *13- by 9-inch (3.5 L) cake pan, greased*

1. In a large bowl, beat butter and sugar until smooth and creamy. Beat in eggs, one at a time, until incorporated. Stir in almond extract. Blend in baking powder and flour. Spread evenly in prepared pan. Top with large spoonfuls of pie filling, 4 along the length and 4 across the width.

2. Bake in preheated oven for 45 to 50 minutes or until golden brown. (The blueberry filling will sink into the cake while baking.) Place pan on a rack to cool completely, then cut into squares.

Makes 36 squares

Blueberry Cheesecake Shortbread Bars

BASE

2 cups	all-purpose flour	500 mL
½ cup	packed brown sugar	125 mL
½ tsp	salt	2 mL
¾ cup	butter	175 mL

TOPPING

1 lb	cream cheese, softened	500 g
¾ cup	granulated sugar	175 mL
2	eggs	2
1 tsp	vanilla	5 mL
¾ cup	blueberry preserves	175 mL

- *Preheat oven to 350°F (180°C)*
- *13- by 9-inch (3.5 L) cake pan, greased*

1. *Base:* In a medium bowl, mix together flour, brown sugar and salt. Using two knives, a pastry blender or your fingers, cut butter in until mixture resembles coarse crumbs. Press evenly into prepared pan. Bake in preheated oven for 18 to 20 minutes, until lightly browned.

2. *Topping:* In a medium bowl, beat cream cheese and sugar until smooth. Add eggs and beat until incorporated. Stir in vanilla.

3. Spread blueberry preserves evenly over hot base. Spread cream cheese mixture evenly over blueberries. Bake 25 to 30 minutes longer or until slightly puffed. Place pan on a wire rack to cool completely, then cut into bars. Store, covered, in refrigerator.

Makes 36 bars

Cherry Cheesecake Bars

BASE

6 tbsp	butter or margarine, melted	90 mL
1½ cups	graham wafer crumbs (about 22 wafers)	375 mL
2 tbsp	granulated sugar	25 mL

TOPPING

12 oz	cream cheese, softened	375 g
½ cup	granulated sugar	125 mL
2	eggs	2
1½ tsp	vanilla	7 mL
1 cup	cherry pie filling	250 mL

- *Preheat oven to 350°F (180°C)*
- *9-inch (2.5 L) square cake pan, greased*

1. *Base:* In a small bowl, mix together butter, sugar and graham crumbs. Press evenly into prepared pan. Bake in preheated oven for 10 minutes or until golden brown. Place pan on a wire rack to cool.

2. *Topping:* In a medium bowl, beat cream cheese and sugar until smooth. Beat in eggs until incorporated. Stir in vanilla.

3. Spread evenly over cooled base. Spoon pie filling over cream cheese mixture, then run a knife through the batter to create a marbling effect.

4. Bake 40 to 45 minutes longer or until top is almost set. Place pan on a wire rack to cool completely, then store in refrigerator until ready to serve. Cut into bars.

Makes 24 bars

Crabapple Jelly Bars

BASE		
1½ cups	all-purpose flour	375 mL
¼ cup	granulated sugar	50 mL
Pinch	salt	Pinch
1 cup	shredded Cheddar cheese	250 mL
½ cup	finely chopped pecans	125 mL
¾ cup	butter or margarine	175 mL
TOPPING		
1 cup	crabapple jelly	250 mL

- Preheat oven to 350°F (180°C)
- 9-inch (2.5 L) square cake pan, greased

1. *Base:* In a large bowl mix together flour, sugar, salt, cheese and nuts. Using two knives, a pastry blender or your fingers, work butter in until mixture resembles coarse crumbs. Press half of mixture evenly into prepared pan.
2. *Topping:* Stir crabapple jelly to loosen; spoon evenly over top. Sprinkle with remaining crumb mixture.
3. Bake in preheated oven for 25 to 30 minutes or until golden brown. Place pan on a wire rack to cool completely, then cut into bars.

Makes 24 bars

Cranberry Streusel Bars

BASE		
⅓ cup	confectioner's (icing) sugar, sifted	75 mL
¾ cup	butter, softened	175 mL
1½ cups	all-purpose flour	375 mL
FILLING		
8 oz	cream cheese, softened	250 g
1	can (10 oz/300 mL) sweetened condensed milk	1
¼ cup	freshly squeezed lemon juice	50 mL
1 tbsp	packed brown sugar	15 mL
2 tbsp	cornstarch	25 mL
1	can (14 oz/398 mL) whole-berry cranberry sauce	1
TOPPING		
⅓ cup	all-purpose flour	75 mL
2 tbsp	packed brown sugar	25 mL
¼ cup	butter, softened	50 mL
¾ cup	chopped walnuts	175 mL

- Preheat oven to 350°F (180°C)
- 13- by 9-inch (3.5 L) cake pan, lightly greased

1. *Base:* In a medium bowl, beat confectioner's sugar and butter until smooth and creamy. Gradually blend in flour. Spread evenly in prepared pan. Bake in preheated oven for 15 minutes or until lightly browned. Place pan on a rack to cool slightly.
2. *Filling:* In another medium bowl, beat cream cheese until smooth. Gradually beat in condensed milk. Stir in lemon juice. Spread mixture evenly over warm base.
3. In another medium bowl, mix together brown sugar and cornstarch. Add cranberry sauce and mix well. Spread over cream cheese layer.
4. *Topping:* In a clean bowl, mix together flour and brown sugar. Using two knives, a pastry blender, or your fingers, cut butter in until mixture resembles coarse crumbs. Stir in nuts. Sprinkle over cranberry layer. Bake 30 to 35 minutes longer or until bubbly and golden brown. Place pan on a rack and cut into bars. Serve warm or cooled.

Makes 36 bars

Fig Newton Lattice Bars

BASE

¾ cups	butter, softened	175 mL
⅓ cup	granulated sugar	75 mL
1	egg	1
2 tsp	vanilla	10 mL
¼ tsp	salt	1 mL
2 cups	all-purpose flour	500 mL

TOPPING

1 cup	water	250 mL
1	package (10 oz/300 g) dried figs, stems cut off	1
1 cup	pitted prunes	250 mL
⅓ cup	packed brown sugar	75 mL
2 tbsp	freshly squeezed lemon juice	25 mL

> **TIP:** To make a lattice base or top, place half the dough strips parallel to each other at equal intervals. Weave a cross-strip through the center of the pie or cake in the opposite direction by folding back every other strip. Continue to weave remaining strips, folding back alternate strips each time a cross-strip is added. Trim ends if necessary.

- *Preheat oven to 375°F (190°C)*
- *13- by 9-inch (3.5 L) cake pan, greased*

1. *Base:* In a medium bowl, beat butter and sugar until smooth and creamy. Add egg, vanilla and salt, beating until incorporated. Blend in flour just until a dough forms. Knead lightly, then divide into two pieces, one slightly larger than the other. Wrap smaller piece in plastic wrap and refrigerate. Press larger piece evenly into prepared pan and refrigerate until ready to use.

2. *Topping:* In a saucepan, over medium heat, combine water, figs, prunes and brown sugar, stirring frequently, until mixture thickens and most of the liquid is absorbed, about 10 minutes. Set aside to cool slightly.

3. In a food processor, process fig mixture with lemon juice until almost smooth. Transfer to a bowl and refrigerate until cool.

4. When ready to bake, spread fig mixture over base. On a floured work surface, divide second piece of dough into two pieces, one slightly larger than the other. Cut the larger piece of dough into 10 equal pieces and, using your hands, roll each into a rope approximately 13 inches (33 cm) long. Repeat with second piece of dough, rolling the 10 pieces into ropes approximately 9 inches (23 cm) long. Top fig mixture with a lattice pattern made from the ropes of dough. (See Tip, at left.) Trim excess dough.

5. Bake in preheated oven for 40 minutes or until golden brown. Place pan on wire rack to cool completely in pan, then cut into bars.

Makes 36 bars

Classic Chocolate Nut Brownies *(page 129)* ➤
Overleaf: Rocky Road Brownies *(page 139)*

Fresh Fruit Fiesta Bars

BASE

1¾ cups	all-purpose flour	425 mL
1½ cups	old-fashioned rolled oats	375 mL
½ tsp	ground cinnamon	2 mL
¾ cup	butter or margarine, softened	175 mL
1 cup	packed brown sugar	250 mL

TOPPING

1	can (10 oz/284 mL) mandarin oranges, drained	1
1	banana, sliced	1
1 cup	cubed peeled apples	250 mL
½ cup	raisins	125 mL
¼ cup	orange juice	50 mL
1 tsp	ground cinnamon	5 mL

- *Preheat oven to 375°F (190°C)*
- *13- by 9-inch (3.5 L) cake pan, ungreased*

1. *Base:* In a medium bowl, mix together flour, rolled oats, and cinnamon.
2. In a large bowl, beat butter and sugar until smooth and creamy. Blend in flour mixture. Set aside 1¼ cups (300 mL) of mixture. Press remainder evenly into pan. Bake in preheated oven for 15 minutes.
3. *Topping:* In a medium bowl, mix together oranges, banana, apples, raisins, orange juice and cinnamon.
4. Spread topping evenly over warm base, leaving a space about ¼ inch (5 mm) from the edges. Sprinkle reserved base mixture over top, patting down gently. Bake 15 to 20 minutes longer or until golden brown. Place pan on a wire rack to cool completely, then cut into bars.

Makes 36 bars

Jam Crumb Bars

BASE

1¾ cups	all-purpose flour	425 mL
½ cup	finely chopped nuts	125 mL
¼ cup	butter or margarine, softened	50 mL
½ cup	confectioner's (icing) sugar, sifted	125 mL
¼ tsp	grated lemon zest	1 mL

TOPPING

¾ cup	jam (any flavor)	175 mL
1 tbsp	all-purpose flour	15 mL

> **TIP:** To soften cold butter quickly, place a small heated saucepan upside-down over the dish of butter for several minutes.

- *Preheat oven to 375°F (190°C)*
- *9-inch (2.5 L) square cake pan, ungreased*

1. *Base:* In a medium bowl mix together flour and nuts.
2. In a large bowl, beat butter, confectioner's sugar and lemon zest until smooth and creamy. Blend in flour mixture until crumbly. Set aside one-third of this mixture. Press remainder evenly into pan.
3. *Topping:* Stir jam until smooth, then spread evenly over base. In a small bowl, mix together reserved base mixture and flour. Sprinkle evenly over jam.
4. Bake in preheated oven for 25 to 30 minutes or until golden brown. Place pan on a wire rack to cool completely, then cut into bars.

Makes 24 bars

◄ Coffee Mocha Cheesecake Diamonds *(page 162)*
Overleaf: Chocolate Chip Blondies *(page 146)*

Almond Lemon Bars

BASE

1¾ cups	all-purpose flour	425 mL
2 tsp	baking powder	10 mL
¼ tsp	salt	1 mL
½ cup	butter or margarine, softened	125 mL
1 cup	granulated sugar	250 mL
1	egg	1
	Grated zest of 1 lemon	

TOPPING

	Milk	
¾ cup	sliced almonds	175 mL

GLAZE

4 tsp	freshly squeezed lemon juice	20 mL
1 cup	confectioner's (icing) sugar, sifted	250 mL

- *Preheat oven to 325°F (160°C)*
- *2 cookie sheets, ungreased*

1. *Base:* In a small bowl, mix together flour, baking powder and salt.
2. In a large bowl, beat butter and sugar until smooth and creamy. Beat in egg and lemon zest until incorporated. Blend in flour mixture.
3. Divide dough into four portions. Shape each portion into a log about 12 inches (30 cm) long. Place two rolls on each sheet, about 4 inches (10 cm) apart. Using your hand, flatten each roll to a width of about 2½ inches (6 cm).
4. *Topping:* Brush rolls with milk. Sprinkle almonds on top and press lightly into dough. Bake 12 to15 minutes longer or until lightly browned. Place pans on wire rack to cool.
5. *Glaze:* In a small bowl, beat lemon juice and confectioner's sugar until smooth and spreadable. Drizzle glaze over top of rolls and set aside until set. Cut diagonally into bars.

Makes about 36 bars

Lemon Coconut Tea Squares

BASE

½ cup	butter or margarine, softened	125 mL
⅓ cup	confectioner's (icing) sugar, sifted	75 mL
¾ cup	all-purpose flour	175 mL
⅓ cup	ground almonds	75 mL

TOPPING

2	eggs	2
1 cup	granulated sugar	250 mL
½ tsp	baking powder	2 mL
¼ tsp	salt	1 mL
1 tsp	grated lemon zest	5 mL
2 tbsp	freshly squeezed lemon juice	25 mL
¾ cup	flaked coconut	175 mL

- *Preheat oven to 350°F (180°C)*
- *8-inch (2 L) square cake pan, ungreased*

1. *Base:* In a medium bowl, beat butter and confectioner's sugar until smooth and creamy. Gradually blend in flour just until a soft dough forms. Stir in almonds. Press mixture evenly into pan. Bake in preheated oven for 20 minutes.
2. *Topping:* In another medium bowl, beat eggs, sugar, baking powder, salt, lemon zest and juice until blended. Stir in coconut.
3. Spread mixture evenly over hot base. Bake 25 to 30 minutes longer or until top is golden brown. Place pan on a wire rack to cool completely, then cut into squares.

Makes 16 squares

Lemon Blueberry Crumb Bars

BASE

3 cups	all-purpose flour	750 mL
2 cups	old-fashioned rolled oats	500 mL
1²⁄₃ cups	packed brown sugar	400 mL
1½ tsp	baking powder	7 mL
1¼ tsp	ground nutmeg	6 mL
½ tsp	salt	2 mL
1 tsp	grated lemon zest	5 mL
1¼ cups	butter or margarine, softened	300 mL
1	egg, beaten	1

TOPPING

1	egg	1
1	can (14 oz/398 mL) sweetened condensed milk	1
2 tsp	grated lemon zest	10 mL
½ cup	freshly squeezed lemon juice	125 mL
2 tbsp	all-purpose flour	25 mL
3 cups	blueberries, thawed if frozen	750 mL

> **TIP:** A cake will be less likely to stick to the pan if the pan is placed on a cold wet towel upon removal from the oven.

- *Preheat oven to 375° F (190° C)*
- *13- by 9-inch (3.5 L) cake pan, greased*

1. *Base:* In a large bowl, mix together flour, oats, brown sugar, baking powder, nutmeg, salt and lemon zest. Using two knives, a pastry blender or your fingers, cut butter in until mixture resembles coarse crumbs. Set 2 cups (500 mL) aside. Add egg to remaining mixture and mix until just combined. Spread evenly in prepared pan. Bake in preheated oven for 10 minutes.

2. *Topping:* In another large bowl, beat egg, condensed milk and lemon juice until smooth and blended. Blend in flour and lemon zest. Stir in blueberries.

3. Spread evenly over base. Sprinkle with reserved crumb mixture. Bake 40 to 45 minutes longer or until lightly browned. Place pan on a wire rack to cool completely, then cut into bars.

Makes about 36 bars

Lemon Cream Cheese Bars

BASE

1	package (18¼ oz/515 g) yellow cake mix	1
1	egg	1
⅓ cup	vegetable oil	75 mL

TOPPING

8 oz	cream cheese, softened	250 g
⅓ cup	granulated sugar	75 mL
1	egg	1
1 tsp	freshly squeezed lemon juice	5 mL

- *Preheat oven to 350° F (180° C)*
- *13- by 9-inch (3.5 L) cake pan, ungreased*

1. *Base:* In a medium bowl, mix together cake mix, egg and oil until mixture resembles coarse crumbs. Set aside 1 cup (250 mL) of mixture. Press remainder evenly into prepared pan. Bake in preheated oven for 15 minutes.

2. *Topping:* In another medium bowl, beat cream cheese and sugar until smooth. Add egg and beat until incorporated. Stir in lemon juice.

3. Spread evenly over hot base. Sprinkle with reserved crumb mixture. Bake 15 minutes longer or until lightly browned. Place pan on a wire rack to cool completely, then cut into bars.

Makes 36 bars

Deluxe Lemon Bars

BASE

1 cup	butter or margarine, softened	250 mL
½ cup	confectioner's (icing) sugar, sifted	125 mL
2 cups	all-purpose flour	500 mL

TOPPING

4	eggs	4
1½ cups	granulated sugar	375 mL
2 tsp	grated lemon zest	10 mL
⅓ cup	freshly squeezed lemon juice	75 mL
¼ cup	all-purpose flour	50 mL
½ tsp	baking powder	2 mL
	Confectioner's (icing) sugar	

- *Preheat oven to 350°F (180°C)*
- *13- by 9-inch (3.5 L) cake pan, ungreased*

1. *Base:* In a medium bowl, beat butter and confectioner's sugar until smooth and creamy. Gradually blend in flour, just until a soft dough forms. Press evenly into pan. Bake in preheated oven for 20 to 25 minutes or until golden brown.

2. *Topping:* In another medium bowl, beat eggs, sugar, lemon juice and zest until blended. Gradually blend in flour and baking powder.

3. Spread evenly over base. Bake 25 minutes longer. Place pan on a wire rack to cool completely. Sift confectioner's sugar over top and cut into bars.

Makes 36 bars

TIP: Cool bars, squares and brownies thoroughly before slicing. They will cut more easily and keep their shape better.

Lemon Sunburst Bars

1 cup	all-purpose flour	250 mL
1 tsp	baking powder	5 mL
¼ tsp	ground cinnamon	1 mL
¼ tsp	ground nutmeg	1 mL
1⅓ cups	packed brown sugar	325 mL
¾ cup	shortening, softened	175 mL
2	eggs	2
½ tsp	vanilla	2 mL
½ tsp	grated lemon zest	2 mL
2 tbsp	freshly squeezed lemon juice	25 mL
1 cup	quick-cooking rolled oats	250 mL
½ cup	chopped walnuts	125 mL
	Lemon Glaze or Lemon Butter Frosting (see recipes, page 364) (optional)	

- *Preheat oven to 350°F (180°C)*
- *13- by 9-inch (3.5 L) cake pan, greased*

1. In a small bowl, mix together flour, baking powder, cinnamon and nutmeg.
2. In a large bowl, beat brown sugar and shortening until smooth and creamy. Beat in eggs, one at a time, until incorporated. Stir in vanilla, lemon zest and juice. Blend in flour mixture. Stir in oats and walnuts.
3. Spread evenly in prepared pan. Bake in preheated oven for 20 to 25 minutes or until golden brown. (If desired, top with Lemon Glaze while still warm or allow to cool and frost with Lemon Butter Frosting.) When cool, cut into bars.

Makes 36 bars

Lemon Pecan Diamonds

BASE		
2 cups	all-purpose flour	500 mL
½ cup	chopped pecans	125 mL
⅓ cup	granulated sugar	75 mL
¼ tsp	salt	1 mL
¾ cup	shortening	175 mL
TOPPING		
4	eggs	4
1½ cups	granulated sugar	375 mL
1 tbsp	grated lemon zest	15 mL
½ cup	freshly squeezed lemon juice	125 mL
1 tsp	baking powder	5 mL
	Confectioner's (icing) sugar (optional)	

- *Preheat oven to 350°F (180°C)*
- *13- by 9-inch (3.5 L) cake pan, ungreased*

1. *Base:* In a food processor, combine flour, pecans, sugar and salt. Pulse twice to combine, then add shortening and process until mixture resembles fine crumbs. Press evenly into pan. Bake in preheated oven for 15 to 18 minutes, until golden brown. Place pan on a wire rack to cool slightly.
2. *Topping:* In a medium bowl, beat eggs and sugar until blended and thick. Stir in lemon zest and juice. Add baking powder and mix well. Spread mixture evenly over warm base. Bake 25 minutes longer or until topping sets. Place pan on a wire rack to cool completely. Sift confectioner's sugar over top, if desired. Cut into diamonds. (For technique, see Coffee Mocha Cheesecake Diamonds, page 162.)

Makes 36 bars

Favorite Glazed Lemon Raspberry Bars

BASE

1½ cups	all-purpose flour	375 mL
½ cup	confectioner's (icing) sugar, sifted	125 mL
¾ cup	butter	175 mL

TOPPING

½ cup	raspberry jam	125 mL
4	eggs	4
1½ cups	granulated sugar	375 mL
½ cup	freshly squeezed lemon juice	125 mL
3 tbsp	all-purpose flour	45 mL
1 tsp	baking powder	5 mL

GLAZE

½ cup	confectioner's (icing) sugar, sifted	125 mL
1 tbsp	butter or margarine, melted	15 mL
1 tbsp	freshly squeezed lemon juice	15 mL

- *Preheat oven to 350°F (180°C)*
- *13- by 9-inch (3.5 L) cake pan, greased*

1. *Base:* In a medium bowl, mix together flour and confectioner's sugar. Using two knives, a pastry blender or your fingers, cut butter in until mixture resembles coarse crumbs. Press evenly into prepared pan. Bake in preheated oven for 15 to 18 minutes, until golden brown.

2. *Topping:* Stir jam until smooth and spread evenly over warm base.

3. In a medium bowl, beat eggs and sugar until thick. Stir in lemon juice. Blend in flour and baking powder. Spread over jam. Bake 20 to 25 minutes longer or until golden brown. Place pan on a rack to cool completely.

4. *Glaze:* In a small bowl, beat confectioner's sugar, melted butter and lemon juice until smooth. Spread over cooled cake, then cut into bars.

Makes 36 bars

TIP: To sprinkle lemon juice, use a small plastic or glass salt shaker with a non-metallic top.

Sour Cream–Topped Lemon Bars

BASE

1½ cups	all-purpose flour	375 mL
½ cup	confectioner's (icing) sugar, sifted	125 mL
1 tsp	grated lemon zest	5 mL
1 tsp	grated orange zest	5 mL
¾ cup	cold butter or margarine, cut into cubes	175 mL

FILLING

2 cups	granulated sugar	500 mL
¼ cup	all-purpose flour	50 mL
1 tsp	baking powder	5 mL
4	eggs, beaten	4
2 tsp	grated lemon zest	10 mL
⅓ cup	freshly squeezed lemon juice	75 mL
2 tsp	grated orange zest	10 mL

TOPPING

⅓ cup	granulated sugar	75 mL
2 cups	sour cream	500 mL
½ tsp	vanilla	2 mL

TIP: Use a pastry brush to dislodge pieces of lemon or orange zest from the holes of a grater before washing.

- *Preheat oven to 350°F (180°C)*
- *13- by 9-inch (3.5 L) cake pan, greased*

1. *Base:* In a food processor, combine flour and confectioner's sugar. Pulse twice to combine. Add zests and butter and process until mixture begins to form a ball. Press evenly into prepared pan. Bake in preheated oven for 12 to 15 minutes or until lightly browned.

2. *Filling:* In a bowl, mix together sugar, flour and baking powder. Add eggs, lemon zest and juice and orange zest and mix until blended.

3. Spread mixture evenly over hot base. Bake 14 to 16 minutes longer or until set.

4. *Topping:* In a medium bowl, mix together sugar, sour cream and vanilla. Spread over filling.

5. Bake 8 to 10 minutes longer or until set. Place pan on a wire rack to cool completely, then store, covered, in refrigerator. Before serving, cut into bars.

Makes 36 bars

Lemon Ginger Bars

3 cups	all-purpose flour	750 mL
1½ tsp	baking soda	7 mL
1½ tsp	salt	7 mL
1 tsp	ground cinnamon	5 mL
1 tsp	ground ginger	5 mL
1 cup	shortening, softened	250 mL
1 cup	granulated sugar	250 mL
2	eggs	2
1 cup	fancy molasses	250 mL
1 cup	hot water	250 mL
LEMON SAUCE		
1 cup	water	250 mL
½ cup	granulated sugar	125 mL
2 tsp	cornstarch	10 mL
Pinch	salt	Pinch
Pinch	ground nutmeg	Pinch
2	egg yolks	2
2 tbsp	butter or margarine	25 mL
½ tsp	grated lemon zest	2 mL
2 tbsp	freshly squeezed lemon juice	25 mL

> **VARIATION**
> Top each bar with a dollop of whipped cream cheese and spoon lemon sauce over top.

- *Preheat oven to 350°F (180°C)*
- *13- by 9-inch (3.5 L) cake pan, greased*

1. In a medium bowl, mix together flour, baking soda, salt, cinnamon and ginger.
2. In another large bowl, beat shortening and sugar until smooth and creamy. Add eggs, one at a time, beating until incorporated. Beat in molasses. Gradually blend in flour mixture alternately with hot water, stirring until just incorporated.
3. Spread evenly in prepared pan. Bake in preheated oven for 35 to 40 minutes or until a tester inserted in the center comes out clean. Place pan on a rack to cool completely then cut into bars.
4. *Lemon Sauce:* In a saucepan, over medium heat, stir water, sugar, cornstarch, salt and nutmeg until smooth and bubbly. Cook and stir for 2 minutes longer. Remove from heat.
5. In a small bowl, beat egg yolks with 2 tbsp (25 mL) of the cornstarch mixture. Stir into remaining cornstarch mixture and return to heat. Cook over low heat, stirring constantly, for 2 minutes longer. Remove from heat and stir in butter, zest and juice until blended. Serve over warm or cold cake. Store, covered, in refrigerator.

Makes 36 bars

Glazed Lemon Poppy Seed Squares

BASE

1½ cups	all-purpose flour	375 mL
¾ tsp	baking soda	4 mL
1 cup + 2 tbsp	granulated sugar	275 mL
¾ cup	butter, softened	175 mL
3	eggs, separated	3
2 tsp	vanilla	10 mL
¾ cup	sour cream	175 mL
¼ cup	poppy seeds	50 mL
2 tbsp	grated lemon zest	25 mL

GLAZE

¼ cup	freshly squeezed lemon juice	50 mL
½ cup	granulated sugar	125 mL

TOPPING

1 cup	whipping (35%) cream	250 mL
2 tbsp	granulated sugar	25 mL
1 tsp	lemon extract	5 mL
	Grated lemon zest (optional)	

> **TIP:** For an attractive dessert, cut lemons in half, scoop out the pulp and hollow out shells. Then fill the shells with scoops of lemon sherbet or fresh fruit salad.

- *Preheat oven to 350°F (180°C)*
- *8-inch (2 L) square cake pan, greased*

1. *Base:* In a small bowl, mix together flour and baking soda.
2. In a large bowl, beat the 1 cup (250 mL) of sugar and butter until smooth and creamy. Beat in egg yolks, one at a time, until incorporated. Stir in vanilla. Gradually blend in flour mixture, alternately with sour cream, until just incorporated. Stir in poppy seeds and lemon zest.
3. In a clean bowl, beat egg whites until foamy. Add remaining 2 tbsp (25 mL) sugar and beat until stiff peaks form. Fold into batter and spread evenly in prepared pan.
4. Bake in preheated oven for 60 to 65 minutes or until a tester inserted in the center comes out clean. Place pan on a wire rack to cool for 10 minutes, then invert cake onto rack with waxed paper placed underneath.
5. *Glaze:* Mix together lemon juice and sugar until blended. Spoon over warm cake.
6. *Topping:* In a large bowl, beat cream until frothy. Add sugar and lemon extract and beat until soft peaks form. Spread evenly over glaze. Sprinkle lemon zest over top, if desired. Cut into squares.

Makes 16 squares

Coconut Crisp Lemon Squares

BASE

1 cup	all-purpose flour	250 mL
¾ cup	finely crushed saltine crackers (about 18 crackers)	175 mL
½ cup	flaked coconut	125 mL
½ tsp	baking soda	2 mL
½ tsp	salt	2 mL
6 tbsp	butter or margarine, softened	90 mL
¾ cup	packed brown sugar	175 mL

TOPPING

1 cup	water	250 mL
¾ cup	granulated sugar	175 mL
2 tbsp	cornstarch	25 mL
¼ tsp	salt	1 mL
2	egg yolks, beaten	2
½ tsp	grated lemon zest	2 mL
½ cup	freshly squeezed lemon juice	125 mL

TIP: A medium-sized lemon yields about 2 to 3 tbsp (25 to 45 mL) of juice and 1 tbsp (15 mL) grated zest.

- *Preheat oven to 350°F (180°C)*
- *8-inch (2 L) square cake pan, ungreased*

1. *Base:* In a medium bowl, mix together flour, cracker crumbs, coconut, baking soda and salt.

2. In a large bowl, beat butter and sugar until smooth and creamy. Blend in flour mixture. Set aside half of mixture and press remainder evenly into prepared pan. Bake in preheated oven for 10 minutes or until lightly browned. Place pan on a wire rack to cool slightly.

3. *Topping:* In a saucepan, over medium heat, stir water, sugar, cornstarch and salt until smooth and bubbly. Cook, stirring constantly, for 2 minutes longer. Remove from heat.

4. In a small bowl, beat egg yolks with 2 tbsp (25 mL) of the cornstarch mixture. Stir into remaining cornstarch mixture and return to heat. Cook over low heat, stirring constantly, for 2 minutes more. Stir in lemon zest and juice.

5. Spread evenly over baked base and sprinkle reserved crumb mixture over top. Bake 30 minutes longer or until golden brown. Place pan on a rack to cool completely, then cut into squares.

Makes 16 squares

Orange, Lemon and Lime Bars

BASE		
¾ cup	butter or margarine, softened	175 mL
½ cup	confectioner's (icing) sugar, sifted	125 mL
1½ cups	all-purpose flour	375 mL

TOPPING		
3	eggs	3
1 cup	granulated sugar	250 mL
½ tsp	grated orange zest	2 mL
½ tsp	grated lemon zest	2 mL
½ tsp	grated lime zest	2 mL
2 tbsp	freshly squeezed orange juice	25 mL
2 tbsp	freshly squeezed lemon juice	25 mL
2 tbsp	freshly squeezed lime juice	25 mL
3 tbsp	all-purpose flour	45 mL
½ tsp	baking powder	2 mL
½ tsp	salt	2 mL
1 tbsp	confectioner's (icing) sugar	15 mL

> **TIP:** Before squeezing a lemon, lime or orange for juice, grate the peel and freeze it for use in recipes requiring zest.

- *Preheat oven to 350°F (180°C)*
- *13- by 9-inch (3.5 L) cake pan, lined with greased foil*

1. *Base:* In a medium bowl, beat butter and confectioner's sugar until smooth and creamy. Gradually blend in flour, just until dough forms. Press evenly into prepared pan. Bake in preheated oven for 20 to 25 minutes or until lightly browned.

2. *Topping:* In a medium bowl, beat eggs, sugar, zests and juices until smooth and blended. Blend in flour, baking powder and salt.

3. Spread mixture evenly over hot base. Bake 15 minutes longer or until topping is just set and golden brown. Sift confectioner's sugar over top. Place pan on a wire rack to cool completely, then transfer cake, with foil, to a cutting board and cut into bars.

Makes 36 bars

"Groovy" Raspberry Lemon Bars

BASE

1 cup	butter, softened	250 mL
½ cup	confectioner's (icing) sugar, sifted	125 mL
1	egg yolk	1
1 tsp	vanilla	5 mL
2½ cups	all-purpose flour	625 mL

FILLING

	Raspberry jam	
½ cup	confectioner's (icing) sugar, sifted	125 mL
2 tsp	milk or whipping (35%) cream	10 mL
2 tsp	freshly squeezed lemon juice	10 mL

> **TIP:** If a recipe calls for softened butter (at room temperature) and you are short of time, grate butter into a warm bowl. It will soften in no time.

- *Preheat oven to 350°F (180°C)*
- *Cookie sheet, ungreased*

1. *Base:* In a large bowl, beat butter and confectioner's sugar until smooth and creamy. Beat in egg yolk and vanilla until incorporated. Gradually blend in flour. Wrap dough tightly in plastic wrap and refrigerate for at least 1 hour or up to 4 days.

2. When ready to use, divide dough into four portions. Shape each portion into a rope, about ¾ inches (2 cm) wide and 12 inches (30 cm) long. Place ropes on cookie sheet, about 2 inches apart. With your little finger, press a groove down the center of each rope. Bake in preheated oven for 10 minutes or until firm to the touch.

3. *Filling:* Spoon raspberry jam into the grooves, down each rope. Return to preheated oven and bake for 5 to 10 minutes or until golden brown. Place pan on a wire rack.

4. In a small bowl, beat confectioner's sugar, milk and lemon juice until smooth and blended. Drizzle over hot strips. Cool slightly, then cut, at an angle, into bars. The number of bars will depend on the thickness of the slices.

Makes 20 bars

Mixed Fruit Squares

BASE

2 cups	all-purpose flour	500 mL
¾ tsp	salt	4 mL
1 cup	shortening	250 mL
1	egg	1
1 tbsp	white vinegar	15 mL
2 tbsp	cold water	25 mL

FILLING

1 cup	coarsely chopped dried apricots	250 mL
2	pears, peeled and sliced	2
2	apples, peeled and sliced	2
1½ tbsp	all-purpose flour	22 mL
¾ cup	water	175 mL
¼ cup	packed brown sugar	50 mL
¼ tsp	ground cinnamon	1 mL
1 tsp	grated lemon zest	5 mL
1 tbsp	lemon juice	15 mL
	Confectioner's (icing) sugar	

- *Preheat oven to 400°F (200°C)*
- *Cookie sheet, lightly greased*

1. *Base:* In a medium bowl, combine flour and salt. Using two knives, a pastry blender or your fingers, cut shortening in until mixture resembles coarse crumbs.

2. In another medium bowl, beat egg, vinegar and water just until blended. Blend in flour mixture and stir just until a soft dough forms. Divide dough in half, shaping each half into a ball. Wrap tightly in plastic wrap and chill for 15 to 20 minutes.

3. *Filling:* In a saucepan, over low heat, combine apricots, pears, apples and flour and stir to blend. Add water, brown sugar, cinnamon, zest and juice. Bring to a boil, stirring frequently, then cover and simmer for 15 minutes or until fruit is tender. Set aside to cool.

4. On a floured work surface, roll out one portion of dough to a 12- by 9-inch (30 by 23 cm) rectangle. Place on prepared cookie sheet. Spoon filling evenly over top, leaving a ½-inch (1 cm) border all around. With your fingertips, moisten the edges with a little water.

5. Roll out remaining dough as for the first. Place on top of the fruit and crimp edges together. Using a knife, make some slashes on the top.

6. Bake in preheated oven for 10 minutes, then lower heat to 350°F (180°C) and bake 25 to 30 minutes longer, until golden brown. Place pan on wire rack to cool slightly and, while still warm, sift confectioner's sugar over top and cut into squares.

Makes 30 squares

Velvet Orange Squares

BASE

1⅔ cups	all-purpose flour	400 mL
1 tsp	baking powder	5 mL
½ tsp	baking soda	2 mL
¼ tsp	salt	1 mL
½ cup	butter or margarine, softened	125 mL
1 cup	granulated sugar	250 mL
2	eggs	2
1 tbsp	grated orange zest	15 mL
½ cup	orange juice	125 mL
½ tsp	lemon extract	2 mL

GLAZE

½ cup	apricot jam	125 mL
½ cup	granulated sugar	125 mL
⅓ cup	water	75 mL
2	oranges, thinly sliced	2
	Granulated sugar	

VARIATIONS

If desired, substitute Orange Butter Frosting (see recipe, page 360) or Easy Orange Frosting (see recipe, page 365) for the glaze.

- *Preheat oven to 350°F (180°C)*
- *8-inch (2 L) square cake pan, greased*

1. *Base:* In a small bowl, mix together flour, baking powder, baking soda and salt.
2. In a large bowl, beat butter and sugar until smooth and creamy. Add eggs and beat until incorporated. Stir in orange zest, orange juice juice and lemon extract. Gradually blend in flour mixture.
3. Spread evenly in prepared pan. Bake in preheated oven for 35 to 40 minutes or until a tester inserted in the center comes out clean. Place pan on a wire rack to cool for 10 minutes. Invert onto rack to cool completely.
4. *Glaze:* In a saucepan, over low heat, stir jam for 5 to 10 minutes, until melted and smooth. Set aside to cool slightly. In another saucepan, over low heat, combine sugar and water, stirring constantly until sugar is syrupy. Add orange slices and simmer until softened and translucent. Using a slotted spoon, transfer orange slices onto a sheet of waxed paper. Sprinkle lightly with sugar. Cool just enough to handle, then cut slices into quarters.
5. Spread half the jam over top of cake. Arrange orange pieces evenly over the jam layer, then brush with remaining jam. Chill for at least 1 hour, then cut into squares.

Makes 16 squares

Chocolate Date Nut Bars

BASE

½ cup	semi-sweet chocolate chips or chunks	125 mL
½ cup	butter or margarine	125 mL
¼ cup	granulated sugar	50 mL
1 tbsp	milk	15 mL
1⅓ cups	all-purpose flour	325 mL

TOPPING

⅓ cup	granulated sugar	75 mL
2	eggs	2
2 tbsp	all-purpose flour	25 mL
½ tsp	baking powder	2 mL
1 cup	finely chopped pitted dates	250 mL
½ cup	chopped walnuts	125 mL

- *Preheat oven to 350°F (180°C)*
- *9-inch (2.5 L) square cake pan, lightly greased*

1. *Base:* In a large saucepan over low heat, melt chocolate and butter. Stir in sugar and milk until blended. Blend in flour. Spread evenly in prepared pan. Bake in preheated oven for 10 minutes. Place pan on a wire rack to cool slightly.

2. *Topping:* In a medium bowl, beat sugar and eggs until blended. Blend in flour and baking powder. Stir in dates and walnuts.

3. Spread evenly over warm base. Bake 20 to 25 minutes longer or until a tester inserted in the center comes out clean. Place pan on a wire rack to cool completely, then cut into bars.

Makes 24 bars

Matrimonial Date Bars

FILLING

2 cups	chopped pitted dates	500 mL
⅔ cup	cold water	150 mL
2 tbsp	packed brown sugar	25 mL
2 tsp	grated orange zest	10 mL
2 tbsp	orange juice	25 mL
1 tsp	freshly squeezed lemon juice	5 mL

BASE

1½ cups	all-purpose flour	375 mL
1 tsp	baking powder	5 mL
½ tsp	baking soda	2 mL
¼ tsp	salt	1 mL
1½ cups	old-fashioned rolled oats	375 mL
1 cup	packed brown sugar	250 mL
1 cup	butter or margarine	250 mL

- *Preheat oven to 325°F (160°C)*
- *13- by 9-inch (3.5 L) cake pan, greased*

1. *Filling:* In a saucepan, combine dates, water, brown sugar and zest. Cook, stirring, over medium heat until thick and smooth. Remove from heat, then stir in orange and lemon juices. Set aside to cool slightly.

2. *Base:* In a large bowl, mix together flour, baking powder, baking soda and salt. Stir in oats and brown sugar. Using two knives, a pastry blender or your fingers, cut butter in until mixture resembles coarse crumbs. Set half aside and press remainder evenly into prepared pan.

3. Spread filling evenly over base. Top with the remaining crumb mixture; smooth lightly with your hands. Bake in preheated oven for 30 to 35 minutes, then increase heat to 350°F (180°C) and bake 5 minutes longer or until lightly browned. Remove from oven and cut into bars while still hot. Place pan on a wire rack to cool completely.

Makes 36 bars

Double Date Nut Squares

2 cups	boiling water	500 mL
2 cups	chopped pitted dates	500 mL
2 tbsp	baking soda	25 mL
2 tbsp	butter or margarine, softened	25 mL
2 cups	granulated sugar	500 mL
2	eggs	2
2 tsp	vanilla	10 mL
2½ cups	cake flour, sifted	625 mL
½ cup	chopped walnuts	125 mL
	Date Frosting (see recipe, page 368)	

- *Preheat oven to 350°F (180°C)*
- *13- by 9-inch (3.5 L) cake pan, greased*

1. In a medium bowl, mix together water, dates and baking soda.
2. In a large bowl, beat butter, sugar, eggs and vanilla until blended. Add date mixture and mix thoroughly. Blend in flour. Stir in walnuts.
3. Spread evenly in prepared pan. Bake in preheated oven for 45 to 50 minutes or until a tester inserted in the center comes out clean. Place pan on a wire rack to cool completely. Frost with Date Frosting, then cut into squares.

Makes 36 squares

TIP: Keep some vegetable oil in a squeeze bottle for when a small amount is needed.

Full of Prunes Bars

BASE

1 cup	chopped pitted prunes	250 mL
2 cups	all-purpose flour	500 mL
1½ cups	granulated sugar	375 mL
½ cup	chopped walnuts	125 mL
1¼ tsp	baking soda	6 mL
1 tsp	salt	5 mL
1 tsp	ground cinnamon	5 mL
1 tsp	ground nutmeg	5 mL
3	eggs, beaten	3
½ cup	vegetable oil	125 mL

TOPPING

½ cup	granulated sugar	125 mL
2 tbsp	all-purpose flour	25 mL
2 tbsp	butter	25 mL

- *Preheat oven to 350°F (180°C)*
- *13- by 9-inch (3.5 L) cake pan, greased*

1. *Base:* In a covered saucepan, over low heat, simmer prunes, with water to cover, for 15 to 20 minutes or until tender. Drain, reserving ⅔ cup (150 mL) of cooking liquid. (If you do not have sufficient liquid, add required amount of water.)
2. In a large bowl, mix together flour, sugar, walnuts, baking soda, salt, cinnamon and nutmeg. Make a well in the center. Add eggs, oil, and reserved prune liquid and mix until blended. Stir in prunes. Spread evenly in prepared pan.
3. *Topping:* In a small bowl, mix together sugar and flour. Using two knives, a pastry blender or your fingers, cut butter in until mixture resembles coarse crumbs.
4. Sprinkle evenly over base. Bake in preheated oven for 30 to 35 minutes or until a tester inserted in the center comes out clean. Place pan on a wire rack to cool completely, then cut into bars.

Makes 36 bars

Spicy Prune Bars

1½ cups	all-purpose flour	375 mL
¾ cup	granulated sugar	175 mL
¼ cup	packed brown sugar	50 mL
1 tsp	baking powder	5 mL
½ tsp	baking soda	2 mL
½ tsp	ground cinnamon	2 mL
¼ tsp	salt	1 mL
¼ tsp	ground ginger	1 mL
1	egg, beaten	1
1 tsp	vanilla	5 mL
½ cup	vegetable oil	125 mL
½ cup	cold water	125 mL
½ cup	strained prunes (baby food)	125 mL
½ cup	chopped walnuts	125 mL
GLAZE (OPTIONAL)		
1 tbsp	light (5%) cream	15 mL
Pinch	ground cinnamon	Pinch
½ cup	confectioner's (icing) sugar, sifted	125 mL

- *Preheat oven to 350°F (180°C)*
- *9-inch (2.5 L) square cake pan, greased*

1. In a bowl mix together flour, sugars, baking powder, baking soda, cinnamon, salt and ginger. Make a well in the center. Add egg, vanilla, oil, water and prunes and mix just until incorporated.
2. Spread batter evenly in prepared pan. Sprinkle nuts evenly over top. Bake in preheated oven for 25 to 30 minutes or until a tester inserted in center comes out clean. Place pan on a rack to cool.
3. Glaze (optional): In a bowl combine cream and cinnamon. Gradually beat in confectioner's sugar. Drizzle over top of cake. When cool, cut into bars.

Makes 24 bars

Raisin Bars

2¾ cups	Mix-Ahead Bar Mix (see recipe, page 210)	675 mL
1 cup	raisins	250 mL
¼ tsp	ground cinnamon	1 mL
¼ tsp	ground nutmeg	1 mL
2	eggs, beaten	2
⅓ cup	unsweetened applesauce	75 mL
1 tbsp	milk	15 mL
1 tsp	vanilla	5 mL
	Frosting (optional)	

- *Preheat oven to 350°F (180°C)*
- *9-inch (2.5 L) square cake pan, greased*

1. In a large bowl, mix together Bar Mix, raisins, cinnamon and nutmeg.
2. In another large bowl, beat eggs, applesauce, milk and vanilla. Blend in dry ingredients.
3. Spread evenly in prepared pan. Bake in preheated oven for 20 to 25 minutes or until a tester inserted in the center comes out clean. Place pan on a rack to cool completely. If desired, spread with a frosting, such as Butter Frosting (see recipe, page 360) or Banana Frosting (see recipe, page 358), before cutting into bars.

TIP: To freshen raisins that have dried out, place them in a strainer and steam over hot water.

Makes 24 bars

Mix-Ahead Bar Mix

4 cups	all-purpose flour	1 L
1 cup	packed brown sugar	250 mL
1 cup	granulated sugar	250 mL
2 tsp	baking powder	10 mL
1½ cups	shortening	375 mL

1. In a large bowl, mix together flour, brown sugar, sugar and baking powder. Using two knives, a pastry blender or your fingers, cut shortening in until mixture resembles coarse crumbs. Store in an airtight container, at room temperature, for up to 6 weeks, or in freezer for up to 6 months.

Makes about 8 cups (2 L)

Strawberry Rhubarb Meringue Bars

Base		
1¾ cups	all-purpose flour	425 mL
2 tbsp	confectioner's (icing) sugar, sifted	25 mL
½ cup	butter or margarine	125 mL
FILLING		
1½ cups	granulated sugar	375 mL
¼ cup	all-purpose flour	50 mL
¼ tsp	salt	1 mL
6	egg yolks	6
1 cup	evaporated milk	250 mL
2 cups	sliced strawberries, thawed if frozen	500 mL
4 cups	sliced rhubarb (1 inch/2.5 cm thick), thawed if frozen	1 L
½ tsp	freshly squeezed lemon juice	2 mL
TOPPING		
6	egg whites	6
½ cup	granulated sugar	125 mL

- *Preheat oven to 350°F (180°C)*
- *13- by 9-inch (3.5 L) cake pan, ungreased*

1. *Base:* In a medium bowl, mix together flour and confectioner's sugar. Using two knives, a pastry blender or your fingers, cut butter in until mixture resembles coarse crumbs. Press evenly into pan. Bake in preheated oven for 10 to 12 minutes. Place pan on a rack to cool slightly.

2. *Filling:* In a large bowl, mix together sugar, flour and salt. In another bowl, whisk egg yolks and milk. Add to flour mixture and mix until blended. Stir in strawberries, rhubarb and lemon juice.

3. Spread filling evenly over warm base and bake 55 to 60 minutes longer or until filling is firm.

4. *Topping:* In a clean bowl, beat egg whites until foamy. Gradually add sugar, beating until stiff peaks form.

5. Spread over filling. Bake 10 minutes longer or until meringue is nicely browned. Place pan on a wire rack to cool completely, then cut into bars.

Makes 36 bars

TIP: Use only unsweetened strawberries and rhubarb in this recipe.

Peaches 'n' Cream Dessert Bars

BASE		
2 cups	graham wafer crumbs	500 mL
1/3 cup	granulated sugar	75 mL
1/2 cup	sliced almonds	125 mL
6 tbsp	butter, melted	90 mL

FILLING		
1 1/2 cups	cream cheese, softened	375 mL
1/2 cup	granulated sugar	125 mL
2	eggs	2
1 tsp	vanilla	5 mL

TOPPING		
2 tbsp	all-purpose flour	25 mL
2 tbsp	cold butter, cut into pieces	25 mL
1/4 cup	packed brown sugar	50 mL
1/2 cup	sliced almonds	125 mL
1 cup	peach jam	250 mL

- *Preheat oven to 350°F (180°C)*
- *13- by 9-inch (3.5 L) cake pan, greased*

1. *Base:* In a medium bowl, mix together graham wafer crumbs, sugar, almonds and melted butter. Press evenly into prepared pan. Bake in preheated oven for 10 minutes or until lightly browned. Place pan on a rack to cool slightly.
2. *Filling:* In a medium bowl, beat cream cheese and sugar until smooth. Beat in eggs until incorporated. Stir in vanilla.
3. Spread filling evenly over warm base. Bake 15 minutes longer, until slightly puffed.
4. *Topping:* In a small bowl, combine flour, butter, brown sugar and almonds and mix together until crumbly. Set aside.
5. Stir jam until smooth, then spread evenly over filling. Sprinkle topping evenly over jam. Bake 15 minutes longer or until hot and bubbly. Place pan on a wire rack to cool completely.

Makes 36 bars

Oatmeal Peach Crumble Squares

BASE		
4 cups	peeled sliced peaches (about 6 peaches)	1 L
1 cup	granulated sugar	250 mL
2 tbsp	freshly squeezed lemon juice	25 mL

TOPPING		
3 cups	oatmeal muffin mix	750 mL
1/4 tsp	ground nutmeg	1 mL
1/2 cup	butter or margarine	125 mL

- *Preheat oven to 375°F (190°C)*
- *8-inch (2 L) square cake pan, ungreased*

1. *Base:* In a large bowl, mix together peaches, sugar and lemon juice. Spread evenly in pan.
2. *Topping:* In another large bowl, combine muffin mix and nutmeg. Using two knives, a pastry blender or your fingers, cut butter in until mixture resembles coarse crumbs.
3. Spoon over fruit. Bake in preheated oven for 40 to 45 minutes or until golden brown. Cool slightly, then cut into squares.

Makes 16 squares

TIP: These squares are particularly delicious served warm with ice cream.

Cinnamon Nut Pear Bars

BASE

2 cups	packaged biscuit mix	500 mL
¼ cup	granulated sugar	50 mL
1 tsp	ground cinnamon	5 mL
1	can (28 oz/796 mL) pears, drained, sliced, ½ cup (125 mL) of liquid reserved	1
1	egg	1
½ tsp	vanilla	2 mL

TOPPING

¼ cup	packed brown sugar	50 mL
¼ cup	all-purpose flour	50 mL
2 tbsp	butter	25 mL
¼ cup	chopped walnuts	50 mL

TIP: For an added touch, thinly slice a fresh pear, leaving the skin, on and place a slice on top of each bar.

- *Preheat oven to 375° F (190° C)*
- *9-inch (2.5 L) square cake pan, greased*

1. *Base:* In a bowl, mix together biscuit mix, sugar and cinnamon.
2. In a small bowl, whisk together reserved pear juice, egg and vanilla. Add to biscuit mixture, mixing just until a dough forms. Spread evenly in prepared pan. Arrange pears evenly over top.
3. *Topping:* In a small bowl mix together brown sugar and flour. Using two knives, a pastry blender or your fingers, cut butter in until mixture resembles coarse crumbs. Stir in walnuts.
4. Spoon evenly over pears. Bake in preheated oven for 30 to 35 minutes or until lightly browned around the edges. Place pan on a wire rack to cool completely, then cut into bars.

Makes 24 bars

Lemon Walnut Squares

BASE

½ cup	butter	125 mL
¼ cup	confectioner's (icing) sugar, sifted	50 mL
Pinch	salt	Pinch
1 cup	all-purpose flour	250 mL
⅓ cup	finely chopped walnuts	75 mL

TOPPING

¾ cup	granulated sugar	175 mL
2	eggs	2
1 tbsp	grated lemon zest	15 mL
¼ cup	freshly squeezed lemon juice	50 mL
2 tbsp	all-purpose flour	25 mL
½ tsp	baking powder	2 mL
	Confectioner's (icing) sugar (optional)	

- *Preheat oven to 350°F (180°C)*
- *8-inch (2 L) square cake pan, lightly greased*

1. *Base:* In a medium bowl, beat butter and sugar until smooth and creamy. Add salt and blend well. Gradually blend in flour, mixing until crumbly. Stir in walnuts. Press evenly into prepared pan. Bake in preheated oven for 20 to 25 minutes or until golden brown. Place pan on a rack to cool slightly.
2. *Topping:* In a small bowl, beat sugar, eggs, lemon zest and juice until blended. Blend in flour and baking powder. Spoon over baked base. Bake 25 to 30 minutes longer or until center is set. Place pan on a rack to cool completely. If desired, sift confectioner's sugar lightly over top. Cut into squares.

Makes 16 squares

Pineapple Carrot Bars

½ cup	all-purpose flour	125 mL
½ cup	whole wheat flour	125 mL
1 tbsp	ground cinnamon	15 mL
1 tsp	baking powder	5 mL
1 tsp	baking soda	5 mL
½ cup	packed brown sugar	125 mL
2 tbsp	vegetable oil	25 mL
1	egg, beaten	1
1 tsp	vanilla	5 mL
¼ cup	milk	50 mL
1 cup	finely grated carrots	250 mL
½ cup	raisins	125 mL
⅔ cup	crushed unsweetened pineapple, drained	150 mL

- *Preheat oven to 350°F (180°C)*
- *13- by 9-inch (3.5 L) cake pan, lightly greased*

1. In a large bowl, mix together all-purpose flour, whole wheat flour, cinnamon, baking powder and baking soda. Add sugar, oil, egg, vanilla and milk and mix until just blended. Stir in carrots, raisins, and pineapple.
2. Spread evenly in prepared pan. Bake in preheated oven for 25 minutes or until top is golden brown. Place pan on a wire rack to cool completely, then cut into bars. Store, covered, in refrigerator.

Makes 36 bars

Rhubarb Crisp Squares

FILLING		
4 cups	chopped rhubarb, thawed if frozen	1 L
1 cup	granulated sugar	250 mL
2 tbsp	cornstarch	25 mL
1 tsp	grated orange zest	5 mL
BASE		
1½ cups	all-purpose flour	375 mL
½ cup	packed brown sugar	125 mL
½ cup	chopped pecans	125 mL
1 tsp	ground cinnamon	5 mL
¼ tsp	salt	1 mL
½ cup	butter or margarine, softened	125 mL

TIP: Allow bars, squares and brownies to cool completely before cutting. Then use a sharp knife and a gentle, sawing motion to avoid squashing the cake.

- *Preheat oven to 350°F (180°C)*
- *8-inch (2 L) square cake pan, greased*

1. *Filling:* In a saucepan, combine rhubarb, sugar, cornstarch and zest. Cook over medium heat, stirring constantly, for 5 minutes or until mixture thickens. Set aside to cool.
2. *Base:* In a medium bowl, mix together flour, sugar, pecans, cinnamon and salt. Using two knives, a pastry blender or your fingers, cut butter in until mixture resembles coarse crumbs. Set aside 1 cup (250 mL) and press remainder evenly in prepared pan.
3. Spread filling evenly over base and sprinkle reserved flour mixture evenly over top. Bake in preheated oven for 35 to 40 minutes or until golden brown. Place pan on a rack to cool completely, then cut into squares.

Makes 16 squares

Strawberry Rhubarb Crisp Bars

BASE

½ cup	butter or margarine, melted	125 mL
¼ cup	granulated sugar	50 mL
1½ cups	graham wafer crumbs (about 22 wafers)	375 mL

TOPPING

3 cups	chopped rhubarb (1-inch/2.5 cm pieces), thawed if frozen	750 mL
1 cup	granulated sugar	250 mL
3 tbsp	cornstarch	45 mL
Pinch	ground cinnamon	Pinch
½ cup	cold milk	125 mL
1½ tsp	unflavored gelatin	7 mL
8 oz	cream cheese, softened	250 g
2 tbsp	granulated sugar	25 mL
1 cup	sliced fresh strawberries	250 mL

TIP: If desired, garnish each bar with sliced strawberries.

- *Preheat oven to 350°F (180°C)*
- *9-inch (2.5 L) square cake pan, greased*

1. *Base:* In a medium bowl, mix together butter, sugar and crumbs. Set aside one-quarter of the mixture and press remainder evenly into prepared pan. Bake in preheated oven for 10 minutes or until golden brown. Place pan on a rack to cool slightly.

2. *Topping:* In a saucepan, combine rhubarb, sugar, cornstarch and cinnamon. Cook over low heat, stirring constantly, until sugar dissolves and mixture thickens. Simmer 5 minutes longer, until rhubarb is tender. Remove from heat and set aside to cool.

3. In the top of a double boiler, sprinkle gelatin over milk. Let stand for 5 minutes, then stir over hot (not boiling) water until gelatin dissolves. Set aside to cool.

4. In a large bowl, beat cream cheese and sugar until smooth. Gradually add dissolved gelatin mixture and mix until blended. Stir in rhubarb mixture. Spread evenly over baked base. Sprinkle with reserved crumbs. Chill for at least 1 hour, then cut into bars.

Makes 24 bars

Scrumptious Strawberry Swirls

BASE

2¼ cups	graham wafer crumbs (about 30 wafers)	550 mL
½ cup	butter, melted	125 mL

TOPPING

2	packages (4 servings each) strawberry-flavored gelatin dessert mix	2
1⅓ cups	boiling water	325 mL
2	packages (each 10 oz/300 g) frozen unsweetened strawberries, thawed	2
1	package (10½ oz/300 g) miniature marshmallows	1
½ cup	milk	125 mL
1 cup	whipping (35%) cream, whipped	250 mL

TIP: If desired, set aside ¼ cup (50 mL) of graham wafer crumb mixture and sprinkle over top.

- *Preheat oven to 350°F (180°C)*
- *9-inch (2.5 L) square cake pan, ungreased*

1. In a medium bowl, mix together graham crumbs and melted butter. Press evenly into pan.
2. In a large bowl, combine gelatin with boiling water and mix until gelatin dissolves. Add strawberries and mix well. Chill until almost set, stirring occasionally.
3. In the top of a double boiler, melt marshmallows in milk, stirring constantly until smooth. Transfer to refrigerator and chill until cold. When gelatin mixture is almost set, fold whipped cream into marshmallow mixture.
4. Alternate layers of marshmallow and gelatin mixtures over base, then run a knife through the layers to create a marbling effect. Refrigerate until ready to serve, then cut into squares.

Makes 24 squares

Old-Fashioned Gingerbread Spice Bars

2½ cups	all-purpose flour	625 mL
2 tsp	baking powder	10 mL
1 tsp	ground cinnamon	5 mL
1 tsp	ground ginger	5 mL
½ tsp	baking soda	2 mL
½ tsp	salt	2 mL
Pinch	ground cloves	Pinch
½ cup	shortening, softened	125 mL
½ cup	granulated sugar	125 mL
2	eggs	2
1 cup	fancy molasses	250 mL
1 cup	boiling water	250 mL

- *Preheat oven to 350°F (180°C)*
- *13- by 9-inch (3.5 L) cake pan, greased*

1. In a medium bowl, mix together flour, baking powder, cinnamon, ginger, baking soda, salt and cloves.
2. In a large bowl, beat shortening and sugar until smooth and creamy. Add eggs, one at a time, beating until incorporated. Beat in molasses. Gradually blend in flour mixture alternately with boiling water until just incorporated.
3. Pour into prepared pan. Bake in preheated oven for 40 to 45 minutes, until a tester inserted in the center comes out clean. Place pan on a wire rack to cool completely, then cut into bars.

Makes 36 bars

Spiced Pumpkin Bars

BASE

1 cup	all-purpose flour	250 mL
½ cup	quick-cooking rolled oats	125 mL
½ cup	packed brown sugar	125 mL
½ cup	cold butter, cut into cubes	125 mL

FILLING

2 cups	scalded milk	500 mL
¾ cup	granulated sugar	175 mL
2 cups	pumpkin purée (not pie filling)	500 mL
3	eggs, beaten	3
1 tsp	ground cinnamon	5 mL
½ tsp	salt	2 mL
½ tsp	ground ginger	2 mL
¼ tsp	ground cloves	1 mL

TOPPING

2 tbsp	all-purpose flour	25 mL
1 cup	packed brown sugar	250 mL
1 cup	chopped nuts	250 mL
¼ cup	butter, softened	50 mL

- *Preheat oven to 350° F (180° C)*
- *13- by 9-inch (3.5 L) cake pan, greased*

1. *Base:* In a medium bowl, mix together flour, oats and sugar. Using two knives, a pastry blender or your fingers, cut butter in until mixture resembles coarse crumbs. Press evenly into prepared pan. Bake in preheated oven for 12 to 15 minutes or until golden brown.

2. *Filling:* In a large bowl, mix together milk, sugar and pumpkin. Add eggs, cinnamon, salt, ginger and cloves and mix until thoroughly blended.

3. Spread evenly over baked base. Bake 15 to 20 minutes longer or until set.

4. *Topping:* In another medium bowl, mix together flour, brown sugar and nuts. Using two knives, a pastry blender or your fingers, cut butter in until mixture is crumbly.

5. Sprinkle evenly over hot cake. Bake 10 to 15 minutes longer or until topping is golden brown. Place pan on a wire rack to cool completely, then cut into bars.

Makes 36 bars

TIP: No time to bake it? Fake it! Surprise guests or your family with the aroma of freshly baked cookies, bars, squares or brownies — without baking! Just heat 2 tsp (10 mL) vanilla and ¼ cup (50 mL) water in a metal pan, in a warm oven. No one will ever guess your secret.

Pumpkin Cheesecake Bars

BASE

2 tbsp	butter, melted	25 mL
2 tbsp	maple syrup	25 mL
1⅓ cups	graham wafer crumbs	325 mL

TOPPING

½ cup	granulated sugar	125 mL
1½ lbs	cream cheese, softened	750 g
4	eggs	4
½ cup	maple syrup	125 mL
1 tsp	vanilla	5 mL
1⅔ cups	pumpkin purée (not pie filling)	400 mL
	Whipped cream (optional)	

- *Preheat oven to 375° F (190° C)*
- *9-inch (2.5 L) square cake pan, lightly greased*

1. *Base:* In a small bowl, mix together butter, syrup and wafer crumbs. Press evenly into prepared pan. Bake in preheated oven for 8 to 10 minutes or until lightly browned. Place pan on a wire rack to cool. Lower oven heat to 350°F (180°C).

2. *Topping:* In a large bowl, beat sugar and cream cheese until smooth. Add eggs, one at a time, beating until incorporated. Stir in syrup and vanilla. Blend in pumpkin.

3. Pour over base. Bake 55 to 60 minutes longer or until center is just set. Run a knife around the edge of the cake, then place pan on a wire rack to cool completely. Chill overnight. When ready to serve, cut into bars. Top with a dollop of whipped cream, if desired.

Makes 24 bars

Pumpkin Pie Dessert Bars

BASE

1½ cups	quick-cooking rolled oats	375 mL
1½ cups	packed brown sugar	375 mL
1½ cups	all-purpose flour	375 mL
½ tsp	salt	2 mL
¾ cup	butter	175 mL
1	egg	1

FILLING

3 cups	pumpkin purée (not pie filling)	750 mL
¾ cup	packed brown sugar	175 mL
1½ tsp	ground cinnamon	7 mL
¾ tsp	ground nutmeg	4 mL
¾ tsp	ground ginger	4 mL
3	eggs	3
1 cup	evaporated milk	250 mL
¾ cup	chopped pecans	175 mL

- *Preheat oven to 350°F (180°C)*
- *13- by 9-inch (3.5 L) cake pan, ungreased*

1. *Base:* In a large bowl, mix together oats, brown sugar, flour and salt. Using two knives, a pastry blender or your fingers, cut butter in until mixture resembles coarse crumbs. Add egg and mix well. Set aside 1½ cups (375 mL) of mixture and press remainder evenly in pan. Bake in preheated oven for 20 minutes or until golden brown. Place pan on a rack to cool slightly.

2. *Filling:* In a large bowl, combine pumpkin, brown sugar, cinnamon, nutmeg and ginger. Add eggs, one at a time and beat until blended. Gradually stir in milk. Pour evenly over baked base.

3. In a small bowl, mix together reserved oat mixture and nuts. Sprinkle evenly over filling. Bake 30 to 35 minutes longer or until center is set. Place pan on a wire rack to cool completely, then cut into bars.

Makes 36 bars

Frosted Carrot Bars

1¼ cups	all-purpose flour	300 mL
1 cup	granulated sugar	250 mL
1 tsp	baking soda	5 mL
1 tsp	ground cinnamon	5 mL
½ tsp	salt	2 mL
1	jar (7½ oz/213 mL) strained carrots (baby food)	1
1	jar (7½ oz/213 mL) strained applesauce (baby food)	1
2 tbsp	vegetable oil	25 mL
2	eggs	2
FROSTING		
3 oz	cream cheese, softened	90 g
1 tsp	milk (approximate)	5 mL
1 tsp	vanilla	5 mL
2 cups	confectioner's (icing) sugar, sifted	500 mL

- *Preheat oven to 350°F (180°C)*
- *13- by 9-inch (3.5 L) cake pan, greased*

1. In a large bowl, mix together flour, sugar, baking soda, cinnamon and salt. Add baby foods, oil and eggs and mix until just blended.

2. Spread evenly in prepared pan. Bake in preheated oven for 20 to 25 minutes or until tester inserted in the center comes out clean. Place pan on a wire rack to cool completely, then cut into bars.

3. *Frosting:* In a medium bowl, beat cream cheese, milk and vanilla until smooth. Gradually add confectioner's sugar, beating until smooth and spreadable, adjusting consistency with more milk if necessary. Drop a spoonful of frosting on top of each bar.

Makes 36 bars

TIP: A wet knife does a smoother job of cutting fresh bars, squares or brownies.

Carrot Pumpkin Bars

BASE

2 cups	all-purpose flour	500 mL
2 tsp	baking powder	10 mL
1½ tsp	ground cinnamon	7 mL
1 tsp	baking soda	5 mL
½ tsp	salt	2 mL
½ tsp	ground ginger	2 mL
Pinch	ground cloves	Pinch
⅓ cup	butter or margarine, softened	75 mL
1 cup	granulated sugar	250 mL
½ cup	packed brown sugar	125 mL
2	eggs	2
2	egg whites	2
1 cup	finely shredded carrots	250 mL
2 cups	pumpkin, cooked and puréed or canned pumpkin purée (not pie filling)	500 mL

TOPPING

4 oz	light cream cheese, softened	125 g
¼ cup	granulated sugar	50 mL
1 tbsp	milk	15 mL

> **TIP:** If you prefer, substitute 2 tsp (10 mL) pumpkin pie spice for the cinnamon, ginger and cloves.

- *Preheat oven to 350°F (180°C)*
- *13- by 9-inch (3.5 L) cake pan, greased*

1. *Base:* In a medium bowl, mix together flour, baking powder, cinnamon, baking soda, salt, ginger and cloves.
2. In a large bowl, beat butter, granulated sugar and brown sugar until smooth and creamy. Add eggs and egg whites, beating until incorporated. Stir in carrots and pumpkin. Gradually blend in flour mixture. Spread evenly in prepared pan.
3. *Topping:* In a small bowl, beat cream cheese and sugar until smooth. Beat in milk.
4. Drop teaspoonfuls of mixture over top of pumpkin batter. Run a knife through batters to create a marbling effect. Bake in preheated oven for 30 to 35 minutes or until a tester inserted in the center comes out clean. Place pan on a wire rack to cool completely, then cut into bars.

Makes 36 bars

Raspberry Oat Granola Bars

BASE		
⅓ cup	quick-cooking rolled oats	75 mL
17	graham wafers, finely crushed	17
2 tbsp	granulated sugar	25 mL
1	egg white	1
1 tbsp	butter or margarine, melted	15 mL
1 tbsp	fruit juice or water	15 mL
⅓ cup	raisins	75 mL
TOPPING		
1½ cups	raspberry jam	375 mL

- *Preheat oven to 375°F (190°C)*
- *8-inch (2 L) square cake pan, greased*

1. *Base:* In a medium bowl, mix together oats, graham crumbs, sugar, egg white, butter and fruit juice. Set aside ¼ cup (50 mL) of mixture; stir raisins into the remainder.
2. Spread evenly in prepared pan. Bake in preheated oven for 7 minutes. Place pan on a wire rack to cool completely.
3. *Topping:* Stir jam until smooth.
4. Spread evenly over cooled base. Sprinkle with reserved crumb mixture. Bake in preheated oven for 30 to 40 minutes or until bubbly. Run a knife around the edges of the pan, then place pan on a rack to cool completely. Cut into bars.

Makes 16 bars

Banana Chocolate Chip Oatmeal Bars

1 cup	packed brown sugar	250 mL
¾ cup	butter or margarine, softened	175 mL
1	egg	1
½ tsp	salt	2 mL
1¼ cups	mashed ripe bananas (4 medium)	300 mL
4 cups	old-fashioned rolled oats	1 L
½ cup	chocolate chips	125 mL
½ cup	raisins	125 mL

- *Preheat oven to 350°F (180°C)*
- *13- by 9-inch (3.5 L) cake pan, greased*

1. In a large bowl, beat brown sugar and butter until smooth and creamy. Beat in egg, salt and bananas until well combined. Stir in oats, chocolate chips and raisins and mix thoroughly.
2. Spread evenly in prepared pan. Bake in preheated oven for 50 to 60 minutes or until a tester inserted in the center comes out clean. Place pan on a wire rack to cool completely, then cut into bars.

Makes 36 bars

TIP: To ripen green bananas quickly, wrap them in newspaper.

Raisin-Spice Pumpkin Bars

2 cups	all-purpose flour	500 mL
2 cups	granulated sugar	500 mL
2 tsp	baking powder	10 mL
1 tsp	baking soda	5 mL
1 tsp	ground cinnamon	5 mL
1 tsp	ground nutmeg	5 mL
1/2 tsp	salt	2 mL
1/2 tsp	ground cloves	2 mL
4	eggs, beaten	4
1 cup	vegetable oil	250 mL
2 cups	pumpkin purée (not pie filling)	500 mL
1/2 cup	raisins	125 mL
1/2 cup	chopped nuts	125 mL
FROSTING (OPTIONAL)		
4 oz	cream cheese, softened	125 g
1/3 cup	butter or margarine, softened	75 mL
2 tsp	milk	10 mL
1 tsp	vanilla	5 mL
2 cups	confectioner's (icing) sugar, sifted	500 mL

> **TIP:** Replace ground spices annually; they lose their flavor over time.

- *Preheat oven to 350°F (180°C)*
- *13- by 9-inch (3.5 L) cake pan, greased*

1. In a large bowl, mix together flour, sugar, baking powder, baking soda, cinnamon, nutmeg, salt and cloves. Make a well in the center. Add eggs, oil and pumpkin and mix until blended. Stir in raisins and nuts.

2. Bake in preheated oven for 30 to 35 minutes or until a tester inserted in the center comes out clean. Place pan on a wire rack to cool completely.

3. *Frosting (optional):* In a medium bowl, beat cream cheese and butter until smooth. Beat in milk and vanilla. Gradually add confectioner's sugar, beating until smooth and spreadable. Spread frosting over top of cooled cake. Cut into bars.

Makes 36 bars

Wheat Germ Date Bars

1¼ cups	chopped pitted dates (8 oz/250 g package)	300 mL
1¼ cups	water	300 mL
BASE		
1 cup	wheat germ	250 mL
1 cup	whole wheat flour	250 mL
½ cup	packed brown sugar	125 mL
½ cup	butter or margarine, softened	125 mL
TOPPING		
⅔ cup	whole wheat flour	150 mL
½ cup	granulated sugar	125 mL
1 tsp	baking powder	5 mL
½ tsp	salt	2 mL
2	eggs, beaten	2
¼ tsp	almond extract	1 mL

> **TIP**: To soften brown sugar that has hardened, place sugar in a glass jar with half an apple. Seal tightly and let stand for 1 day. Remove the apple and, using a fork, fluff up sugar. Reseal the jar.

- *Preheat oven to 350°F (180°C)*
- *9-inch (2.5 L) square cake pan, greased*

1. In a saucepan, over medium heat, bring dates and water to a boil. Reduce heat and simmer, uncovered, for 15 to 20 minutes or until water is absorbed and dates thicken. Set aside.

2. *Base:* In a medium bowl, mix together wheat germ, whole-wheat flour and sugar. Using two knives, a pastry blender or your fingers, cut butter in until mixture resembles coarse crumbs. Press 2 cups (500 mL) into prepared pan. Set remainder aside. Bake in preheated oven for 10 minutes. Place pan on a rack.

3. *Topping:* In another bowl, mix together whole-wheat flour, sugar, baking powder and salt. Blend in eggs, almond extract and reserved dates.

4. Spread evenly over hot base. Sprinkle reserved crumb mixture evenly over top, pressing down lightly. Bake 25 minutes longer or until topping is set. Place pan on a wire rack to cool completely, then cut into bars.

Makes 24 bars

Glazed Zucchini Raisin Bars

2 cups	whole wheat flour (see Tip, below)	500 mL
2 tsp	baking soda	10 mL
¾ tsp	ground cinnamon	4 mL
½ tsp	ground nutmeg	2 mL
¼ tsp	ground cloves	1 mL
1 cup	raisins	250 mL
½ cup	butter or margarine, softened	125 mL
1¼ cups	packed brown sugar	300 mL
2	eggs	2
1 tsp	vanilla	5 mL
1½ cups	shredded zucchini	375 mL
LEMON GLAZE		
2 tbsp	butter or margarine, softened	25 mL
1 to 2 tbsp	freshly squeezed lemon juice	15 to 25 mL
1½ cups	confectioner's (icing) sugar, sifted	375 mL

TIP: If desired, use 1 cup (250 mL) each of whole wheat and all-purpose flour.

- *Preheat oven to 350°F (180°C)*
- *13- by 9-inch (3.5 L) cake pan, greased*

1. In a medium bowl, mix together flour, baking soda, cinnamon, nutmeg, cloves and raisins.
2. In a large bowl, beat butter and brown sugar until smooth and creamy. Beat in eggs, then vanilla, until incorporated. Blend in flour mixture. Stir in zucchini.
3. Spread evenly in prepared pan. Bake in preheated oven for 30 to 35 minutes or until a tester inserted in the center comes out clean. Place pan on a wire rack to cool.
3. *Glaze:* In a small bowl, beat butter and lemon juice until smooth. Gradually add confectioner's sugar, beating until smooth and spreadable. Spread over warm cake, then cut into bars. Store, covered, in refrigerator.

Makes 36 bars

Pineapple Upside-Down Bars

2 tbsp	butter or margarine	25 mL
½ cup	packed brown sugar	125 mL
1¼ cups	all-purpose flour	300 mL
2 tsp	baking powder	10 mL
½ tsp	salt	2 mL
1	can (8 oz/250 mL) pineapple slices, drained, ½ cup (125 mL) juice reserved	1
4	maraschino cherries	4
⅓ cup	shortening, softened	75 mL
½ cup	granulated sugar	125 mL
1	egg	1
½ tsp	grated lemon zest (optional)	2 mL

- *Preheat oven to 350°F (180°C)*
- *8-inch (2 L) square cake pan, ungreased*

1. In preheated oven, melt butter in baking pan. Remove from oven. Sprinkle brown sugar evenly over pan. Arrange 4 pineapple slices over the sugar and place a cherry in the center of each. Set aside.

2. In a small bowl, mix together, flour, baking powder and salt.

3. In another bowl, beat shortening and granulated sugar until smooth and creamy. Beat in egg until incorporated. Stir in lemon zest, if using. Gradually blend in flour mixture alternately with reserved pineapple juice until just incorporated.

4. Spread mixture evenly over pineapple. Bake in preheated oven for 30 to 35 minutes or until golden. Let stand for about 10 minutes and then invert onto a platter, leaving pan on top for a few minutes to allow the butter–brown sugar liquid to pour onto the cake. Cool, then cut into bars. Top with whipped cream or ice cream, if desired.

Makes 12 large bars

Nut and Peanut Butter Bars and Squares

continued on next page

Almond Rocca Bars

BASE

1 cup	butter, softened	250 mL
½ cup	packed brown sugar	125 mL
½ cup	granulated sugar	125 mL
2	egg yolks	2
1 tsp	vanilla	5 mL
1 cup	all-purpose flour	250 mL
1 cup	old-fashioned rolled oats	250 mL

TOPPING

3	milk chocolate bars (each about 1.45 oz/43 g)	3
2 tbsp	butter	25 mL
½ cup	finely chopped almonds	125 mL

- *Preheat oven to 350°F (180°C)*
- *9-inch (2.5 L) square cake pan, greased*

1. *Base:* In a medium bowl, beat butter and sugars until smooth and creamy. Beat in egg yolks until incorporated. Stir in vanilla. Blend in flour and oats.

2. Spread evenly in prepared pan. Bake in preheated oven for 30 to 35 minutes or until browned.

2. *Topping:* In the top of a double boiler, over hot (not boiling) water, melt chocolate bars and butter, stirring until smooth. Pour over warm base. Sprinkle almonds evenly over top. Place pan on a wire rack to cool completely, then cut into bars.

Makes 24 bars

Cherry Nut Fingers

BASE

1¼ cups	all-purpose flour	300 mL
¼ tsp	salt	1 mL
⅔ cup	packed brown sugar	150 mL
½ cup	butter, softened	125 mL
2	egg yolks	2
½ tsp	vanilla	2 mL

TOPPING

2	egg whites	2
2 tbsp	all-purpose flour	25 mL
½ cup	chocolate sundae topping	125 mL
½ cup	shredded coconut	125 mL
½ cup	chopped maraschino cherries	125 mL
½ cup	chopped nuts	125 mL

- *Preheat oven to 350°F (180°C)*
- *9-inch (2.5 L) square cake pan, greased*

1. *Base:* In a small bowl, mix together flour and salt.

2. In a medium bowl, beat brown sugar and butter until smooth and creamy. Beat in egg yolks until incorporated. Stir in vanilla. Blend in flour mixture.

3. Spread evenly in prepared pan. Bake in preheated oven for 15 minutes. Place pan on a wire rack to cool slightly.

4. *Topping:* In a clean bowl, beat egg whites until soft peaks form. Fold in flour, then chocolate topping, coconut, cherries and nuts.

5. Spread evenly over top of warm base. Bake 18 to 20 minutes longer. Place pan on a rack to cool completely, then cut into bars.

Makes 24 bars

> **TIP:** Prefer cake with a finer texture? When baking bars or squares, try adding 2 tbsp (25 mL) boiling water to the creamed butter and sugar mixture.

Jammin' Almond Bars

BASE

1¾ cups	old-fashioned rolled oats	425 mL
1 cup	all-purpose flour	250 mL
1 cup	packed brown sugar	250 mL
1 tsp	baking powder	5 mL
¼ tsp	salt	1 mL
¾ cup	butter or margarine, melted	175 mL

TOPPING

¾ cup	raspberry jam	175 mL
½ cup	coarsely chopped almonds	125 mL

- *Preheat oven to 375° F (190° C)*
- *9-inch (2.5 L) square cake pan, greased*

1. *Base:* In a large bowl, mix together oats, flour, brown sugar, baking powder and salt. Add butter and mix until combined. Set aside one-third and press remainder into prepared pan.
2. *Topping:* Stir jam until smooth and spread evenly over base.
3. In a small bowl, mix together almonds and reserved crumb mixture.
4. Sprinkle over jam layer, pressing down lightly. Bake in preheated oven for 25 to 30 minutes or until golden brown. Place pan on a wire rack to cool completely, then cut into bars.

Makes 24 bars

Coffee Raisin Nut Bars

1½ cups	all-purpose flour	375 mL
½ tsp	baking powder	2 mL
½ tsp	baking soda	2 mL
½ tsp	salt	2 mL
½ tsp	ground cinnamon	2 mL
¼ cup	shortening, softened	50 mL
1 cup	packed brown sugar	250 mL
1	egg	1
½ cup	hot coffee	125 mL
½ cup	raisins	125 mL
½ cup	chopped nuts	125 mL
	Coffee Frosting (see recipe, page 363) (optional)	

- *Preheat oven to 350°F (180°C)*
- *13- by 9-inch (3.5 L) cake pan, greased*

1. In a small bowl, mix together flour, baking powder, baking soda, salt and cinnamon.
2. In a large bowl, beat shortening and brown sugar until smooth and creamy. Add egg and beat until incorporated. Stir in coffee. Blend in flour mixture. Stir in raisins and nuts.
3. Spread evenly in prepared pan. Bake in preheated oven for 20 to 25 minutes or until golden brown. Place pan on a wire rack to cool completely. If desired, frost with Coffee Frosting or a frosting of your choice, then cut into bars.

Makes 36 bars

Date Nut Squares

6 tbsp	all-purpose flour	90 mL
1 tsp	baking powder	5 mL
½ tsp	ground cinnamon	2 mL
1 tsp	grated orange zest	5 mL
¾ cup	packed brown sugar	175 mL
2	eggs	2
½ tsp	vanilla	2 mL
1 cup	chopped pitted dates	250 mL
1 cup	chopped nuts	250 mL
6	maraschino cherries, chopped	6
	Confectioner's (icing) sugar	

- *Preheat oven to 325° F (160° C)*
- *8-inch (2 L) square cake pan, greased*

1. In a small bowl, mix together flour, baking powder, cinnamon and orange zest.
2. In a large bowl, beat brown sugar, eggs and vanilla until combined. Blend in flour mixture. Stir in dates, nuts and cherries.
3. Spread evenly in prepared pan. Bake in preheated oven for 35 to 40 minutes or until tester inserted in center comes out clean. Place pan on a wire rack to cool. Sift confectioner's sugar over top, then cut into squares.

Makes 16 squares

Raspberry Hazelnut Bars

BASE

⅓ cup	granulated sugar	75 mL
½ cup	butter or margarine, softened	125 mL
1	egg	1
2 cups	all-purpose flour	500 mL

TOPPING

¾ cup	seedless raspberry jam	175 mL
½ cup	chopped toasted hazelnuts (see Tip, below)	125 mL

TIP: To toast hazelnuts: Place on a cookie sheet and bake at 325° F (160° C) for about 15 minutes, stirring occasionally. Wrap hot nuts in a clean tea towel or paper towel for 1 to 2 minutes. Using your hands, rub nuts together until skins fall off. Cool, then chop, if desired.

- *Preheat oven to 350° F (180° C)*
- *13- by 9-inch (3.5 L) cake pan, lightly greased*

1. *Base:* In a medium bowl, beat sugar and butter until smooth and creamy. Beat in egg until incorporated. Gradually blend in flour just until a dough forms. Spread evenly in prepared pan.
2. *Topping:* Stir jam until smooth and spread over dough, stopping just short of edges. Sprinkle nuts over top of jam.
3. Bake in preheated oven for 20 to 25 minutes or until golden brown. Place pan on a wire rack to cool completely, then cut into bars.

Makes 36 bars

Dutch Jan Hagels

BASE

1¼ cups	all-purpose flour	300 mL
½ cup	granulated sugar	125 mL
½ tsp	ground cinnamon	2 mL
½ cup	butter or margarine, softened	125 mL
1	egg yolk	1

TOPPING

1	egg white	1
¼ cup	granulated sugar	50 mL
½ cup	sliced almonds	125 mL

- *Preheat oven to 350°F (180°C)*
- *13- by 9-inch (3.5 L) cake pan, greased*

1. *Base:* In a medium bowl, mix together flour, sugar and cinnamon. Using two knives, a pastry blender or your fingers, cut butter in until mixture resembles coarse crumbs. Mix in egg yolk until dough forms. Press evenly into prepared pan.

2. *Topping:* Beat egg white slightly and brush over dough. Sprinkle sugar and almonds over top and press down into dough.

3. Bake in preheated oven for 18 to 20 minutes or until golden brown. Place pan on a wire rack to cool slightly, then cut into bars. Cool completely before removing from pan.

Makes 36 bars

Macadamia Nut Triangles

BASE

1 cup	all-purpose flour	250 mL
¼ cup	granulated sugar	50 mL
Pinch	salt	Pinch
6 tbsp	butter or margarine	90 mL
3 tbsp	water	45 mL

TOPPING

1¼ cups	macadamia nuts, divided	300 mL
⅔ cup	packed brown sugar	150 mL
1	egg	1
2 tsp	vanilla	10 mL

TIP: To cut cake into triangles, cut into 4 long strips. Cut each strip into 4 squares. Cut each square in half on the diagonal to form triangles.

- *Preheat oven to 425°F (220°C)*
- *9-inch (2.5 L) square cake pan, greased*

1. *Base:* In a small bowl, mix together flour, sugar and salt. Using two knives, a pastry blender, or your fingers, cut butter in until mixture resembles coarse crumbs. Sprinkle with water, 1 tbsp (15 mL) at a time, mixing lightly with a fork until dough is just moist enough to hold together. (You may not need to use all the water.) Press evenly into prepared pan and bake in preheated oven for 15 to 20 minutes or until golden brown. Place pan on a wire rack to cool and reduce oven temperature to 375°F (190°C).

2. *Topping:* Coarsely chop ½ cup (125 mL) of the nuts and set aside. In food processor, combine remaining nuts with brown sugar and process until nuts are finely ground. Add egg and vanilla and pulse to blend.

3. Spread topping evenly over base. Sprinkle reserved nuts over top. Bake 20 minutes longer. Cool completely and cut into triangles (see Tip, left).

Makes 32 triangles

Pecan Pie Bars

BASE

2 cups	all-purpose flour	500 mL
½ cup	granulated sugar	125 mL
¾ cup	butter or margarine	175 mL

TOPPING

¼ cup	butter or margarine, melted	50 mL
1 cup	granulated sugar	250 mL
1 cup	corn syrup	250 mL
4	eggs	4
1⅔ cups	butterscotch chips (10 oz/300 g package)	400 mL
1⅓ cups	coarsely chopped pecans	325 mL

TIP: These bars are particularly delicious served warm, like pecan pie, with ice cream. If you don't like pecans, use a different kind of nut.

- *Preheat oven to 350°F (180°C)*
- *13- by 9-inch (3.5 L) cake pan, lightly greased*

1. *Base:* In a medium bowl, mix together flour and sugar. Using two knives, a pastry blender or your fingers, cut butter in until mixture resembles coarse crumbs. Spread evenly in prepared pan. Bake in preheated oven for 15 to 18 minutes or until golden brown.
2. *Topping:* In a large bowl, beat butter, sugar, syrup and eggs until blended. Stir in butterscotch chips and pecans.
3. Spread evenly over base. Bake 30 minutes longer or until set and golden brown. Serve warm or cool completely, then cut into bars.

Makes 36 bars

Caramel Oatmeal Bars

BASE

1½ cups	all-purpose flour	375 mL
¾ cup	packed brown sugar	175 mL
½ cup	quick-cooking rolled oats	125 mL
½ cup	butter or margarine	125 mL
1	egg, beaten	1
½ cup	chopped pecans	125 mL

TOPPING

1¼ cups	milk or sweetened condensed milk	300 mL
25	soft caramels, unwrapped	25
¼ cup	butter or margarine	50 mL

- *Preheat oven to 350°F (180°C)*
- *13- by 9-inch (3.5 L) cake pan, greased*

1. *Base:* In a large bowl, mix together flour, brown sugar and oats. Using two knives, a pastry blender or your fingers, cut butter in until mixture resembles coarse crumbs. Add egg and mix until blended. Stir in pecans. Set aside 1½ cups (375 mL) and press remainder evenly into prepared pan. Bake in preheated oven for 15 to 18 minutes or until lightly browned. Place pan on a rack to cool slightly.
2. *Topping:* In a saucepan, over low heat, melt caramels with milk, stirring constantly until smooth. Pour over baked base. Sprinkle reserved crumb mixture evenly over top. Bake 20 to 25 minutes longer, until bubbly and golden brown. Place pan on a rack to cool completely, then cut into bars.

Makes 36 bars

NUT AND PEANUT BUTTER BARS AND SQUARES

Chocolate Nut Squares

BASE

1 cup	all-purpose flour	250 mL
¼ tsp	salt	1 mL
½ cup	butter, softened	125 mL
2 tbsp	confectioner's (icing) sugar, sifted	25 mL
1	egg yolk	1

TOPPING

2 tbsp	all-purpose flour	25 mL
¼ tsp	salt	1 mL
½ cup	packed brown sugar	125 mL
3	eggs	3
⅔ cup	corn syrup	150 mL
1 tbsp	freshly squeezed lemon juice	15 mL
1 cup	chocolate chips	250 mL
1 cup	chopped pecans or walnuts	250 mL

- *Preheat oven to 350°F (180°C)*
- *8-inch (2 L) square cake pan, lightly greased*

1. Base: In a small bowl, mix together flour and salt.
2. In a medium bowl, beat butter and confectioner's sugar until smooth and creamy. Beat in egg yolk until incorporated. Blend in flour mixture. Press evenly into prepared pan. Bake in preheated oven for 15 minutes or until golden brown. Place pan on a rack to cool slightly.
3. *Topping:* In a small bowl, mix together flour and salt. In a large bowl, beat brown sugar, eggs, corn syrup and lemon juice until blended. Blend in flour mixture. Stir in chocolate chips and nuts.
4. Spread topping evenly over top of warm base. Bake 35 to 40 minutes longer or until top is set. Place pan on a rack to cool completely, then cut into squares.

Makes 16 squares

Carrot Walnut Bars

1½ cups	all-purpose flour	375 mL
1 cup	packed brown sugar	250 mL
1 tsp	baking powder	5 mL
1 tsp	ground cinnamon	5 mL
½ tsp	baking soda	2 mL
⅔ cup	vegetable oil	150 mL
2	eggs, beaten	2
1 tsp	vanilla	5 mL
½ cup	shredded coconut	125 mL
½ cup	finely shredded carrots	125 mL
¾ cup	chopped walnuts	175 mL
	Cream Cheese Frosting (see recipe, page 363)	

- *Preheat oven to 350°F (180°C)*
- *13- by 9-inch (3.5 L) cake pan, greased*

1. In a bowl mix together flour, brown sugar, baking powder, cinnamon and baking soda. Make a well in the center. Add oil, eggs and vanilla and mix just until incorporated. Stir in coconut, carrots and walnuts.
2. Spread batter evenly in prepared pan. Bake in preheated oven for 20 to 25 minutes or until a tester inserted in the center comes out clean. Place pan on a wire rack to cool completely.
2. Spread cream cheese frosting over top of cooled cake. Cut into bars. Store, covered, in refrigerator.

Makes about 36 bars

Glazed Walnut Jam Bars

BASE

1 cup	all-purpose flour	250 mL
1 tsp	baking powder	5 mL
½ cup	shortening, softened	125 mL
1 tbsp	milk	15 mL
1	egg	1

TOPPING

½ cup	raspberry jam	125 mL
2 tbsp	all-purpose flour	25 mL
¼ tsp	salt	1 mL
¼ tsp	baking powder	1 mL
1 cup	packed brown sugar	250 mL
2	eggs	2
1 tsp	vanilla	5 mL
½ cup	flaked coconut	125 mL
1 cup	chopped walnuts	250 mL

GLAZE

1½ cups	confectioner's (icing) sugar, sifted	375 mL
1 ½ tbsp	freshly squeezed lemon juice	22 mL
1 to 2 tbsp	milk or light (5%) cream	15 to 25 mL

- *Preheat oven to 350°F (180°C)*
- *9-inch (2.5 L) square cake pan, greased*

1. *Base:* In a medium bowl, mix together flour and baking powder. Using two knives, a pastry blender or your fingers, cut shortening in until mixture resembles coarse crumbs. Add milk and eggs; mix just until incorporated. Press evenly into prepared pan.
2. *Topping:* Stir jam until smooth and spread over base.
3. In a small bowl mix together flour, salt and baking powder. In another bowl, beat brown sugar, eggs and vanilla until blended. Blend in flour mixture. Stir in coconut and walnuts.
4. Spread evenly over jam and bake in preheated oven for 35 to 40 minutes or until set and golden brown. Place pan on a wire rack to cool.
5. *Glaze:* In a small bowl, combine confectioner's sugar and lemon juice. Stir in enough milk to make a spreadable consistency. Spread over warm cake. Cool completely, then cut into bars.

Makes 24 bars

Chinese Nut Chews

1 cup	granulated sugar	250 mL
¾ cup	all-purpose flour	175 mL
1 tsp	baking powder	5 mL
¼ tsp	salt	1 mL
3	eggs, beaten	3
1 cup	chopped pitted dates	250 mL
1 cup	chopped walnuts	250 mL
	Confectioner's (icing) sugar	

- *Preheat oven to 350°F (180°C)*
- *13- by 9-inch (3.5 L) cake pan, greased*

1. In a large bowl, mix together sugar, flour, baking powder and salt. Add eggs, dates and walnuts and mix well.
2. Spread evenly in prepared pan. Bake in preheated oven for 20 minutes or until top is golden brown. Place pan on a wire rack and cut into bars. Cool completely, then sift confectioner's sugar over top.

Makes 36 bars

Peanut-Butterscotch Bars

BASE

½ cup	packed brown sugar	125 mL
½ cup	butter or margarine, softened	125 mL
1⅓ cups	all-purpose flour	325 mL

TOPPING

⅔ cup	light corn syrup	150 mL
⅔ cup	granulated sugar	150 mL
¾ cup	butterscotch chips	175 mL
½ cup	chunky peanut butter	125 mL
2 cups	corn flakes cereal	500 mL

- *Preheat oven to 350°F (180°C)*
- *13- by 9-inch (3.5 L) cake pan, ungreased*

1. *Base:* In a medium bowl, beat brown sugar and butter until smooth and creamy. Blend in flour just until crumbly. Press evenly into pan. Bake in preheated oven for 15 minutes. Place pan on a wire rack to cool slightly.

2. *Topping:* In a saucepan, over low heat, stir together corn syrup and sugar until dissolved. Increase heat and bring to a boil. Remove from heat and stir in butterscotch chips and peanut butter until chips are melted and mixture is smooth. Stir in corn flakes. Spread evenly over baked base. Cool completely, then cut into bars.

Makes 36 bars

Caramel Peanut Cup Bars

BASE

1	package (18¼ oz/515 g) yellow cake mix	1
½ cup	butter or margarine, softened	125 mL
1	egg	1
20	miniature peanut butter cups, chopped	20

TOPPING

2½ cups	caramel sundae sauce	625 mL
2 tbsp	cornstarch	25 mL
¼ cup	peanut butter	50 mL
1 cup	chopped salted peanuts, divided	250 mL
1	container (15 oz/450 g) ready-to-serve chocolate frosting	1

- *Preheat oven to 350°F (180°C)*
- *13- by 9-inch (3.5 L) cake pan, greased*

1. *Base:* In a large bowl, mix together cake mix, butter and egg, until smooth. Fold in peanut butter cups. Spread mixture evenly in prepared pan. Bake in preheated oven for 18 to 20 minutes or until lightly browned. Place pan on a wire rack to cool slightly.

2. *Topping:* In a saucepan, over low heat, stir together caramel sauce, cornstarch and peanut butter. Increase heat and bring to a boil; cook, stirring constantly, for 2 minutes, until smooth. Remove from heat. Stir in ½ cup (125 mL) of the peanuts and spread evenly over warm base.

3. Bake 6 to 8 minutes longer or until almost set. Place pan on a rack to cool completely. Spread frosting over top. Sprinkle with remaining peanuts. Chill at least 1 hour before cutting into bars.

Makes 36 bars

Chocolate-Drizzled Peanut Butter Bars

1½ cups	all-purpose flour	375 mL
1 tsp	baking powder	5 mL
¼ tsp	salt	1 mL
1 cup	packed brown sugar	250 mL
½ cup	granulated sugar	125 mL
½ cup	butter or margarine, softened	125 mL
¼ cup	smooth peanut butter	50 mL
2	eggs	2
1 tsp	vanilla	5 mL
½ cup	chopped unsalted peanuts	125 mL
24	miniature peanut butter cups, cut into quarters	24

CHOCOLATE DRIZZLE

¼ cup	semi-sweet chocolate chips	50 mL
1 tsp	butter or margarine	5 mL

- *Preheat oven to 350°F (180°C)*
- *13- by 9-inch (3.5 L) cake pan, lightly greased*

1. In a small bowl, mix together flour, baking powder and salt.
2. In a large bowl, beat sugars, butter and peanut butter until smooth. Beat in eggs, one at a time, until incorporated. Stir in vanilla. Blend in flour mixture. Stir in peanuts. Spread evenly in prepared pan. Sprinkle pieces of peanut butter cups over batter and press down slightly. Bake in preheated oven for 20 to 25 minutes or until a tester inserted in the center of cake comes out clean. Place pan on a wire rack to cool slightly.
3. *Chocolate Drizzle:* In the top of a double boiler, over hot (not boiling) water, melt chocolate chips with butter, stirring until smooth. Drizzle over top of warm cake. Cool completely, then cut into bars.

Makes 36 bars

Nutty Mix Bars

1	package (18¼ oz/515 g) yellow cake mix	1
½ cup	chunky peanut butter	125 mL
1⅔ cups	milk	400 mL
3	eggs	3

NUTTY FROSTING

4¾ cups	confectioner's (icing) sugar, sifted	1.25 L
½ cup	unsweetened cocoa powder, sifted	1.25 mL
¼ tsp	salt	1 mL
⅓ cup	butter or margarine	75 mL
¼ cup	chunky peanut butter	50 mL
1 tsp	vanilla	5 mL
⅓ cup	boiling water	75 mL

- *Preheat oven to 350°F (180°C)*
- *13- by 9-inch (3.5 L) cake pan, greased*

1. In a large bowl, beat cake mix, peanut butter, milk and eggs until blended and smooth. Spread evenly in prepared pan. Bake in preheated oven for 35 to 40 minutes or until a tester inserted in the center comes out clean. Place pan on a wire rack to cool completely.
2. *Frosting:* In a large bowl, mix together confectioner's sugar, cocoa and salt. In another large bowl, beat butter, peanut butter and vanilla until smooth and creamy. Beat in boiling water. Gradually add sugar mixture, beating until mixture is smooth and spreadable. Spread frosting on cooled cake, then cut into bars.

Makes 36 bars

Peanut Butter Marshmallow Treats

BASE		
1½ cups	packed brown sugar	375 mL
½ cup	butter, softened	125 mL
½ cup	peanut butter (smooth or crunchy)	125 mL
2	eggs	2
1 tsp	vanilla	5 mL
1½ cups	quick-cooking rolled oats	375 mL
1 cup	all-purpose flour	250 mL
TOPPING		
3 cups	miniature marshmallows	750 mL
FROSTING		
¼ cup	smooth peanut butter	50 mL
¼ cup	butter or margarine, softened	50 mL
2 tbsp	milk	25 mL
1 tsp	vanilla	5 mL
1⅓ cups	confectioner's (icing) sugar, sifted	325 mL

- *Preheat oven to 325°F (160°C)*
- *13- by 9-inch (3.5 L) cake pan, greased*

1. *Base:* In a large bowl, beat brown sugar, butter and peanut butter until smooth. Beat in eggs, then vanilla, until blended. Blend in oats and flour. Press evenly into prepared pan. Bake in preheated oven for 25 to 30 minutes or until lightly browned around the edges.

2. *Topping:* Sprinkle marshmallows evenly over base. Bake 1 to 2 minutes longer or until marshmallows puff up slightly. Place pan on a wire rack to cool completely.

3. *Frosting:* In a small bowl, beat peanut butter, butter, milk and vanilla until smooth and creamy. Gradually add confectioner's sugar, beating until mixture is smooth and spreadable. Spread evenly over marshmallow layer, then cut into bars.

Makes 36 bars

Savannah Cake Bars

1	package (18¼ oz/515 g) yellow cake mix	1
½ cup	butter or margarine	125 mL
1 cup	packed brown sugar	250 mL
½ cup	crunchy peanut butter	125 mL
1¼ cups	flaked coconut	300 mL
⅓ cup	half-and-half (10 %) cream	75 mL

- *Preheat oven to 350° F (180°C)*
- *13- by 9-inch (3.5 L) cake pan, greased*

1. Prepare and bake cake mix according to package directions. Place pan on a wire rack.

2. In a saucepan, over low heat, melt butter. Remove from heat and add brown sugar, peanut butter, coconut and cream, mixing until well blended. Spread evenly over cake.

3. Preheat broiler. Place cake about 5 to 6 inches (13 to 15 cm) from heat and broil for 1 to 2 minutes or just until frosting bubbles. Place pan on a rack to cool completely, then cut into bars.

Makes 36 bars

Chocolate Raisin Peanut Bars

1 cup	all-purpose flour	250 mL
1½ tsp	baking powder	7 mL
½ cup	butter or margarine	125 mL
½ cup	smooth peanut butter	125 mL
1½ cups	granulated sugar	375 mL
2	eggs	2
1 tbsp	vanilla	15 mL
1½ cups	raisins	375 mL
2	squares (each 1 oz/28 g) semi-sweet chocolate, melted	2

> **TIP:** If you have forgotten to remove eggs from the refrigerator to allow them to come to room temperature, place them in a bowl of warm water for several minutes.

- *Preheat oven to 350°F (180°C)*
- *13- by 9-inch (3.5 L) cake pan, greased*

1. In a small bowl, mix together flour and baking powder.
2. In a large saucepan, over medium heat, stir butter and peanut butter until melted. Remove from heat. Beat in sugar until blended. Add eggs and vanilla and beat until smooth. Blend in flour mixture. Stir in raisins.
3. Spread evenly in prepared pan. Bake in preheated oven for about 25 minutes or until a tester inserted in the center comes out clean. Place pan on a wire rack to cool completely.
4. Drizzle melted chocolate over the top. Allow chocolate to set, then cut into bars.

Makes 36 bars

Oatmeal Chip Peanut Squares

½ cup	packed brown sugar	125 mL
½ cup	corn syrup	125 mL
½ cup	butter or margarine, softened	125 mL
1 tsp	vanilla	5 mL
3 cups	quick-cooking rolled oats	750 mL
½ cup	semi-sweet chocolate chips	125 mL
¼ cup	smooth peanut butter	50 mL

- *Preheat oven to 350°F (180°C)*
- *8-inch (2 L) square cake pan, greased*

1. In a large bowl, beat sugar, syrup, butter and vanilla until blended and smooth. Stir in oats. Press evenly into prepared pan. Bake in preheated oven for 25 to 30 minutes or until lightly browned. Place pan on a wire rack to cool for 5 minutes.
2. Sprinkle chocolate chips evenly over top, then drop small spoonfuls of peanut butter over top of the chips. Let stand for about 5 minutes, until chips and peanut butter have softened, then run a knife through the topping to create a marbling effect. Chill for 15 to 20 minutes, until topping is firm, then cut into squares.

Makes 16 squares

Grandma's Traditional Almond Squares

1 cup	ground almonds	250 mL
¾ cup	all-purpose flour	175 mL
¼ tsp	salt	1 mL
1 cup	granulated sugar	250 mL
1 cup	butter, softened	250 mL
6	egg yolks	6
16	whole blanched almonds	16

TIP: To blanch almonds, cover shelled nuts with boiling water. Let stand for a few minutes, then rinse under cold water. Almonds will pop out of their skins.

- *Preheat oven to 350°F (180°C)*
- *8-inch (2 L) square cake pan, greased*

1. In a small bowl, mix together ground almonds, flour and salt.
2. In a large bowl, beat sugar and butter until smooth and creamy. Beat in egg yolks, one at a time, until incorporated. Gradually add flour mixture, mixing until blended. Spread evenly in prepared pan. Lightly mark off 16 squares and place an almond in the center of each. Bake in preheated oven for 30 to 35 minutes or until golden brown. Place pan on a wire rack to cool slightly, then cut into squares.

Makes 16 squares

Banana Cream Walnut Squares

BASE

1 cup	granulated sugar	250 mL
1	egg, beaten	1
1 cup	chopped walnuts	250 mL

TOPPING

1	package (4-serving size) vanilla instant pudding mix	1
1 cup	milk	250 mL
1 cup	sour cream	250 mL
2	medium bananas, sliced	2

TIP: To toast nuts, spread them in a single layer on a baking sheet. Bake at 350°F (180°C) for 5 to 10 minutes, stirring occasionally until lightly browned.

- *Preheat oven to 350°F (180°C)*
- *Baking sheet, greased*
- *8-inch (2 L) square cake pan, ungreased*

1. *Base:* In a medium bowl, mix together sugar, egg and nuts until blended. Spread a thin layer on prepared baking sheet. Bake in preheated oven for 18 to 20 minutes or until golden brown. Place pan on a wire rack to cool. When cooled, crush into crumbs. Set aside half and spread remainder evenly in cake pan.
2. *Topping:* In a medium bowl, beat pudding mix, milk and sour cream until well blended. Fold in bananas. Pour over base and sprinkle with reserved crumbs. Chill for 3 to 4 hours, then cut into squares.

Makes 16 squares

Caramel Double-Nut Squares

¾ cup	all-purpose flour	175 mL
1 tsp	baking powder	5 mL
¼ tsp	salt	1 mL
1 cup	packed brown sugar	250 mL
¼ cup	butter	50 mL
1	egg	1
1 tsp	vanilla	5 mL
1 cup	shredded coconut	250 mL
½ cup	ground pecans	125 mL
½ cup	chopped walnuts	125 mL

- *Preheat oven to 350°F (180°C)*
- *8-inch (2 L) square cake pan, greased*

1. In a small bowl, mix together flour, baking powder and salt.
2. In a small saucepan, over medium heat, melt brown sugar and butter, stirring until smooth and blended. Set aside to cool, then beat in egg and vanilla. Gradually blend in flour mixture. Stir in coconut, pecans and walnuts. Spread evenly in prepared pan. Bake in preheated oven for 25 to 30 minutes or until golden brown. Place pan on a rack to cool, then cut into squares.

Makes 16 squares

Marbled Pistachio Bars

½ cup	butter or margarine	125 mL
3	eggs	3
1½ cups	granulated sugar	375 mL
½ tsp	vanilla	2 mL
¼ tsp	almond extract	1 mL
1 cup	cake flour, sifted	250 mL
¼ cup	finely chopped pistachio nuts	50 mL
Half	square (1 oz/28 g) semi-sweet chocolate, grated	Half
	Confectioner's (icing) sugar (optional)	
	Vanilla Frosting (optional) (see recipe, page 368)	

- *Preheat oven to 350°F (180°C)*
- *9-inch (2.5 L) square cake pan, greased*

1. In a saucepan, over low heat, melt butter. Set aside to cool.
2. In a large bowl, beat eggs until foamy. Gradually beat in sugar, beating continually until mixture has tripled in volume, about 15 minutes. Beat in vanilla and almond extract. Fold flour into egg mixture, alternately with cooled butter, just until combined. Spread half evenly in prepared pan. Sprinkle half the nuts and half the grated chocolate evenly over top. Spoon remaining batter over top and sprinkle with the remaining nuts and grated chocolate. Run a knife through the batters to create a marbling effect.
3. Bake in preheated oven for 25 to 30 minutes or until a tester inserted in the center comes out clean. Place pan on a wire rack to cool for 5 minutes, then transfer cake from pan to rack to cool completely. Sift confectioner's sugar lightly over top or frost with Vanilla Frosting. Cut into bars.

Makes 24 bars

Orange Nut Oatmeal Bars

BASE

1¼ cups	boiling water	300 mL
1 cup	quick-cooking rolled oats	250 mL
1¾ cups	all-purpose flour	425 mL
1 tsp	baking powder	5 mL
1 tsp	baking soda	5 mL
½ tsp	salt	2 mL
½ tsp	ground cinnamon	2 mL
½ cup	butter or margarine, softened	125 mL
½ cup	packed brown sugar	125 mL
1 cup	granulated sugar	250 mL
2	eggs	2
1 tsp	vanilla	5 mL
¼ cup	frozen orange juice concentrate, thawed	50 mL

TOPPING

½ cup	packed brown sugar	125 mL
¼ cup	butter or margarine	50 mL
2 tbsp	frozen orange juice concentrate, thawed	25 mL
1 cup	flaked coconut	250 mL
½ cup	chopped walnuts	125 mL

- *Preheat oven to 350°F (180°C)*
- *13- by 9-inch (3.5 L) cake pan, greased*

1. *Base:* In a medium bowl, combine boiling water and oats. Set aside.
2. In another medium bowl, mix together flour, baking powder, baking soda, salt and cinnamon.
3. In a large bowl, beat butter and sugars until smooth and creamy. Beat in eggs, one at a time, until incorporated. Stir in vanilla and orange juice concentrate. Gradually blend in flour mixture alternately with oat mixture.
4. Spread evenly in prepared pan. Bake in preheated oven for 40 minutes or until a tester inserted in the center comes out clean. Place pan on a wire rack to cool.
5. *Topping:* Preheat broiler. In a saucepan, over low heat, stir together brown sugar, butter and orange juice concentrate until dissolved. Increase heat and bring to a boil, stirring constantly; cook for 1 minute. Remove from heat and stir in coconut and nuts. Spread evenly over top of cooled cake and place pan under broiler for 1 to 2 minutes or until golden brown. Place pan on a rack to cool slightly, then cut into bars.

Makes 36 bars

> **TIP:** To toast nuts in a skillet, stir often over medium heat until nuts become golden brown. To toast nuts in the microwave, spread the nuts out on a paper plate or a shallow dish. Cook on High, 1½ minutes for ½ cup (125 mL) nuts and 2 minutes for 1 cup (250 mL) nuts. Stir, then microwave for 2 minutes longer or until golden.

Cinnamon Applesauce Squares *(page 187)* ➤

Raisin Nut Coffee Cake Bars

BASE

2 cups	all-purpose flour	500 mL
1½ tsp	baking powder	7 mL
1 tsp	baking soda	5 mL
¼ tsp	salt	1 mL
1 cup	granulated sugar	250 mL
½ cup	butter or margarine, softened	125 mL
2	eggs	2
1 tsp	vanilla	5 mL
1 cup	sour cream	250 mL

FILLING

1 cup	chopped walnuts	250 mL
½ cup	granulated sugar	125 mL
1 tsp	ground cinnamon	5 mL
1½ cups	raisins	375 mL

- *Preheat oven to 350°F (180°C)*
- *9-inch (2.5 L) square cake pan, greased*

1. *Base:* In a medium bowl, mix together flour, baking powder, baking soda and salt.
2. In a large bowl, beat sugar and butter until smooth and creamy. Beat in eggs until incorporated. Stir in vanilla and sour cream. Blend in flour mixture. Set half aside and spread remainder evenly in prepared pan.
3. *Filling:* In a small bowl, mix together nuts, sugar and cinnamon. Sprinkle half evenly over batter in pan. Sprinkle raisins evenly over top. Top with remaining batter. Sprinkle remaining nut mixture evenly over top of batter.
4. Bake in preheated oven for 35 to 40 minutes or until a tester inserted in the center comes out clean. Place pan on a wire rack to cool slightly, then cut into bars. Serve warm.

Makes 24 bars

Walnut Squares

BASE

1 cup	all-purpose flour	250 mL
½ cup	butter or margarine, softened	125 mL

TOPPING

2	eggs	2
1 cup	packed brown sugar	250 mL
1 tbsp	all-purpose flour	15 mL
½ tsp	baking powder	2 mL
1 cup	chopped walnuts	250 mL
½ cup	flaked coconut	125 mL
	Butter Frosting (see recipe, page 179) (optional)	

- *Preheat oven to 325°F (160°C)*
- *8-inch (2 L) square cake pan, greased*

1. *Base:* In a small bowl, mix together flour and butter. Press evenly into prepared pan. Bake in preheated oven for 8 to 10 minutes or until lightly browned. Place pan on a wire rack to cool slightly.
2. *Topping:* In a medium bowl, beat eggs, brown sugar, flour and baking powder until blended. Stir in nuts and coconut. Spread evenly over warm base. Bake 20 to 25 minutes longer or until golden brown. Place pan on a rack to cool completely, then cut into squares. If desired, frost with your favorite Butter Frosting.

Makes 16 squares

◄ Rhubarb Crisp Squares *(page 213)*

Raspberry Nut Meringue Bars

BASE

½ cup	butter or margarine, softened	125 mL
½ cup	confectioner's (icing) sugar, sifted	125 mL
2	egg yolks	2
1¼ cups	all-purpose flour	300 mL

FILLING

¾ cup	raspberry jam	175 mL

TOPPING

2	egg whites	2
Pinch	cream of tartar	Pinch
½ cup	granulated sugar	125 mL
1 cup	ground toasted pecans	250 mL

> **TIP:** Always use large-size eggs for baking, unless a recipe states otherwise.

> ## VARIATIONS
>
> **Strawberry Nut Meringue Bars**
> Substitute ¾ cup (175 mL) strawberry jam for the raspberry.
>
> **Apricot Nut Meringue Bars**
> Substitute ¾ cup (175 mL) apricot jam for the raspberry.

- *Preheat oven to 350°F (180°C)*
- *9-inch (2.5 L) square cake pan, greased*

1. *Base:* In a medium bowl, beat butter and confectioner's sugar until smooth and creamy. Beat in eggs yolks until incorporated. Blend in flour. Press evenly into prepared pan. Bake in preheated oven for 10 to 12 minutes or until golden brown. Place pan on a wire rack to cool slightly.

2. *Filling:* Stir jam until smooth and spread evenly over warm base.

3. *Topping:* In a clean bowl, beat egg whites and cream of tartar until soft peaks form. Gradually add sugar, beating until stiff peaks form. Fold in nuts.

4. Spread evenly over jam. Bake 20 to 25 minutes longer or until lightly browned. Place pan on a rack to cool completely, then cut into bars.

Makes 24 bars

Sour Cream Coffee Cake Bars

BASE		
1½ cups	all-purpose flour	375 mL
1½ tsp	baking powder	7 mL
1 tsp	baking soda	5 mL
Pinch	salt	Pinch
½ cup	granulated sugar	125 mL
½ cup	butter or margarine, softened	125 mL
2	eggs	2
1 tsp	vanilla	5 mL
1 cup	sour cream	250 mL

TOPPING		
¼ cup	granulated sugar	50 mL
¼ cup	chopped walnuts	50 mL
2 tsp	ground cinnamon	10 mL

- *Preheat oven to 350°F (180°C)*
- *9-inch (2.5 L) square cake pan, lightly greased*

1. *Base:* In a small bowl, combine flour, baking powder, baking soda and salt.
2. In a large bowl, beat sugar and butter until smooth and creamy. Add eggs and beat until incorporated. Stir in vanilla. Gradually blend in flour mixture, alternately with sour cream. Spread half in prepared pan. Set remainder aside.
3. *Topping:* In a small bowl, mix together sugar, nuts and cinnamon. Sprinkle half evenly over base.
4. Spread reserved batter over nut mixture. Sprinkle remaining topping evenly over batter. Bake in preheated oven for 40 minutes or until a tester inserted in the center comes out clean. Place pan on a wire rack to cool completely, then cut into squares.

Makes 24 bars

Walnut Cheesecake Bars

BASE		
2 cups	all-purpose flour	500 mL
⅔ cup	packed brown sugar	150 mL
½ tsp	salt	2 mL
1 cup	finely chopped walnuts	250 mL
⅔ cup	cold butter or margarine, cut into cubes	150 mL

TOPPING		
1 lb	cream cheese, softened	500 g
½ cup	granulated sugar	125 mL
2	eggs	2
¼ cup	milk	50 mL
1 tsp	vanilla	5 mL

- *Preheat oven to 350°F (180°C)*
- *13- by 9-inch (3.5 L) cake pan, greased*

1. *Base:* In a large bowl, mix together flour, brown sugar, salt and walnuts. Using two knives, a pastry blender or your fingers, cut butter in until mixture resembles coarse crumbs. Set half aside and press remainder evenly in prepared pan. Bake in preheated oven for 10 to 15 minutes or until lightly browned. Place pan on a wire rack to cool slightly.
2. *Topping:* In a bowl, beat cream cheese and sugar until smooth. Beat in eggs until incorporated. Stir in milk and vanilla. Spread evenly over warm base. Sprinkle reserved base mixture over top. Bake 20 to 25 minutes longer or until just set. Place pan on a rack to cool completely, then cut into bars. Store, covered, in refrigerator.

Makes 36 bars

Butterscotch Peanut Butter Krunchies

BASE

1⅓ cups	all-purpose flour	325 mL
½ cup	packed brown sugar	125 mL
½ cup	butter or margarine	125 mL

TOPPING

⅔ cup	granulated sugar	150 mL
⅔ cup	light corn syrup	150 mL
½ cup	crunchy peanut butter	125 mL
1 cup	butterscotch chips	250 mL
2 cups	corn flakes cereal	500 mL

- *Preheat oven to 350°F (180°C)*
- *13- by 9-inch (3.5 L) cake pan, ungreased*

1. *Base:* In a medium bowl, mix flour and brown sugar. Using two knives, a pastry blender or your fingers, cut butter in until mixture resembles coarse crumbs. Press evenly into pan. Bake in preheated oven for 15 minutes or until lightly browned. Place pan on a wire rack to cool slightly.

2. *Topping:* In a saucepan, over low heat, stir together sugar and syrup until dissolved. Increase heat and bring to boil. Remove from heat. Add peanut butter and butterscotch chips, stirring until chips are melted and mixture is smooth. Stir in corn flakes until blended. Spread evenly over baked base. Place pan on a rack to cool completely, then cut into squares.

Makes 30 squares

Chocolate Chip Peanut Butter Squares

1 cup	all-purpose flour	250 mL
1 tsp	baking powder	5 mL
¼ tsp	salt	1 mL
½ cup	smooth peanut butter	125 mL
⅓ cup	butter or margarine, softened	75 mL
½ cup	packed brown sugar	125 mL
½ cup	granulated sugar	125 mL
2	eggs	2
1 tsp	vanilla	5 mL
1 cup	semi-sweet chocolate chips	250 mL

- *Preheat oven to 350°F (180°C)*
- *8-inch (2 L) square cake pan, lightly greased*

1. In a small bowl, mix together flour, baking powder and salt.

2. In a large bowl, beat peanut butter, butter and sugars until smooth and creamy. Beat in eggs until incorporated. Stir in vanilla. Gradually blend in flour mixture. Stir in chocolate chips.

3. Spread evenly in prepared pan. Bake in preheated oven for 30 to 35 minutes until golden brown. Place pan on a rack to cool completely.

Makes 16 squares

TIP: Allow cakes to cool completely before frosting, then cut into squares.

Chunky-Style Peanut Squares

1¼ cups	packed brown sugar, divided	300 mL
1 cup	all-purpose flour	250 mL
2 tsp	baking powder	10 mL
½ tsp	salt	2 mL
⅓ cup	crunchy peanut butter	75 mL
½ cup	milk	125 mL
2 tbsp	vegetable oil	25 mL
1 tsp	vanilla	5 mL
1½ cups	hot water	375 mL

- *Preheat oven to 350°F (180°C)*
- *8-inch (2 L) square cake pan, greased*

1. In a large bowl, mix together ¾ cup (175 mL) of the brown sugar, flour, baking powder and salt. Make a well in the center. Add peanut butter, milk, oil and vanilla and mix just until incorporated.
2. Spread evenly in prepared pan. Sprinkle remaining brown sugar over top and slowly pour hot water over all. Bake in preheated oven for 45 minutes or until golden brown. Place pan on a wire rack to cool slightly, then cut into squares. Serve warm.

Makes 16 squares

Peanut Butter Chip Bars

BASE		
1⅓ cups	graham wafer crumbs (about 18 wafers)	325 mL
1¼ cups	all-purpose flour	300 mL
½ cup	granulated sugar	125 mL
1 cup	butter or margarine, melted	250 mL
TOPPING		
¾ cup	unsweetened cocoa powder	175 mL
1¼ cups	sweetened condensed milk	300 mL
1	1 package (10 oz/300 g) peanut butter chips	1
1 cup	flaked coconut	250 mL
¾ cup	chopped peanuts, divided	175 mL

- *Preheat oven to 350°F (180°C)*
- *13- by 9-inch (3.5 L) cake pan, ungreased*

1. *Base:* In a large bowl combine crumbs, flour and sugar. Add butter and mix well. Press evenly into pan. Bake in preheated oven for 15 to 20 minutes or until golden brown. Place pan on a rack.
2. *Topping:* In a large bowl, sift cocoa. Gradually stir in condensed milk until blended. Add peanut butter chips, coconut and ½ cup (125 mL) of the peanuts and mix well.
3. Spread evenly over hot base. Sprinkle remaining peanuts over top. Bake 20 to 25 minutes longer or until topping is set. Place pan on a wire rack to cool completely, then cut into bars.

Makes 36 bars

TIP: Most bars, squares and brownies should be cooled completely before cutting. But when the filling is sticky, you should run a knife around the edge of the pan as soon as you remove it from the oven.

Peanut Butter Chews

BASE		
½ cup	butter or margarine, softened	125 mL
½ cup	packed brown sugar	125 mL
1 cup	all-purpose flour	250 mL
FILLING		
½ cup	semi-sweet chocolate pieces	125 mL
TOPPING		
1 cup	smooth peanut butter	250 mL
5 cups	miniature marshmallows	1.25 L
½ cup	packed brown sugar	125 mL
¼ cup	table (18%) cream	50 mL
¼ cup	halved maraschino cherries	50 mL
4 cups	dry chow mein noodles	1 L

- *Preheat oven to 350°F (180°C)*
- *9-inch (2.5 L) square cake pan, greased*

1. *Base:* In a small bowl, beat butter and brown sugar until smooth and creamy. Blend in flour. Press evenly into prepared pan. Bake in preheated oven for 15 to 20 minutes or until golden brown. Place pan on a wire rack.

2. *Filling:* Sprinkle chocolate pieces evenly over hot base.

3. *Topping:* In the top of a double boiler, over low heat, melt peanut butter and marshmallows. Add brown sugar and cream, stirring constantly until melted and blended. Remove top of double boiler from heat. Stir in cherries and noodles. Spread evenly over chocolate layer. Place pan on a rack to cool completely, then cut into squares.

Makes 16 squares

Honey Double-Peanut Bars

BASE		
2 cups	packaged biscuit mix	500 mL
2 tbsp	granulated sugar	25 mL
⅔ cup	milk	150 mL
1	egg, lightly beaten	1
¼ cup	smooth peanut butter	50 mL
¼ cup	liquid honey	50 mL
TOPPING		
½ cup	packaged biscuit mix	125 mL
½ cup	packed brown sugar	125 mL
½ tsp	ground cinnamon	2 mL
2 tbsp	butter or margarine, softened	25 mL
2 tbsp	smooth peanut butter	25 mL
¼ cup	chopped peanuts	50 mL

- *Preheat oven to 400°F (200°C)*
- *9-inch (2.5 L) square cake pan, greased*

1. *Base:* In a medium bowl, mix together biscuit mix, sugar, milk and egg. Add peanut butter and honey and mix just until blended. (Mixture will not be smooth.) Spread evenly in prepared pan. Set aside.

2. *Topping:* In a small bowl, mix together biscuit mix, brown sugar and cinnamon. Stir in butter and peanut butter until mixture resembles coarse crumbs. Stir in peanuts.

3. Sprinkle evenly over top of batter. Bake in preheated oven for 20 to 25 minutes or until a tester inserted in the center comes out clean. Place pan on a rack to cool completely, then cut into bars.

Makes 24 bars

Peanut Butter 'n' Jelly Bars

BASE		
2 cups	all-purpose flour	500 mL
1 tbsp	baking powder	15 mL
1 tsp	salt	5 mL
1½ cups	granulated sugar	375 mL
⅓ cup	shortening, softened	75 mL
2	eggs	2
⅓ cup	peanut butter	75 mL
1 cup	milk	250 mL
TOPPING		
1 cup	red currant jelly	250 mL
1	container (15 oz/450 g) vanilla ready-to-serve frosting or Vanilla Frosting (see recipe, page 368)	1
½ cup	chopped peanuts	125 mL

- *Preheat oven to 350°F (180°C)*
- *13- by 9-inch (3.5 L) cake pan, greased*

1. *Base:* In a medium bowl, mix together flour, baking powder and salt.
2. In a large bowl, beat sugar and shortening until smooth and creamy. Add eggs and beat until incorporated. Beat in peanut butter. Gradually blend in flour mixture, alternately with milk, just until incorporated.
3. Spread evenly in prepared pan. Bake in preheated oven for 45 to 50 minutes, until a tester inserted into center comes out clean. Place pan on a wire rack to cool.
4. *Topping:* Stir jelly until smooth and spread evenly over top of cake. When cake has cooled completely, frost. Sprinkle chopped peanuts over top and cut into bars.

Makes 36 bars

Shortbread Peanut Butter Favorites

2 cups	cake flour, sifted	500 mL
½ tsp	baking powder	2 mL
Pinch	salt	Pinch
½ cup	crunchy peanut butter	125 mL
¾ cup	confectioner's (icing) sugar, sifted	175 mL
¾ cup	unsalted butter, softened	175 mL
1	egg	1
½ tsp	vanilla	2 mL
½ cup	coarsely chopped salted peanuts	125 mL

- *Preheat oven to 350°F (180°C)*
- *9-inch (2.5 L) square cake pan, lightly greased*

1. In a medium bowl, mix together flour, baking powder and salt.
2. In another bowl, beat peanut butter, confectioner's sugar and butter until blended. Beat in egg until incorporated. Stir in vanilla. Gradually blend in flour mixture.
3. Spread evenly in prepared pan. Press peanuts into the surface of the batter. Bake in preheated oven for 25 to 30 minutes or until a tester inserted in the center comes out clean. Place pan on a wire rack to cool completely, then cut into squares.

Makes 16 squares

TIP: To determine if an egg is fresh, place it in a large bowl filled with water. A fresh egg will sink; a stale one will float.

Buttermilk Nut Squares

BASE

1 cup	all-purpose flour	250 mL
½ tsp	baking powder	2 mL
½ tsp	ground cinnamon	2 mL
¼ tsp	baking soda	1 mL
⅓ cup	butter or margarine, softened	75 mL
½ cup	granulated sugar	125 mL
¼ cup	packed brown sugar	50 mL
1	egg	1
½ cup	buttermilk	125 mL

TOPPING

¼ cup	packed brown sugar	50 mL
¼ cup	finely chopped pecans	50 mL
¼ tsp	ground cinnamon	1 mL
Pinch	ground nutmeg	Pinch

- *Preheat oven to 350°F (180°C)*
- *8-inch (2 L) square cake pan, greased*

1. *Base:* In a small bowl, mix together flour, baking powder, cinnamon and baking soda.

2. In a medium bowl, beat butter and sugars until smooth and creamy. Beat in egg until incorporated. Blend in flour mixture alternately with the buttermilk, just until incorporated. Spread evenly in prepared pan.

3. *Topping:* In a bowl, mix together brown sugar, pecans, cinnamon and nutmeg. Sprinkle evenly over base. Bake in preheated oven for 40 to 45 minutes or until a tester inserted in the center comes out clean. Place pan on a rack to cool completely, then cut into squares.

Makes 16 squares

> **TIP:** To prevent freshly baked brownies, bars or squares from sticking to a serving plate, sprinkle a thin layer of sugar evenly over the plate before adding the cake.

Chocolate Chip Granola Bars

3 cups	old-fashioned rolled oats	750 mL
1 cup	raisins	250 mL
1 cup	sunflower seeds	250 mL
1 cup	chopped peanuts	250 mL
1 cup	semi-sweet chocolate chips	250 mL
1	can (14 oz/398 mL) sweetened condensed milk	1
½ cup	butter or margarine, melted	125 mL

- *Preheat oven to 325°F (160°C)*
- *13- by 9-inch (3.5 L) cake pan, lined with greased foil*

1. In a large bowl, mix together oats, raisins, sunflower seeds, peanuts and chocolate chips. Add condensed milk and mix thoroughly. Stir in melted butter until blended.

2. Spread evenly in prepared pan. Bake in preheated oven for 25 to 30 minutes or until top is lightly browned. Place pan on a wire rack to cool slightly, then transfer cake, with foil, to a cutting board and cut into bars.

Makes 36 bars

No-Bake Cookies, Bars and Squares

What could be easier than making cookies, bars and squares that you don't even have to bake? Some of these tasty treats require a bit of stovetop cooking, others are just mixed, shaped and chilled. All are simple, failproof, fun and delicious.

Almond-Coated Chocolate Fig Balls

2¾ cups	trimmed dried figs	675 mL
¼ cup	water	50 mL
½ cup	bourbon, divided	125 mL
3¼ cups	crushed vanilla wafers (about 68 cookies)	800 mL
1 cup	confectioner's (icing) sugar, sifted	250 mL
1 cup	ground almonds or pecans, divided	250 mL
3 tbsp	all-purpose flour	45 mL
¼ tsp	ground cinnamon	1 mL
1 cup	mini chocolate chips	250 mL
2 tbsp	light corn syrup	25 mL
¼ cup	granulated sugar	50 mL

1. In a saucepan, combine figs, water and ¼ cup (50 mL) bourbon. Bring to a boil over low heat, then simmer, covered, for 10 minutes. Set aside to cool.

2. In a large bowl, mix together vanilla wafers, confectioner's sugar, ½ cup (125 mL) ground pecans, flour, cinnamon and chocolate chips.

3. In a food processor, combine cooled fig mixture, corn syrup and remaining bourbon. Process until figs are puréed and mixture is smooth. Add to vanilla wafer mixture and mix until blended.

4. In a small bowl, mix remaining ½ cup (125 mL) ground almonds or pecans with granulated sugar.

5. Shape dough into 1-inch (2.5 cm) balls, then roll in the sugar-nut mixture. Place in an airtight container and allow to mellow for at least 24 hours.

Makes about 4 dozen

No-Bake Granola Peanut Treats

6 cups	miniature marshmallows	1.5 L
¼ cup	butter or margarine	50 mL
½ cup	smooth or crunchy peanut butter	125 mL
4 cups	granola cereal	1 L
1 cup	semi-sweet chocolate chips	250 mL

- *Large platter or cookie sheet, lined with waxed paper*

1. In a saucepan, over low heat, melt marshmallows and butter or margarine, stirring until mixture is smooth. Remove from heat. Add peanut butter and mix well. Stir in granola and chocolate chips.

2. Shape mixture into 1-inch (2.5 cm) balls and place on platter or prepared cookie sheet. Refrigerate until firm.

Makes about 3 dozen

Chocolate Haystacks

6	squares (each 1 oz/28 g) semi-sweet chocolate	6
1 cup	mini butterscotch chips	250 mL
2 cups	dried chow mein noodles	500 mL
1 cup	salted peanuts	250 mL
1 cup	miniature marshmallows	250 mL

TIP: To freshen up stale marshmallows, store them in an airtight container with a slice of fresh bread.

• *Large platter or cookie sheet, lined with waxed paper*

1. In the top of a double boiler, over hot water, melt chocolate and butterscotch chips, stirring constantly, until smooth. Add noodles, peanuts and marshmallows, stirring until well coated with chocolate mixture.
2. Drop by rounded teaspoonfuls (5 mL) onto platter or prepared cookie sheet. Refrigerate until firm.

Makes about 3 dozen

Crispy Caramel Haystacks

2½ cups	miniature marshmallows	625 mL
3 tbsp	butter or margarine	45 mL
2 cups	dried chow mein noodles	500 mL
12	caramels	12
1 tbsp	water	15 mL
2 tbsp	smooth or crunchy peanut butter	25 mL

• *Large platter or cookie sheet, lined with waxed paper*

1. In a large saucepan, over low heat, melt marshmallows and butter or margarine, stirring constantly until smooth. Add noodles and stir until well coated.
2. Drop mixture by teaspoonfuls (5 mL) onto platter or prepared cookie sheet.
3. In a saucepan, over low heat, melt caramels in water, stirring until smooth. Add peanut butter and mix well. Drizzle caramel mixture over haystacks. Refrigerate until firm.

Makes about 2 dozen

No-Bake Peanut Butter–Rice Chews

²⁄₃ cup	corn syrup	150 mL
²⁄₃ cup	smooth peanut butter	150 mL
½ cup	lightly packed brown sugar	125 mL
2½ cups	crisp rice cereal	625 mL
1 cup	shredded coconut	250 mL
½ cup	chopped nuts	125 mL

> **TIP:** To ease cleanup when measuring 1-cup (250 mL) quantities of messy ingredients such as honey or syrup, use 8-oz (250 mL) paper cups in place of glass measuring cups. When through, just throw them away.

- *Large platter or cookie sheet, lined with waxed paper*

1. In a large saucepan, over low heat, combine corn syrup, peanut butter and brown sugar, stirring constantly, until sugar is dissolved. Remove from heat. Stir in rice cereal, coconut and nuts until thoroughly blended.
2. Drop mixture by tablespoonfuls (15 mL) onto prepared cookie sheet and refrigerate until firm.

Makes about 3 dozen

Barnyard Cow Pies

2 cups	milk chocolate chips	500 mL
1 tbsp	shortening	15 mL
½ cup	raisins	125 mL
½ cup	chopped slivered almonds	125 mL

- *Large platter or cookie sheet, lined with waxed paper*

1. In the top of a double boiler, over hot water, melt chocolate chips with shortening, stirring constantly, until smooth. Remove from heat. Stir in raisins and almonds until well blended.
2. Drop by tablespoonfuls (15 mL) onto platter or prepared cookie sheet and refrigerate until firm.

Makes about 2 dozen

No-Bake Cocoa Orange Balls

¼ cup	unsweetened cocoa powder, sifted	50 mL
1 cup	confectioner's (icing) sugar, sifted	250 mL
1 cup	graham wafer crumbs (about 14 crackers)	250 mL
2 tbsp	corn syrup	25 mL
1 tsp	vanilla	5 mL
¼ cup	frozen orange juice concentrate, thawed	50 mL
	Cocoa powder or confectioner's sugar for coating	

• *Small baking cups (optional)*

1. In a large bowl, mix together cocoa, confectioner's sugar and graham wafer crumbs. Make a well in the center.
2. In a small bowl, combine corn syrup, vanilla and orange juice concentrate. Add to cocoa mixture and stir until blended. Cover and refrigerate for 30 minutes.
3. Shape mixture into 1-inch (2.5 cm) balls and roll in cocoa or confectioner's sugar. Place in baking cups for decoration, if desired. Store in the refrigerator, but bring to room temperature before serving.

Makes about 2½ dozen

Chocolate-Covered Peanut Graham Balls

3 tbsp	butter, softened	45 mL
½ cup	smooth peanut butter	125 mL
1 cup	confectioner's (icing) sugar, sifted	250 mL
1 cup	graham wafer crumbs (about 14 wafers)	250 mL
8	squares (each 1 oz/28 g) semi-sweet chocolate, melted (see page 14)	8

• *Large platter or cookie sheet, lined with waxed paper*

1. In a medium bowl, beat butter, peanut butter and confectioner's sugar until smooth. Add wafer crumbs and mix until well blended.
2. Shape mixture into 1-inch (2.5 cm) balls and place on platter or prepared cookie sheet. Refrigerate 30 minutes until firm.
3. Using a spoon or your fingers, dip balls in melted chocolate and roll around until all surfaces are covered. Return to cookie sheet and refrigerate until chocolate sets. Store, tightly covered, in refrigerator.

Makes about 2 dozen

Pineapple Snowballs

4 oz	cream cheese, softened	125 g
2½ cups	confectioner's (icing) sugar, sifted	625 mL
1 cup	vanilla wafer crumbs (about 20 cookies)	250 mL
¼ tsp	salt	1 mL
½ cup	crushed pineapple, drained	125 mL
½ cup	quartered miniature marshmallows	125 mL
	Shredded coconut	

• *Large platter or cookie sheet, lined with waxed paper*

1. In a large bowl, beat cream cheese until smooth. Gradually add confectioner's sugar, mixing until creamy. Stir in wafer crumbs and salt and mix well. Add pineapple, then marshmallows, stirring until well combined. Cover bowl with plastic wrap and refrigerate for 1 hour.
2. Shape mixture into 1-inch (2.5 cm) balls and roll in coconut until well coated. Place on platter or prepared cookie sheet and refrigerate until firm.

Makes about 3 dozen

Fruit 'n' Nut Snowballs

4 cups	All-Bran cereal	1 L
1 cup	pitted prunes	250 mL
1⅔ cups	raisins	400 mL
1½ cups	dried apricots	375 mL
2 cups	chopped pecans	500 mL
	Confectioner's (icing) sugar	

1. Place cereal and prunes in a food processor and process until cereal is crumbled. Add raisins, apricots and pecans and process until fruit is finely chopped.
2. Shape mixture into 1-inch (2.5 cm) balls, then roll in confectioner's sugar. Store in a tightly covered container. Before serving, roll again in confectioner's sugar.

Makes about 5 dozen

TIP: To keep dried fruit fresh after the package has been opened, place in an airtight container and refrigerate. To soften hardened fruit, soak in hot water or juice.

Rocky Road Specials

8	squares (each 1 oz/28 g) semi-sweet chocolate	8
1 cup	miniature marshmallows	250 mL
1 cup	chopped walnuts	250 mL
1/3 cup	white chocolate, coarsely chopped, about 2 oz (56 g)	75 mL

TIP: To freshen up stale marshmallows, store them in an airtight container with a slice of fresh bread.

- *Large platter or cookie sheet, lined with waxed paper*

1. In top of a double boiler, over hot water, melt semi-sweet chocolate, stirring occasionally, until smooth. Remove pot from hot water and let stand for 10 to 15 minutes, until chocolate has cooled slightly. Stir in marshmallows, walnuts and white chocolate until well blended.
2. Drop by rounded tablespoonfuls (15 mL) onto platter or prepared cookie sheet and refrigerate until chocolate has set.

Makes about 2 dozen

Stovetop Cookies

1/2 cup	chopped pitted dates	125 mL
2	eggs, beaten	2
3/4 cup	granulated sugar	175 mL
1 tsp	vanilla	5 mL
Pinch	salt	Pinch
1 cup	crisp rice cereal	250 mL
1 cup	coarsely crushed corn flakes cereal	250 mL
	Flaked or shredded coconut	

TIP: To color coconut, add food coloring to 1 tsp (5 mL) water and toss the coconut until evenly colored.

1. In a heavy frying pan, over low heat, stirring constantly, cook dates, eggs and sugar for 8 minutes. Remove from heat. Stir in vanilla and salt, then rice cereal and corn flakes. Mix together until well blended.
2. Wet hands and roll dough into balls or fingers. On a plate, roll balls in coconut until well coated.

Makes about 2 dozen

Stovetop Sugarplum Gems

½ cup	cooking dates, cut into thin strips	125 mL
½ cup	dried apricots, cut into thin strips	125 mL
3 tbsp	water	45 mL
2 tbsp	liquid honey	25 mL
2 tbsp	orange juice	25 mL
1 tsp	grated orange zest	5 mL
¼ cup	finely chopped pecans	50 mL
¾ cup	shredded coconut	175 mL
	Confectioner's (icing) sugar	

> **TIP:** If shredded or flaked coconut dries out, sprinkle with milk and let stand until it softens to the desired consistency. If you won't be using coconut for a while, to prevent it from becoming moldy, toast in a skillet, then store.

- *Large platter or cookie sheet, lined with waxed paper*

1. In a saucepan, combine dates, apricots, water, honey and orange juice. Cover and cook over medium heat until simmering. Reduce heat to low and, stirring constantly, cook for 10 minutes, until fruit is very tender and liquid has evaporated. (If liquid evaporates before the fruit softens, add about 1 tbsp/15 mL water.) Remove from heat and set aside until mixture is lukewarm, then process in a food processor until mixture is a fairly smooth paste.
2. Transfer mixture to a bowl and stir in orange zest and pecans, mixing until well blended.
3. Spread coconut out on a shallow dish. Pinch off a rounded teaspoonful (5 mL) of dough and, using the palms of your hands, roll into a ball. Drop into coconut and roll until well coated. Repeat with remaining dough.
4. Place on platter or prepared cookie sheet and sprinkle with confectioner's sugar.

Makes about 2½ dozen

Chocolate Rum Balls

1 cup	vanilla wafer crumbs (about 20 cookies)	250 mL
1½ cups	chopped pecans	375 mL
1 cup	confectioner's (icing) sugar, sifted	250 mL
¼ cup	unsweetened cocoa powder	50 mL
2 tbsp	corn syrup	25 mL
¼ cup	dark rum	50 mL
½ cup	fine granulated sugar	125 mL

1. In a large bowl, mix together wafer crumbs, pecans, confectioner's sugar and cocoa. Stir in syrup and rum until well blended.
2. Shape dough into 1-inch (2.5 cm) balls and roll in sugar. Store in tightly covered container.

Makes 2½ dozen

Chocolate Peppermint Bars

BASE

¼ cup	butter or margarine, melted	50 mL
1¼ cups	vanilla wafer crumbs (about 28 cookies)	300 mL

FILLING

4 cups	peppermint-flavored ice cream, softened	1 L

TOPPING

2	squares (each 1 oz/28 g) unsweetened chocolate	2
½ cup	butter or margarine	125 mL
3	eggs, separated	3
1½ cups	confectioner's (icing) sugar, sifted	375 mL
1 tsp	vanilla	5 mL
½ cup	chopped pecans	125 mL

> **TIP:** Raw eggs can be a potentially dangerous source of salmonella. To reduce this food-safety risk, add egg yolk to butter and chocolate in Step 3 and cook over low heat. Use pasteurized egg whites in Step 4.

- *9-inch (2.5 L) square cake pan, greased*

1. *Base:* In a small bowl, mix together butter and crumbs. Set aside ¼ cup (50 mL) and press remainder evenly into prepared pan.
2. *Filling:* Spread softened ice cream evenly over top of base, then freeze until solid.
3. *Topping:* In a large saucepan, over low heat, melt butter and chocolate, stirring until smooth. Set aside to cool slightly, then beat in egg yolks. Stir in vanilla. Gradually add confectioner's sugar, beating until blended and smooth. Fold in nuts.
4. In a clean bowl, beat egg whites until soft peaks form. Gently fold into chocolate mixture until combined, then spread mixture over top of ice cream. Sprinkle reserved base mixture over top and freeze. When ready to serve, cut into bars.

Makes 18 long bars

No-Bake Eatmore Bars

¾ cup	packed brown sugar	175 mL
¾ cup	liquid honey	175 mL
¾ cup	smooth peanut butter	175 mL
½ cup	unsweetened cocoa powder, sifted	125 mL
1¼ cups	quick-cooking rolled oats	300 mL
2½ cups	crisp rice cereal	625 mL
1 cup	chopped peanuts	250 mL
1 cup	chopped, mixed dried fruit (such as dates, raisins, apples, apricots, cranberries, etc.)	250 mL

• *13- by 9-inch (3.5 L) cake pan, lightly greased*

1. In a saucepan, over low heat, combine brown sugar, honey and peanut butter. Cook, stirring, until sugar dissolves and mixture is smooth. Stir in cocoa.
2. In a large bowl, mix together oats, cereal, peanuts and dried fruit. Add brown sugar mixture and mix until blended (mixture will be a bit crumbly). Press batter evenly into prepared pan. Chill until set, then cut into bars.

Makes 36 bars

Ice Cream Peanut Krispies

½ cup	peanut butter (smooth or crunchy)	125 mL
½ cup	corn syrup	125 mL
4 cups	crisp rice cereal (cocoa flavored, if desired)	1 L
2 cups	chocolate or vanilla ice cream	500 mL

• *13- by 9-inch (3.5 L) cake pan, greased with butter*

1. In a large bowl, beat peanut butter and corn syrup until smooth and creamy. Stir in cereal and mix until well coated. Press evenly into prepared pan. Chill until firm.
2. When ready to serve, cut cake into 12 large bars. Place a slice of ice cream on half the bars, then top with remaining bars. Cut each bar in half. Store in freezer.

Makes 12 bars

The Ultimate Nanaimo Bar

BASE

½ cup	butter, melted	125 mL
¼ cup	granulated sugar	50 mL
1	egg, beaten	1
⅓ cup	unsweetened cocoa powder, sifted	75 mL
1 tsp	vanilla	5 mL
2 cups	graham wafer crumbs (about 30 wafers)	500 mL
1 cup	shredded coconut	250 mL
½ cup	chopped walnuts	125 mL

FILLING

¼ cup	butter, softened	50 mL
2 tbsp	vanilla custard powder or vanilla instant pudding mix	25 mL
2 tbsp	milk (approximate)	25 mL
2 cups	confectioner's (icing) sugar, sifted	500 mL

TOPPING

4	squares (each 1 oz/28 g) unsweetened chocolate	4
1 tbsp	butter	15 mL

> **TIP:** Classic Nanaimo Bars are made with Bird's Custard Powder. If you can't find it, substitute an equal quantity of vanilla instant pudding powder (sold in tins).

- *9-inch (2.5 L) square cake pan, greased with butter*

1. *Base:* In a small bowl, mix together melted butter, sugar, egg, cocoa and vanilla until blended.
2. In a large bowl, mix together crumbs, coconut and walnuts. Add butter mixture and mix well. Press evenly into prepared pan. Chill at least 1 hour.
3. *Filling:* In a medium bowl, cream butter. Beat in custard powder, milk and confectioner's sugar until blended. If mixture is too thick, add a few drops more milk. Spread evenly over base and chill for 30 minutes or until firm.
4. *Topping:* In a saucepan, over low heat, melt chocolate and butter, stirring until smooth. Spread evenly over topping, then cut into bars. Store, covered, in the refrigerator.

Makes 24 bars

Noble Napoleons

BASE

40	graham wafers	40
1	package (6 oz/170 g) chocolate pudding and pie filling (not instant pudding)	1
2 cups	milk	500 mL
1 cup	whipping (35%) cream, whipped	250 mL

TOPPING

2 tbsp	butter or margarine	25 mL
1 cup	semi-sweet chocolate chips	250 mL

FROSTING

1 tbsp	butter or margarine, softened	15 mL
1 tbsp	milk	15 mL
¾ cup	confectioner's (icing) sugar, sifted	175 mL

- 13- by 9-inch (3.5 L) cake pan, lined with wax paper

1. *Base:* In prepared pan, place half of the graham wafers in a single layer, cutting end pieces to fit. Set aside.
2. Prepare pudding mix according to package directions, using 2 cups (500 mL) of milk. Place a layer of plastic wrap directly on pudding (to prevent a skin from forming) and chill.
3. When pudding is chilled, fold in whipped cream. Spread evenly over wafers in pan. Cover with remaining graham wafers, cutting as necessary to cover top completely. Chill for several hours or overnight.
4. *Topping:* In a saucepan, over low heat, melt butter and chocolate chips. Spread evenly over top layer of graham wafers. Chill until chocolate is firm.
5. *Frosting:* Mix together butter, milk and confectioner's sugar until blended and smooth. Using a cake decorator's bag, or any appropriate method, make a checkerboard design over top of chocolate. Chill until set.
6. Before serving, leave at room temperature for about 15 minutes, then cut into bars. Store, covered, in refrigerator.

Makes 36 bars

Puffed Wheat Bars

½ cup	butter or margarine	125 mL
½ cup	corn syrup	125 mL
1 cup	packed brown sugar	250 mL
2 tbsp	unsweetened cocoa powder, sifted	25 mL
1 tsp	vanilla	5 mL
½ cup	salted peanuts	125 mL
8 cups	puffed wheat cereal	2 L

- 13- by 9-inch (3.5 L) cake pan, greased

1. In a saucepan, over low heat, bring butter, corn syrup, brown sugar and cocoa to a boil. Cook, stirring for 3 minutes. Remove from heat. Stir in vanilla. Stir in peanuts and puffed wheat.
2. Press evenly into prepared pan. Set aside until firm, then cut into bars.

Makes about 40 bars

Blueberry and White Chocolate Squares

BASE		
¼ cup	butter or margarine, melted	50 mL
2 cups	amaretto cookie crumbs	500 mL

TOPPING		
1½ cups	blueberries, fresh or individually frozen and thawed	375 mL
⅓ cup	whipping (35%) cream	75 mL
8	squares (each 1 oz/28 g) white chocolate, finely chopped	8

- 8-inch (2 L) square cake pan, lined with foil, ends extending

1. *Base:* In a medium bowl, mix together butter and cookie crumbs. Press evenly into prepared pan

2. *Topping:* Sprinkle blueberries evenly over base.

3. In a large saucepan, heat whipping cream to boiling. Remove from heat and add chocolate, stirring until melted and smooth.

4. Spoon evenly over blueberries. Chill for 2 hours or until firm. Transfer cake, with foil, to a cutting board and cut into squares.

Makes 16 squares

Honey Nut Chocolate Squares

1 cup	smooth peanut butter	250 mL
¾ cup	liquid honey	175 mL
1 tsp	vanilla	5 mL
3 cups	crisp rice cereal	750 mL
1 cup	salted peanuts	250 mL
1 cup	semi-sweet chocolate chips	250 mL

- 8-inch (2 L) or 9-inch (2.5 L) square cake pan, greased

1. In a saucepan over medium heat, bring peanut butter and honey to a boil, stirring until smooth. Remove from heat and stir in vanilla. Add cereal, peanuts and chocolate chips and mix well.

2. Press evenly into prepared pan. Chill for 1 hour, until firm. Cut into squares.

Makes 16 squares

Chocolate Peanut Krispies

⅔ cup	smooth peanut butter	150 mL
2 cups	semi-sweet chocolate chips	500 mL
3 cups	miniature marshmallows	750 mL
6 cups	crisp rice cereal	1.5 L

- 13- by 9-inch (3.5 L) cake pan, lightly greased

1. In a large saucepan, over low heat, melt peanut butter and chocolate chips, stirring constantly until smooth. Remove from heat. Stir in marshmallows and cereal, mixing until combined.

2. Press evenly into prepared pan and chill until firm, about 1 hour. Cut into squares and store, covered, in refrigerator.

Makes 30 squares

Coconut Custard Icebox Bars

BASE

¼ cup	granulated sugar	50 mL
¼ cup	unsweetened cocoa powder, sifted	50 mL
½ cup	butter or margarine	125 mL
2 cups	graham wafer crumbs (about 30 wafers)	500 mL
1	egg, beaten	1
1 tsp	vanilla	5 mL
1 cup	flaked coconut	250 mL
½ cup	finely ground walnuts	125 mL

TOPPING

¼ cup	butter or margarine, softened	50 mL
3 tbsp	custard powder	45 mL
Pinch	salt	Pinch
2 cups	confectioner's (icing) sugar, sifted	500 mL
3 tbsp	boiling water	45 mL

FROSTING (OPTIONAL)

6	squares (each 1 oz/28 g) semi-sweet chocolate	6
1 tbsp	butter	15 mL

TIP: Raw eggs can be a potentially dangerous source of salmonella. To reduce this food-safety risk, use pasteurized egg in Step 1.

- *13- by 9-inch (3.5 L) cake pan, ungreased*

1. *Base:* In a large saucepan, over low heat, stir together sugar, cocoa and butter until butter is melted and sugar dissolves. Remove from heat and sprinkle graham crumbs over top. Let stand for 1 minute, then stir until blended. Stir in egg and vanilla. Stir in coconut and walnuts. Spread mixture evenly in pan. Chill until firm (about 30 minutes).

2. *Topping:* In a medium bowl, beat butter, custard powder and salt until creamy. Gradually add confectioner's sugar, beating until mixture resembles coarse crumbs. Slowly add boiling water, beating until mixture is smooth and spreadable. Spread over base and chill 30 minutes longer or until topping has hardened.

3. *Frosting (optional):* In a small saucepan, over low heat, melt chocolate and butter, stirring until melted and smooth. Drizzle over cake. Chill until chocolate is firm. Cut into bars.

Makes 36 bars

Luscious Lemon Squares

BASE

¼ cup	butter or margarine, melted	50 mL
1¼ cups	graham wafer crumbs (about 18 wafers)	300 mL

FILLING

¾ cup	boiling water	175 mL
1	large package (6 oz/170 g) lemon-flavored gelatin dessert mix	1
¼ cup	freshly squeezed lemon juice	50 mL
¼ cup	liquid honey	50 mL
1	can (14 oz/385 mL) chilled evaporated milk	1
1 tsp	grated lemon zest	5 mL

> **TIP:** When buying lemons, look for fine-textured skin. The lemon will be juicier. If there is a bit of greenish colouring, the juice will be more acidic.

- *13- by 9-inch (3.5 L) cake pan, ungreased*

1. *Base:* In a small bowl, mix together butter and wafer crumbs. Set aside ¼ cup (50 mL) and press remainder into pan.
2. *Filling:* In a heatproof bowl, combine boiling water and gelatin, stirring until gelatin is completely dissolved. Add lemon juice and honey. Set aside to cool.
3. In another bowl, beat evaporated milk until stiff. Gently fold in lemon zest, then gelatin mixture. Spoon over base and sprinkle remaining crumbs evenly over top. Chill for 4 hours or until set. Cut into squares.

Makes 12 large squares

Raspberry Patch Shortcake

1	pound cake (about 10 oz/300 g), cut into 12 slices	1
⅓ cup	cranberry juice	75 mL
2 cups	fresh whole raspberries	500 mL
2	packages (each 4-serving size) vanilla instant pudding mix	2
2½ cups	milk	625 mL
4 cups	whipped topping, divided	1 L

- *13- by 9-inch (3.5 L) cake pan, ungreased*

1. Line pan with sliced cake. Drizzle cranberry juice evenly over top. Spread raspberries evenly over top.
2. Prepare pudding according to package directions, using 2½ cups (625 mL) of milk for both packages. Fold in 1 cup (250 mL) of the whipped topping and spoon over the raspberries. Spread remaining topping evenly over top. Chill for at least 1 hour. Cut into squares.

Makes 30 squares

No-Bake Crispy Peanut Butter Squares

1 cup	smooth peanut butter	250 mL
¼ cup	butter or margarine	50 mL
½ cup	packed brown sugar	125 mL
½ cup	corn syrup	125 mL
1 tsp	vanilla	5 mL
Pinch	salt	Pinch
2 cups	corn flakes cereal	500 mL
1 cup	crispy rice cereal	250 mL

- *8-inch (2 L) square cake pan, lightly greased*

1. In a saucepan, over low heat, stir together peanut butter, butter, brown sugar and corn syrup until blended and smooth. Remove from heat and stir in vanilla and salt.
2. In a large bowl, mix together cereals. Add peanut butter mixture and mix well.
3. Press evenly into prepared pan. Chill for 6 hours or until firm. Cut into squares.

Makes 16 squares

Pineapple Graham Bars

BASE		
2 cups	graham wafer crumbs (about 30 wafers)	500 mL
½ cup	butter or margarine, melted	125 mL

TOPPING		
2 cups	milk	500 mL
1	package (16 oz/500 g) miniature marshmallows (about 60 to 70)	1
1½ tsp	lemon extract	7 mL
2 cups	drained crushed pineapple	500 mL
2 cups	whipping (35%) cream, whipped	500 mL

- *13- by 9-inch (3.5 L) cake pan, greased*

1. *Base:* In a medium bowl, mix together graham crumbs and butter. Set aside ½ cup (125 mL) and press remainder evenly into prepared pan.
2. *Topping:* In a saucepan, over low heat, combine milk and marshmallows, stirring until melted and smooth. Remove from heat and stir in lemon extract. Set aside to cool, stirring occasionally.
3. When cooled, gently fold in pineapple, then whipped cream, until well combined. Spread mixture evenly over base, then sprinkle with remaining crumb mixture. Chill for 3 to 4 hours, then cut into bars. Store, covered, in refrigerator.

Makes 24 bars

TIP: Make whipped cream fluffy by adding 1 tsp (5 mL) of honey as you whip. Finish off by beating in some confectioner's sugar.

Coconut Date Refrigerator Squares

BASE

½ cup	finely chopped pitted dates	125 mL
⅓ cup	granulated sugar	75 mL
½ cup	butter or margarine	125 mL
⅓ cup	unsweetened cocoa powder, sifted	75 mL
1	egg	1
1 tsp	vanilla	5 mL
2 cups	graham wafer crumbs (about 30 wafers)	500 mL
1 cup	shredded coconut	250 mL
½ cup	chopped walnuts	125 mL

FILLING

⅓ cup	butter or margarine	75 mL
2 tbsp	vanilla custard powder	25 mL
¼ cup	milk	50 mL
2 cups	confectioner's (icing) sugar, sifted	500 mL

TOPPING

1 tbsp	butter or margarine	15 mL
4	squares (each 1 oz/28 g) semi-sweet chocolate	4

> **TIP:** Raw eggs can be a potentially dangerous source of salmonella. To reduce this food-safety risk, use pasteurized egg in Step 1.

- *8-inch (2 L) square cake pan, ungreased*

1. *Base:* In a saucepan, combine dates, sugar, butter and cocoa. Cook, stirring over medium heat until butter melts. Remove from heat and stir in egg and vanilla until blended. Add crumbs, coconut and nuts and mix well. Press evenly into pan. Chill for 2 to 3 hours.

2. *Filling:* In a medium bowl, cream butter. Beat in custard powder, milk and confectioner's sugar until blended and smooth. Spread evenly over chilled base. Chill for 30 minutes.

3. *Topping:* In a small saucepan, melt chocolate and butter over low heat, stirring constantly, until smooth. Spread over chilled layers. Chill until chocolate hardens, then cut into squares.

Makes 16 squares

Hawaiian Cheesecake Bars

BASE

1 cup	graham wafer crumbs (about 14 wafers)	250 mL
¼ cup	granulated sugar	50 mL
¼ cup	butter or margarine, melted	50 mL

TOPPING

1	can (20 oz/568 mL) pineapple chunks packed in juice	1
1	package (4-serving size) lemon-flavored gelatin dessert mix	1
8 oz	cream cheese, softened	250 g

- *9-inch (2.5 L) square cake pan, ungreased*

1. *Base:* In a small bowl, mix together wafer crumbs, sugar and butter until blended. Press evenly into pan. Chill until firm.
2. *Topping:* Drain pineapple, reserving juice. Cover pineapple and refrigerate until ready to use. Add water to the juice to make 1 cup (250 mL). In a saucepan, over medium heat, bring to a boil.
3. In a heatproof bowl, combine lemon gelatin and boiling liquid. Stir until gelatin dissolves. Set half aside. Add cream cheese to remainder and beat until smooth and blended. Spread evenly over base. Chill until set.
4. Arrange pineapple chunks over top and spoon reserved gelatin mixture over top of pineapple. Refrigerate until set, then cut into bars.

Makes 24 bars

Specialty Cookies, Bars and Squares

In this section of the book I've collected recipes for cookies, bars and squares that are a bit unusual. They may be special because they are put to extraordinary uses, such as being shaped into cups or cones and packed with a filling or, like Best Spritz Cookies, they are pressed into interesting patterns and designs using an uncommon technique. Try browsing through this chapter when you're in the mood to make cookies, bars and squares but feel you want something different.

continued on next page

Apricot Cheddar Pillows

2 cups	all-purpose flour	500 mL
1/2 tsp	salt	2 mL
1/3 cup	butter	75 mL
2/3 cup	shortening	150 mL
1/2 lb	old Cheddar cheese, crumbled, about 1 cup (250 mL)	250 g
1 to 2 tbsp	cold water (optional)	15 to 25 mL
1/2 cup	apricot jam	125 mL

- *Preheat oven to 400°F (200°C)*
- *Cookie sheet, ungreased*
- *Round cookie cutter*

1. In a large bowl, mix together flour and salt. Using two knives, a pastry blender or your fingers, cut in butter and shortening until mixture resembles coarse crumbs. Mix in crumbled cheese. If necessary, add enough cold water to dough to achieve a pastry-like consistency. Knead lightly and refrigerate for at least 30 minutes.

2. On a lightly floured surface, roll dough out to 1/8-inch (0.25 cm) thickness. Using a round cookie cutter or glass dipped in flour, cut out circles. Place a level teaspoonful (5 mL) apricot jam in the center of each round. Fold dough in half to form a semi-circle. Seal edges with the tines of a fork. Place about 1/2 inch (1 cm) apart on cookie sheet. Bake in preheated oven for 12 to 15 minutes or until golden brown. Immediately transfer to wire racks to cool.

Makes about 3 dozen

Chocolate Puffs

1	package (8 oz/235 g) refrigerated crescent rolls	1
1	milk chocolate or bittersweet chocolate bar (4 oz/100 g), broken into four equal pieces	1

- *Preheat oven to 375°F (190°C)*
- *Cookie sheet, ungreased*

1. On a floured surface, separate dough into four rectangles and press the perforated seams together to form a seamless piece. Place a piece of chocolate in the center of each rectangle. Fold up the sides of dough to cover the chocolate, making certain the chocolate is totally enclosed and won't leak out. Pinch the seams together to form a new rectangle about 4 1/2 by 2 1/2 inches (11 by 6 cm). Repeat with remaining dough. Place about 2 inches (5 cm) apart on cookie sheet. Bake in preheated oven for 10 to 12 minutes or until golden brown. Cool on sheet for a few minutes, then transfer to a serving plate.

Makes 4 puffs

Cookie Cups

½ cup	all-purpose flour	125 mL
½ cup	granulated sugar	125 mL
Pinch	salt	Pinch
1	egg	1
1	egg white	1
1 tsp	orange liqueur	5 mL
1 tsp	grated orange zest	5 mL
3 tbsp	butter or margarine, melted	45 mL
¼ cup	sliced blanched almonds, toasted (see page 14)	50 mL
	Pudding, mousse or fresh fruit for filling	
	Whipped cream	

- *Preheat oven to 350°F (180°C)*
- *Cookie sheet, greased*
- *Small custard cups, inverted, or overturned muffin tin, brushed with butter*

1. In a small bowl, combine flour, sugar and salt.

2. In a medium bowl, whisk together egg, egg white, liqueur and zest. Gradually stir in flour mixture and mix until blended and smooth. Fold in toasted almonds.

3. Drop batter by heaping tablespoons (15 mL), 4 inches (10 cm) apart and 4 inches (10 cm) from the edge, onto prepared cookie sheet. Bake only two cookies at a time in preheated oven for 5 to 7 minutes or until edges are lightly browned.

4. Working quickly, with a spatula, drape warm cookies, one at a time, over the inverted cups and press down lightly with your hand to make a cup shape. When cookies become firm, about 30 minutes, lift gently and place on a wire rack to cool.

5. *To serve:* Fill cookie cups with pudding, mousse or fresh fruit topped with whipped cream.

Makes 1 dozen cookie cups

Cinnamon Pretzels

¾ cup	warm water	175 mL
1	package (16 oz/500 g) hot roll mix with yeast or frozen pizza dough, thawed	1
⅓ cup	granulated sugar	75 mL
3	egg yolks	3
¼ cup	orange juice	50 mL
1 tsp	grated orange zest (optional)	5 mL
2 tbsp	melted butter	25 mL
1 tsp	ground cinnamon	5 mL
1 tsp	vanilla	5 mL
TOPPING		
2 tbsp	granulated sugar	25 mL
½ tsp	ground cinnamon	2 mL

- *Preheat oven to 350°F (180°C)*
- *Cookie sheet, greased*

1. In a large bowl, mix the hot roll mix with yeast package, or the frozen pizza dough, with water, sugar, 2 egg yolks, juice, zest, if using, butter, cinnamon and vanilla. Mix together until well blended and a soft dough forms.

2. On a lightly floured surface, knead dough for 5 minutes, until smooth and elastic. Cover and let rest for 5 minutes.

3. Divide dough into 16 portions. Roll each portion out into a 6-inch (15 cm) long rope. Place one portion on prepared sheet.

4. Shape into a heart shape. Twist dough ends twice where they meet and attach ends to the curved bottom of the heart to form a pretzel shape. Repeat with remaining dough.

5. In a small bowl, whisk remaining egg yolk with 1 tbsp (15 mL) water. Brush over top of pretzels.

6. *Topping:* In another small bowl, mix together sugar and cinnamon. Sprinkle over pretzels. Let rise for 10 minutes.

7. Bake in preheated oven for 20 minutes or until golden brown. Immediately transfer to wire racks to cool.

Makes 16 pretzels

Swedish Rosettes

1 cup	all-purpose flour	250 mL
2 tbsp	granulated sugar	25 mL
Pinch	salt	Pinch
2	eggs	2
1 cup	milk	250 mL
	Oil for frying	
¾ cup	confectioner's (icing) sugar, sifted	175 mL

TIP: Rosette irons can be purchased at kitchen accessory stores.

- *Rosette iron*
- *Deep fryer or Dutch oven*

1. In a medium bowl, mix together flour, sugar and salt. Make a well in the center.
2. In a small bowl, whisk eggs and milk until blended. Gradually spoon into well, stirring until blended and smooth. Cover and chill in refrigerator for 1 hour.
3. In a deep fryer or Dutch oven, heat oil to 375°F (190°C). Dip rosette iron into hot oil for about 1 minute. Tap off excess oil and dip iron into batter until about three-quarters of it is submerged in the batter. However, do not allow batter to cover the top of the iron. If the batter won't stick, the iron is probably too hot, so allow it to cool slightly.
4. Return iron to oil and fry until the rosette slips off the iron. Continue cooking the rosette for 35 to 40 seconds or until golden. If rosette does not come off iron, loosen sides gently with a knife. With a slotted spoon, transfer the rosette from the oil to paper towels to drain. Repeat, stirring the batter each time before dipping, until all batter is used up. When cooled, sprinkle rosettes with confectioner's sugar.

Makes about 6 dozen

Almond Cookie Cones

2 tbsp	corn syrup	25 mL
4 tsp	maple syrup	20 mL
2 tbsp	butter, softened	25 mL
4 tsp	liquid honey	20 mL
½ cup	granulated sugar	125 mL
3 tbsp	whipping (35%) cream	45 mL
1 tsp	all-purpose flour	5 mL
¾ cup	ground almonds	175 mL

WHITE CHOCOLATE CREAM FILLING

3	squares (each 1 oz/28 g) white chocolate, chopped	3
¾ cup	whipping (35%) cream, divided	175 mL

TIPS: Leftover whipped cream will retain its lightness and texture for a day or more, refrigerated, if you add 1 tsp (5 mL) light corn syrup to each ½ pint cream. You won't notice any more sweetness with this addition.
Fill the cones with plain whipped cream or whipped cream mixed with chopped strawberries.

- *Preheat oven to 400°F (200°C)*
- *Lightly oiled cookie sheet, lined with parchment or waxed paper*

1. In a medium saucepan, combine syrups, butter, honey, sugar, cream and flour. Bring to a boil and, over medium heat, cook, stirring, for about 5 minutes. Remove from heat and stir in almonds.

2. Using a ladle or large spoon, drop one-sixth of the batter onto prepared cookie sheet to form a round cookie. Repeat two more times, so there are three cookies on the sheet, leaving enough room between each cookie to allow for considerable spreading.

3. Bake in preheated oven for 5 to 6 minutes until cookies are golden. Cool on sheet for 3 minutes, then carefully loosen the edges with a spatula or knife. Lift cookie and wrap it around well-greased handles of several spoons held together to form a cone. Cool, then slide off gently. Or place lacy side of a cooled cookie on a foil-lined baking sheet and heat in a 350°F (180°C) oven for 2 to 3 minutes until it softens slightly. Remove from foil, one cookie at a time, and roll, lacy side out, to form cones. Repeat with remaining batter.

4. *White Chocolate Cream Filling:* In a small saucepan, over low heat, melt chocolate and ¼ cup (50 mL) cream, stirring until smooth. Set aside to cool. In a small bowl, beat remaining ½ cup (125 mL) cream until soft peaks form. Fold in chocolate mixture and refrigerate until ready to use. When ready to serve, spoon about 2 tbsp (25 mL) mixture into each cornucopia.

Makes 6 cones

Almond Crescents

2 cups	cake flour	500 mL
½ cup	confectioner's (icing) sugar, sifted	125 mL
1 cup	butter, softened	250 mL
1 tsp	vanilla	5 mL
1 cup	finely chopped almonds	250 mL
	Confectioner's (icing) sugar, sifted	

- *Preheat oven to 350°F (180°C)*
- *Cookie sheet, lined with parchment or waxed paper*

1. In a medium bowl, sift flour and confectioner's sugar.
2. In a large bowl, cream butter until smooth. Add vanilla and mix well. Stir in flour mixture until well blended. Fold in almonds. Refrigerate dough for at least 4 hours, until firm.
3. On a lightly floured surface, shape 1 tbsp (15 mL) dough into a roll 2 to 2½ inches (5 to 6 cm) long. Bend ends inward to form a crescent shape. Repeat with remaining dough. Place about 2 inches (5 cm) apart on prepared cookie sheet. Bake in preheated oven for 12 to 15 minutes, until firm to the touch and golden brown. Transfer to wire racks to cool, then sprinkle with confectioner's sugar.

Makes about 4 dozen

Sugar-Coated Walnut Crescents

1½ cups	butter, softened	375 mL
2 tbsp	confectioner's (icing) sugar, sifted	25 mL
1	egg yolk, beaten	1
1 cup	finely chopped walnuts	250 mL
3¼ cups	all-purpose flour	800 mL
	Additional confectioner's (icing) sugar, sifted, for coating	

- *Preheat oven to 300°F (150°C)*
- *Cookie sheet, lined with parchment or waxed paper*

1. In a large bowl, cream butter and confectioner's sugar until smooth. Add beaten egg yolk and chopped walnuts. Mix together until well blended. Gradually add flour and mix until a soft dough forms. Cover and refrigerate for 1 hour until firm.
2. On a lightly floured surface, form dough into 1¼-inch (3 cm) balls. Shape each into a tapered log about 3 inches (7.5 cm) long. Bend each end inward to form a crescent. Place about 2 inches (5 cm) apart on prepared cookie sheet. Bake in preheated oven for 35 to 40 minutes, until lightly browned on the bottom and almost firm to the touch. Cool slightly on sheet. Coat with confectioner's sugar (see Tip, left).

TIP: To coat crescents with confectioner's sugar, sift sugar onto a clean cookie sheet until it forms a thin layer. Arrange crescents on sugar and sift additional confectioner's sugar over tops. Let stand until cool.

Makes about 3 dozen

Cheddar-Chive Tomato Pinwheels

4½ cups	all-purpose flour	1.125 L
1	package (¼ oz/7 g) active dry yeast	1
2 tbsp	granulated sugar	25 mL
1¼ tsp	salt	6 mL
¼ cup	butter or margarine, softened	50 mL
½ cup	warm water (not hot)	125 mL
¾ cup	warmed tomato juice	175 mL
1	egg	1
2 tbsp	finely chopped chives	25 mL
2 cups	finely shredded Cheddar cheese	500 mL

- *Preheat oven to 400°F (200°C)*
- *Cookie sheet, greased*

1. In a large bowl, mix together flour, yeast, sugar and salt.

2. In another large bowl, combine butter or margarine, water, tomato juice and egg and beat well. Gradually add flour mixture until a soft dough forms. (You may not use all the flour.)

3. Shape dough into a ball and place in a greased bowl, turning to ensure that all sides of the dough are greased. Cover and refrigerate for 2 to 3 hours, until dough has doubled in size. Using your fists, as in making bread, punch dough down. Divide into two portions.

4. On a floured surface, roll one portion of dough into a 15- by 12-inch (38 by 30 cm) rectangle, about ⅛ inch (0.25 cm) thick. Using a pastry wheel or a sharp knife, cut into 3-inch (7.5 cm) squares. Place about 1 inch (2.5 cm) apart on prepared cookie sheet. Cut 1-inch (2.5 cm) slits from each corner to the center.

5. In a small bowl, mix together chives and cheese.

6. Place 1 rounded teaspoonful (5 mL) chive mixture in the center of each square. Bring alternate corners up to the center, overlapping slightly, to form a pinwheel. Press firmly in the center to seal. Repeat with remaining dough.

7. Bake in preheated oven for 8 to 10 minutes or until golden brown. Immediately transfer to wire racks to cool.

Makes about 40 pinwheels

Cookie Cards

2¼ cups	all-purpose flour	550 mL
1½ tsp	baking powder	7 mL
¼ tsp	salt	1 mL
¾ cup	shortening, softened	175 mL
1 cup	granulated sugar	250 mL
2	eggs	2
1 tsp	vanilla	5 mL
	Icings	
	Cake decorator for printing names	
	Strands of red shoestring licorice, colored ribbon, wool or string	

> These cookies are a unique and fun way to make place cards.

- *Preheat oven to 375°F (190°C)*
- *Rectangular cookie cutter, preferably with fluted edges*
- *Cookie sheet, ungreased*
- *Drinking straw*
- *Cookie cutter*

1. In a medium bowl, mix together flour, baking powder and salt.
2. In a large bowl, beat shortening and sugar until smooth and creamy. Add eggs, one at a time, beating until well incorporated. Stir in vanilla. Gradually add flour mixture and mix until a dough forms.
3. On a lightly floured surface, roll dough out to ⅛-inch (0.25 cm) thickness. Using a cookie cutter dipped in flour, cut out shapes and place 2 inches (5 cm) apart on sheet. Using a drinking straw, punch two holes into the dough on one long side of the rectangle. Bake in preheated oven for 6 to 8 minutes or until lightly browned. Immediately transfer to wire racks to cool.
4. Decorate and print names on with icing.
5. *To make place cards:* Place two cookies together and thread a ribbon or licorice through the holes. Make a bow or a knot in the back and stand cards up.

Makes about 18 name cards, depending on the size of cookie cutter used

Homemade Ladyfingers

2	egg yolks	2
½ tsp	vanilla	2 mL
Pinch	salt	Pinch
3	egg whites, room temperature	3
⅓ cup + 3 tbsp	granulated sugar	120 mL
⅓ cup	all-purpose flour	75 mL

> **TIP:** Ladyfinger tins are molds that ladyfingers are baked in. If you have them, just spoon the mixture into each mold and bake as above.

- *Preheat oven to 350°F (180°C)*
- *Cookie sheet, greased*
- *Pastry bag*

1. In a medium bowl, whisk together egg yolks, vanilla and salt until thick and pale yellow in color.

2. In a clean bowl, beat egg whites until soft peaks form. Gradually add ⅓ cup (75 mL) sugar, beating until stiff peaks form. Fold into egg yolk mixture, then gradually fold in flour until well combined.

3. Fill a pastry bag with batter. Pipe fingers, about 4 to 5 inches (10 to 13 cm) long and 2 inches (5 cm) apart, onto prepared cookie sheet. Sprinkle lightly with remaining sugar. Bake in preheated oven for 10 to 12 minutes or until lightly browned. Immediately transfer to wire racks to cool.

Makes about 20 ladyfingers

Special Wonton Cookies

1½ cups	packed brown sugar	375 mL
1 cup	chopped dried apricots	250 mL
1½ cups	chopped prunes	375 mL
1 cup	chopped almonds	250 mL
1½ cups	flaked or shredded coconut	375 mL
24	wonton squares	24
	Vegetable oil for frying	

> *Wonton wrappers, or squares of dough, can be purchased at most major grocery stores.*

> **TIP:** Next time you buy cooking oil, don't pull off the silver seal. Instead, cut a small slit in it. It makes it much easier to pour without spilling.

- *Deep fryer or Dutch oven*

1. In a large bowl, mix together sugar, apricots, prunes, almonds and coconut.

2. Lay half the wonton squares out on a work surface. Place about 2 tsp (10 mL) filling in the center of each. Moisten edges with water and fold in half to form a triangle. Press edges together firmly to seal. Repeat until all wrappers are filled. Cover filled wontons with a cloth to keep moist.

3. Fill a deep fryer or Dutch oven with oil to a depth of about 1½ inches (4 cm). Heat to 360°F (185°C). Using a slotted spoon, drop four wontons at a time into the hot oil and cook, turning, until golden brown. Lift out with the slotted spoon and drain on paper towel.

Makes 2 dozen

Fortune Cookies

½ cup	all-purpose flour	125 mL
1 tbsp	cornstarch	15 mL
¼ cup	granulated sugar	50 mL
Pinch	salt	Pinch
¼ cup	cooking oil	50 mL
2	egg whites	2
1 tsp	almond extract	5 mL

> *Before beginning these cookies, make up about 24 paper fortunes, about 2- by ½-inches (5 by 1 cm), with clever little sayings, to place inside.*

> **TIP:** If a cookie cools before you can form it, heat in a preheated 300°F (150°C) oven for about 1 minute.

- *Preheat oven to 300°F (150°C)*
- *Cookie sheet, greased*
- *Muffin tin, ungreased*

1. In a medium bowl, mix together flour, cornstarch, sugar and salt. Make a well in the center.

2. In a small bowl, whisk oil, egg whites and almond extract. Pour into well and stir until mixture is blended and smooth.

3. Spoon a heaping teaspoonful (5 mL) batter onto prepared cookie sheet. Using the back of a spoon, spread into a 3-inch (7.5 cm) circle. Make three other circles. (Cookies will spread, so bake only four at a time.) Bake in preheated oven for 10 minutes or until golden brown.

4. Working quickly, one cookie at a time, and using a wide spatula, flip cookies from baking sheet onto a sheet of waxed paper. Place a paper fortune in the center and fold cookie in half. Gently bring tips of cookie together to form a slight crease or bend in the middle. Place cookie in an ungreased muffin cup to cool and to hold its shape. Repeat with remaining dough.

Makes about 2 dozen

Sugar-Cinnamon Twists

¾ cup	warm water, divided	175 mL
1	package (¼ oz/7 g) active dry yeast	1
¼ cup	butter or margarine, softened	50 mL
¼ cup	granulated sugar	50 mL
1	egg	1
4 to 4½ cups	all-purpose flour, divided	1 to 1.125 L
1½ tsp	salt	7 mL
½ cup	warm milk	125 mL

FILLING

½ cup	packed brown sugar	125 mL
4 tsp	ground cinnamon	20 mL
¼ cup	melted butter or margarine	50 mL

> **TIP:** If your recipe calls for eggs at room temperature and you forgot to remove them from the refrigerator, place them in warm water for several minutes.

- *Preheat oven to 350°F (180°C)*
- *Cookie sheet, greased*

1. In a large bowl, combine yeast and ¼ cup/50 mL water. Stir until dissolved.
2. Add butter or margarine, sugar, egg, 2 cups (500 mL) flour, salt, remaining water and milk. Beat for 2 to 3 minutes, until blended. Gradually add more flour, mixing until a soft dough forms.
3. On a floured surface, knead dough for 6 to 8 minutes, until smooth and elastic. Place dough in a greased bowl, turning to ensure that all sides of the dough are greased. Cover and let rise in a warm place for about 1 hour, until dough doubles in size. Punch down, then roll out to a 16- by 12-inch (40 by 30 cm) rectangle.
4. *Filling:* In a small bowl, mix together brown sugar and cinnamon. Brush dough with melted butter or margarine, then sprinkle with sugar-cinnamon mixture.
5. Let dough rest for 5 minutes, then cut lengthwise into three strips, 16 by 4 inches (40 by 10 cm). Cut each strip into 16 pieces, 4 by 1 inches (10 by 2.5 cm). Twist each strip and place on prepared sheets. Cover with a cloth and let rise for about 30 minutes, until doubled in size.
6. Bake in preheated oven for 5 minutes or until golden brown. Immediately transfer to wire racks to cool.

Makes 4 dozen twists

Oatmeal Pecan Turnovers

2½ cups	all-purpose flour	625 mL
1 tsp	baking powder	5 mL
½ tsp	baking soda	2 mL
1 tsp	salt	5 mL
2 cups	old-fashioned rolled oats	500 mL
½ cup	chopped pecans	125 mL
½ cup	butter or margarine, softened	125 mL
1 cup	packed brown sugar	250 mL
1	egg	1
1 tsp	vanilla	5 mL
½ cup	milk	125 mL
8 oz	cream cheese, softened	250 g
1 cup	fruit pie filling	250 mL
	Confectioner's (icing) sugar, sifted	

> **TIP:** Don't waste milk that is just about to pass its "best before" date. Pour the milk into an ice-cube tray and freeze. These cubes can be added to hot liquids such as coffee or hot chocolate.

- *Preheat oven to 375°F (190°C)*
- *Cookie sheet, greased*

1. In a medium bowl, mix together flour, baking powder, baking soda, salt, oats and pecans.

2. In a large bowl, beat butter or margarine and brown sugar until smooth and creamy. Beat in egg until incorporated. Stir in vanilla and milk. Mix in dry ingredients until well blended and a soft dough forms. Cover and refrigerate for 30 minutes.

3. Place dough between two sheets of waxed paper and roll out to ¼-inch (0.5 cm) thickness. Remove paper and cut into 4-inch (10 cm) squares. Spoon 1 tbsp (15 mL) cream cheese onto half of each square. Top with 1 tbsp (15 mL) fruit pie filling. Fold into a triangle and press edges with the tines of a fork dipped in flour to seal.

4. Place about 2 inches (5 cm) apart on prepared cookie sheet. Bake in preheated oven for 20 to 25 minutes, until crispy and golden brown. Transfer to wire racks to cool. Sprinkle with confectioner's sugar.

Makes 16 turnovers

Fancy Lattice Cookies

⅔ cup	all-purpose flour	150 mL
¼ tsp	ground cinnamon	1 mL
¼ tsp	ground cloves	1 mL
¼ tsp	ground nutmeg	1 mL
1	package (18 oz/540 g) refrigerated sugar cookie dough	1
	Seedless raspberry jam	
	Confectioner's (icing) sugar, sifted	

1. In a large bowl, mix together flour, cinnamon, cloves and nutmeg. Add sugar cookie dough and knead together until well combined.

2. Place dough between two sheets of waxed paper and roll out to ⅛-inch (0.25 cm) thickness. Remove top sheet and, using a cookie cutter or a glass dipped in flour, cut out 2-inch (5 cm) rounds. Shape remaining scraps of dough into a disk and set aside.

3. Place rounds about 1 inch (2.5 cm) apart on cookie sheet. Spread each with ½ tsp (2 mL) jam.

4. Place disk of scrap dough between two sheets of waxed paper and roll out to ⅛-inch (0.25 cm) thickness. Cut dough into 2- by ¼-inch (5 by 0.5 cm) strips. Place strips over the jam on each cookie to form a lattice pattern, two strips horizontally and two strips intertwined vertically. Trim to fit.

5. Bake in preheated oven for 15 minutes or until golden brown. Cool on sheet for 2 minutes, then transfer to wire racks to cool completely. Sprinkle with confectioner's sugar.

Makes about 2½ dozen

Peak Frean Vanilla Napoleons

1	package (4-serving size) vanilla pudding and pie filling mix	1
1½ cups	milk	375 mL
½ cup	confectioner's (icing) sugar, sifted	125 mL
1 tbsp	water	15 mL
¼ tsp	vanilla	1 mL
24	Peak Frean Nice cookies	24
1	square (1 oz/28 g) unsweetened chocolate, melted (see page 14)	1

1. Prepare pudding following package directions, but using only 1½ cups (375 mL) milk. Allow to cool, stirring frequently.
2. In a small bowl, mix together sugar, water and vanilla to make a glaze.
3. Place eight cookies on a work surface. Spread tops with the glaze. Using a spoon, drizzle with chocolate in thin horizontal lines about ½ inch (1 cm) apart. Draw a knife across the lines in the opposite direction (vertically) to make a design. Set aside.
4. Place eight more cookies on work surface. Spread each with pudding. Top with eight more cookies and spread with pudding. Top with glazed cookies. Refrigerate for 6 hours.

Makes 8 napoleons

Delicate Lace Baskets

¼ cup	butter	50 mL
¼ cup	granulated sugar	50 mL
2½ tbsp	dark molasses	32 mL
¼ tsp	ground cinnamon	1 mL
Pinch	ground ginger	Pinch
½ tbsp	vanilla	7 mL
⅓ cup	all-purpose flour	75 mL
	Pudding, mousse or ice cream for filling	

- *Preheat oven to 300°F (150°C)*
- *Cookie sheet, greased*
- *4-inch (10 cm) diameter bowl, brushed with melted butter*

1. In a saucepan, over medium heat, melt butter with sugar, molasses, cinnamon and ginger, stirring until mixture is smooth. Stir in vanilla, then flour, until blended.
2. Using a large spoon, drop 2½ tbsp (32 mL) batter, about 4 inches (10 cm) apart, onto prepared cookie sheet. (Cookies will spread, so bake only three at a time.) Bake in preheated oven for 18 minutes. Cool on sheet for 30 seconds, then, using a wide spatula, lift cookies up and carefully shape over the bottom of prepared bowl. Allow to cool on bowl until cookie is firm, then gently lift off. Repeat with remaining batter.
3. Fill cooled baskets with pudding, mousse or ice cream.

Makes 6 baskets

Best Spritz Cookies

1 cup	butter, softened	250 mL
1 cup	granulated sugar	250 mL
1	egg	1
¼ tsp	salt	1 mL
2 tsp	vanilla	10 mL
2¼ cups	all-purpose flour	550 mL

> *"Spritz" are cookies put through a cookie press. They are great fun because you can make so many interesting patterns and designs.*

VARIATIONS

Lemon Spritz
Omit egg and vanilla and add ¼ cup (50 mL) frozen lemonade concentrate.

Cinnamon Spritz
Substitute 1⅓ cups (325 mL) lightly packed brown sugar for the granulated sugar. Add 1 tsp (5 mL) cinnamon.

Chocolate Spritz
Add 2 squares (each 1 oz/28 oz) melted unsweetened chocolate.

- *Preheat oven to 400°F (200°C)*
- *Cookie press*
- *Cookie sheet, ungreased*

1. In a large bowl, beat butter and sugar until smooth and creamy. Add egg and beat until well incorporated. Stir in salt and vanilla. Add flour and beat until blended. If dough is too soft, cover and chill in refrigerator for about 30 minutes, until firm.

2. Pack dough into cookie press and press cookies onto baking sheet about 1 inch (2.5 cm) apart. Bake in preheated oven for 6 to 8 minutes or until edges are lightly browned. Cool on sheet for 5 minutes, then transfer to wire racks to cool completely.

Makes about 7 dozen

Blueberry Graham Cheesecake Bars

BASE

1¼ cups	graham wafer crumbs (about 16 wafers)	300 mL
½ cup	butter or margarine, softened	125 mL
¼ cup	granulated sugar	50 mL

FILLING

8 oz	cream cheese, softened	250 g
½ cup	granulated sugar	125 mL
2	eggs	2
1 tsp	vanilla	5 mL
	Ground cinnamon	

TOPPING

2 tbsp	cornstarch	25 mL
½ cup	granulated sugar	125 mL
1	can (19 oz/540 mL) blueberry pie filling	1
2 tbsp	freshly squeezed lemon juice	25 mL

- *Preheat oven to 300°F (150°C)*
- *9-inch (2.5 L) square cake pan, ungreased*

1. *Base:* In a small bowl, mix together crumbs, butter and sugar. Press evenly into pan. Set aside.
2. *Filling:* In a medium bowl, beat cream cheese and sugar until smooth. Beat in eggs and vanilla until blended.
3. Spread evenly over base. Bake in preheated oven for 30 minutes. Sprinkle cinnamon over top and place pan on a wire rack to cool.
3. *Topping:* In a small bowl, mix together blueberry pie filling and lemon juice. Spread over warm cake. Chill thoroughly, then cut into bars.

Makes 24 bars

Coffee Lover's Bars

2 tsp	instant coffee powder	10 mL
2 tbsp	boiling water	25 mL
½ cup	all-purpose flour	125 mL
½ cup	unsweetened cocoa powder, sifted	125 mL
½ cup	butter or margarine, softened	125 mL
1 cup	granulated sugar	250 mL
2	eggs	2
1 tsp	vanilla	5 mL
FROSTING		
2 tbsp	butter or margarine, softened	25 mL
4 oz	cream cheese, softened	125 g
2 tsp	instant coffee powder	10 mL
1 tsp	vanilla	5 mL
1½ cups	confectioner's (icing) sugar, sifted	375 mL
	Unsweetened cocoa powder	

- *Preheat oven to 350°F (180°C)*
- *9-inch (2.5 L) square cake pan, greased*

1. In a cup, mix instant coffee with boiling water until dissolved. Set aside.
2. In a small bowl, mix together flour and cocoa.
3. In a large bowl, beat butter and sugar until smooth and creamy. Beat in eggs and vanilla just until blended. Blend in flour mixture.
4. Spread evenly in prepared pan. Bake in preheated oven for 20 to 25 minutes or until tester inserted in center comes out clean. Place pan on a wire rack to cool completely.
5. *Frosting:* In a medium bowl, beat butter, cream cheese, instant coffee and vanilla until smooth and blended. Gradually add confectioner's sugar, beating until frosting is smooth and spreadable. Spread evenly over cake. Sift cocoa lightly over top, then cut into bars.

Makes 24 bars

Cola Honey Cake Bars

4 cups	all-purpose flour	1 L
2 tsp	baking powder	10 mL
1 tsp	ground cinnamon	5 mL
½ tsp	baking soda	2 mL
½ tsp	ground cloves, nutmeg or allspice	2 mL
4	eggs	4
1 cup	granulated sugar	250 mL
½ cup	vegetable oil	125 mL
1½ cups	liquid honey	375 mL
1 cup	cola	250 mL
½ cup	raisins (optional)	125 mL

- *Preheat oven to 325°F (160°C)*
- *13- by 9-inch (3.5 L) cake pan, greased*

1. In a large bowl, mix together flour, baking powder, cinnamon, baking soda and cloves.
2. In another large bowl, beat eggs, sugar, oil and honey until smooth and blended. Gradually blend in flour mixture, alternately with cola, just until incorporated. Stir in raisins, if using.
3. Spread evenly in prepared pan. Bake in preheated oven for 50 to 60 minutes or until tester inserted in center comes out clean. Place pan on a rack to cool completely, then cut into bars.

Makes 36 bars

Lebkuchen (Honey Cake Bars)

2 cups	all-purpose flour	500 mL
1 ½ tsp	ground cinnamon	7 mL
½ tsp	baking soda	2 mL
½ tsp	ground ginger	2 mL
½ tsp	ground nutmeg	2 mL
¼ tsp	salt	1 mL
¼ tsp	ground cloves	1 mL
½ cup	raisins	125 mL
½ cup	chopped blanched almonds	125 mL
1 cup	liquid honey	250 mL
¾ cup	packed brown sugar	175 mL
1	egg	1
3 tbsp	freshly squeezed lemon juice, divided	45 mL
1 tsp	grated lemon zest	5 mL
1 cup	confectioner's (icing) sugar, sifted	250 mL
	Candied red cherries, halved	

- *Preheat oven to 350° F (180° C)*
- *Two 9-inch (2.5 L) square cake pans, greased*

1. In a medium bowl, mix together flour, cinnamon, baking soda, ginger, nutmeg, salt and cloves. Stir in raisins and almonds.

2. In a large saucepan, over medium heat, bring honey and brown sugar to a boil, stirring constantly, until sugar dissolves. Allow to cool, then beat in egg, 1 tbsp (15 mL) lemon juice and the lemon zest. Blend in flour mixture. Chill overnight.

3. Divide dough in half and spread evenly in prepared pans. Bake in preheated oven for 30 minutes or until firm. Place pans on wire racks, score into bars and press a cherry half, cut side down, in the center of each bar.

4. Meanwhile, in a bowl, beat confectioner's sugar with remaining 2 tbsp (25 mL) of lemon juice until smooth and blended. Drizzle glaze over top of cake. Cool completely, then cut into bars.

Makes 36 bars

> **TIP:** If you prefer, substitute 1 tbsp (15 mL) pumpkin pie spice for the cinnamon, ginger, nutmeg and cloves.

Dainty Petit-Four Bars

2 cups	cake flour	500 mL
1 tbsp	baking powder	15 mL
¼ tsp	salt	1 mL
¼ cup	shortening, softened	50 mL
¼ cup	butter or margarine, softened	50 mL
1¼ cups	granulated sugar, divided	300 mL
½ tsp	vanilla	2 mL
¼ tsp	almond extract	1 mL
¾ cup	milk	175 mL
6	egg whites	6

FROSTING

1½ cups	hot water	375 mL
3 cups	granulated sugar	750 mL
¼ tsp	cream of tartar	1 mL
1 tsp	vanilla	5 mL
2¼ cups	confectioner's (icing) sugar, sifted	550 mL

TIP: For a special touch, tint the frosting with food coloring and place a nut or candy decoration on top of each bar.

- *Preheat oven to 350° F (180° C)*
- *13- by 9-inch (3.5 L) cake pan, lightly greased*

1. In a medium bowl, sift together flour, baking powder and salt.
2. In a large bowl, beat shortening, butter and 1 cup (250 mL) of the sugar until smooth and creamy. Beat in vanilla and almond extracts. Blend in flour mixture, alternately with milk, just until incorporated.
3. In a clean bowl, beat egg whites until foamy. Gradually add remaining sugar beating until stiff peaks form. Fold into batter.
4. Bake in preheated oven for 35 to 40 minutes or until a tester inserted in center comes out clean. Place pan on a rack to cool for 5 minutes, then remove cake and cool completely on rack.
4. *Frosting:* In a saucepan, over low heat, stir together water, sugar and cream of tartar until mixture resembles a thin syrup. Cool until lukewarm, then beat in vanilla and confectioner's sugar until smooth and spreadable. Cut cake into bars or diamond shapes. Spoon frosting over cakes.

Makes 36 bars

Powdered Poppy Seed Squares

1 cup	poppy seeds	250 mL
1 cup	milk	250 mL
2 cups	all-purpose flour	500 mL
2 tsp	baking powder	10 mL
½ tsp	salt	2 mL
½ cup	butter, softened	125 mL
1 cup	granulated sugar	250 mL
2	eggs, separated	2
½ tsp	almond extract	2 mL
	Confectioner's (icing) sugar	

- *Preheat oven to 350°F (180°C)*
- *8-inch (2 L) square cake pan, greased*

1. In a small bowl, combine poppy seeds and milk. Let stand for 1 hour.
2. In a medium bowl, mix together flour, baking powder and salt.
3. In a large bowl, beat butter and sugar until smooth and creamy. Beat in egg yolks until incorporated. Stir in almond extract. Gradually blend in flour mixture alternately with poppy seed mixture, just until incorporated.
4. In a clean bowl, beat egg whites until soft peaks form. Fold into batter.
5. Spread evenly in prepared pan. Bake in preheated oven for 40 to 45 minutes or until a tester inserted in the center comes out clean. Place pan on a wire rack to cool completely, then sift confectioner's sugar over top. Cut into squares.

Makes 16 squares

Raisin-Spice Hermit Bars

2 cups	all-purpose flour	500 mL
⅔ cup	packed brown sugar	150 mL
2 tsp	ground cinnamon	10 mL
1½ tsp	ground ginger	7 mL
½ tsp	baking soda	2 mL
½ tsp	salt	2 mL
6 tbsp	butter or margarine, melted	90 mL
2	eggs	2
⅔ cup	fancy molasses	150 mL
2 tsp	vanilla	10 mL
¾ cup	dark seedless raisins	175 mL

- *Preheat oven to 375° F (190° C)*
- *13- by 9-inch (3.5 L) cake pan, lined with greased foil*

1. In a medium bowl, mix together flour, brown sugar, cinnamon, ginger, baking soda and salt.
2. In a large bowl, beat butter, eggs, molasses and vanilla until blended. Blend in flour mixture. Stir in raisins.
3. Spread evenly in prepared pan. Bake in preheated oven for 20 to 25 minutes or until edges are golden brown. Place pan on a wire rack to cool completely. Transfer cake, with foil, to a cutting board and cut into bars.

Makes 36 bars

TIP: To plump raisins, soak them in orange juice and store in refrigerator.

Delicate Lace Baskets *(page 282)* ➤

Rice Pudding Bars

2	eggs	2
1/3 cup	packed brown sugar	75 mL
1/2 tsp	ground cinnamon	2 mL
1/2 tsp	vanilla	2 mL
1 cup	milk	250 mL
1 cup	cooked rice	250 mL
1/4 cup	raisins	50 mL

- *Preheat oven to 325°F (160°C)*
- *9-inch (2.5 L) square cake pan, greased*

1. In a medium bowl, beat eggs, brown sugar, cinnamon, vanilla and milk until well blended. Stir in rice and raisins.
2. Spread evenly in prepared pan. Bake in preheated oven for 40 to 45 minutes or until firm. Place pan on a wire rack and cut into bars. Serve warm or cool.

Makes 24 bars

Strawberry Cheesecake Bars

BASE		
3/4 cup	butter or margarine, softened	175 mL
1/3 cup	light corn syrup	75 mL
1/4 cup	granulated sugar	50 mL
2 cups	all-purpose flour	500 mL
1/2 tsp	salt	2 mL
TOPPING		
1 lb	cream cheese, softened	500 g
3	eggs	3
2 tsp	vanilla	10 mL
1 cup	light corn syrup	250 mL
3/4 cup	strawberry jam	175 mL

- *Preheat oven to 375°F (190°C)*
- *13- by 9-inch (3.5 L) cake pan, greased*

1. *Base:* In a medium bowl, beat butter, corn syrup and sugar until smooth. Blend in flour and salt until a dough forms. Press evenly into prepared pan.
2. *Topping:* In another medium bowl, beat cream cheese, eggs and vanilla until smooth and creamy. Beat in corn syrup.
3. Spread evenly over dough. Bake in preheated oven for 35 to 40 minutes or until lightly browned and topping is set. Place pan on a wire rack.
4. Stir jam until smooth. Spread evenly over hot topping. Cool for 30 minutes, then chill 3 hours, or overnight, before cutting into bars. Store, covered, in the refrigerator.

Makes 36 bars

◄ Rainbow Gelatin Squares *(page 291)*

Trail Mix Squares

1 cup	all-purpose flour	250 mL
1 tsp	baking powder	5 mL
¾ cup	packed brown sugar	175 mL
½ cup	butter or margarine, softened	125 mL
2	eggs	2
1 tsp	vanilla	5 mL
½ cup	trail mix, chopped	125 mL
½ cup	semi-sweet chocolate chips	125 mL

- *Preheat oven to 325°F (160°C)*
- *8-inch (2 L) square cake pan, greased*

1. In a small bowl, mix together flour and baking powder.
2. In a medium bowl, beat brown sugar and butter until smooth and creamy. Beat in eggs until incorporated. Stir in vanilla. Blend in flour mixture. Stir in trail mix and chocolate chips.
3. Spread evenly in prepared pan. Bake in preheated oven for 30 to 35 minutes or until a tester inserted in the center comes out clean. Place pan on a wire rack to cool completely, then cut into squares.

Makes 16 squares

Greek Baklava Diamonds

BASE

3½ cups	finely chopped walnuts	875 mL
½ cup	granulated sugar	125 mL
1 tsp	ground cinnamon	5 mL
2	packages (each 8 oz /250 g) refrigerated crescent rolls	2

GLAZE

2 tbsp	butter or margarine	25 mL
¼ cup	granulated sugar	50 mL
2 tbsp	freshly squeezed lemon juice	25 mL
½ cup	liquid honey	125 mL

TIP: To keep honey or molasses from sticking to a measuring cup, grease the cup first — or, if the recipe calls for oil, measure that before measuring the sticky ingredient.

- *Preheat oven to 350°F (180°C)*
- *13- by 9-inch (3.5 L) cake pan, ungreased*

1. *Base:* In a large bowl, mix together nuts, sugar and cinnamon.
2. On a work surface, separate each package of dough into two long rectangles. Line bottom of pan with half, spreading ½ inch (1 cm) up the sides. Spread evenly with nut mixture. Place remaining dough on top, pressing down. Using the dough edges and the perforations in the dough as guidelines, take a sharp knife and score the dough five times lengthwise and seven times diagonally to make diamond-shaped pieces.
3. *Glaze:* In a saucepan, over medium-high heat, combine butter, sugar, lemon juice and honey. Bring to a boil. Remove from heat and spoon half evenly over top of the dough.
4. Bake in preheated oven for 25 to 30 minutes or until golden brown. Spoon the remaining glaze over hot pastry. Place pan on a wire rack to cool completely, then cut into diamonds.

Makes 28 diamonds

Rainbow Gelatin Squares

CLEAR LAYERS

4	packages (4 servings each) gelatin dessert mix, assorted flavors	4
3 cups	boiling water, divided	750 mL
3 cups	cold water, divided	750 mL

CREAMY LAYERS

3	packages (4 servings each) gelatin dessert mix, assorted flavors	3
2¼ cups	boiling water, divided	300 mL
¾ cup	cold water, divided	175 mL
1½ cups	evaporated milk, divided	375 mL
4 cups	frozen whipped topping, thawed	1 L
	Sliced fresh strawberries (optional)	

- *13- by 9-inch (3.5 L) cake pan, greased*

1. *Clear layers:* In a small bowl, combine gelatin dessert mix with ¾ cup (175 mL) boiling water, stirring until completely dissolved. Add ¾ cup (175 mL) cold water and mix thoroughly. Pour into prepared baking pan and refrigerate for 35 to 40 minutes or until almost set.

2. *Creamy layers:* In another small bowl, combine gelatin dessert mix with ¾ cup (175 mL) boiling water, stirring until completely dissolved. Add ¼ cup (50 mL) cold water and ½ cup (125 mL) evaporated milk; mix thoroughly. Spoon over chilled clear layer and refrigerate until almost set.

3. Repeat clear and creamy layers, making seven in all, chilling each layer before adding another. (See photo opposite page 289 for color ideas.)

4. When all layers are completed and gelatin is set, cut into squares. Decorate squares with topping and garnish with sliced strawberries, if using.

Makes 30 squares

Butterscotch Pudding Bars

BASE

1 cup	all-purpose flour	250 mL
½ cup	chopped pecans	125 mL
½ cup	butter	125 mL

FILLING

1 cup	confectioner's (icing) sugar, sifted	250 mL
8 oz	cream cheese, softened	250 g
3 cups	frozen whipped topping, thawed, divided	750 mL

TOPPING

2	package (each a 4-serving size) butterscotch instant pudding mix	2
3½ cups	milk	875 mL
¼ cup	chopped pecans	50 mL

TIP: Plastic wrap will cling better to the rim of a bowl or pan if you moisten the rim with a few drops of water.

- *Preheat oven to 350°F (180°C)*
- *13- by 9-inch (3.5 L) cake pan, ungreased*

1. *Base:* In a medium bowl, mix together flour and pecans. Using two knives, a pastry blender or your fingers, cut butter in until mixture resembles coarse crumbs. Press evenly into pan. Bake in preheated oven for 15 to 20 minutes or until lightly browned. Place pan on a wire rack to cool.
2. *Filling:* In a medium bowl, beat sugar and cream cheese until smooth. Fold in 1 cup (250 mL) of the whipped topping and spread evenly over baked base.
3. *Topping:* In another medium bowl, beat pudding mix and milk until blended and smooth. Spoon over filling. Chill for 15 to 20 minutes until set. Top with remaining whipped topping and pecans. Chill for 2 hours. Cut into bars.

Makes 36 bars

Chocolate Peanut Butter Coconut Gems

BASE

1½ cups	graham wafer crumbs (about 22 wafers)	375 mL
½ cup	butter or margarine, melted	125 mL

FILLING

1⅓ cups	flaked coconut	325 mL
1	can (10 oz/300 mL) sweetened condensed milk	1

TOPPING

½ cup	smooth peanut butter	125 mL
1½ cups	semi-sweet chocolate chips	375 mL

- *Preheat oven to 325°F (160°C)*
- *13- by 9-inch (3.5 L) cake pan, ungreased*

1. *Base:* In a small bowl, mix together crumbs and melted butter. Press evenly into pan.
2. *Filling:* Sprinkle coconut evenly over base. Pour condensed milk evenly over coconut.
3. Bake in preheated oven for 20 to 25 minutes or until lightly browned.
4. *Topping:* In a saucepan, over low heat, melt peanut butter and chocolate chips, stirring until smooth. Spread evenly over filling. Place pan on a wire rack to cool for 30 minutes, then chill thoroughly. Cut into squares.

Makes 24 squares

Frosted Chocolate Nut Bars

2 cups	all-purpose flour	500 mL
½ tsp	salt	2 mL
2 cups	granulated sugar	500 mL
1 cup	butter or margarine, softened	250 mL
4	eggs	4
1 tbsp	vanilla	15 mL
2 cups	chopped walnuts	500 mL
2	squares (each 1 oz/28 g) unsweetened chocolate, melted	2

FROSTING

1 cup	milk	250 mL
5 tbsp	all-purpose flour	75 mL
1 cup	confectioner's (icing) sugar, sifted	250 mL
1 cup	butter or margarine, softened	250 mL
2 tsp	vanilla	10 mL

TIP: To prevent cakes from becoming soggy, always cool them in their pans, on a wire rack, so the bottom of the pan will be cooled by circulating air.

- *Preheat oven to 350°F (180°C)*
- *13- by 9-inch (3.5 L) cake pan, greased*

1. In a small bowl, mix together flour and salt.
2. In a large bowl, beat sugar and butter until smooth and creamy. Beat in eggs until incorporated. Stir in vanilla. Blend in flour mixture. Stir in nuts.
3. Set aside half the batter and spread remainder evenly in prepared pan. Blend melted chocolate into reserved batter. Spread carefully over the batter in the pan. Bake in preheated oven for 30 to 35 minutes or until a tester inserted in the center comes out clean. Place pan on a wire rack to cool completely.
4. *Frosting:* In a saucepan, whisk milk and flour until smooth. Cook, stirring constantly, over medium heat, until thickened (about 10 minutes). Remove from heat and set aside.
5. In a medium bowl, beat sugar, butter and vanilla until smooth and blended. Gradually add milk mixture, beating until smooth and spreadable. Spread frosting over top of cake. Cut into bars.

Makes 36 bars

Krispie Toffee Triangles

BASE

½ cup	all-purpose flour	125 mL
¼ tsp	baking soda	1 mL
Pinch	salt	Pinch
⅓ cup	butter or margarine, melted	75 mL
⅓ cup	packed brown sugar	75 mL
¾ cup	crisp rice cereal	175 mL

FILLING

½ cup	butter or margarine	125 mL
1¼ cups	sweetened condensed milk	300 mL
½ cup	packed brown sugar	125 mL

TOPPING

½ cup	semi-sweet chocolate chips	125 mL
1 ¼ cups	crisp rice cereal	300 mL

> **TIP:** After placing batter in your baking pan, bang the pan on the counter two or three times. This will get rid of any large air pockets that will create holes in the cake.

- *Preheat oven to 350°F (180°C)*
- *8-inch (2 L) square cake pan, greased*

1. *Base:* In a medium bowl, mix together flour, baking soda and salt. Make a well in the center. Add melted butter, brown sugar and rice cereal and mix until blended. Press evenly into prepared pan. Bake in preheated oven for 10 to 12 minutes or until lightly browned. Place pan on a wire rack.

2. *Filling:* In a saucepan, over low heat, stir together butter, condensed milk and brown sugar until sugar is dissolved. Increase heat and bring to a boil, stirring constantly; boil for 5 minutes. Spoon evenly over baked base.

3. *Topping:* In another saucepan, over low heat, melt chocolate chips. Stir in cereal and mix until well coated. Spread evenly over filling. Chill for at least 3 hours, then cut into 16 squares. Cut each square in half diagonally to form two triangles.

Makes 32 triangles

Glazed Boston Cream Bars

CAKE

1⅓ cups	all-purpose flour	325 mL
1½ tsp	baking powder	7 mL
¼ tsp	salt	1 mL
3	egg whites	3
½ cup	granulated sugar, divided	125 mL
¼ cup	butter or margarine, softened	50 mL
2 tsp	vanilla	10 mL
⅔ cup	skim milk	150 mL

FILLING

1½ cups	skim milk	375 mL
1	package (4-serving size) vanilla instant pudding mix	1

CHOCOLATE GLAZE

3 tbsp	granulated sugar	45 mL
2 tbsp	unsweetened cocoa powder, sifted	25 mL
1¼ tsp	cornstarch	6 mL
⅓ cup	skim milk	75 mL
½ tsp	vanilla	2 mL

TIP: To determine whether an egg is fresh, immerse it in a pan of cool, salted water. If it sinks, it is fresh. If it rises to the top, it has passed its peak and is best discarded.

- *Preheat oven to 350°F (180°C)*
- *9-inch (2.5 L) square cake pan, lightly greased*

1. *Cake:* In a small bowl, mix together flour, baking powder and salt.
2. In a clean bowl, beat egg whites until frothy. Gradually beat in ¼ cup (50 mL) of the sugar, until stiff peaks form.
3. In a large bowl, beat remaining ½ cup (50 mL) sugar and butter until smooth and creamy. Stir in vanilla. Gradually blend in flour mixture, alternately with milk, just until incorporated. Stir in ⅓ of egg white mixture until well blended, then fold in remainder.
4. Spread evenly in prepared pan. Bake in preheated oven for 35 minutes or until a tester inserted in the center comes out clean. Place pan on a wire rack to cool for 10 minutes, then turn cake out onto rack to cool completely.
5. *Filling:* Prepare pudding according to the instructions on the package but use 1½ cups (375 mL) of milk. Chill for 30 minutes or until thickened.
6. *Glaze:* In a saucepan, combine sugar, cocoa, cornstarch and milk. Bring to a boil over medium heat and cook for 1 to 2 minutes, stirring constantly, until slightly thickened. Remove from heat and stir in vanilla. Cool in refrigerator for about 20 minutes.
7. Using a serrated knife, cut the cake in half horizontally and place the bottom piece, cut side up, on a plate. Spoon filling evenly over top. Top with second layer, cut side down. Spoon glaze over top, allowing some to drip down the sides. Chill for 3 to 4 hours, until glaze hardens, then cut into bars.

Makes 24 bars

Old-Fashioned Butter Tart Bars

BASE

1 cup	all-purpose flour	250 mL
2 tbsp	granulated sugar	25 mL
1/2 cup	butter or margarine, softened	125 mL

FILLING

1 1/2 cups	packed brown sugar	375 mL
1 cup	chopped walnuts	250 mL
1/2 cup	raisins	125 mL
3	eggs, beaten	3
3 tbsp	all-purpose flour	45 mL
1/2 tsp	baking powder	2 mL
1 tsp	vanilla	5 mL

- *Preheat oven to 350°F (180°C)*
- *9-inch (2.5 L) square cake pan, ungreased*

1. *Base:* In a small bowl, mix together flour and sugar. Using two knives, a pastry blender or your fingers, cut butter in until mixture resembles coarse crumbs. Press evenly into pan. Bake in preheated oven for 15 to 18 minutes or until golden brown. Place pan on a wire rack.

2. *Filling:* In a medium bowl, combine brown sugar, walnuts and raisins. Add eggs, flour, baking powder and vanilla and beat until well blended.

3. Spread evenly over hot base and bake 20 to 25 minutes longer or until golden brown. Place pan on a wire rack to cool completely. (The filling may seem a bit jiggly at first but will become firm when completely cooled.) Cut into bars.

Makes about 24 bars

Buttermilk Spice Squares

2 1/2 cups	cake flour, sifted	625 mL
2 tsp	baking powder	10 mL
2 tsp	ground cinnamon	10 mL
1/2 tsp	baking soda	2 mL
1/2 tsp	ground cloves	2 mL
1/4 tsp	ground allspice	1 mL
1/4 tsp	ground nutmeg	1 mL
1/4 tsp	ground mace	1 mL
1/2 cup	butter or shortening, softened	125 mL
1 cup	packed brown sugar	250 mL
2	eggs	2
1 cup	buttermilk	250 mL

- *Preheat oven to 350°F (180°C)*
- *8-inch (2 L) square cake pan , greased*

1. In a medium bowl, mix together flour, baking powder, cinnamon, baking soda, cloves, allspice, nutmeg and mace.

2. In a large bowl, beat butter and sugar until smooth and creamy. Beat in eggs until incorporated. Gradually blend in flour mixture, alternately with buttermilk, just until incorporated.

3. Spread evenly in prepared pan. Bake in preheated oven for 45 to 50 minutes or until a tester inserted in the center comes out clean. Place pan on a wire rack to cool completely, then cut into squares.

Makes 16 squares

TIP: If you don't have any buttermilk, here's an easy substitute: For each cup of buttermilk needed, just add 1 tbsp (15 mL) lemon juice to 1 cup (250 mL) regular milk and stir well.

Coffee-Bran Squares

½ cup	whole bran cereal	125 mL
1 cup	cold, strong coffee	250 mL
1 cup	granulated sugar	250 mL
1 cup	whole wheat flour	250 mL
½ cup	all-purpose flour	125 mL
1 tsp	baking soda	5 mL
1 tsp	ground cinnamon	5 mL
½ tsp	salt	2 mL
½ tsp	ground nutmeg	2 mL
¼ tsp	ground cloves	1 mL
¼ cup	vegetable oil	50 mL
1 tsp	vanilla	5 mL
1 tbsp	vinegar	15 mL

- *Preheat oven to 350°F (180°C)*
- *8-inch (2 L) square cake pan, lightly greased*

1. In a small bowl, mix together cereal and coffee. Let stand for 2 minutes or until coffee is almost completely absorbed.
2. In a medium bowl, mix together sugar, flours, baking soda, cinnamon, salt, nutmeg and cloves.
3. In a large bowl, whisk together oil, vanilla and vinegar. Stir in cereal mixture until blended. Blend in flour mixture.
4. Spread evenly in prepared pan. Bake in preheated oven for 35 to 40 minutes or until a tester inserted in center comes out clean. Place pan on a wire rack to cool completely, then cut into squares.

Makes 16 squares

TIP: For a quick dessert, take 1 can of refrigerated biscuit dough and separate the biscuits. Dip each biscuit in melted butter, then in a mixture of 1 tsp (5 mL) ground cinnamon and ¾ cup (175 mL) granulated sugar. Place biscuits in a greased cake pan, sides touching, and bake in a preheated 450°F (230°C) oven for 10 minutes or until golden brown. Place pan on a wire rack to cool completely, then cut into squares.

Cinnamon Raisin Bars

3 cups	raisins	750 mL
1½ cups	all-purpose flour	375 mL
1 tsp	baking soda	5 mL
1 tsp	salt	5 mL
1 tsp	ground cinnamon	5 mL
1 tsp	ground nutmeg	5 mL
1 cup	packed brown sugar	250 mL
½ cup	butter or margarine, softened	125 mL
3	eggs	3

- *Preheat oven to 350° F (180°C)*
- *9-inch (2.5 L) square cake pan, greased*

1. In a saucepan, over medium heat, add sufficient water to cover raisins. Bring to a boil and cook for 5 minutes. Remove from heat and strain cooking liquid into a 1-cup (250 mL) measure. Add water, if required, to make 1 cup (250 mL) of liquid. Set raisins and liquid aside.

2. In a medium bowl, mix together flour, baking soda, salt, cinnamon and nutmeg.

3. In a large bowl, beat brown sugar and butter until smooth and creamy. Beat in eggs until incorporated. Gradually blend in flour mixture, alternately with reserved raisin liquid, until just incorporated. Stir in reserved raisins.

4. Spread evenly in prepared pan. Bake in preheated oven for 35 to 40 minutes or until a tester inserted in the center comes out clean. Place pan on a wire rack to cool completely, then cut into bars.

Makes 24 bars

Scottish Cottage Pudding Squares

1¾ cups	all-purpose flour	425 mL
2½ tsp	baking powder	12 mL
½ tsp	salt	2 mL
¼ cup	shortening, softened	50 mL
1 cup	granulated sugar	250 mL
1	egg	1
½ tsp	vanilla	2 mL
¼ tsp	almond extract	1 mL
1 tbsp	grated orange zest	15 mL
⅔ cup	milk	150 mL

- *Preheat oven to 350°F (180°C)*
- *8-inch (2 L) square cake pan, greased*

1. In a small bowl, mix together flour, baking powder and salt.

2. In a large bowl, beat shortening and sugar until smooth and creamy. Beat in egg until incorporated. Stir in vanilla, almond extract and orange zest. Blend in flour mixture, alternately with milk, until just incorporated.

3. Spread evenly in prepared pan. Bake in preheated oven for 30 to 35 minutes or until a tester inserted in the center comes out clean. Cut into squares immediately and serve while still hot.

Makes 16 squares

TIP: These squares are even more delicious with a lemon or orange sauce.

Dutch Crumb Squares

2½ cups	cake flour, sifted	625 mL
½ tsp	baking soda	2 mL
½ tsp	salt	2 mL
½ cup	butter or margarine, softened	125 mL
¾ cup	packed brown sugar	175 mL
1 cup	seedless raisins, ground in a food processor	250 mL
1	egg, beaten	1
¾ cup	buttermilk	175 mL
2 tbsp	granulated sugar	25 mL
Pinch	ground cinnamon	Pinch

TIP: When working with a sticky or fluffy batter, wet your spatula, or hands, before patting or spreading the batter in the pan.

- *Preheat oven to 350°F (180°C)*
- *Greased 8-inch (2 L) square cake pan*

1. In a medium bowl, mix together flour, baking soda and salt.
2. In a large bowl, beat butter and brown sugar until smooth and creamy. Gradually blend in flour mixture. Set aside ¾ cup (175 mL). To remaining mixture, add raisins, egg and buttermilk, beating until well blended.
3. Spread evenly in prepared pan. Sprinkle reserved crumb mixture evenly over top. Sprinkle sugar and cinnamon over top of crumb mixture. Bake in preheated oven for 20 to 25 minutes or until a tester inserted in the center comes out clean. Place pan on a wire rack to cool completely, then cut into squares.

Makes 16 squares

Orange Nut Dessert Layers

BASE

1½ cups	all-purpose flour	375 mL
½ cup	packed brown sugar	125 mL
¼ tsp	salt	1 mL
1 tbsp	grated orange zest	15 mL
½ cup	butter or margarine	125 mL

FILLING

1 cup	semi-sweet chocolate chips	250 mL

TOPPING

¼ cup	all-purpose flour	50 mL
½ tsp	baking powder	2 mL
¼ tsp	salt	1 mL
2	eggs	2
1 cup	packed brown sugar	250 mL
1 tsp	vanilla	5 mL
1½ cups	chopped walnuts	375 mL

- *Preheat oven to 375°F (190°C)*
- *13- by 9-inch (3.5 L) cake pan, ungreased*

1. *Base:* In a medium bowl, mix together flour, brown sugar, salt and orange zest. Using two knives, a pastry blender or your fingers, cut butter in until mixture resembles coarse crumbs. Press evenly into pan. Bake in preheated oven for 10 minutes. Place pan on a rack.
2. *Filling:* Sprinkle chocolate over hot base. Let stand for about 2 minutes or until chocolate softens. Using a knife, spread evenly over base.
3. *Topping:* In a small bowl, mix together flour, baking powder and salt. In another bowl, beat eggs, brown sugar and vanilla until blended. Blend in flour mixture. Stir in walnuts.
4. Spread mixture evenly over chocolate. Bake 20 minutes longer or until top is firm and golden brown. Place pan on a rack to cool completely, then cut into squares.

Makes 24 squares

Honey Cake Spice Bars

2 tbsp	packed brown sugar	25 mL
1/4 cup+ 2 tsp	vegetable oil	60 mL
1/4 cup	water	50 mL
1/4 cup	liquid honey	50 mL
3/4 cup	frozen apple juice concentrate, thawed	175 mL
2	eggs	2
1/2 cup	ground almonds	125 mL
2 1/4 cups	all-purpose flour	550 mL
1 1/2 tsp	baking powder	7 mL
1 tsp	ground cinnamon	5 mL
1/2 tsp	ground ginger	2 mL
1/4 tsp	ground allspice	1 mL

- *Preheat oven to 375°F (190°C)*
- *13- by 9-inch (3.5 L) cake pan, lightly greased*

1. In a saucepan, combine sugar, oil, water, honey and apple juice concentrate. Bring to a boil and remove from heat. Set aside to cool. Add eggs and mix to blend.
2. In a large bowl, mix together almonds, flour, baking powder, cinnamon, ginger and allspice. Make a well in the center. Add apple juice mixture and stir until blended. Shape dough into a ball, wrap tightly in plastic wrap and chill for 2 hours.
3. Press dough evenly into prepared pan. Bake in preheated oven for 25 to 30 minutes or until golden brown. Place pan on a wire rack to cool completely, then cut into bars.

Makes 36 bars

TIP: For a decorative touch, use a sharp knife to gently score center of each bar before baking and place a whole, blanched almond in each. Bake as directed.

Spicy Oatmeal Bars with Citrus Glaze

1¾ cups	all-purpose flour	425 mL
1½ tsp	baking soda	7 mL
¾ tsp	ground cinnamon	4 mL
¼ tsp	ground nutmeg	1 mL
¼ tsp	ground cloves	1 mL
½ cup	butter or margarine, softened	125 mL
1 cup	packed brown sugar	250 mL
2	eggs	2
1 tsp	vanilla	5 mL
1 cup	unsweetened applesauce	250 mL
1½ cups	quick-cooking rolled oats	375 mL
1 cup	raisins	250 mL
½ cup	chopped walnuts	125 mL
CITRUS GLAZE		
½ cup	confectioner's (icing) sugar, sifted	125 mL
2 tsp	water	10 mL
2 tsp	freshly squeezed lemon juice	10 mL

- *Preheat oven to 375°F (190°C)*
- *13- by 9-inch (3.5 L) cake pan, greased*

1. In a small bowl, mix together flour, baking soda, cinnamon, nutmeg and cloves.
2. In a large bowl, beat butter and brown sugar until smooth and creamy. Beat in eggs until incorporated. Stir in vanilla. Gradually blend in flour mixture, alternately with applesauce, until just incorporated. Stir in oats, raisins and walnuts.
3. Spread evenly in prepared pan. Bake in preheated oven for 30 to 35 minutes or until a tester inserted in the center comes out clean. Place pan on a wire rack to cool.
3. *Glaze:* In a small bowl, beat confectioner's sugar, water and juice until smooth and spreadable. Drizzle glaze over top of warm cake. Cool completely, then cut into bars.

Makes 36 bars

Orange-Raisin Bars

BASE

2 cups	all-purpose flour	500 mL
1 cup	granulated sugar	250 mL
1 tsp	baking powder	5 mL
1 cup	butter or margarine	250 mL
1	egg, beaten	1

FILLING

1⅓ cups	raisins	325 mL
¾ cup	granulated sugar	175 mL
2 tbsp	all-purpose flour	25 mL
1 cup	boiling water	250 mL
½ tsp	orange juice	2 mL
Pinch	salt	Pinch

> **TIP:** For a more pronounced orange flavor, increase amount of orange juice in filling to 1 tsp (5 mL).

- *Preheat oven to 350°F (180°C)*
- *9-inch (2.5 L) square cake pan, lightly greased*

1. *Base:* In a large bowl, mix together flour, sugar and baking powder. Using two knives, a pastry blender or your fingers, cut butter in until mixture resembles coarse crumbs. Mix in egg just until dough forms. Form dough into a ball, then divide in half. Press one portion into prepared pan. Set other aside.

2. *Filling:* In a saucepan, over low heat, stir together raisins, sugar, flour and boiling water until sugar is dissolved. Increase heat and bring to a boil. Reduce heat to simmer and cook, stirring constantly, for 5 to 8 minutes or until thickened. Remove from heat. Stir in orange juice and salt. Set aside to cool slightly.

3. Spread filling evenly over dough. On lightly floured work surface, press remaining dough to make a 9-inch (23 cm) square and place over the raisin filling. (Disregard any small holes in the dough.) Bake in preheated oven for 25 to 35 minutes or until lightly browned. Place pan on a wire rack to cool completely, then cut into bars.

Makes 24 bars

Peachy Topped Bars

BASE

1½ cups	all-purpose flour	375 mL
¼ cup	granulated sugar	50 mL
2 tsp	baking powder	10 mL
½ tsp	salt	2 mL
1	egg	1
3 tbsp	butter or shortening, melted	45 mL
½ cup	milk	125 mL

PEACH TOPPING

1½ cups	thinly sliced peaches	375 mL
2 tbsp	granulated sugar	25 mL
½ tsp	ground cinnamon	2 mL

- *Preheat oven to 400°F (200°C)*
- *8-inch (2 L) square cake pan, greased*

1. *Base:* In a medium bowl, mix together flour, sugar, baking powder and salt. Make a well in the center.

2. In a small bowl, beat egg, butter and milk until blended. Add to flour mixture and mix until just incorporated. Spread evenly in prepared pan.

3. *Topping:* In a small bowl, mix together peaches, sugar and cinnamon.

4. Spread evenly over batter. Cover pan with aluminum foil and bake in preheated oven for 10 minutes. Remove foil, bake 15 minutes longer, cool and cut into bars.

Makes 12 bars

Pink Lemonade Bars

BASE

2 cups	vanilla wafer crumbs (about 40 cookies)	500 mL
½ cup	butter or margarine, melted	125 mL

TOPPING

¾ cup	water	175 mL
½	can (12 oz/355 mL) frozen pink lemonade concentrate	½
48	miniature marshmallows	48
1 cup	whipping (35%) cream	250 mL

- *Preheat oven to 325°F (160°C)*
- *8-inch (2 L) square cake pan, ungreased*

1. *Base:* In a medium bowl, mix together crumbs and butter. Set aside ½ cup (125 mL) and press remainder evenly into bottom and halfway up the sides of pan. Bake in preheated oven for 15 minutes. Place pan on a wire rack to cool completely.

2. *Topping:* In a saucepan, combine water and lemonade concentrate. Heat over low heat until lemonade thaws and mixture is hot. Stir in marshmallows until melted and smooth. Chill for 3 to 4 hours or overnight, until mixture is thick and syrupy.

3. In a medium bowl, whip cream until stiff. Fold gently into marshmallow mixture until blended. Spoon into cooled base. Sprinkle remaining crumb mixture evenly over top. Freeze for 3 to 4 hours or until firm. Cut into bars. Allow to stand at room temperature for about 30 minutes before serving. Store, covered, in the freezer.

Makes 12 bars

Plantation Marble Squares

2 cups	cake flour, sifted	500 mL
2 tsp	baking powder	10 mL
¼ tsp	salt	1 mL
½ cup	butter or margarine, softened	125 mL
1 cup	granulated sugar	250 mL
2	eggs	2
½ cup	milk	125 mL
1 tsp	ground cinnamon	5 mL
½ tsp	ground nutmeg	2 mL
½ tsp	ground cloves	2 mL
2 tbsp	fancy molasses	25 mL

TIP: If desired, frost with a Butter Frosting (see recipes, page 360), then sprinkle with nuts and/or raisins.

• *Preheat oven to 350°F (180°C)*
• *8-inch (2 L) square cake pan, greased*

1. In a medium bowl, mix together flour, baking powder and salt.
2. In a large bowl, beat butter and sugar until smooth and creamy. Beat in eggs until incorporated. Gradually blend in flour mixture alternately with milk, until just incorporated.
3. Divide batter into two bowls. Stir cinnamon, nutmeg, cloves and molasses into one of the bowls; spread mixture evenly in prepared pan. Drop batter from remaining bowl, by spoonfuls, over top. Run a knife through batters to create a marbling effect.
4. Bake in preheated oven for 45 to 50 minutes or until a tester inserted in the center comes out clean. Place pan on a wire rack to cool completely, then cut into squares.

Makes 16 squares

Poppy Seed Squares

1 cup	poppy seeds	250 mL
1 cup	milk	250 mL
2 cups	all-purpose flour	500 mL
2 tsp	baking powder	10 mL
½ tsp	salt	2 mL
½ cup	butter or margarine, softened	125 mL
1 cup	granulated sugar	250 mL
2	eggs, separated	2
	Grated zest of 1 orange or ½ tsp (2 mL) almond extract	
	Confectioner's (icing) sugar	

• *Preheat oven to 350°F (180°C)*
• *8-inch (2 L) square cake pan, greased*

1. In a small bowl, combine poppy seeds and milk. Let stand for 1 hour.
2. In a medium bowl, mix together flour, baking powder and salt.
3. In a large bowl, beat butter and sugar until smooth and creamy. Beat in egg yolks until incorporated. Blend in flour mixture alternately with poppy seed mixture, mixing just until incorporated. Stir in orange zest.
4. In a clean bowl, beat egg whites until stiff. Fold gently into batter.
5. Spread evenly in prepared pan. Bake in preheated oven for about 45 minutes or until a tester inserted in the center comes out clean. Place pan on a rack to cool completely. Sift confectioner's sugar over top. Cut into squares.

Makes 16 squares

Holiday Treats

Many people associate holiday memories with special foods. The Thanksgiving turkey, Christmas pudding, Hanukah rugelach and special baked goods are, for many, cherished traditions of the holidays. But homemade cookies, bars and squares are more than a holiday treat. They also make an ideal present. Wrapped in pretty paper or presented in elegant tins, they are always appreciated. From Peppermint Candy Canes to Poppy Seed Hamantashen, I hope these recipes will enhance your holiday celebrations.

Bird's Nest Cookies

3 cups	all-purpose flour	750 mL
1 tsp	baking powder	5 mL
1 tsp	salt	5 mL
1 cup	shortening, softened	250 mL
1 cup	lightly packed brown sugar	250 mL
2	eggs, separated	2
1 tsp	vanilla	5 mL
½ cup	milk	125 mL
1¼ cups	sweetened shredded coconut	300 mL
½ cup	apricot or raspberry jam	125 mL

- *Preheat oven to 350°F (180°C)*
- *Cookie sheet, ungreased*

1. In a medium bowl, mix together flour, baking powder and salt.
2. In a large bowl, beat shortening and sugar until smooth and creamy. Add egg yolks, one at a time, beating until incorporated. Stir in vanilla. Gradually add flour mixture, alternating with milk to form a dough. Shape into 1½-inch (4 cm) balls.
3. In a clean bowl, whisk egg whites. Spread coconut on a plate. One at a time, dip balls into egg whites. Shake off excess, then roll in coconut. Place about 2 inches (5 cm) apart on cookie sheet and, using a thimble or your thumb, make a small dent in the center of each. Fill with jam.
4. Bake in preheated oven for 12 to 15 minutes or until lightly browned. Immediately transfer to wire racks to cool.

Makes about 40 cookies

Xmas Chocolate Log Cookies

1⅓ cups	granulated sugar	325 mL
2 tbsp	all-purpose flour	25 mL
Pinch	ground cinnamon	Pinch
2½ cups	ground almonds	625 mL
2	egg whites	2
4	squares (each 1 oz/28 g) semi-sweet chocolate, melted (see page 14)	4
	Granulated sugar	

- *Preheat oven to 425°F (220°C)*
- *Cookie sheet, ungreased*

1. In a small bowl, mix together sugar, flour, cinnamon and almonds.
2. In a clean bowl, beat egg whites until soft peaks form. Fold in melted chocolate. Gradually add sugar mixture, mixing until a stiff dough forms.
3. On a lightly floured surface, shape dough, 2 tbsp (25 mL) at a time, into logs about 5 inches (13 cm) long, then roll in sugar.
4. Place logs about 2 inches (5 cm) apart on cookie sheet. Bake in preheated oven for 10 minutes or until browned. Using a lifter, carefully transfer to wire racks to cool.

Makes 4 dozen

Holiday Cranberry Cookies

1½ cups	all-purpose flour	375 mL
¾ tsp	baking powder	4 mL
¼ tsp	baking soda	1 mL
¼ tsp	salt	1 mL
¼ cup	butter, softened	50 mL
⅓ cup	packed brown sugar	75 mL
½ cup	granulated sugar	125 mL
1	egg	1
3 tbsp	frozen orange juice concentrate, thawed	45 mL
1 tsp	grated orange zest	5 mL
1½ cups	fresh cranberries, halved, or 1 cup (250 mL) dried cranberries	375 mL
½ cup	chopped pecans or walnuts	125 mL
FROSTING		
¼ cup	butter, softened	50 mL
2 cups	confectioner's (icing) sugar, sifted	500 mL
3 tbsp	frozen orange juice concentrate, thawed	45 mL
1 tsp	vanilla	5 mL
	Pecan or walnut halves (optional)	

- *Preheat oven to 375°F (190°C)*
- *Cookie sheet, ungreased*

1. In a small bowl, mix together flour, baking powder, baking soda and salt.

2. In a large bowl, beat butter and sugars until smooth and creamy. Beat in egg until well incorporated. Stir in concentrate and zest until blended. Gradually add flour mixture and mix until well blended. Fold in cranberries and nuts until thoroughly combined.

3. Drop dough by rounded tablespoonfuls (15 mL), about 2 inches (5 cm) apart, onto cookie sheet. Bake in preheated oven for 10 to 12 minutes or until lightly browned. Cool on cookie sheet.

4. *Frosting:* In a small bowl, beat butter until creamy. Add confectioner's sugar, orange juice and vanilla and mix until smooth. Spread on cooled cookies. Garnish with nuts, if desired.

Makes about 3 dozen

TIP: To prevent a crust from forming on icings and frostings, press a piece of plastic wrap against their surfaces until ready to use.

Glazed Holiday Wreaths

1¼ cups	all-purpose flour	300 mL
½ cup	confectioner's (icing) sugar, sifted	125 mL
Pinch	salt	Pinch
½ cup	butter, softened	125 mL
½ tsp	vanilla	2 mL
1	egg	1
GLAZE		
1	egg, beaten	1
¼ cup	finely chopped blanched almonds	50 mL
2 tbsp	granulated sugar	25 mL

- *Preheat oven to 350°F (180°C)*
- *Round cookie cutters or two glasses, 2½ inches (6 cm) and 1 inch (2.5 cm) in diameter*
- *Cookie sheet, ungreased*

1. In a small bowl, sift together flour, confectioner's sugar and salt.

2. In a large bowl, beat butter, vanilla and egg until smooth and creamy. Add flour mixture and, using your hands, knead into a dough.

3. Divide dough into three portions. Wrap each tightly in plastic wrap and refrigerate for 1 to 2 hours, until firm.

4. On a lightly floured surface, roll out dough to ⅛-inch (0.25 cm) thickness. Cut out circles with wide cutter, then, using the smaller cutter, cut a circle in the center of each round.

5. Place about 2 inches (5 cm) apart on cookie sheet. Brush with beaten egg, then top with almonds and sugar. Bake in preheated oven for 10 to 15 minutes until golden brown. Cool on baking sheets for 5 minutes, then transfer to wire racks to cool completely.

Makes about 2½ dozen

Cherry Bell Cookies

¾ cup	butter, softened	175 mL
½ cup	granulated sugar	125 mL
1	egg yolk	1
1 tsp	vanilla	5 mL
1¾ cups	all-purpose flour	425 mL
12	maraschino cherries, drained and halved	12

TIP: Make extra dough when making cookies. Roll out and cut, shape and slice, then wrap tightly in plastic wrap and freeze. Unwrap and pop frozen dough into the oven whenever you want warm cookies in a hurry.

- *Preheat oven to 375°F (190°C)*
- *Cookie sheet, ungreased*

1. In a large bowl, beat butter and sugar until smooth and creamy. Beat in egg yolk and vanilla until well incorporated. Gradually beat in flour until a soft dough forms.
2. On a floured surface, roll dough into a log, 8 by 1½ inches (20 by 4 cm). Wrap tightly in plastic wrap and refrigerate at least 3 hours or overnight.
3. Using a knife, cut log into slices ¼ inch (0.5 cm) wide and place about 2 inches (5 cm) apart on cookie sheet. Allow dough to reach room temperature, then fold two edges of each cookie over the center so they overlap, with one end more pointed and the other a rounded bell shape. Tuck a cherry half into the rounded end to resemble a clapper. Bake in preheated oven for 10 to 12 minutes or until just lightly browned. Immediately transfer to wire racks to cool.

Makes about 2½ dozen

Chocolate Chunk Snowballs

2 cups	butter, softened	500 mL
1 cup	confectioner's (icing) sugar, sifted	250 mL
3½ cups	all-purpose flour	875 mL
½ cup	cornstarch	125 mL
6	squares (each 1 oz/28 g) coarsely chopped bittersweet chocolate	6
1 cup	coarsely chopped pecans, toasted (see page 14)	250 mL
	Confectioner's (icing) sugar, sifted	

- *Preheat oven to 350°F (180°C)*
- *Cookie sheet, ungreased*

1. In a large bowl, beat butter and sugar until smooth and creamy. Gradually stir in flour, then cornstarch, mixing until well blended. Fold in chocolate and pecans.
2. Shape dough into 1-inch (2.5 cm) balls. Place about 2 inches (5 cm) apart on cookie sheet. Bake in preheated oven for 15 minutes or until lightly browned. Immediately transfer to wire racks to cool. When cool, dust lightly with confectioner's sugar.

Makes about 5 dozen

Pfeffernüesse

4 cups	all-purpose flour	1 L
1 tsp	baking soda	5 mL
½ tsp	salt	2 mL
¼ tsp	freshly ground black pepper	1 mL
1 tbsp	ground cinnamon	15 mL
1 tsp	ground nutmeg	5 mL
1 tsp	ground cloves	5 mL
1 tsp	ground allspice	5 mL
1 tbsp	ground cardamom seeds (optional)	15 mL
¼ lb	candied orange peel	125 g
½ lb	citron (see Tip, page 71)	250 g
2 tbsp	butter, softened	25 mL
2½ cups	confectioner's (icing) sugar, sifted	625 mL
5	eggs, separated	5
1½ tsp	grated lemon zest	7 mL
	Confectioner's sugar for frosting (optional)	

GLAZE (OPTIONAL)

1 cup	confectioner's (icing) sugar	250 mL
¼ cup	water	50 mL

- *Preheat oven to 350°F (180°C)*
- *Cookie sheet, ungreased*

1. In a large bowl, mix together flour, baking soda, salt, pepper, cinnamon, nutmeg, cloves, allspice, cardamom seeds, if using, orange peel and citron.

2. In another large bowl, beat butter and confectioner's sugar until smooth and creamy. Beat in egg yolks and lemon zest until well blended. Add flour mixture and mix well.

3. In a clean bowl, beat egg whites until peaks form. Fold into flour-butter mixture. Wrap dough tightly in plastic wrap and refrigerate for 2 hours, until firm.

4. Shape dough into 1-inch (2.5 cm) balls and place about 2 inches (5 cm) apart on cookie sheet. Bake in preheated oven for 15 minutes or until lightly browned.

5. *Glaze:* In a small bowl, beat confectioner's sugar with water until smooth and spreadable. Spread lightly over tops of cookies and return to hot oven for 2 minutes. Immediately transfer to wire racks to cool.

Makes about 6 dozen

These tasty cookies, traditionally served at Christmas in many European countries, are so called because they contain an ingredient not usually found in cookies — black pepper.

TIP: Eggs separate easier when they are cold. However, egg whites will gain more volume if they are allowed to reach room temperature before being beaten.

Rum-Glazed Xmas Fruitcake Cookies

½ cup + 2 tbsp	butter, softened, divided	150 mL
⅓ cup	packed brown sugar	75 mL
½ tsp	ground cinnamon	2 mL
¼ tsp	ground nutmeg	1 mL
½ tsp	ground ginger	2 mL
Pinch	salt	Pinch
1 cup + 2 tbsp	all-purpose flour, divided	275 mL
½ cup	moist dried figs, cut into ½-inch (1 cm) pieces	125 mL
½ cup	large dates, cut into ½-inch (1 cm) pieces	125 mL
½ cup	blanched almonds, toasted and chopped (see page 14)	125 mL
½ cup	coarsely chopped pecans	125 mL
2 tbsp	liquid honey	25 mL
1 tsp	rum	5 mL
1	egg, lightly beaten	1

RUM GLAZE

½ cup	confectioner's (icing) sugar, sifted	125 mL
2 tbsp	dark rum	25 mL

> **TIP:** Just like Christmas fruitcake, these cookies will be better if they are allowed to mellow for 2 to 3 days after they are baked. Store in an airtight container for up to 2 weeks.

- *Preheat oven to 400°F (200°C)*
- *2-inch (5-cm) round cookie cutter, fluted if possible*
- *Cookie sheet, lightly greased*

1. In a small bowl, beat 6 tbsp (90 mL) butter and brown sugar until smooth and creamy. Add cinnamon, nutmeg, ginger and salt and beat until well combined. Add ¾ cup (175 mL) flour and mix until a soft dough forms. Wrap tightly in plastic wrap and refrigerate for 15 to 30 minutes, until firm.

2. In a medium bowl, mix together figs, dates, almonds and pecans.

3. In a clean bowl, beat remaining 4 tbsp (60 mL) butter, honey and rum until smooth and creamy. Gradually beat in egg until incorporated. Add remaining flour and mix well. Add to fruit mixture, mixing until pieces are completely coated. Set aside.

4. On a lightly floured surface, roll dough out to ¼-inch (0.5 cm) thickness. Using a cookie cutter dipped in flour, cut out rounds and place 2 inches (5 cm) apart on prepared cookie sheet. Drop a rounded tablespoonful (15 mL) of the fruit and nut mixture onto each cookie and, using your fingers, shape into mounds. Bake in preheated oven for 10 to 12 minutes until cookies begin to brown on the top.

5. *Rum Glaze:* In a bowl, beat confectioner's sugar and rum until smooth. Spread over hot cookies and immediately return to preheated oven to bake for 1 minute, until glaze bubbles. Cool on cookie sheet for 5 minutes, then transfer to wire racks to cool completely.

Makes about 2 dozen

Springerle Cookies

4 cups	all-purpose flour	1 L
1 tsp	baking soda	5 mL
4	eggs	4
2 cups	granulated sugar	500 mL
2 tsp	anise extract	10 mL
2 tbsp	crushed anise seeds	25 mL

Springerle are German cookies, usually made at Christmas. They are noted for their beautiful designs, achieved by using either a special rolling pin or individual molds.

TIP: An egg left at room temperature for one hour deteriorates as much as it would if stored for a week in the refrigerator. Eggs should be stored in their carton, in the refrigerator, not on the refrigerator door.

- *Preheat oven to 300°F (150°C)*
- *Springerle rolling pin or molds*
- *Lightly floured cookie sheet*

1. In a large bowl, mix together flour and baking soda.

2. In another large bowl, beat eggs and sugar until smooth and creamy. Stir in anise extract. Stir in flour, one-third at a time, mixing after each addition, until a stiff dough forms.

3. Divide dough into three portions. On a lightly floured surface, using a plain rolling pin, roll dough out to ½-inch (1 cm) thickness. Flour the springerle rolling pin, if using, and roll slowly, only once, over the dough, pressing down firmly to make clear designs. Your cookies will now be about ¼ inch (0.5 cm) thick. Cut cookies apart on dividing lines. Lift each cookie carefully and transfer to lightly floured cookie sheet. Repeat with remaining dough. Cover with towels and let stand overnight. If using springerle molds, roll the dough a bit thinner with the plain rolling pin and press molds firmly into the dough. Then transfer to floured sheets.

4. Grease a clean cookie sheet and sprinkle lightly with anise seeds. Brush excess flour from cookie bottoms and, using a finger dipped in water, moisten bottom of each cookie.

5. Place about 2 inches (5 cm) apart on prepared cookie sheet. Bake in preheated oven for 15 minutes, until firm and dry but not browned. Immediately transfer to wire racks to cool. Allow cookies to mellow in a covered, airtight container for at least 1 week.

Makes about 6 dozen

Peppermint Candy Canes

2½ cups	all-purpose flour	625 mL
1 tsp	salt	5 mL
½ cup	shortening, softened	125 mL
½ cup	butter or margarine, softened	125 mL
1 cup	confectioner's (icing) sugar, sifted	250 mL
1	egg	1
1 tsp	vanilla	5 mL
1 tsp	peppermint extract	5 mL
½ tsp or more	red food coloring	2 mL or more

- *Preheat oven to 375°F (190°C)*
- *Cookie sheet, ungreased*

1. In a medium bowl, mix together flour and salt.
2. In a large bowl, beat shortening, butter or margarine and confectioner's sugar until smooth. Beat in egg until well incorporated. Stir in vanilla and peppermint extract and mix well. Gradually add flour mixture and mix until a dough forms.
3. On a lightly floured surface, divide dough into two portions. Knead red food coloring into one portion until well blended. Leave other portion as is.
4. Shape 1 tsp (5 mL) of dough from each half into a rope 4 inches (10 cm) long, rolling back and forth until smooth and even. Place plain rope and a red-colored one side by side. Twist together to make a candy cane. Repeat with remaining dough.
5. Place canes on cookie sheet and, using your hand, curve the top of each to form the handle of a cane. Bake in preheated oven for 8 to 10 minutes or until firm and lightly browned. Immediately transfer to wire racks to cool.

Makes about 4 dozen

Christmas Fruit Cookies

4 cups	all-purpose flour	1 L
2 tsp	baking powder	10 mL
½ tsp	salt	2 mL
¾ cup	butter or margarine, softened	175 mL
¾ cup	shortening, softened	175 mL
1¼ cups	packed brown sugar	300 mL
2	eggs	2
1 tsp	vanilla	5 mL
1	can (8 oz/250 mL) crushed pineapple, drained	1
½ cup	chopped red maraschino cherries	125 mL
½ cup	chopped green maraschino cherries	125 mL
½ cup	chopped pitted dates	125 mL
½ cup	chopped pecans or walnuts	125 mL
½ cup	shredded coconut (optional)	125 mL

- *Preheat oven to 375°F (190°C)*
- *Cookie sheet, ungreased*

1. In a large bowl, mix together flour, baking powder and salt.
2. In another large bowl, beat butter or margarine, shortening and brown sugar until smooth and creamy. Beat in eggs, one at a time, until incorporated. Stir in vanilla. Gradually add flour mixture, mixing until well combined. Stir in pineapple, red and green cherries, dates, nuts and coconut, if desired. Mix well until thoroughly combined.
3. On a lightly floured surface, divide dough into three portions. Shape each portion into a roll 10 inches (25 cm) long. Wrap each roll tightly in plastic wrap and refrigerate for 2 hours, until firm.
4. On a cutting board, cut dough into slices ¼ inch (0.5 cm) thick. Place about 2 inches (5 cm) apart on cookie sheets. Bake in preheated oven for 8 to 10 minutes or until golden brown. Immediately transfer to wire racks to cool.

Makes about 10 dozen

Chocolate Thumbprint Cookies

2 cups	all-purpose flour	500 mL
1/4 cup	unsweetened cocoa powder	50 mL
1 cup	butter, softened	250 mL
1/2 cup	granulated sugar	125 mL
2	eggs	2
1 tsp	vanilla	5 mL
1 cup	finely chopped pecans	250 mL
18	glacé cherries, halved	18
	Melted semi-sweet or bittersweet chocolate (see page 14) (optional)	

- *Preheat oven to 325°F (160°C)*
- *Cookie sheet, greased*

1. In a medium bowl, mix together flour and cocoa.
2. In a large bowl, beat butter and sugar until smooth and creamy. Beat in eggs, one at a time, until incorporated. Stir in vanilla. Gradually add flour mixture, mixing until well incorporated. Fold in pecans.
3. Shape dough into 1-inch (2.5 cm) balls and press a cherry half into the center. Place about 2 inches (5 cm) apart on prepared cookie sheet. Bake in preheated oven for 15 minutes or until golden brown. Immediately transfer to wire racks to cool. When cool, drizzle melted chocolate over tops in a zig-zag pattern, if desired.

Makes about 3 dozen

Mincemeat Drop Cookies

1 1/2 cups	all-purpose flour	375 mL
1 1/2 tsp	baking soda	7 mL
1/2 tsp	ground cinnamon	2 mL
1/4 tsp	ground nutmeg	1 mL
1/4 tsp	salt	1 mL
1/4 cup	butter or margarine, softened	50 mL
3/4 cup	packed brown sugar	175 mL
2	eggs	2
3/4 cup	mincemeat	175 mL
1 1/2 cups	semi-sweet chocolate chips	375 mL
1/2 cup	chopped walnuts	125 mL

- *Preheat oven to 350°F (180°C)*
- *Cookie sheet, greased*

1. In a small bowl, mix together flour, baking soda, cinnamon, nutmeg and salt.
2. In a large bowl, beat butter or margarine and brown sugar until smooth and creamy. Add eggs, one at a time, beating until well incorporated. Stir in mincemeat. Add flour mixture and mix until thoroughly combined. Fold in chocolate chips and nuts.
3. Drop by tablespoonfuls (15 mL), about 2 inches (5 cm) apart, onto prepared cookie sheet. Bake in preheated oven for 10 to 12 minutes or until golden brown. Immediately transfer to wire racks to cool.

Makes about 4 dozen

Checkerboard Squares

1 cup	butter or margarine, softened	250 mL
½ cup	granulated sugar	125 mL
6 tbsp	packed brown sugar	90 mL
1	egg	1
2 tsp	vanilla	10 mL
1½ tsp	baking powder	7 mL
1⅔ cups	all-purpose flour	400 mL
2	squares (each 1 oz/28 g) unsweetened chocolate, melted (see page 14)	2

- *Preheat oven to 375°F (190°C)*
- *Cookie sheet, ungreased*

1. In a large bowl, beat butter or margarine and sugars until smooth and creamy. Beat in egg until incorporated. Stir in vanilla and baking powder. Gradually add flour, mixing in as much as possible, then stirring in remainder with a wooden spoon.

2. Divide dough in half. Knead melted chocolate into one portion of dough until combined. Divide plain and chocolate doughs in half. Shape each portion into 8-inch (20 cm) logs. (You will have two plain logs and two chocolate logs.) Wrap each tightly in plastic wrap and refrigerate for 2 hours, until firm.

3. On a floured surface, place one plain roll and one chocolate roll side by side. Top the plain roll with another chocolate roll and the chocolate roll with a plain roll. Press logs together firmly so they adhere and, using your hands, square the sides to make a square-shaped log. Wrap tightly in plastic wrap and refrigerate 6 hours, until firm.

4. Using a knife, cut log into slices ¼ inch (0.5 cm) thick. Place about 2 inches (5 cm) apart on cookie sheet. Bake in preheated oven for 8 to 10 minutes or until bottoms are lightly browned. Immediately transfer to wire racks to cool.

Makes about 6 dozen

Double Chocolate Swirl Cookies

1 tbsp	hot water (not boiling)	15 mL
1½ tsp	instant coffee (espresso) granules	7 mL
2¼ cups	all-purpose flour	550 mL
¼ cup	unsweetened cocoa powder	50 mL
1 cup	butter or margarine, softened	250 mL
⅓ cup	firmly packed brown sugar	75 mL
⅓ cup	granulated sugar	75 mL
1	egg	1
1 tsp	vanilla	5 mL
2	squares (each 1 oz/28 g) semi-sweet chocolate, melted and cooled (see page 14)	2

CHOCOLATE DIP

3	squares (each 1 oz/28 g) white chocolate, melted	3
3	squares (each 1 oz/28 g) semi-sweet chocolate, melted	3

TIP: Before pouring hot liquid into a glass, place a stainless steel spoon in the glass. Add the liquid slowly so the spoon can absorb the heat and the glass won't crack.

- *Preheat oven to 375°F (190°C)*
- *Pastry bag with star tip*
- *Cookie sheet, lightly greased*
- *Large platter or cookie sheet, lined with waxed paper*

1. In a cup, mix hot water and coffee granules until coffee dissolves. Set aside to cool.
2. In a medium bowl, mix together flour and cocoa.
3. In a large bowl, beat butter or margarine and sugars until smooth and creamy. Beat in egg until incorporated. Stir in vanilla and melted chocolate until blended. Add coffee and mix well. Gradually add flour mixture, beating until just blended.
4. Using a pastry bag with a star tip, pipe dough onto prepared cookie sheet, making a 2-inch (5 cm) circle with a swirled design. Bake in preheated oven for 8 to 10 minutes or until lightly browned. Immediately transfer to wire racks to cool.
5. Holding a cookie with your fingers, dip top half in white chocolate. Place on a platter or cookie sheet lined with waxed paper. Repeat with 13 additional cookies. Drizzle top of the dipped half with semi-sweet chocolate. Repeat procedure for remaining cookies, but dip in semi-sweet chocolate and drizzle with white chocolate.

Makes 2½ dozen

Chocolate Chip Holiday Stars

2½ cups	all-purpose flour	625 mL
½ tsp	salt	2 mL
1 cup	butter or margarine, softened	250 mL
⅓ cup	granulated sugar	75 mL
½ cup	packed brown sugar	125 mL
1	egg yolk	1
2 tsp	vanilla	10 mL
2 cups	mini semi-sweet chocolate chips, divided	500 mL
	Vanilla Icing (see recipe, page 367)	

TIP: To decorate cookies with frosting when you don't have a decorator, cut an envelope from one of the top corners to the middle of the bottom of the envelope. Cut a little piece off the corner. Fill with some frosting and squeeze out as you would with a decorator.

- *Preheat oven to 350°F (180°C)*
- *Star-shaped cookie cutter*
- *Cookie sheet, ungreased*
- *Cake decorating tube with a fine tip*

1. In a medium bowl, mix together flour and salt.

2. In a large bowl, beat butter or margarine and sugars until smooth and creamy. Add egg yolk and beat until incorporated. Stir in vanilla. Gradually add flour mixture, mixing until a soft dough forms. Stir in 1½ cups (375 mL) chocolate chips.

3. Divide dough in half. Flatten each half into a disk and wrap tightly in plastic wrap. Cover and refrigerate for 1 to 2 hours, until firm.

4. Place one portion of dough between two sheets of waxed paper and roll out to ¼-inch (0.5 cm) thickness. Using a star cookie cutter, cut into star shapes and place about 2 inches (5 cm) apart on cookie sheet. Cover with a clean towel and refrigerate for 10 minutes.

5. Bake in preheated oven for 10 to 12 minutes or until golden brown. Cool 5 minutes on sheet, then transfer to wire racks to cool completely.

6. Melt remaining ½ cup (125 mL) chocolate chips (see page 14). Using a cake decorator tube with a fine, straight-line tip, pipe a thin line of chocolate close to outer edge of cookie, following the shape of the star. Repeat with vanilla icing, drawing a second line inside the chocolate outline.

Makes about 3 dozen

Raspberry Bows

2¼ cups	all-purpose flour, divided	550 mL
1	package (¼ oz/7 g) quick-rising active dry yeast	1
½ cup	sour cream	125 mL
1 tbsp	water	15 mL
½ cup	butter, softened	125 mL
1	egg	1
	Granulated sugar	

RASPBERRY FILLING

2 tbsp	butter, softened	25 mL
⅓ cup	raspberry jam	75 mL
¼ cup	plain bread crumbs	50 mL
¼ cup	granulated sugar	50 mL
	Confectioner's (icing) sugar, sifted	

TIP: If something spills in your oven while baking, immediately sprinkle salt over the spill. Once the oven has cooled, brush off the burnt food and wipe clean with a damp sponge.

- *Preheat oven to 375°F (190°C)*
- *Cookie sheet lined with parchment or waxed paper*

1. In a large bowl, combine ½ cup (125 mL) flour with the yeast.
2. In a small saucepan, heat sour cream with water until warm (not hot). Stir into flour mixture. Add butter, egg and as much of the remaining flour as necessary to make a soft dough.
3. Knead dough into a ball. Divide in half and wrap each half tightly in plastic wrap. Refrigerate for 2 to 3 hours.
4. *Raspberry Filling:* In a small bowl, mix together butter, jam, bread crumbs and sugar. Set aside.
5. On a work surface sprinkled with granulated sugar, roll one portion of dough into an 18- by 8-inch (45 by 20 cm) rectangle. Spread half of the filling, lengthwise, over half of the dough. Fold dough in half, lengthwise, and trim the edges. Cut crosswise into 12 strips and twist each in the center to form a bow. Repeat with remaining dough.
6. Place bows about 2 inches (5 cm) apart on prepared cookie sheet. Bake in preheated oven for 15 to 20 minutes or until golden brown. Immediately transfer to wire racks. When cool, dust with sifted confectioner's sugar.

Makes 2 dozen

Hickory Nut Macaroons

2	egg whites	2
2 cups	confectioner's (icing) sugar, sifted	500 mL
1 cup	chopped hickory nuts or toasted pecans (see page 14)	250 mL

- *Preheat oven to 325°F (160°C)*
- *Cookie sheet, greased*

1. In a clean bowl, beat egg whites until soft peaks form. Add confectioner's sugar, ¼ cup (50 mL) at a time, beating until stiff peaks form. Fold in nuts.

2. Drop by rounded teaspoonfuls (5 mL), about 2 inches (5 cm) apart, onto prepared cookie sheet. Bake in preheated oven for 15 minutes or until edges are lightly browned. (Cookies may split around the edges as they bake, which is acceptable.) Immediately transfer to wire racks to cool. Recipe can be doubled.

Makes about 1½ dozen

Hanukah Sugar Cookies

2 cups	all-purpose flour	500 mL
1½ tsp	baking powder	7 mL
½ tsp	salt	2 mL
¼ tsp	ground nutmeg	1 mL
¾ cup	butter or margarine, softened	175 mL
1 cup	granulated sugar	250 mL
2	eggs	2
1 tsp	vanilla	5 mL
	Vanilla Icing (see Recipe, page 365) (optional)	

TIP: Dip cookie cutters in salad oil before cutting out cookies. It will make a cleaner cut and be less sticky.

- *Preheat oven to 375°F (190°C)*
- *Cookie cutters in Hanukah shapes, such as a dreidel, menorah or Star of David*
- *Cookie sheet, ungreased*

1. In a medium bowl, mix together flour, baking powder, salt and nutmeg.

2. In a large bowl, beat butter or margarine and sugar until smooth and creamy. Beat in eggs, one at a time, until incorporated. Stir in vanilla. Gradually add flour mixture, mixing until a soft dough forms. Cover tightly and refrigerate for 2 to 3 hours, until firm.

3. On a lightly floured surface, roll dough out to ⅛-inch (0.25 cm) thickness. Using cookie cutters, cut into a variety of Hanukah shapes.

4. Place 2 inches (5 cm) apart on cookie sheet. Bake in preheated oven for 8 to 10 minutes or until lightly browned. Immediately transfer to wire racks to cool. Decorate cookies with icing, if desired.

Makes about 3 dozen

Cinnamon Nut Rugelach

1 cup	butter, softened	250 mL
8 oz	cream cheese, softened	250 g
2	eggs	2
1 tsp	salt	5 mL
2½ cups	all-purpose flour	625 mL

CINNAMON-NUT FILLING

¾ cup	finely chopped raisins	175 mL
⅔ cup	finely chopped walnuts	150 mL
1 cup	granulated sugar	250 mL
½ tsp	ground cinnamon	2 mL
½ cup	melted butter	125 mL

VARIATION

Chocolate-Coconut Filling
In a small bowl, mix together ½ cup (125 mL) finely chopped slivered toasted almonds, ¾ cup (175 mL) sweetened shredded coconut, ½ cup (125 mL) semi-sweet mini chocolate chips and ¼ cup (50 mL) granulated sugar. Using a spatula, thinly coat a large circle of dough with 2 tbsp (25 mL) apricot preserves. Sprinkle with a quarter of the almond mixture. Proceed with Step 5, right.

- *Preheat oven to 375°F (190°C)*
- *Cookie sheet, lined with parchment or waxed paper*

1. In a large bowl, beat butter and cream cheese until smooth. Add eggs, one at a time, beating until incorporated. Mix in salt, then gradually beat in flour until a sticky dough forms. Transfer dough to a lightly floured surface and knead, adding up to ½ cup (125 mL) flour until dough is not sticky.

2. Divide dough into four portions. Wrap each in plastic wrap and refrigerate for 3 to 4 hours, until firm.

3. *Cinnamon-Nut Filling:* In a small bowl, combine raisins and walnuts. Add sugar and cinnamon and mix well. Set aside.

4. On floured surface, roll one portion of dough into a 10-inch (25 cm) circle. Brush with melted butter and sprinkle about ⅓ cup (75 mL) nut mixture over the circle.

5. Using a knife or pastry cutter, cut circle into 12 pie-shaped wedges. Roll up tightly, beginning from the wide edge and finishing with the point in the middle. Bend the rolls slightly inward to form crescents and place, point side down, about 2 inches (5 cm) apart, on prepared cookie sheet. Brush with melted butter. Repeat with remaining dough.

6. Bake in preheated oven for 20 to 25 minutes or until golden brown. Immediately transfer to wire racks to cool.

Makes about 4 dozen

Passover Almond Cookies

3	eggs	3
1/2 cup	granulated sugar	125 mL
1 tbsp	matzo meal	15 mL
2 tbsp	brandy	25 mL
2 1/4 cups	finely ground almonds or hazelnuts	550 mL
	Halved blanched almonds	

- *Preheat oven to 300°F (150°C)*
- *Cookie sheet, lightly greased*

1. In a medium bowl, whisk eggs until light and fluffy. Add sugar and matzo meal and mix well. Stir in brandy. Fold in nuts until well combined.
2. Shape dough into 1-inch (2.5 cm) balls. Place about 2 inches (5 cm) apart on prepared cookie sheet and gently press half a nut in the center of each. Bake in preheated oven for 20 minutes or until lightly browned. Immediately transfer to wire racks to cool.

Makes about 2 1/2 dozen

Passover Coconut Macaroons

2	egg whites	2
1/2 cup	granulated sugar	125 mL
1 tbsp	liquid honey	15 mL
2 tbsp	potato starch	25 mL
1 3/4 cups	finely shredded coconut (see Tip, below)	425 mL

TIP: This recipe works best if the coconut is very fine. Add required quantity to a food processor and process to the desired consistency.

- *Preheat oven to 325°F (160°C)*
- *Cookie sheet, greased and dusted with potato starch*

1. In a clean bowl, beat egg whites until soft peaks form. Add sugar and honey and beat until shiny, stiff peaks form. Gradually fold in potato starch, then coconut.
2. Drop by tablespoonfuls (15 mL), about 2 inches (5 cm) apart, onto prepared cookie sheet. Bake in preheated oven for 15 to 18 minutes or until lightly browned. Immediately transfer to wire racks to cool.

Makes about 2 1/2 dozen

Poppy Seed Hamantashen

6	eggs	6
1 cup	vegetable oil	250 mL
1 cup	granulated sugar	250 mL
	Juice of ½ lemon or ½ cup (125 mL) orange juice	
6 cups	all-purpose flour	1.5 L
4 tsp	baking powder	20 mL
¼ tsp	salt	1 mL
POPPY SEED FILLING		
2 cups	poppy seeds	500 mL
¾ cup	milk	175 mL
½ cup	liquid honey	125 mL
¼ cup	packed brown sugar	50 mL
Pinch	salt	Pinch
1	egg, beaten	
GLAZE		
1	egg yolk, lightly beaten	1

These cookies, which are made in the shape of a three-cornered hat, are traditionally made to celebrate the Jewish feast of Purim. (For prune filling, see Olga's Hamantashen, page 344.)

- *Preheat oven to 350°F (180°C)*
- *3-inch (7.5-cm) round cookie cutter*
- *Cookie sheet, greased*

1. In a medium bowl, whisk together eggs, oil, sugar and juice until blended.

2. In a large bowl, sift together flour, baking powder and salt. Make a well in the center. Pour in egg mixture and using your hands, mix together until a soft dough forms. Cover and refrigerate for 2 hours or overnight.

3. *Poppy Seed Filling:* In a medium bowl, add boiling water to poppyseeds to cover by 1 inch (2.5 cm). Let stand for 10 minutes, then drain. In a food processor with a metal blade, grind poppy seeds.

4. In a saucepan, combine ground poppy seeds, milk, honey, brown sugar and salt. Cook over low heat for 5 minutes, stirring constantly, until thick. Allow to cool for 15 minutes, then mix in beaten egg. Set aside.

5. On a lightly floured surface, roll dough into a circle about ⅛ inch (0.25 cm) thick. Using a 3-inch (7.5 cm) cookie cutter, cut out circles. Spoon a heaping tablespoonful (15 mL) of filling in the center of each circle. Moisten the edges lightly with a finger dipped in water and pinch together three edges of the dough to form a triangle, leaving a small opening in the center with some filling showing. It will resemble a three-cornered hat. Or pinch the top together tightly to enclose the filling, if desired.

6. Place triangles on prepared cookie sheet. Cover with a cloth and let stand for 1 hour. Then brush tops with egg yolk glaze. Bake in preheated oven for 20 to 25 minutes or until lightly browned. Allow to cool on sheets, then, using a spatula, lift off very carefully.

Makes about 3½ dozen

Chocolate Valentine Hearts

1 cup	butter, softened	250 mL
1 cup	confectioner's (icing) sugar, sifted	250 mL
⅓ cup	unsweetened cocoa powder	75 mL
1½ cups	all-purpose flour	375 mL
	Vanilla Icing (see Recipe, page 367)	
	Cinnamon hearts for decoration	

TIP: When using recipe cards, place a fork, tines up, in a tall glass and wedge the card between the tines.

- *Preheat oven to 300°F (150°C)*
- *3-inch (7.5 cm) heart-shaped cookie cutter*
- *Cookie sheet, ungreased*

1. In a large bowl, cream butter until smooth.
2. In another bowl, sift confectioner's sugar, cocoa and flour. Gradually add to butter and mix until a soft dough forms. If dough is too soft, refrigerate for 30 minutes or until firm.
3. On a lightly floured surface, roll dough to ⅛-inch (0.25 cm) thickness. Using a heart-shaped cookie cutter about 3 inches (7.5 cm) across, cut out cookies.
4. Place about 2 inches (5 cm) apart on cookie sheet and bake in preheated oven for 20 to 25 minutes. Cool on sheet for 5 minutes, then transfer to wire racks to cool completely.
4. Make Vanilla Icing and divide in half. Tint one half with red food coloring. Decorate cookies with red and white icing, cinnamon hearts, whatever strikes your fancy as appropriate for Valentine's Day.

Makes about 3 dozen

Cherry Valentine Cookies

3½ cups	all-purpose flour	875 mL
2 tsp	baking powder	10 mL
1 tsp	baking soda	5 mL
½ tsp	salt	2 mL
½ cup	shortening, softened	125 mL
½ cup	butter or margarine, softened	125 mL
1 cup	granulated sugar	250 mL
1	egg	1
1 tsp	vanilla	5 mL
½ cup	milk	125 mL

CHERRY FILLING

½ cup	granulated sugar	125 mL
4½ tsp	cornstarch	22 mL
½ cup	orange juice	125 mL
1 tbsp	butter or margarine	15 mL
12	red maraschino cherries, chopped	12
¼ cup	cherry juice	50 mL
	Additional sugar	

> **TIP:** To use little hearts from leftover cut-outs, lower oven heat to 325°F (160°C) and bake 5 minutes, until lightly browned. Dip in melted chocolate, if desired.

- *Preheat oven to 375°F (190°C)*
- *Large and small heart-shaped cookie cutters*
- *Cookie sheet, greased*

1. In a large bowl, mix together flour, baking powder, baking soda and salt.
2. In another large bowl, beat shortening, butter or margarine and sugar until smooth and creamy. Add egg and beat until well incorporated. Stir in vanilla and milk until well blended. Gradually add flour mixture, mixing until a soft dough forms. Cover and refrigerate for at least 2 hours, until firm.
3. *Cherry Filling:* In a small saucepan, combine sugar, cornstarch, orange juice, butter or margarine, cherries and cherry juice. Bring to a boil over low heat and cook, stirring, for 1 minute. Transfer saucepan to refrigerator and chill until cool.
4. On a lightly floured surface, roll dough out to ⅛-inch (0.25 cm) thickness. Using a heart-shaped cookie cutter about 2½ inches (6 cm) across, cut cookies out. Place half on prepared cookie sheet. Spoon ½ tsp (2 mL) filling in the center of each. Using a heart-shaped cookie cutter about 1½ inches (4 cm) across, cut hearts out of remaining cookies. Place cut-out hearts over filled hearts and press together gently.
5. Bake in preheated oven for 8 to 10 minutes or until lightly browned. Immediately transfer to wire racks to cool.

Makes about 4½ dozen

Thanksgiving Pumpkin Spice Cookies

4½ cups	all-purpose flour	1.125 L
2 tsp	baking powder	10 mL
1 tsp	baking soda	5 mL
1½ tsp	ground cinnamon	7 mL
½ tsp	ground nutmeg	2 mL
½ tsp	ground ginger	2 mL
1¼ cups	shortening, softened	300 mL
1 cup	packed brown sugar	250 mL
1 cup	granulated sugar	250 mL
2	eggs	2
1 tsp	vanilla	5 mL
1 tsp	finely grated orange zest	5 mL
1	can (16 oz) pumpkin purée (not pie filling)	1
	Confectioner's (icing) sugar, sifted	

- *Preheat oven to 375°F (190°C)*
- *Round cookie cutter or glass, 2 inches (5 cm) in diameter*
- *Cookie sheet, ungreased*

1. In a large bowl, mix together flour, baking powder, baking soda, cinnamon, nutmeg and ginger.

2. In another large bowl, beat shortening and sugars until smooth and creamy. Beat in eggs, one at a time, until incorporated. Stir in vanilla and orange zest. Add half the flour mixture and beat well. Add pumpkin and beat well. Add remaining flour mixture, beating until well combined and a soft dough forms.

3. Divide dough in half. Wrap each portion tightly in plastic wrap and refrigerate for 3 to 4 hours until firm.

4. On a lightly floured surface, roll out one portion of dough to ¼-inch (0.5 cm) thickness. Using a cutter dipped in flour, cut into rounds and place about 2 inches (5 cm) apart on cookie sheet.

5. Bake in preheated oven for 10 minutes or until browned. Immediately transfer to wire racks to cool. When cool, dust with sifted confectioner's sugar.

Makes about 6 dozen

Candied Easter Specials

2 cups	all-purpose flour	500 mL
¼ tsp	baking soda	1 mL
Pinch	salt	Pinch
½ tsp	ground cinnamon	2 mL
¼ tsp	ground nutmeg	1 mL
Pinch	ground cloves	Pinch
1 cup	liquid honey	250 mL
1 tbsp	granulated sugar	15 mL
¼ cup	chopped blanched almonds	50 mL
2 tbsp	butter or margarine, softened	25 mL
1 tbsp	rum or sherry	15 mL
¾ tsp	grated lemon zest	4 mL
½ cup	chopped candied lemon or orange peel	125 mL
	Granulated sugar (optional)	

> **TIP:** These cookies are best stored in an airtight container with a slice of apple to keep them moist.

- *Preheat oven to 300°F (150°C)*
- *Round or rectangular cookie cutter*
- *Cookie sheet, greased*

1. In a medium bowl, sift together flour, baking soda, salt, cinnamon, nutmeg and cloves.

2. In a small saucepan, over low heat, bring honey and sugar to a boil, stirring constantly. Simmer for 5 minutes, then add almonds and simmer 5 minutes more. Set aside to cool.

3. In a large bowl, beat butter or margarine, rum or sherry and lemon zest. Add honey mixture and blend well. Gradually add flour mixture and mix well. Stir in candied peel, mixing until a soft dough forms. Cover and refrigerate for 1 to 2 hours, until firm.

4. On a lightly floured surface, divide dough into three portions. Roll one portion out to ¼- to ½-inch (0.5 to 1 cm) thickness. Using a round or rectangular cookie cutter dipped in flour, cut out shapes. Repeat with remaining dough.

5. Place cookies about 2 inches (5 cm) apart on prepared cookie sheet. Bake in preheated oven for 20 minutes or until browned. Immediately transfer to wire racks to cool. While cookies are still warm, sprinkle with granulated sugar, if desired.

Makes about 3 dozen

Chinese New Year Bursts

2 cups	all-purpose flour	500 mL
1 tsp	baking powder	5 mL
1 tbsp	shortening, softened	15 mL
$\frac{2}{3}$ cup	granulated sugar	150 mL
1	egg	1
3 tbsp	water	45 mL
$\frac{1}{2}$ cup	sesame seeds	125 mL
8 cups	oil for frying	2 L

TIP: If you don't have a deep-frying thermometer, you can test the temperature of the oil by dropping a small piece of bread into it. If it turns golden in color, the oil is hot enough.

• *Deep fryer or Dutch oven*

1. In a small bowl, mix together flour and baking powder.
2. In a large bowl, beat shortening and sugar until smooth and creamy. Beat in egg until well incorporated. Add water and mix until well blended. Stir in flour mixture, mixing until a dough forms.
3. On a lightly floured surface, knead dough until soft. Shape into 1$\frac{1}{2}$-inch (4 cm) balls.
4. Add water to a bowl and spread sesame seeds on a plate. Dip balls in water, then roll in sesame seeds to coat.
5. Heat oil in deep fryer or Dutch oven to 325°F (160°C). Using a slotted spoon, add five or six balls to preheated oil. Cook, turning once, until dough cracks in the center, bursts and is golden brown, about 3 to 5 minutes. Using a slotted spoon, transfer cookies to a paper towel to drain. Repeat with remaining dough.

Makes about 16 bursts

Esther's Favorites

This chapter is a tribute to my family and friends who have provided me with so many wonderful cookie, bars and squares recipes over the years.

continued on next page

Mama's Homemade Cookies

4 cups	all-purpose flour	1 L
1 tsp	baking soda	5 mL
¼ tsp	salt	1 mL
3	eggs	3
½ cup	vegetable oil	125 mL
1 cup	granulated sugar	250 mL
1 tsp	vanilla	5 mL
½ cup	milk	125 mL

- *Preheat oven to 350°F (180°C)*
- *Cookie sheet, ungreased*

1. In a large bowl, mix together flour, baking soda and salt. Make a well in the center.
2. In a separate bowl, whisk together eggs, oil, sugar, vanilla and milk. Pour mixture into well and mix thoroughly.
3. Drop by rounded teaspoonfuls (5 mL), 2 inches (5 cm) apart, onto cookie sheet. Bake in preheated oven for about 20 minutes or until golden brown. Immediately transfer to wire racks to cool.

Makes about 5 dozen

Cecille's One-Bowl Chocolate Cookies

16	squares (each 1 oz/28 g) semi-sweet chocolate, divided	16
¾ cup	firmly packed brown sugar	175 mL
¼ cup	butter or margarine, softened	50 mL
2	eggs	2
1 tsp	vanilla	5 mL
¼ tsp	baking powder	1 mL
½ cup	all-purpose flour	125 mL
2 cups	chopped nuts (optional)	500 mL

- *Preheat oven to 350°F (180°C)*
- *Cookie sheet, ungreased*

1. Coarsely chop half of the chocolate and set aside.
2. In a large bowl, in a microwave oven, melt remaining chocolate (see page 14). Add brown sugar, butter, eggs and vanilla, beating until smooth. Stir in baking powder, then flour, and mix until well blended. Fold in reserved chocolate and nuts, if using, mixing until well combined.
3. Using a ¼-cup (50 mL) measure, drop by cupfuls onto cookie sheet. Bake in preheated oven for 12 to 13 minutes, until cookies are puffed and soft to touch. Cool on cookie sheet for 1 minute, then transfer to wire racks to cool completely.

Makes about 1½ dozen large cookies

TIP: If you do not have enough cookie sheets when baking cookies, use a baking pan instead. Turn it over and set the cookies on the bottom.

Lisa's Chocolate Chip Cookies

1 cup	all-purpose flour	250 mL
½ tsp	baking soda	2 mL
½ tsp	salt	2 mL
½ cup	shortening or butter, softened	125 mL
½ cup	granulated sugar	125 mL
¼ cup	firmly packed brown sugar	50 mL
1	egg	1
1 tsp	vanilla	5 mL
1	package (10 oz/300 g) mini chocolate chips	1

- *Preheat oven to 375°F (190°C)*
- *Cookie sheet, ungreased*

1. In a small bowl, mix together flour, baking soda and salt.
2. In a large bowl, beat shortening or butter and sugars until smooth and creamy. Beat in egg until incorporated. Stir in vanilla. Fold in chocolate chips. Add flour mixture and mix thoroughly.
3. Drop by rounded teaspoonfuls (5 mL), about 2 inches (5 cm) apart, onto cookie sheet. Bake in preheated oven for 8 to 10 minutes or until lightly browned. Immediately transfer to wire racks to cool.

Makes about 2 dozen

Shirley's Meringue Cookies

½ cup	granulated sugar	125 mL
3 tbsp	potato flour or cornstarch	45 mL
3	egg whites	3
1 cup	chocolate chips	250 mL

TIP: Potato flour is available in the baking section of supermarkets.

VARIATION

Coconut Meringues
Substitute 1 cup (250 mL) sweetened shredded coconut for the chocolate chips.

- *Preheat oven to 250°F (120°C)*
- *Cookie sheet lined with waxed paper*

1. In a small bowl, mix together sugar and potato flour or cornstarch.
2. In a large, clean bowl, beat egg whites until soft peaks form. Gradually add sugar mixture to egg whites, beating until stiff, glossy peaks form. Fold in chocolate chips.
3. Drop by teaspoonfuls (5 mL), about 2 inches (5 cm) apart, onto prepared cookie sheet. Bake in preheated oven for 55 to 60 minutes or until lightly browned. Immediately transfer to wire racks to cool.

Makes about 2 dozen

Baba Mary's Jam Delights

2 cups	all-purpose flour	500 mL
2 tsp	baking powder	10 mL
Pinch	salt	Pinch
¾ cup	shortening	175 mL
½ cup	granulated sugar	125 mL
2	eggs	2
	Jam, any flavor, for filling	

• *Preheat oven to 350°F (180°C)*
• *Cookie sheet, lined with parchment or waxed paper*

1. In a medium bowl, sift together flour, baking powder and salt.
2. In a large bowl, beat shortening and sugar until smooth and creamy. Add eggs, one at a time, beating after each addition. Gradually mix in flour mixture until well blended.
3. Shape dough into 1-inch (2.5 cm) balls and place on prepared cookie sheet. Using a thimble or your thumb, make an indentation in the center of each cookie and fill with jam. Bake in preheated oven for 15 minutes or until golden brown. Immediately transfer to wire racks to cool.

Makes about 4 dozen

Shauna's Shortbread Cookies

1½ cups	sifted pastry flour	375 mL
½ cup	cornstarch	125 mL
½ tsp	salt	2 mL
½ lb	butter, softened	250 g
⅔ cup	lightly packed brown sugar	150 mL
½ cup	glacé cherries (optional)	125 mL
½ cup	chopped almonds (optional)	125 mL

• *Preheat oven to 300°F (150°C)*
• *Cookie sheet, ungreased*

1. In a small bowl, mix together pastry flour, cornstarch and salt.
2. In a large bowl, beat butter and brown sugar until smooth and creamy. Stir in cherries and almonds, if using. Gradually add flour mixture, mixing thoroughly after each addition, until a soft dough forms. Knead lightly.
3. On a lightly floured board, knead dough until cracks appear on the surface. Roll out to about ¼-inch (0.5 cm) thickness. Using a knife or a cookie cutter, cut into small oblongs and place on cookie sheet. Bake in preheated oven for 20 to 25 minutes or until golden brown. Immediately transfer to wire racks to cool.

Makes about 2 dozen

Aunty Giza's Lemon Cookies

1¾ cups	all-purpose flour	325 mL
1 tsp	baking powder	5 mL
¼ tsp	salt	1 mL
¼ lb	shortening, softened	125 g
¾ cup	granulated sugar	175 mL
2	egg yolks	2
	Zest and juice of ½ lemon	
½ cup	orange juice	125 mL
2 tsp	red wine (optional)	10 mL
	Egg whites	
	Halved nuts (optional)	

TIP: Leftover egg yolks or whites can be kept in the refrigerator for 3 to 4 days in airtight containers. Yolks should be covered with cold water to keep them from drying up.

- *Preheat oven to 350°F (180°C)*
- *Cookie sheet, lightly greased*

1. In a small bowl, mix together, flour, baking powder and salt.
2. In a large bowl, beat shortening and sugar until smooth and creamy. Beat in egg yolks until incorporated. Stir in lemon zest and juice, orange juice and wine, if using. Add flour mixture and mix until a dough forms.
3. Cut dough in half. Shape into 1-inch (2.5 cm) balls and using your finger, press down on each to flatten slightly. Place about 1-inch (2.5 cm) apart on prepared cookie sheet. Brush egg white on top of each cookie and place a nut, if desired, in the center. Bake in preheated oven for 20 minutes or until golden brown. Immediately transfer to wire racks to cool.

Mom's Peanut Butter Cookies

1 cup	all-purpose flour	250 mL
1 tsp	baking soda	5 mL
¼ tsp	salt	1 mL
½ cup	shortening, softened	125 mL
½ cup	granulated sugar	125 mL
½ cup	lightly packed brown sugar	125 mL
1	egg	1
½ cup	smooth peanut butter (or crunchy, if desired)	125 mL
¼ tsp	vanilla	1 mL

- *Preheat oven to 350°F (180°C)*
- *Cookie sheet, lightly greased*

1. In a small bowl, mix together flour, baking soda and salt.
2. In a large bowl, beat shortening and sugars until smooth and creamy. Beat in egg until incorporated. Stir in peanut butter and vanilla. Gradually add flour mixture, mixing until a soft dough forms.
3. Shape dough into 1-inch (2.5 cm) balls. Place about 2 inches (5 cm) apart on prepared cookie sheet and, using the tines of a fork, press to flatten. Bake in preheated oven for 12 to 15 minutes. Immediately transfer to wire racks to cool.

Makes about 2 dozen

Esther's Famous Komish Bread Cookies

3 cups	all-purpose flour	750 mL
½ tsp	salt	2 mL
1 tsp	baking powder	5 mL
1 to 2 tsp	ground cinnamon	5 to 10 mL
3	eggs	3
1 cup	granulated sugar	250 mL
1 cup	oil	250 mL
1 tsp	vanilla	5 mL
1 cup	chocolate chips	250 mL
SUGAR-CINNAMON MIX		
½ cup	granulated sugar	125 mL
2 tsp	ground cinnamon	10 mL

> *I also refer to these as Chocolate Chip Miniscotti. They are the favorite cookies of my son, Leonard, and daughter, Lisa. Vary the quantity of cinnamon according to your taste. I probably use more than most people, as I love cinnamon.*

- *Preheat oven to 350°F (180°C)*
- *Cookie sheet, greased*

1. In a medium bowl, mix together flour, salt, baking powder and cinnamon.
2. In a large bowl, beat eggs, sugar and oil until blended. Mix in vanilla. Add dry ingredients and mix well. Fold in chocolate chips.
3. On a floured surface, divide dough into three portions. Shape into three rolls about 2 to 3 inches (5 to 7.5 cm) wide. Place at least 2 inches (5 cm) apart on prepared cookie sheet. Bake in preheated oven for 30 to 35 minutes, until lightly browned and a toothpick inserted into center of one of the rolls comes out clean and dry. Remove from oven and turn off heat.
4. *Sugar-Cinnamon Mix:* In a small bowl, mix sugar and cinnamon.
5. On a cutting board, cut hot rolls into slices about ½ inch (1 cm) thick. Dip each slice in sugar-cinnamon mix until well coated. Place on cookie sheet, and leaving heat off, return to oven to dry for 20 to 25 minutes.

Makes about 4 dozen

Lisa's Cinnamon Nut Crescents

1	package (¼ oz/7 g) active dry yeast	1
2 tbsp	granulated sugar	25 mL
½ cup	warm water	125 mL
3 cups	all-purpose flour	750 mL
½ tsp	salt	2 mL
3	egg yolks	3
½ cup	whipping (35%) cream	125 mL
1 tsp	vanilla	5 mL
1 cup	butter or margarine, softened	250 mL

FILLING

2	egg whites	2
1¾ cups	finely chopped walnuts, toasted (see page 14)	425 mL
¾ cup	granulated sugar	175 mL
Pinch	salt	Pinch

SUGAR-CINNAMON MIX

¾ cup	granulated sugar	175 mL
3 tbsp	ground cinnamon	45 mL

Compared to other cookies, these are a lot of work. But they are definitely worth it.

- *Preheat oven to 350°F (180°C)*
- *Foil-lined cookie sheet, greased*

1. In a small bowl, dissolve yeast and 2 tbsp (25 mL) sugar in warm water.

2. In a large bowl, combine flour and salt. Add yeast mixture, mixing until blended, then mix in egg yolks, cream and vanilla. Beat in butter, spoonfuls at a time, until well blended and a dough forms. Wrap tightly in plastic wrap and refrigerate for at least 3 hours or overnight, until dough is firm.

3. *Filling:* In a clean bowl, beat egg whites until soft peaks form. Fold in walnuts, sugar and salt. Set aside.

4. *Sugar-Cinnamon Mix:* In a small bowl, mix sugar and cinnamon.

5. Divide dough into 10 balls and return nine to refrigerator until ready to use. On a work surface, sprinkled with a heaping tablespoonful (15 mL) sugar-cinnamon mixture, roll one dough ball into an 8-inch (20 cm) circle, turning at least once so both sides will be coated with the sugar-cinnamon mixture. Using a knife or a pastry cutter, fluted, if desired, cut into eight pie-shaped wedges. Place 1 tsp (5 mL) walnut filling on the outer edge of each wedge. Beginning with the outer edge and finishing with the point in the center, roll up to form crescents. Repeat with remaining dough.

6. Place, point side down, on prepared sheet and bake in preheated oven for 12 to 15 minutes, until puffy and browned. Immediately transfer to wire racks to cool.

Makes about 6½ dozen

No-Bake Crispy Peanut Butter Squares *(page 264)* ➤

Sima's Passover Cookies

2	eggs	2
½ cup	oil	125 mL
2 tbsp	potato starch	25 mL
1 tbsp	freshly squeezed lemon juice	15 mL
¾ cup	granulated sugar	175 mL
1 cup	cake meal	250 mL
¾ cup	ground almonds, divided	175 mL
½ cup	Sugar-Cinnamon Mix (see page 14)	125 mL

- *Preheat oven to 350°F (180°C)*
- *Cookie sheet, lightly greased*

1. In a large bowl, beat together eggs and oil. Add potato starch and lemon juice and mix well. Add sugar and cake meal, mixing until blended. Fold in ½ cup (125 mL) ground almonds.
2. Roll dough into 1-inch (2.5 cm) balls. Mix remaining ¼ cup (50 mL) ground almonds with sugar-cinnamon mix and roll the ball in this mixture to coat. Flatten a little, if desired.
3. Place about 2 inches (5 cm) apart on prepared cookie sheet. Bake for 10 to 12 minutes, until golden brown. Immediately transfer to wire racks to cool

Makes about 2 dozen

Cecille's Passover Komish Bread

3	eggs	3
¾ cup	granulated sugar	175 mL
¾ cup	oil	175 mL
1 to 2 tsp	ground cinnamon	5 to 10 mL
¾ cup	cake meal	175 mL
¼ cup	matzo meal	50 mL
2 tbsp	potato starch	25 mL
½ cup	chopped walnuts	125 mL

TIP: When you buy cooking oil, instead of removing the protective seal, cut a small slit in it. You'll be able to pour the oil through it without spilling.

- *Preheat oven to 325°F (160°C)*
- *9-inch (2.5 L) square cake pan, greased*

1. In a large bowl, beat eggs and sugar until thick and pale. Beat in oil until well incorporated. Add cinnamon, to taste, cake meal, matzo meal and potato starch, mixing until well blended. Fold in nuts.
2. Using a spatula, scrape batter into prepared pan and bake in preheated oven for 50 to 60 minutes, until a toothpick inserted in the center comes out clean and dry. Cool in pan for 30 minutes, then cut into slices ½ inch (1 cm) thick. Place on wire racks.
3. Increase oven heat to 350°F (180°C) and return rack of slices to oven to dry for 30 minutes. Remove from oven and cool completely before serving.

Makes 4½ dozen

◄ Peppermint Candy Canes *(page 313)*
Checkerboard Squares *(page 316)*

Esther's Rugelach

2 cups	all-purpose flour	500 mL
¼ cup	granulated sugar	50 mL
1 cup	butter, softened	250 mL
8 oz	cream cheese, softened	250 g
FILLING		
½ cup	granulated sugar	125 mL
1 tbsp	ground cinnamon	15 mL
¾ cup	finely chopped walnuts	175 mL
½ cup	raisins (optional)	125 mL
¼ cup	melted butter	50 mL

Rugelach, tiny crescents made from a cream cheese dough, are often served during the Jewish festival of Hanukah, but many people eat them all year round.

VARIATION

Raspberry Hazelnut Rugelach
In a small bowl, mix together ½ cup (125 mL) raspberry jam and ½ cup (125 mL) finely chopped toasted hazelnuts (see page 14). Spread over circle after brushing with butter. Sprinkle lightly with granulated sugar.

- *Preheat oven to 350°F (180°C)*
- *Cookie sheet, lined with parchment or waxed paper*

1. In a large bowl, mix together flour and ¼ cup (50 mL) sugar. Using your fingers, work the butter and cream cheese together to form a dough. (You can also do this in a food processor.)

2. Divide dough into four sections. Wrap tightly in plastic wrap and refrigerate for at least 4 hours.

3. *Filling:* In a medium bowl, mix together ½ cup (125 mL) sugar, cinnamon, walnuts and raisins, if using.

4. On a floured surface, using a floured rolling pin, roll one portion of dough into a 10-inch (25 cm) circle. Brush with 1 tbsp (15 mL) melted butter, then spread one-quarter of the filling evenly over circle.

5. Using a knife or a pastry wheel, cut circle into 12 pie-shaped wedges. Beginning at the wide edge, with the filling inside, roll tightly, finishing with the point in the middle. Curve the rolls slightly to form a crescent and place, point side down on, prepared cookie sheet. Repeat with remaining dough.

6. Bake in preheated oven for 25 to 30 minutes or until delicately browned. Transfer to wire racks to cool.

Makes about 4 dozen

Mildred's Sour Cream Kiffles

1	package (¼ oz/7 g) active dry yeast	1
6 cups	all-purpose flour	1.5 L
6 tbsp	granulated sugar	90 mL
1 tsp	salt	5 mL
1 cup	butter	250 mL
1 cup	margarine	250 mL
4	eggs, beaten	4
1 cup	sour cream	250 mL
2 cups	Sugar-Cinnamon Mix (see page 14)	500 mL

- *Preheat oven to 350°F (180°C)*
- *Cookie sheet, greased*

1. In a small bowl, proof yeast according to package instructions.
2. In a large bowl, mix together flour, sugar and salt. Using two knives, a pastry blender or your fingers, cut in butter and margarine until mixture resembles coarse crumbs. Make a well in the center. Add eggs, sour cream and dissolved yeast and mix well. Cover and refrigerate overnight.
3. Divide dough into four parts. Knead one part until soft, then, on a work surface sprinkled with sugar-cinnamon mix, roll into a large circle, turning at least once so both sides will be coated with the sugar-cinnamon mixture. Using a knife or a pastry cutter, fluted if desired, cut into eight pie-shaped wedges and spread with sugar-cinnamon mix. Beginning with the outer edge and finishing with the point in the center, roll up. Turn ends slightly towards each other to form a crescent. Repeat with remaining dough.
4. Place crescents 2 inches (5 cm) apart on prepared cookie sheet, cover with a clean tea towel and set in a warm place to rise until double in size, approximately 1 hour. Bake in preheated oven for 20 minutes or until golden brown. Immediately transfer to wire racks to cool.

Makes 32 kiffles

Felicia's Mandelbrot

2³⁄₄ cups	all-purpose flour	675 mL
4 tsp	baking powder	20 mL
½ tsp	salt	2 mL
3	eggs	3
1 cup	granulated sugar	250 mL
6 tbsp	vegetable oil	90 mL
	Grated zest of 1 lemon	
½ tsp	vanilla	2 mL
⅓ cup	coarsely chopped blanched almonds	75 mL

> Mandelbrot, like Komish Bread, is a traditional Jewish cookie that is baked and sliced, then returned to the oven to dry. Although it is similar to biscotti, it is not as hard.

- *Preheat oven to 350°F (180°C)*
- *Cookie sheet, lightly greased*

1. In a medium bowl, sift together flour, baking powder and salt.
2. In a large bowl, beat eggs, sugar, oil, zest and vanilla until thoroughly blended. Stir egg mixture into flour mixture and mix well. Fold in almonds and mix until a soft dough forms.
3. On a well-floured surface, divide dough in half. Shape into two long rolls about 3 inches (7.5 cm) wide. Place at least 2 inches (5 cm) apart on prepared sheet. Bake in preheated oven for 40 to 50 minutes, until lightly browned and a toothpick inserted into center of one of the rolls comes out clean and dry. Remove from oven and turn off heat.
4. On a cutting board, cut hot rolls into slices about ½ inch (1 cm) thick. Place on cookie sheet and, leaving heat off, return to oven to dry for 25 minutes.

Makes about 3 dozen

Helen's Mon Cookies

1½ to 2 cups	all-purpose flour	375 to 500 mL
1 tsp	baking powder	5 mL
1 cup	old-fashioned rolled oats	250 mL
½ cup	shortening, softened	125 mL
¼ to ½ cup	vegetable oil	50 to 125 mL
¾ cup	packed brown sugar	175 mL
1	egg	1
¼ cup	poppy seeds	50 mL

> Mon cookies are a traditional Jewish cookie made from poppy seeds.

- *Preheat oven to 350°F (180°C)*
- *Cookie sheet, ungreased*

1. In a medium bowl, mix together flour, baking powder and rolled oats.
2. In a large bowl, cream together shortening, oil and brown sugar. Mix in egg and poppy seeds until well blended. Add flour mixture and mix well.
3. Drop by rounded teaspoonfuls (5 mL), about 2 inches (5 cm) apart, onto cookie sheet. Flatten slightly with a fork. Bake in preheated oven for 10 minutes until golden brown. Transfer to wire racks to cool.

Makes about 3 dozen

Baba Mary's Thimble Cookies

1 cup	butter, softened	250 mL
½ cup	lightly packed brown sugar	125 mL
2	egg yolks	2
2 cups	all-purpose flour	500 mL
2	egg whites, beaten	2
1 cup	chopped walnuts	250 mL
	Jam or jelly	

TIP: Rinse hot cookie sheet under cold water to cool completely before baking any more cookies.

- *Preheat oven to 300°F (150°C)*
- *Cookie sheet, ungreased*

1. In a large bowl, beat butter and brown sugar until smooth and creamy. Beat in egg yolks until well incorporated. Gradually add flour and mix until well blended.
2. Shape dough into 1-inch (2.5 cm) balls. Drop balls into slightly beaten egg whites and then into walnuts. Place about 1 inch (2.5 cm) apart on cookie sheet and, using a fork, flatten slightly. Using a thimble or your thumb, make an indentation in the center of each cookie and fill with jam or jelly. Bake in preheated oven for 15 to 20 minutes or until golden brown. Immediately transfer to wire racks to cool.

Makes about 4 dozen

Colleen's Goosnargh Cakes

1 tbsp	coriander seeds	15 mL
1 tbsp	caraway seeds	15 mL
1 lb	butter, softened	500 g
¼ cup	confectioner's (icing) sugar, sifted	50 mL
3¾ cups	all-purpose flour	925 mL
	Confectioner's (icing) sugar, sifted	

This recipe from a dear friend is for Goosnargh cakes, a barely sweetened shortbread with caraway seeds, which are a specialty of the northwest part of England.

- *Preheat oven to 300°F (150°C)*
- *Cookie sheet, ungreased*

1. Place seeds in a plastic bag and, using a rolling pin, crush finely.
2. In a large bowl, beat butter and confectioner's sugar until smooth and creamy. Add seeds and mix well. Gradually add flour, mixing well after each addition. (You may not need all the flour because dough should be moist, not dry.)
3. On a floured work surface, roll dough out to ¾-inch (2 cm) thickness. Using a small glass, about 2 inch (5 cm) in diameter, cut out cookies. Place 2 inches (5 cm) apart on cookie sheet and bake in preheated oven for 30 to 45 minutes, until just dry. Do not brown. Cookies should be white. Immediately transfer to wire racks to cool. When cool, sprinkle liberally with confectioner's sugar and pat to press down.

Makes 40 cookies

Aunty Giza's Rosettes

1 cup	all-purpose flour	250 mL
1 tbsp	granulated sugar	15 mL
¼ tsp	salt	1 mL
4	egg yolks, beaten	4
1	whole egg, beaten	1
1 tsp	freshly squeezed lemon juice	5 mL
	Oil for frying	
	Confectioner's (icing) sugar, sifted	
	Glacé cherries, each cut into three or four pieces, or red jam or jelly	

Aunty Giza always made her rosettes with glazed cherries, a variation I much prefer to the one made with jam.

TIP: For the smallest cookie cutter, use the top from a narrow-mouthed container, such as ketchup bottle.

- *Round cookie cutters, 2 inches (5 cm), 1 inch (2.5 cm) and ½ inch (1 cm) in diameter*
- *Deep fryer or Dutch oven*

1. In a large bowl, mix together flour, sugar and salt. Make a well in the center. Add egg yolks, egg and lemon juice and mix until well blended.

2. On a floured surface, roll dough out to ⅛-inch (0.25 cm) thickness and, using the three cutters, make as many complete sets of different-sized circles as possible. Slit the edge of each round in five places to make petals. Combine three different-sized circles by placing the largest on the bottom and the smallest on the top. Using your finger, press hard in the center to stick layers together.

3. In a deep fryer or Dutch oven, heat oil to 375°F (190°C). Working with four to six rosettes at a time, fry cookies, turning once, to a golden brown. Using a slotted spoon, lift out carefully and drain on paper towel. While still warm, dust with confectioner's sugar. Place a piece of glacé cherry or ¼ tsp (1 mL) red jam or jelly in the center of each rosette.

Makes about 2 dozen

Shauna's Bow Knots

2	eggs	2
3 tbsp	granulated sugar	45 mL
1 tbsp	sour cream	15 mL
½ tsp	brandy	2 mL
½ tsp	any flavor liqueur	2 mL
1¾ cups	all-purpose flour, divided	425 mL
	Oil for frying (about 10 cups/2.5 L)	
	Confectioner's (icing) sugar, sifted	

- *Deep fryer or Dutch oven*

1. In a medium bowl, beat eggs and sugar until light and fluffy. Add sour cream, brandy and liqueur, mixing until well blended. Gradually add 1⅓ cups flour, in three portions, beating after each addition.
2. On a floured surface, knead in as much of remaining flour as required so dough is not sticky. Cover with a clean tea towel and let rest for 20 to 25 minutes.
3. Divide dough into four rolls. Place three pieces under a damp towel and roll one piece into a rectangle about ¼ inch (0.5 cm) thick. Using a knife, cut into strips, 1- by 4-inches (2.5 by 10 cm). Cut a slit almost through the middle of the long side of the strip and take the two ends of each strip and pull them through the slit. Repeat with remaining dough.
4. Fill a deep fryer or Dutch oven with oil to a depth of about 2 inches (5 cm). Heat to 375°F (190°C). Add bows, a few at a time, and fry just until light golden brown (this will only take a few seconds). Lift out with a slotted spoon and drain on paper towel. Dust heavily with confectioner's sugar.

Makes about 3 dozen

Olga's Hamantashen

PRUNE FILLING

1 cup	pitted prunes	250 mL
1 cup	raisins	250 mL
	Juice of 1 lemon	
	Juice of 1 orange	
½ cup	granulated sugar	125 mL
2 tsp	vanilla	10 mL
3 tbsp	apricot jam or other jam	45 mL
1 cup	finely crushed walnuts	250 mL

DOUGH

⅔ cup	shortening, softened	150 mL
1 tsp	salt	5 mL
3 tbsp	liquid honey	45 mL
3	eggs	3
1 tsp	baking powder	5 mL
3 cups	all-purpose flour	750 mL

TOPPING

1	egg	1
2 tbsp	milk	25 mL
Pinch	sugar	Pinch

- *Preheat oven to 350°F (180°C)*
- *Cookie cutter or glass 2 to 3 inches (5 to 7.5 cm) in diameter*
- *Cookie sheet, lightly greased*

1. *Prune Filling:* In a medium bowl, cover prunes and raisins with boiling water and leave to soak overnight, until softened. Drain.

2. In a food processor or using a mincer, process prunes and raisins until smooth. Transfer to a medium bowl. Add lemon juice, orange juice, sugar, vanilla, jam and walnuts and mix well. Set aside.

3. In a large bowl, cream shortening, salt and honey until smooth. Beat in eggs, one at a time, mixing until well incorporated. Stir in baking powder, then gradually add flour, mixing until a soft dough forms. Cover with a damp towel.

4. On a lightly floured surface, divide dough in half. Return one half to bowl and cover. Roll other half out to a ¼-inch (0.5 cm) thickness. Using a cookie cutter dipped in flour, cut out circles. Spoon a heaping teaspoonful (5 cm) of filling in the center of each circle. Moisten the edges lightly with a finger dipped in water and pinch together three edges of the dough to form a triangle, leaving a small opening in the center with some filling showing. It will resemble a three-cornered hat.

5. *Topping:* In a small bowl, beat the egg, milk and sugar. Brush top of each triangle with the mixture.

6. Place triangles on prepared cookie sheet and bake in preheated oven for 15 to 20 minutes, until nicely browned. Cool on sheet and, using a spatula, lift off very carefully.

Makes about 2 dozen

Betty's Nothings

3	eggs	3
3 tsp	granulated sugar	15 mL
Pinch	salt	Pinch
½ cup	vegetable oil	125 mL
1 cup	all-purpose flour	250 mL

> Nothing could be simpler than this very plain but delicious cookie.

- *Preheat oven to 425°F (220°C)*
- *Cookie sheet, greased*

1. In a large bowl, beat eggs, sugar and salt until light and fluffy. Continue beating, gradually adding oil, alternately with flour. Mix well.
2. Drop by teaspoonfuls (5 mL), about 2 inches (5 cm) apart, onto prepared cookie sheet. Bake in preheated oven for 20 to 25 minutes or until lightly browned. Immediately transfer to wire racks to cool.

Makes about 3 dozen

Betty's Cornflake Macaroons

2	egg whites	2
½ tsp	vanilla	2 mL
1 cup	lightly packed brown or granulated sugar	250 mL
2 cups	crushed corn flakes cereal	500 mL
½ cup	chopped nuts	125 mL
1 cup	shredded coconut	250 mL

> **TIP**: When making recipes that require egg whites only, drop the yolks into a pan of boiling, salted water and hard-cook them for use in salads, sandwiches, etc.

- *Preheat oven to 350°F (180°C)*
- *Cookie sheet, well-greased*

1. Beat egg whites and vanilla until soft peaks form. Gradually beat in sugar until stiff peaks form. Gently fold in corn flakes, nuts and coconut.
2. Drop by rounded teaspoonfuls (5 mL), about 2 inches (5 cm) apart, onto prepared cookie sheet. Bake in preheated oven for 15 to 20 minutes or until delicately browned. Immediately transfer to wire racks to cool.

Makes about 2½ dozen

Felicia's Apple Squares

BASE

2 cups	all-purpose flour	500 mL
1 cup	granulated sugar	250 mL
1 tsp	baking powder	5 mL
½ cup	butter or margarine, melted	125 mL
2	egg yolks, beaten	2

TOPPING

9	medium apples, peeled and coarsely grated (about 3 lbs/1.5 kg)	9
2 tsp	brown sugar	10 mL
1 tsp	freshly squeezed lemon juice	5 mL
2 tbsp	cold butter or margarine, cut into tiny chunks	25 mL
1 tsp	granulated sugar	5 mL

- *Preheat oven to 350°F (180°C)*
- *13- by 9-inch (3.5 L) cake pan, greased*

1. *Base:* In a large bowl mix together flour, sugar and baking powder. Add butter and egg yolks and mix until crumbly. Set aside 1 cup (250 mL) and press remainder evenly into prepared pan.
2. *Topping:* In a large bowl, mix together apples, brown sugar and lemon juice. Spread evenly over base. Sprinkle reserved crumb mixture over top. Sprinkle with butter chunks, then sugar.
3. Bake in preheated oven for 45 to 50 minutes or until golden brown. Place pan on a wire rack to cool completely, then cut into squares.

Makes 30 squares

Christine's Chocolate Nut Bars

1 cup	corn syrup	250 mL
1 cup	packed brown sugar	250 mL
1 cup	smooth peanut butter	250 mL
2 tbsp	butter or margarine	25 mL
1 tsp	vanilla	5 mL
Pinch	salt	Pinch
4 cups	crisp rice cereal	1 L
2 cups	peanuts	500 mL
	Chocolate frosting (see pages 361 to 363 for recipes)	

- *9-inch (2.5 L) square cake pan, greased*

1. In a large saucepan, over low heat, stir together corn syrup, brown sugar, peanut butter and butter until sugar is dissolved. Increase heat and bring to a boil; cook, stirring constantly, until melted and smooth. Remove from heat. Stir in vanilla and salt. Stir in cereal and peanuts until blended.
2. Press evenly into prepared pan. Chill until firm. Frost with a chocolate frosting of your choice. Cut into bars.

Makes 24 bars

TIP: To prevent icings or frostings from running off your cake, try dusting the surface lightly with cornstarch before frosting.

Betty's Sour Cream Chocolate Chip Bars

BASE

1⅓ cups	all-purpose flour	325 mL
1½ tsp	baking powder	7 mL
1 tsp	baking soda	5 mL
1 tsp	ground cinnamon	5 mL
Pinch	salt	Pinch
6 tbsp	butter or margarine, softened	90 mL
1 cup	granulated sugar	250 mL
2	eggs	2
½ tsp	vanilla	2 mL
1 cup	sour cream	250 mL

TOPPING

1 cup	semi-sweet chocolate chips	250 mL
1 tbsp	granulated sugar	15 mL

- *Preheat oven to 350°F (180°C)*
- *13- by 9-inch (3.5 L) cake pan, greased*

1. *Base:* In a small bowl, mix together flour, baking powder, baking soda, cinnamon and salt.
2. In a large bowl, beat butter and sugar until smooth and creamy. Beat in eggs until incorporated. Stir in vanilla. Blend in flour mixture, alternately with sour cream, until just incorporated. Spread evenly in prepared pan.
3. *Topping:* Sprinkle chocolate chips evenly over top. Sprinkle sugar over chocolate chips.
4. Bake in preheated oven for 30 to 35 minutes or until a tester inserted in the center comes out clean. Place pan on a wire rack to cool completely, then cut into bars.

Makes 36 bars

Felicia's Passover Mocha Nut Bars

2	squares (each 1 oz/28 g) bittersweet chocolate	2
½ cup	butter or margarine	125 mL
2	eggs	2
1 cup	granulated sugar	250 mL
½ tsp	salt	2 mL
½ cup	sifted cake meal (Passover)	125 mL
1 cup	chopped nuts	250 mL

TIP: Try substituting carob for chocolate in some of your recipes. Carob is similar to chocolate in flavor but is lower in fat and is caffeine-free.

- *Preheat oven to 350°F (180°C)*
- *9-inch (2.5 L) square cake pan, greased*

1. In a saucepan, over low heat, melt chocolate and butter, stirring until smooth. Set aside.
2. In a medium bowl, beat eggs, sugar and salt until blended and thick. Add cake meal and mix well. Blend in chocolate mixture. Stir in nuts.
3. Spread evenly in prepared pan. Bake in preheated oven for 25 to 30 minutes or until a tester inserted in the center comes out clean. Place pan on a wire rack to cool completely, then cut into bars.

Makes 24 bars

Colleen's "Sex in a Pan"

BASE

1 cup	all-purpose flour	250 mL
½ cup	chopped almonds or pecans	125 mL
3 tbsp	granulated sugar	45 mL
½ cup	butter or margarine	125 mL

FILLING

8 oz	cream cheese, softened	250 g
1 cup	confectioner's (icing) sugar, sifted	250 mL
2 cups	frozen whipped topping (thawed) or whipped (35%) cream, divided	500 mL

TOPPING

2	packages (each a 4-serving size) chocolate or caramel instant pudding mix	2
1	package (4-serving size) vanilla instant pudding mix	1
4 cups	milk	1 L
	Grated chocolate, chopped nuts or cherries for garnish (optional)	

> *I have no idea — and neither does Colleen — how this recipe got its name, but it has been around for a long time and it is delicious!*

> **TIP:** Pack sweetened whipped cream, flavored with vanilla, into freezer trays. Freeze until firm. Cut in squares and serve on warm cakes or pies.

- *Preheat oven to 350°F (180°C)*
- *13- by 9-inch (3.5 L) cake pan, greased*

1. *Base:* In a medium bowl, mix together flour, nuts and sugar. Using two knives, a pastry blender or your fingers, cut butter in until mixture resembles coarse crumbs. Press evenly into prepared pan. Bake in preheated oven for 12 to 15 minutes or until browned. Place pan on a wire rack to cool completely.

2. *Filling:* In another bowl, beat cream cheese and confectioner's sugar until smooth and creamy. Fold in 1 cup (250 mL) of the whipped topping. Spread evenly over cooled base.

3. *Topping:* In a large bowl, beat puddings and milk until blended and smooth. Spread evenly over cream cheese mixture. Spread with remaining whipped topping. If desired, garnish with chocolate, nuts or cherries. Chill until ready to serve. Cut into squares.

Makes 30 squares

Cecille's Cookie Bars

BASE

1½ cups	crushed corn flakes cereal	375 mL
3 tbsp	granulated sugar	45 mL
½ cup	butter or margarine, melted	125 mL

TOPPING

1 cup	semi-sweet chocolate chips	250 mL
1⅓ cups	flaked coconut	325 mL
1 cup	coarsely chopped walnuts	250 mL
1	can (10 oz/300 mL) sweetened condensed milk	1

- *Preheat oven to 350°F (180°C)*
- *13- by 9-inch (3.5 L) cake pan, greased*

1. *Base:* In a medium bowl mix together corn flake crumbs, sugar and butter. Press firmly into prepared pan.
2. *Topping:* Spread chocolate chips evenly over base. Sprinkle coconut evenly over top. Sprinkle nuts evenly over top of coconut. Pour condensed milk evenly over nuts.
3. Bake in preheated oven for 25 minutes or until edges are lightly browned. Place pan on a wire rack to cool completely, then cut into bars.

Makes 36 bars

Sima's Pineapple Squares

TOPPING

3 cups	crushed pineapple, drained, 2 tbsp (25 mL) juice reserved	750 mL
½ cup	granulated sugar	125 mL
2 tbsp	cornstarch	25 mL
1 tbsp	butter	15 mL

BASE

1½ cups	all-purpose flour	375 mL
2 tsp	baking powder	10 mL
Pinch	salt	Pinch
2	eggs	2
¾ cup	granulated sugar	175 mL
½ cup	vegetable oil	125 mL
½ cup	orange juice	125 mL
¼ cup	water	50 mL

- *Preheat oven to 375°F (190°C)*
- *13- by 9-inch (3.5 L) cake pan, greased*

1. *Topping:* In the top of a double boiler, over simmering (not boiling) water, combine pineapple and sugar. In a small bowl, mix cornstarch with reserved pineapple juice. Add to sugar mixture along with butter. Cook, stirring frequently, until mixture thickens. Set aside.
2. *Base:* In a large bowl, mix together flour, baking powder and salt. Make a well in the center. In another bowl, beat eggs, sugar, oil, orange juice and water. Pour into well and mix until just blended. (Batter will be thin.) Set aside one-half of the batter and pour remainder into prepared pan.
3. Spoon pineapple mixture evenly over batter. Drop remaining batter, by spoonfuls, over pineapple, leaving spaces in the form of vertical and horizontal lines between the dollops of batter. Bake in preheated oven for 25 minutes, then reduce heat to 350° F (180° C) and bake 10 minutes longer, until golden brown. Place pan on a wire rack to cool completely, then cut into squares.

Makes 30 squares

Baba Mary's Honey Diamonds

2 cups	all-purpose flour	500 mL
½ tsp	baking soda	2 mL
½ tsp	ground cinnamon	2 mL
¼ tsp	salt	1 mL
¼ cup	butter or shortening, softened	50 mL
1 cup	packed brown sugar	250 mL
2	eggs	2
⅓ cup	liquid honey	75 mL
½ cup	milk	125 mL
	Butter Frosting (see recipe, page 360)	
½ cup	ground nuts	125 mL

TIP: To soften brick-hard brown sugar, transfer it to a paper bag and place in a 350°F (180°C) oven until the bag is warm. Then crush with a rolling pin and spread out on a cookie sheet to cool.

- *Preheat oven to 350°F (180°C)*
- *13- by 9-inch (3.5 L) cake pan, greased*

1. In a medium bowl mix together flour, baking soda, cinnamon and salt.
2. In a large bowl, beat butter and sugar until smooth and creamy. Add eggs and beat until incorporated. Stir in honey. Gradually blend in flour mixture, alternately with milk, until just incorporated.
3. Spread evenly in prepared pan. Bake in preheated oven for 35 to 40 minutes or until a tester inserted in the center comes out clean. Place pan on a wire rack to cool completely.
4. Frost generously with Butter Frosting, then sprinkle with nuts. Cut lengthwise into six strips; cut crosswise at an angle into six strips to make diamonds.

Makes 36 diamonds

Arlene's Pineapple Cheesecake Squares

BASE

2½ cups	finely crushed graham wafer crumbs (about 36 wafers)	625 mL
¼ cup	butter, melted	50 mL

TOPPING

1 lb	cream cheese, softened	500 g
½ cup	granulated sugar	125 mL
3	eggs	3
1 tsp	vanilla	5 mL
10	finely chopped maraschino cherries	10
½ cup	drained crushed pineapple	125 mL

- *Preheat oven to 350° F (180° C)*
- *8-inch (2 L) square cake pan, lightly greased*

1. *Base:* In a medium bowl, mix together wafer crumbs and butter. Set aside ¾ cup (175 mL) and press remainder evenly into prepared pan.
2. *Topping:* In a large bowl, beat cream cheese and sugar until smooth. Beat in eggs, one at a time, until incorporated. Stir in vanilla. Stir in cherries and pineapple.
3. Spread evenly over base. Sprinkle reserved crumb mixture evenly over top. Bake in preheated oven for 35 minutes or until just set. Place pan on a wire rack to cool completely, then chill for 4 hours, or longer, before cutting into squares.

Makes 16 squares

Olga's Blueberry Cake Squares

BASE

2½ cups	all-purpose flour	625 mL
1 tbsp	baking powder	15 mL
½ tsp	salt	2 mL
2	eggs	2
1 cup	granulated sugar	250 mL
3 tbsp	water	45 mL
1 tsp	vanilla	5 mL
1	can (19 oz/540 mL) blueberry pie filling	1

TOPPING

1 tbsp	butter, softened	15 mL
2 tbsp	all-purpose flour	25 mL
1 tbsp	granulated sugar	15 mL
1	egg yolk	1

- *Preheat oven to 350°F (180°C)*
- *13- by 9-inch (3.5 L) cake pan, greased*

1. *Base:* In a medium bowl, mix together flour, baking powder and salt.
2. In a large bowl, beat eggs, sugar, water and vanilla until blended. Gradually blend in flour mixture. Set half aside and spread remainder evenly in prepared pan. Spread pie filling evenly over top.
3. On a floured work surface, divide remaining dough into 14 portions. Shape each into a rope, half to fit vertically across the cake and half to fit horizontally. Place over cake.
4. *Topping:* In a small bowl mix butter, flour, sugar and egg yolk until mixture is crumbly.
5. Sprinkle topping evenly over cake. Bake in preheated oven for 55 to 60 minutes or until golden brown. Place pan on a rack to cool completely, then cut into squares.

Makes 30 squares

Wendy's Chocolate Chip Cream Cheese Bars

1	package (18 oz/510 g) refrigerated chocolate chip cookie dough, softened	1
1 lb	cream cheese, softened	500 g
1 cup	granulated sugar	250 mL
2	eggs	2
1 ½ tsp	vanilla	7 mL
1	package (18 oz/510 g) refrigerated chocolate chip cookie dough, chilled	1

- *Preheat oven to 350°F (180°C)*
- *13- by 9-inch (3.5 L) cake pan, greased*

1. Spread softened cookie dough evenly in prepared pan.
2. In a medium bowl, beat cream cheese and sugar until smooth. Beat in eggs, one at a time, until incorporated. Stir in vanilla. Spread evenly over dough.
3. On a cutting board, cut chilled dough into very thin slices. Completely cover cream cheese mixture with thin cookie slices. (Place dough in freezer for 15 minutes to make slicing easier.) Bake in preheated oven for 40 minutes or until golden brown. Place pan on a wire rack to cool completely. Store in refrigerator, then cut into bars.

Makes 36 bars

Shauna's Cinnamon Apple Squares

BASE

1¾ cups	all-purpose flour	425 mL
2 tsp	baking powder	10 mL
Pinch	salt	Pinch
2	eggs	2
¾ cup	granulated sugar	175 mL
¾ cup	vegetable oil	175 mL
½ cup	cold water	125 mL
1	can (19 oz/540 mL) apple pie filling	1

TOPPING

2 tbsp	granulated sugar	25 mL
½ tsp	ground cinnamon	2 mL

- *Preheat oven to 350°F (180°C)*
- *13- by 9-inch (3.5 L) cake pan, greased*

1. *Base:* In a small bowl, mix together flour, baking powder and salt.
2. In a large bowl, beat eggs and sugar until thickened. Beat in oil until blended. Gradually blend in flour mixture, alternately with water, until just incorporated. Spread a little more than half the batter evenly in prepared pan.
3. *Topping:* Drop spoonfuls of apple pie filling over top of batter. Spread remaining batter evenly over apple filling.
4. In a small bowl, mix together sugar and cinnamon. Sprinkle evenly over top of cake. Bake in preheated oven for 40 to 60 minutes or until golden brown. Place pan on a wire rack to cool completely, then cut into squares.

Makes 30 squares

Shirley's Cornmeal Squares (Malai Cake)

1 cup	all-purpose flour	250 mL
1 tbsp	baking powder	15 mL
1 tsp	salt	5 mL
½ cup	yellow cornmeal	125 mL
2 cups	water	500 mL
½ cup	butter or margarine, melted	125 mL
6	eggs, separated	6
2 cups	creamed cottage cheese	500 mL
2 cups	sour cream	500 mL
½ cup	granulated sugar	125 mL

TIP: This cake is delicious when served warm with sour cream and strawberries.

- *Preheat oven to 350°F (180°C)*
- *13- by 9-inch (3.5 L) cake pan, greased*

1. In a small bowl, mix together flour, baking powder and salt.
2. In the top of a double boiler, combine cornmeal and water. Cook over low heat until mixture thickens. Stir in butter until melted. Set aside to cool.
3. In a large bowl, beat egg yolks, cottage cheese, sour cream and sugar until blended. Blend in flour mixture, alternating with cornmeal mixture, just until incorporated.
4. In a clean bowl, beat egg whites until stiff peaks form. Fold into batter. Spoon into prepared cake pan, spreading evenly. Bake in preheated oven for 55 to 60 minutes or until golden brown. Place pan on a wire rack to cool completely, or cool slightly and serve warm. Cut into squares.

Makes 30 squares

Betty's Fruit Cocktail Squares

BASE

1 cup	all-purpose flour	250 mL
1 tsp	baking soda	5 mL
¼ tsp	salt	1 mL
¾ cup	granulated sugar	175 mL
1	egg, beaten	1
2 cups	fruit cocktail, partially drained	500 mL

TOPPING

⅓ cup	packed brown sugar	75 mL
1 tsp	ground cinnamon	5 mL

- *Preheat oven to 350°F (180°C)*
- *8-inch (2 L) square cake pan, greased*

1. *Base:* In a small bowl, mix together flour, baking soda and salt.
2. In a large bowl, mix together, sugar, egg and fruit cocktail. Blend in flour mixture. Spread evenly in prepared pan.
3. *Topping:* In a small bowl, mix together brown sugar and cinnamon.
4. Sprinkle evenly over top of cake. Bake in preheated topping oven for 40 to 45 minutes, until golden brown. Place pan on a wire rack to cool completely, then cut into squares.

Makes 16 squares

Cecille's Walnut Squares

BASE

1½ cups	all-purpose flour	375 mL
1 tbsp	packed brown sugar	15 mL
Pinch	baking powder	Pinch
½ cup	butter or margarine	125 mL

TOPPING

1¼ cups	finely chopped walnuts, divided	300 mL
2	eggs	2
¾ cup	packed brown sugar	175 mL
2 tbsp	all-purpose flour	25 mL
Pinch	baking powder	Pinch
1 tsp	vanilla	5 mL
	Butter Frosting (see recipe, page 360)	

- *Preheat oven to 325°F (160°C)*
- *13- by 9-inch (3.5 L) cake pan, ungreased*

1. *Base:* In a bowl mix together flour, brown sugar and baking powder. Using two knives, a pastry blender or your fingers, cut butter in until mixture resembles coarse crumbs. Press evenly into pan. Bake in preheated oven for 15 to 20 minutes or until golden brown. Place pan on a wire rack to cool slightly.
2. *Topping:* Set aside ½ cup (125 mL) of the chopped walnuts. In a bowl, beat eggs and brown sugar until blended. Blend in flour, baking powder and vanilla. Stir in remaining ¾ cup (175 mL) walnuts.
3. Spread evenly over warm base. Bake 15 to 20 minutes longer, until golden brown. Place pan on a wire rack to cool completely. Frost with Butter Frosting and sprinkle reserved walnuts over top. Cut into squares.

Makes 30 squares

Mama's Icebox Cake Bars

1	package (4-serving size) gelatin dessert mix, any flavor	1

WALNUT FILLING

1 cup	graham wafer crumbs (about 14 wafers)	250 mL
1 cup	finely chopped walnuts	250 mL
	Grated zest of 1 lemon	
½ cup	packed brown sugar	125 mL

SOUR CREAM FILLING

1½ cups	sour cream	375 mL
½ cup	packed brown sugar	125 mL
2 tsp	freshly squeezed lemon juice	10 mL
1 tsp	vanilla	5 mL
1	package (14 oz/400 g) whole graham wafers	1

> *How this recipe got its name: The story is that an ingenious cook, a lady with a flair, created a reasonable facsimile of a cake by alternating layers of cookies with flavored whipped cream. This creation was placed in an old-fashioned ice-box to mellow — hence the name Ice-Box Cakes.*

- *13- by 9-inch (3.5 L) cake pan, ungreased*

1. Prepare gelatin according to package directions, allowing to set partially. Gelatin should be firm enough to spread.
2. *Walnut Filling:* In a medium bowl, mix together wafer crumbs, walnuts, zest and brown sugar.
3. *Sour Cream Filling:* In another medium bowl, mix sour cream, brown sugar, lemon juice and vanilla until thoroughly blended.
4. Line bottom of pan with half of the whole graham wafers. Spoon half of sour cream filling over top, spreading evenly. Place remaining graham wafers on top and spread evenly with remaining sour cream filling.
5. Spoon half the walnut filling evenly over cream cheese layer; spread evenly with the partially set gelatin. Spoon remaining walnut filling over top, spreading evenly. Chill for 3 to 4 hours, until cold and set. Cut into bars before serving.

Makes 24 bars

Lisa's Midas Squares

BASE

1 cup	smooth peanut butter	250 mL
½ cup	cane sugar syrup (golden syrup)	125 mL
½ cup	packed brown sugar	125 mL
2 cups	corn flakes cereal, lightly crushed	500 mL
1 cup	crisp rice cereal	250 mL

FROSTING

½ cup	packed brown sugar	125 mL
3 tbsp	milk	45 mL
1 tbsp	margarine, softened	15 mL
1 cup	confectioner's (icing) sugar, sifted	250 mL
½ tsp	vanilla	2 mL

- *8-inch (2 L) square cake pan, ungreased*

1. *Base:* In a saucepan, over low heat, stir peanut butter, syrup and brown sugar, until sugar dissolves and mixture is smooth. Stir in corn flakes and rice cereal. Press firmly and evenly into pan.

2. *Frosting:* In a small bowl, beat brown sugar, milk, margarine, confectioner's sugar and vanilla until smooth and spreadable. Spread over base. Chill for 3 to 4 hours or overnight. When serving, cut into squares.

Makes 16 squares

Colleen's Fruit Cake Squares

1½ cups	water	375 mL
1½ cups	raisins	375 mL
2 tsp	baking soda	10 mL
3 cups	all-purpose flour	750 mL
1 tsp	ground cinnamon	5 mL
1 tsp	ground nutmeg	5 mL
1 tsp	ground ginger	5 mL
2 cups	granulated sugar	500 mL
1 cup	vegetable oil	250 mL
3	eggs	3
2 tsp	vanilla	10 mL
½ cup	chopped nuts (optional)	125 mL
½ cup	chocolate chips (optional)	125 mL

- *Preheat oven to 400°F (200°C)*
- *13- by 9-inch (3.5 L) cake pan, greased*

1. In a saucepan, over low heat, stir together water, raisins and baking soda. Increase heat and bring to a boil. Cook, stirring occasionally, for 5 minutes. Set aside to cool.

2. In a large bowl, mix together flour, cinnamon, nutmeg and ginger. Make a well in the center.

3. In another large bowl, beat sugar, oil, eggs and vanilla until blended. Stir in raisin mixture. Pour into flour mixture and stir just until incorporated. Stir in nuts and chocolate chips, if using.

4. Spread evenly in prepared pan. Bake in preheated oven for 1 hour and 10 minutes or until a tester inserted in the center comes out clean. Place pan on a wire rack to cool completely, then cut into squares.

Makes 30 squares

Jeanette's Filled Coffee Cake Squares

BASE

3 cups	all-purpose flour	750 mL
2 tsp	baking powder	10 mL
½ tsp	salt	2 mL
½ cup	butter or margarine, softened	125 mL
2 cups	granulated sugar	500 mL
4	eggs	4
1 tsp	vanilla	5 mL
1 cup	milk	250 mL

FILLING

1 cup	packed brown sugar	250 mL
2 tbsp	butter, softened	25 mL
2 tbsp	all-purpose flour	25 mL
1 cup	chopped nuts	250 mL
1 tsp	ground cinnamon	5 mL

- *Preheat oven to 350°F (180°C)*
- *13- by 9-inch (3.5 L) cake pan, greased*

1. *Base:* In a medium bowl, mix together flour, baking powder and salt.
2. In a large bowl, beat butter and sugar until smooth and creamy. Beat in eggs, one at a time, until incorporated. Stir in vanilla. Gradually blend in flour mixture, alternately with milk, until just incorporated. Set half aside and spread remainder evenly in prepared pan.
3. *Filling:* In a medium bowl, beat sugar and butter until smooth and creamy. Blend in flour, nuts and cinnamon.
4. Spoon half the filling over batter in pan. Spread reserved batter evenly over filling. Spread remaining filling evenly over batter. Bake in preheated oven for 40 to 50 minutes or until a tester inserted in the center comes out clean. Place pan on a wire rack to cool completely, then cut into squares.

Makes 30 squares

Christine's Lemon Squares

BASE

½ cup	butter or margarine, softened	125 mL
¼ cup	confectioner's (icing) sugar, sifted	50 mL
½ tsp	salt	2 mL
1 cup	all-purpose flour	250 mL

TOPPING

2	eggs, beaten	2
1 cup	granulated sugar	250 mL
2 tbsp	all-purpose flour	25 mL
1½ tsp	grated lemon zest	7 mL
2 tbsp	freshly squeezed lemon juice	25 mL
	Confectioner's (icing) sugar	

- *Preheat oven to 350°F (180°C)*
- *8-inch (2 L) square cake pan, lightly greased*

1. *Base:* In a small bowl, beat butter and confectioner's sugar until smooth and creamy. Beat in salt, then gradually blend in flour until a soft dough forms. Press evenly into prepared pan. Bake in preheated oven for 20 minutes or until lightly browned. Place pan on a wire rack to cool slightly.
2. *Topping:* In a small bowl, mix together eggs, sugar, 2 tbsp (25 mL) flour, zest and juice until blended.
3. Spoon evenly over warm base. Bake 20 to 25 minutes longer. Remove from oven and sift confectioner's sugar over top. Place pan on a wire rack to cool completely, then cut into squares.

Makes 16 squares

Frostings, Glazes and Toppings

Apricot Brandy Glaze

1	jar (12 oz/340 mL) apricot preserves	1
¼ cup	apricot brandy	50 mL

1. In a small saucepan, over low heat, cook apricot preserves until very warm. Add apricot brandy and cook, stirring, for 1 to 2 minutes. Remove from heat. Strain through a fine sieve and allow to cool.

Makes enough for a 13- by 9-inch (3.5 L) pan

Banana Frosting

½ cup	butter or margarine, softened	125 mL
½ cup	mashed bananas (about 1 or 2 medium)	125 mL
3½ cups	confectioner's (icing) sugar, sifted	825 mL
1 tbsp	freshly squeezed lemon juice	15 mL
1 tsp	vanilla	5 mL

1. In a large bowl, cream butter and bananas until blended. Gradually add confectioner's sugar, lemon juice and vanilla and mix well. Chill until mixture is the right consistency for spreading.

Makes enough for a 13- by 9-inch (3.5 L) pan

TIP: If your frosting becomes hard or too stiff while beating, just add a little lemon juice.

VARIATION
To make this recipe a banana filling, chop 2 bananas with a little pulverized sugar and lemon juice.

Quick Banana Frosting

1	ripe mashed banana	1
½ tsp	almond extract	2 mL
2 cups	confectioner's (icing) sugar, sifted	500 mL

1. In a medium bowl, beat banana, almond extract and confectioner's sugar until blended and spreadable.

Makes enough for a 8- or 9-inch (2 or 2.5 L) pan

Broiled Topping

½ cup	packed brown sugar	125 mL
¼ cup	butter or margarine, softened	50 mL
3 tbsp	evaporated milk	45 mL
½ cup	shredded coconut or chopped nuts	125 mL
1 tbsp	grated orange zest (optional)	15 mL

1. In a small bowl, mix together brown sugar, butter, milk, coconut and, if using, orange zest.
2. Spread mixture evenly over cake before cutting into squares or bars, then put under broiler for 2 to 3 minutes or until topping is bubbly and golden brown.

Makes enough for an 8- or 9-inch (2 L or 2.5 L) pan

TIP: This is especially good with a butter, chocolate, orange or carrot cake.

Brown Sugar Meringue

2	egg whites	2
1 tbsp	freshly squeezed lemon juice	15 mL
1 cup	packed brown sugar	250 mL

1. In a small bowl, with an electric mixer, beat egg whites until doubled in volume. Beat in lemon juice. Beat in brown sugar, 1 tbsp (15 mL) at a time, until meringue stands in firm peaks.
2. Spread over cake and bake in a 350°F (180°C) oven for about 10 minutes or until meringue is browned. Place pan on a rack to cool completely, then cut into bars or squares.

Makes enough for an 8- or 9-inch (2 L or 2.5 L) pan

TIP: Meringues are often called "angel crust" because of their gossamer texture.

Butter Frosting

⅓ cup	butter, softened	75 mL
4 cups	confectioner's (icing) sugar, sifted	1 L
1½ tsp	vanilla	7 mL
2 tbsp	light (5%) cream or milk (approximate)	25 mL

1. In a large bowl, cream butter. Slowly add about half of the confectioner's sugar, blending well. Beat in vanilla and gradually blend in the remaining confectioner's sugar. Add only enough cream to make the right spreading consistency.

Makes enough for a 13- by 9-inch (3.5 L) pan

VARIATIONS

Chocolate Butter Frosting
When adding vanilla, also add 2 squares (each 1 oz/28 g) unsweetened chocolate, melted and cooled, and mix to blend.

Lemon Butter Frosting
To creamed butter, add ½ tsp (2 mL) grated lemon zest. Replace light cream with lemon juice, only enough to make frosting the right spreading consistency.

Mocha Coffee Butter Frosting
To creamed butter, add ¼ cup (50 mL) unsweetened cocoa powder and ½ tsp (2 mL) instant coffee.

Orange Butter Frosting
To creamed butter, add 2 tsp (10 mL) grated orange zest and replace light cream with 2 tbsp (25 mL) orange juice.

Pineapple Butter Frosting
Omit vanilla and light cream, and add ⅓ cup (75 mL) pineapple juice and ⅔ cup (150 mL) granulated sugar. Combine the butter, juice and sugar in a small saucepan and heat until sugar is dissolved. Remove from heat and gradually beat in the confectioner's sugar, just enough to give a good spreading consistency.

Caramel Frosting

1½ cups	packed brown sugar	375 mL
½ cup	granulated sugar	125 mL
1 cup	milk	250 mL
1 tbsp	butter or margarine	15 mL

TIP: For a different topping or spread, place caramel candies in the bottom of your baking pan before pouring in batter. Bake as usual, then invert the cake, spread melted caramel evenly over top of cake; cool and cut into bars or squares.

1. In a saucepan, over medium-low heat, combine brown sugar, granulated sugar and milk; cook until sugar is dissolved. Increase heat and bring to a boil; cook until syrup forms a soft ball in cold water. Add butter and stir until melted. Remove from heat. Cool to lukewarm. Beat until thick and creamy and of right consistency for spreading.

Makes enough for a 13- by 9-inch (3.5 L) pan

Chocolate Icing

3	squares (each 1 oz/28 g) unsweetened chocolate	3
½ tbsp	butter	7 mL
5 tbsp	milk	75 mL
3½ cups	confectioner's (icing) sugar, sifted	825 mL
1 tsp	vanilla	5 mL

TIP: For easier handling of icings and frostings when decorating cakes, use a squeeze bottle with a pointed tip, like your ketchup and mustard squeeze bottles.

1. In the top of a double boiler, combine chocolate, butter and milk until melted and smooth.
2. Transfer to a large bowl and gradually beat in confectioner's sugar, then vanilla, until smooth and creamy.

Makes enough for a 13- by 9-inch (3.5 L) pan

Chocolate Chip Frosting

1½ cups	granulated sugar	375 mL
½ cup	butter or margarine	125 mL
⅓ cup	evaporated milk	75 mL
½ cup	semi-sweet chocolate chips	125 mL

1. In a small saucepan, over low heat, combine sugar, butter and milk until sugar is dissolved. Increase heat and bring to boil; cook, stirring constantly, for 1 minute. Add chocolate chips and stir until melted. Allow to cool slightly before using.

Makes enough for a 13- by 9-inch (3.5 L) pan

White Chocolate Buttercream Frosting

¼ cup	whipping (35%) cream	50 mL
6	squares (each 1 oz/28 g) white chocolate	6
1 cup	confectioner's (icing) sugar, sifted	250 mL
1 cup	cold unsalted butter, cut into chunks	250 mL

1. In a saucepan, over low heat, heat cream and chocolate, stirring constantly, until chocolate is melted and mixture is smooth. Set aside to cool for about 15 minutes.
2. Pour cooled chocolate mixture into the small bowl of an electric mixer. Blend in sugar. With motor running, add butter a little at a time. Beat on high speed for 2 minutes or until smooth and fluffy.

Makes enough for an 8- or 9-inch (2 L or 2.5 L) pan

Chocolate Velvet Frosting

1½ cups	granulated sugar	375 mL
¼ tsp	salt	1 mL
6 tbsp	cornstarch	90 mL
1½ cups	boiling water	375 mL
3	squares (each 1 oz/28 g) unsweetened chocolate	3
¼ cup	butter or margarine	50 mL
1 tsp	vanilla	5 mL

1. In a saucepan, over low heat, combine sugar, salt and cornstarch. Stir in the boiling water until well blended. Cook, stirring constantly, until mixture thickens. Add chocolate and butter; cook, stirring until melted. Remove from heat. Stir in vanilla.
2. Pour into a bowl and chill, stirring several times, until thick enough to spread.

Makes enough for a 13- by 9-inch (3.5 L) pan

TIP: Need a garnish? Sprinkle bars or squares with sugar and spice, or glaze with a thin mixture of orange juice and confectioner's sugar.

Cocoa Frosting

3 tbsp	butter or margarine, softened	45 mL
⅓ cup	unsweetened cocoa powder	75 mL
2 cups	confectioner's (icing) sugar, sifted	500 mL
3 tbsp	milk	45 mL
½ tsp	vanilla	2 mL
¼ tsp	salt	1 mL

1. In a small bowl, with an electric mixer, cream together butter and cocoa until smooth and blended. Stir in confectioner's sugar alternately with milk, blending until smooth and of the right consistency for spreading. Stir in vanilla and salt.

Makes enough for an 8- or 9-inch (2 L or 2.5 L) pan

Coffee Frosting

½ cup	butter or margarine, softened	125 mL
2 cups	confectioner's (icing) sugar, sifted	500 mL
3 tbsp	coffee liqueur	45 mL
2 tbsp	milk	25 mL
1 tbsp	instant coffee powder	15 mL

1. In a small bowl, with an electric mixer, cream butter and about half of the confectioner's sugar, until smooth and fluffy.
2. In a measuring cup, mix together liqueur, milk and instant coffee until blended. Add to the creamed mixture alternately with the remaining confectioner's sugar, beating until smooth.

Makes enough for an 8- or 9-inch (2 L or 2.5 L) pan

No-Cook Fudge Frosting

1 cup	confectioner's (icing) sugar, sifted	250 mL
3 tbsp	milk	45 mL
1	egg	1
1 tsp	vanilla	5 mL
2	squares (each 1 oz/28 g) unsweetened chocolate, melted and cooled slightly	2
3 tbsp	butter or margarine, softened	45 mL

1. In a small bowl, combine confectioner's sugar, milk, egg and vanilla, stirring constantly until blended. Stir in melted chocolate, then butter, beating well after each addition. Chill for 10 minutes in refrigerator.
2. Place bowl in ice water. Beat frosting over ice water until the right consistency for spreading.

Makes enough for an 8- or 9-inch (2 L or 2.5 L) pan

> **TIP:** Raw eggs can be a potentially dangerous source of salmonella. To reduce this food-safety risk, use a pasteurized egg.

Cream Cheese Frosting

6 oz	cream cheese, softened	180 g
½ cup	butter or margarine, softened	125 mL
2 tsp	vanilla	10 mL
4½ cups to 5 cups	confectioner's (icing) sugar, sifted	1.125 L to 1.25 L

1. In a large bowl, beat together cream cheese, butter and vanilla until light and fluffy. Gradually add 2 cups (500 mL) of the confectioner's sugar, beating well. Gradually beat in as much of the remaining sugar as required to make the right consistency for spreading.

Makes enough for a 13- by 9-inch (3.5 L) pan

Lemon Glaze

1 cup	confectioner's (icing) sugar, sifted	250 mL
4 tsp	freshly squeezed lemon juice	20 mL

1. In a small bowl, mix together confectioner's sugar and lemon juice until smooth and blended.

Makes enough for a 13- by 9-inch (3.5 L) pan

VARIATION

Pineapple Glaze
Add another 1/2 cup (125 mL) confectioner's sugar and replace lemon juice with 1/4 cup (50 mL) pineapple juice.

Creamy Lemon Frosting

1/4 cup	butter or margarine, softened	50 mL
1/4 cup	shortening, softened	50 mL
1/4 tsp	salt	1 mL
1	egg	1
3 cups	confectioner's (icing) sugar, sifted	750 mL
1/4 cup	light corn syrup	50 mL
3 tbsp	freshly squeezed lemon juice	45 mL

1. In a large bowl, beat butter and shortening until creamy. Beat in salt and egg. Gradually beat in confectioner's sugar, then slowly add corn syrup and lemon juice, beating until fluffy and spreadable.

Makes enough for a 13- by 9-inch (3.5 L) pan

TIP: To remove lumps from confectioner's sugar, press through a sieve, or sift until smooth.

Lemon Butter Frosting

1 1/2 cups	confectioner's (icing) sugar, sifted	375 mL
2 tbsp	butter or margarine, softened	25 mL
1 tbsp	milk	15 mL
1/2 tsp	lemon zest	2 mL
1 tsp	freshly squeezed lemon juice	5 mL

1. In a small bowl, mix together confectioner's sugar, butter or margarine, milk, lemon zest and juice until smooth and spreadable.

Makes enough for an 8- or 9-inch (2 L or 2.5 L) pan

Easy Orange Frosting

2	egg whites	2
1¼ cups	granulated sugar	300 mL
¼ cup	frozen orange juice concentrate, thawed	50 mL
1 tbsp	light corn syrup	15 mL

1. In the top of a double boiler over simmering (not boiling) water, combine egg whites, sugar, concentrate and syrup. Cook, beating constantly with an electric mixer, on high speed, for about 10 minutes or until frosting forms stiff peaks. Remove from heat. Cool slightly.

Makes enough for an 8- or 9-inch (2 L or 2.5 L) pan

Orange Butter Icing

3 tbsp	butter or margarine, softened	45 mL
1½ cups	confectioner's (icing) sugar, sifted	375 mL
2 tsp	orange zest	10 mL
1 tbsp	orange juice	15 mL

1. In a medium bowl, beat butter or margarine and sugar until smooth and creamy. Stir in orange zest and juice. Beat until smooth and the right consistency for spreading.

Makes enough for an 8- or 9-inch (2 L or 2.5 L) pan

Penuche Nut Icing

1 cup	packed brown sugar	250 mL
¼ cup	milk	50 mL
¼ cup	shortening	50 mL
½ tsp	vanilla	2 mL
¼ tsp	salt	1 mL
½ cup	chopped nuts	125 mL

TIP: To keep frosting from hardening in the bowl, cover it with a damp towel.

1. In a saucepan, over medium-low heat, combine brown sugar, milk, shortening and salt. Slowly bring to a rolling boil, stirring constantly, and boil for 2 minutes.
2. Remove from heat and beat with an electric mixer until lukewarm. Add the vanilla and beat until thick enough to spread. If too thick, add a little cream. Stir in nuts.

Makes enough for an 8- or 9-inch (2 L or 2.5 L) pan

Pink Lemonade Frosting

½ cup	frozen pink lemonade concentrate, thawed	125 mL
3½ to 4 cups	confectioner's (icing) sugar, sifted	825 mL to 1 L
2	egg whites	2
Pinch	salt	Pinch

1. In a large bowl, with an electric mixer, combine concentrate, confectioner's sugar, egg whites and salt. Beat, on high speed, until thick enough to spread.

Makes enough for a 13- by 9-inch (3.5 L) pan

TIP: Raw eggs can be a potentially dangerous source of salmonella. To reduce this food-safety risk, use pasteurized egg whites.

Rocky Road Frosting

2	squares (each 1 oz/28 g) unsweetened chocolate	2
2 cups	miniature marshmallows, divided	500 mL
¼ cup	water	50 mL
¼ cup	butter or margarine	50 mL
2 cups	confectioner's (icing) sugar, sifted	500 mL
1 tsp	vanilla	5 mL
½ cup	chopped walnuts	125 mL

1. In a small saucepan, combine chocolate, 1 cup (250 mL) of the marshmallows, water and butter. Cook over low heat, stirring constantly, until blended. Remove from heat and cool slightly.
2. Slowly beat in confectioner's sugar, then vanilla. Beat until smooth and thick, about 2 minutes. Stir in the remaining 1 cup (250 mL) of marshmallows and the nuts; mix until well combined.

Makes enough for an 8- or 9-inch (2 L or 2.5 L) pan

Praline Topping

2	squares (each 1 oz/28 g) unsweetened chocolate	2
2 cups	miniature marshmallows, divided	500 mL
¼ cup	water	50 mL
¼ cup	butter or margarine	50 mL
2 cups	confectioner's (icing) sugar, sifted	500 mL
1 tsp	vanilla	5 mL
½ cup	chopped walnuts	125 mL

1. In a small bowl, combine nuts, brown sugar, butter and cream. Mix together until well blended.
2. Spread evenly over a hot or cooled cake and broil about 3 inches (7.5 cm) from the heat for 1 to 2 minutes, or until pale brown.

Makes enough for an 8- or 9-inch (2 L or 2.5 L) pan

Fresh Strawberry Frosting

1 cup	fresh, ripe strawberries	250 mL
½ tsp	freshly squeezed lemon juice	2 mL
1½ cups	confectioner's (icing) sugar, sifted	375 mL

TIP: To keep cake crumbs from getting into your frosting, first spread cake with a thin layer of frosting and let it set. Then frost as usual.

1. In a medium bowl, mash strawberries with a fork. Add lemon juice and mix until blended. Gradually add confectioner's sugar, beating briskly with a whisk or a hand beater until fluffy. Add up to an additional ½ cup (125 mL) confectioner's sugar, if necessary, until mixture is the right consistency for spreading.

Makes enough for an 8- or 9-inch (2 L or 2.5 L) pan

Strawberry Buttercream Frosting

4 oz	cream cheese, softened	125 g
¼ cup	butter or margarine, softened	50 mL
⅓ cup	mashed fresh strawberries	75 mL
2 cups	confectioner's (icing) sugar, sifted	500 mL

1. In a medium bowl, with an electric mixer, cream butter and cream cheese until fluffy. Beat in strawberries. Stir in the confectioner's sugar and beat until the right consistency for spreading.

Makes enough for an 8- or 9-inch (2 L or 2.5 L) pan

Vanilla Icing

⅓ cup	butter or margarine, softened	75 mL
3 cups	confectioner's (icing) sugar, sifted	750 mL
1½ tsp	vanilla	7 mL
2 tbsp	milk or cream	25 mL

1. In a medium bowl, beat butter and confectioner's sugar until smooth and blended. Stir in vanilla and milk and beat until mixture is smooth and the right consistency for spreading.

Makes enough for a 13- by 9-inch (3.5 L) pan

Vanilla Frosting

3 cups	confectioner's (icing) sugar, sifted	750 mL
1/3 cup	butter or margarine, softened	75 mL
2 tbsp	milk	25 mL
1 1/2 tsp	vanilla	7 mL

1. In a large bowl, with an electric mixer, cream confectioner's sugar and butter. Stir in milk and vanilla and beat until smooth and the right consistency for spreading.

Makes enough for an 8- or 9-inch (2 L or 2.5 L) pan

Vanilla Glaze

1 cup	granulated sugar	250 mL
1/2 tsp	baking soda	2 mL
1/2 cup	buttermilk	125 mL
1 tbsp	light corn syrup	15 mL
1/2 cup	butter or margarine	125 mL
1 tsp	vanilla	5 mL

1. In a saucepan, over low heat, combine sugar, baking soda, buttermilk, syrup and butter. Heat slowly, stirring constantly, to boiling. Continue cooking for 2 minutes. Remove from heat. Stir in vanilla.

Makes enough for a 13- by 9-inch (3.5 L) pan

Date Frosting

1	package (8 oz/250 g) pitted dates, chopped	1
1 cup	boiling water	250 mL
1 cup	granulated sugar	250 mL
1/2 cup	butter or margarine	125 mL
1/2 cup	chopped pecans	125 mL

1. In a saucepan, combine dates, boiling water, granulated sugar and butter; cook over medium heat, stirring constantly, for about 20 minutes or until mixture is very thick. Remove from heat; stir in pecans. Cool to lukewarm.

Makes enough for a 13- by 9-inch (3.5 L) pan

Make-Ahead Whipped Cream Frosting

½ tsp	unflavored gelatin	2 mL
1 tbsp	cold water	15 mL
1 cup	whipping (35%) cream	250 mL
Pinch	salt	Pinch
½ tsp	vanilla	2 mL
1 tbsp	granulated sugar (optional)	15 mL

1. In a small bowl, sprinkle gelatin over the water. Set bowl in 1 inch (2.5 cm) of hot water in a saucepan. Let stand until gelatin dissolves. Remove and let mixture cool for 1 minute.
2. In the small bowl of an electric mixer, whip the cream until almost stiff, then add dissolved gelatin mixture, salt and vanilla, and sugar (if using). Continue beating until stiff peaks form. Cover and chill in refrigerator.
3. Before spreading, beat with a spoon to blend.

Makes enough for an 8- or 9-inch (2 L or 2.5 L) pan

TIP: This recipe will keep for up to 4 days in the refrigerator without separating. Be sure to use very fresh cream.

VARIATION

Chocolate-Dotted Whipped Frosting
Grate 1 square (1 oz/28 g) semi-sweet chocolate (about ¼ cup/50 mL) and fold into frosting; cover and chill in refrigerator.

White Fluffy Frosting

2	egg whites	2
¼ tsp	cream of tartar	1 mL
2½ tbsp	water	32 mL
2 tbsp	light corn syrup	25 mL
1½ tsp	vanilla	7 mL
½ tsp	lemon extract	2 mL
2 cups	confectioner's (icing) sugar, sifted	500 mL

1. In a medium bowl, with an electric mixer, beat egg whites and cream of tartar until stiff peaks form.
2. In another bowl, whisk together syrup, water, vanilla and lemon extract.
3. Add to the egg white mixture alternately with the confectioner's sugar, beating well after each addition, until creamy and stiff and easy to spread.

Makes enough for an 8- or 9-inch (2 L or 2.5 L) pan

TIP: Raw eggs can be a potentially dangerous source of salmonella. To reduce food-safety risk, use pasteurized egg whites in this recipe.

Index

National Library of Canada Cataloguing in Publication

Brody, Esther
    500 best cookies, bars & squares / Esther Brody.

Previously published under titles:
The best 250 cookie recipes and The 250 best brownies, bars & squares.
Includes index.
ISBN 0-7788-0103-9

1. Cookies. 2. Bars (Desserts)
I. Title. II. Title: Five hundred best cookies, bars & squares.

TX772.B758 2004   641.8'654   C2004-902894-4

More Great Books from Robert Rose

Appliance Cooking

- 125 Best Microwave Oven Recipes
  by Johanna Burkhard

- 125 Best Pressure Cooker Recipes
  by Cinda Chavich

- The 150 Best Slow Cooker Recipes
  by Judith Finlayson

- Delicious & Dependable Slow Cooker Recipes
  by Judith Finlayson

- 125 Best Vegetarian Slow Cooker Recipes
  by Judith Finlayson

- America's Best Slow Cooker Recipes
  by Donna-Marie Pye

- Canada's Best Slow Cooker Recipes
  by Donna-Marie Pye

- The Best Family Slow Cooker Recipes
  by Donna-Marie Pye

- 125 Best Indoor Grill Recipes
  by Ilana Simon

- The Best Convection Oven Cookbook
  by Linda Stephen

- 125 Best Toaster Oven Recipes
  by Linda Stephen

- 250 Best American Bread Machine Baking Recipes
  by Donna Washburn and Heather Butt

- 250 Best Canadian Bread Machine Baking Recipes
  by Donna Washburn and Heather Butt

Baking

- 250 Best Cakes & Pies
  by Esther Brody

- 250 Best Cobblers, Custards, Cupcakes, Bread Puddings & More
  by Esther Brody

- 500 Best Cookies, Bars & Squares
  by Esther Brody

- 500 Best Muffin Recipes
  by Esther Brody

- 125 Best Cheesecake Recipes
  by George Geary

- 125 Best Chocolate Recipes
  by Julie Hasson

- 125 Best Chocolate Chip Recipes
  by Julie Hasson

- Cake Mix Magic
  by Jill Snider

- Cake Mix Magic 2
  by Jill Snider

Healthy Cooking

- 125 Best Vegetarian Recipes
  by Byron Ayanoglu with contributions from Alexis Kemezys

- The Juicing Bible
  by Pat Crocker and Susan Eagles

- The Smoothies Bible
  by Pat Crocker

- Better Baby Food
  by Daina Kalnins, RD, CNSD and Joanne Saab, RD

- Better Food for Kids
  by Daina Kalnins, RD, CNSD and Joanne Saab, RD

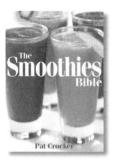

- 500 Best Healthy Recipes
Edited by Lynn Roblin, RD

- 125 Best Gluten-Free Recipes
by Donna Washburn and Heather Butt

- America's Everyday Diabetes Cookbook
Edited by Katherine E. Younker, MBA, RD

- Canada's Everyday Diabetes Choice Recipes
Edited by Katherine E. Younker, MBA, RD

- The Diabetes Choice Cookbook for Canadians
Edited by Katherine E. Younker, MBA, RD

- The Best Diabetes Cookbook (U.S.)
Edited by Katherine E. Younker, MBA, RD

Recent Bestsellers

- 300 Best Comfort Food Recipes
by Johanna Burkhard

- The Convenience Cook
by Judith Finlayson

- The Spice and Herb Bible
by Ian Hemphill

- 125 Best Ice Cream Recipes
by Marilyn Linton and Tanya Linton

- 125 Best Casseroles & One-Pot Meals
by Rose Murray

- The Cook's Essential Kitchen Dictionary
by Jacques Rolland

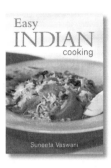

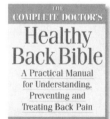

- 125 Best Ground Meat Recipes
by Ilana Simon

- Easy Indian Cooking
by Suneeta Vaswani

- Simply Thai Cooking
by Wandee Young and Byron Ayanoglu

Health

- The Complete Natural Medicine Guide to the 50 Most Common Medicinal Herbs
by Dr. Heather Boon, B.Sc.Phm., Ph.D. and Michael Smith, B.Pharm, M.R.Pharm.S., ND

- The Complete Kid's Allergy and Asthma Guide
Edited by Dr. Milton Gold

- The Complete Natural Medicine Guide to Breast Cancer
by Sat Dharam Kaur, ND

- The Complete Doctor's Stress Solution
by Penny Kendall-Reed, MSc, ND and Dr. Stephen Reed, MD, FRCSC

- The Complete Doctor's Healthy Back Bible
by Dr. Stephen Reed, MD and Penny Kendall-Reed, MSc, ND with Dr. Michael Ford, MD, FRCSC and Dr. Charles Gregory, MD, ChB, FRCP(C)

- Everyday Risks in Pregnancy & Breastfeeding
by Dr. Gideon Koren, MD, FRCP(C), ND

Also Available
from Robert Rose

500 BEST **muffin** RECIPES

Esther Brody

For more great books see previous pages